DEATH ROW FILES

The Trial of
David Westerfield

Written By
Brennon Jones

MONSTER PUBLISHING

PROLOGUE

In the early hours of Saturday, February 2, 2002, seven year old Danielle Van Dam was abducted from her bedroom by an unknown assailant. Located in Poway, a wealthy suburb of San Diego, Danielle's home was in a pristine, beautiful, and safe neighborhood with one of the lowest crime rates in southern California. In the hours immediately following Danielle's disappearance an immense and comprehensive search was launched.

Three weeks later, with no signs of Danielle, police arrested David Alan Westerfield, a fifty year old design engineer who lived just a few houses away and had a successful career and two children in college. He had no criminal history and in no way resembled the monster the people of San Diego assumed had committed such a terrible crime.

Less than one week later, about thirty feet from a remote road in an area littered with dumped appliances, furniture, and trash, at the eastern edge of civilization approximately twenty-seven miles southeast of her home, Danielle's naked body was discovered.

Mr. Westerfield was charged with kidnapping, murder, and possession of child pornography. Because Danielle had died during a kidnapping, if found guilty, Mr. Westerfield would face the death penalty.

On June 7, 2002, the trial of David Alan Westerfield began. From start to finish, the trial was shown live on local television and discussed nightly on numerous cable shows.

DAY 1

The trial of David Westerfield, for the kidnapping and murder of seven year old Danielle Van Dam, started in San Diego, California on Tuesday, June 4, 2002, and was presided over by Judge William Mudd, a fifty-seven year old graduate of Hastings College of Law in San Francisco who had worked as a criminal defense attorney before becoming a judge in 1984. With a long history of working cases involving a variety of violent crimes including, rape, robbery, assault, and murder, Judge Mudd had earned a reputation as a blunt, independent, and fair arbiter who was respected for his dedication to the pursuit of justice.

At 9:50am Judge William Mudd welcomed the jury into the courtroom. "Good morning, ladies and gentleman, and welcome back. I had hoped when we next met the Padres would be on a lengthy winning streak. Unfortunately, that was not to be. As you all know, you folks have already been through the jury selection process and are now the twelve jurors selected to hear this matter. I shall now instruct you as to your basic functions, duties, and conduct. At the conclusion of the case, I will give you further instructions on the law that applies to this case."

Judge Mudd started his initial jury instructions with directions for jurors to base their ultimate decision solely on the facts presented within the trial and not any outside source. "You must not read or listen to any accounts or discussions of the case reported by the newspapers or other news media including radio and television. You must not be influenced by pity for the defendant or by prejudice against him. You must not be biased against the defendant because he has been arrested for this offense, charged with a crime, or brought to trial. None of these circumstances are evidence of guilt."

Judge Mudd warned the jury not to, "be influenced by mere sentiment, conjecture, sympathy, passion, prejudice, public opinion, or public feeling. Both the people and Mr. Westerfield have a right to expect that you will conscientiously consider and weigh the evidence, apply the law, and reach a verdict regardless of the consequences."

Judge Mudd advised the jury against accepting statements or questions made by the attorneys as fact and directed them not to consider evidence stricken by the court as a result of objections. "You must not independently investigate the facts or the law, or consider or discuss facts as to which there is no evidence."

Regarding the substantial media attention the trial was receiving in both local and national news, Judge Mudd assured jurors their names would remain under seal by court order and noted they would only be known by their juror number. "None of you will be photographed in any way."

Stressing the vital importance of jurors avoiding all news stories about the trial, Judge Mudd predicted most stories would contain inaccuracies and noted the jurors would have a much better understanding of the trial than the reporters. Although the defense had requested jury sequestration, Judge Mudd was trusting them to, "self-police," so they could continue going home at night and seeing their families for what would be a multi-month long trial.

Moving on, Judge Mudd mentioned that each juror had been given a notebook for the trial. "As you can see, it's basically a steno pad. Attached to that is a County of San Diego ink pen which means it has about a fifty/fifty chance of having ink in it throughout the course of this trial. But the county has spared no expense and we have as many of these cheap pens as we need." Jurors were informed each notebook had their number on it and were not allowed outside the courtroom until their deliberation began.

Judge Mudd instructed the jury to open their notebook to the first page before giving them the private phone number for the court. Jurors were asked to call the number if they were running late and told that would be their emergency contact number if their family needed to reach them while court was in session.

Their weekly schedule would consist of full days, 9:00am to 4:30pm Monday through Thursday. Lunch breaks would start at noon and last ninety minutes. He was providing the lawyers an extra thirty minutes in hopes they could use that time to better organize their case and improve the overall speed of the trial. They would have additional days off the week of July 4 and there would be no trial the week of July 15 because he and his wife were going on a vacation. "I treasure my thirty-three year marriage and if I don't make this trip, my wife will have my head."

Citing the OJ Simpson trial, Judge Mudd informed jurors they were prohibited from publishing for profit details of their experience for ninety days following the trial's conclusion and were directed to inform the court if a member of the media attempted to "improperly influence any member of this jury."

Judge Mudd directed the jury not to discuss the case with anyone, including each other until the trial concluded and deliberations began. "During the course of this trial and before you begin your deliberations, you will keep an open mind on this case and upon all of the issues you will be asked to decide. In other words, you must not form or express any opinions on this case until the matter is finally submitted to you."

With initial jury instructions completed, the opening statement began.

"Okay, Mr. Dusek, on behalf of the people."

"Thank you, your honor."

The prosecution was led by Deputy District Attorney Jeff Dusek, a former minor league baseball player and a career prosecutor who had already won numerous high profile homicide cases in San Diego. At his side stood George Woody Clarke, the prosecutor who had presented the DNA evidence at the OJ

Simpson trial in 1995.

"This trial will be about two people," Mr. Dusek began. "David Westerfield and Danielle Van Dam. Specifically, it will be about what David Westerfield did to Danielle Van Dam. The evidence in this case will indicate that somebody sneaked into the Van Dam home in the late evening of February 1st going into February 2nd. That somebody was able to get upstairs to Danielle's room and was able to get her out of the house. That somebody killed her, murdered her. We will show you who that is and that somebody dumped her body like trash along the road."

Starting at the beginning, Mr. Dusek recalled that when Danielle's parents, Brenda and Damon, fell asleep in the early hours of Saturday, February 2, everything was normal. When they woke the following morning and realized Danielle was gone, their nightmare began. By the time the Van Dams called 911 and the search for Danielle began, David Westerfield, who lived just three houses away, had left the neighborhood in his motorhome on a spontaneous road trip in which he would drive approximately five hundred miles in the next forty-five hours on an aimless, meandering journey through the southwest that included stops at the Silver Strand State Beach south of San Diego and Glamis, a tiny, one intersection town in the middle of the desert about one hundred and fifty miles east of his home in Poway.

After a long weekend of highly unusual and uncharacteristic behavior, Mr. Westerfield arrived at his drycleaners shortly after 7:00am on Monday morning wearing only a t-shirt and boxer shorts. With no shoes or pants, he handed over his clothes along with some bedding and asked if they could be cleaned by the end of the day.

For the next three weeks, the search for Danielle continued until on February 27 search volunteers found her badly decomposed body a short walk from Dehesa Road, a remote area at the base of a desert mountain about twenty-seven miles southeast of Mr. Westerfield's home and just a few miles south of Interstate 8, the road he would have driven on his way home from Glamis.

Mr. Dusek then revealed for the jury that a search of Mr. Westerfield's house, SUV, and motorhome had recovered multiple pieces of trace evidence linking Danielle to those locations and had also found child pornography on Mr. Westerfield's computer for which he was also being charged.

"Ladies and gentleman, that is some of the evidence you will hear. By the time we finish this case you will be able to answer the question and the evidence will indicate that it was David Westerfield who went into the Van Dam home. You will understand, based on the evidence, what he did to Danielle Van Dam, and what he did with her, and where he dumped her. And you will understand, based upon the evidence in this case, what he did and what he has done to try to get away with this. You will find the evidence is sufficient to convict him of murdering, kidnapping, special circumstances, and possession of child pornography. Thank you."

Before breaking for lunch, Judge Mudd informed the jury that water and cups were available as needed and noted that the water, "in those pitchers comes from a filtered water fountain in the back so it is the best the city of San Diego has to offer." If they wanted something different, they could bring in their own water bottle, coffee, or soda bottle as long as it had a screw top. After the jury exited the room, Judge Mudd informed the spectators that buttons, t-shirts with images, and placards could not be worn inside the courtroom. "You're welcome to remain in this courtroom, but the jury will not be intimidated nor will anyone else."

Following lunch, lead defense attorney, Steven Feldman, expressed his concern about the jury's exposure to the media and requested that the court reconsider sequestration. He additionally said people in the hallway outside the courtroom were handing out the buttons they had been directed not to wear inside the courtroom and requested they be ordered to stop.

After denying the request for sequestration, Judge Mudd agreed with Mr. Feldman's concern about the activity in the hallways. "The public certainly must understand what form of intimidation that is and I'm not going to tolerate it. Period. All right. Let's get the jury."

With the jury back in their seats, Judge Mudd revealed they would soon be receiving a new court phone number to contact in case of emergency because the public had learned the number provided early that morning and, "every weirdo, wacko, and dime store comedian in this country was calling my line with suggestions about my hairdo and my weight." Judge Mudd additionally directed the jury to disregard any photos or badges they saw people wearing and focus their attention only on what was presented inside the courtroom.

"All right. Mr. Feldman on behalf of Mr. Westerfield."

The defense was led by Steven Feldman, a seasoned defense attorney who had attended the University of California Berkeley in the late 1960's when he was arrested during a protest of the war in Vietnam. Mr. Feldman had been practicing law for more than twenty-five years and had worked on several high-profile cases including the case of Robert Corenevsky who was found not guilty for the murder of a jeweler as well as a death penalty case in which he was able to win a life sentence for his client. Assisting Mr. Feldman was Robert Boyce, a defense attorney who had earned his law degree at Capital University in Ohio in 1977 and who specialized in criminal law.

After starting his opening statement by accusing the state of presenting a purely circumstantial case, Mr. Feldman spoke about his client, the person.

"Ladies and gentleman, David Westerfield is a fifty year

old man. He's a design engineer. He has patents, inventions that he's been involved in that benefit many in our society. He's divorced. He has two grown children, each in college. He parents them, he supports them, he provides for them, and has done so all of his life. Two weeks a month he has custody of his children. Coincidentally, on Super Bowl weekend as law enforcement flooded his house, his son was upstairs in that house."

Moving on to the details of the case, Mr. Feldman revealed that Brenda and her friends had smoked marijuana the Friday night before Danielle was abducted. "This wasn't just a girls night out, this was a girls night out to party. The girls were getting down, which in my slang means they were dancing, they were drinking, they were rocking out. No question about it. In fact, the bartender later said those girls were partying so hard, they were being flirtatious. You're gonna learn they're among her closest friends in the world in every sense of the word."

Mr. Feldman informed the jury that Mr. Westerfield had actually been at the same bar that night and had purchased drinks for Brenda and her friends. "They didn't know each other, at least that's the testimony of Brenda Van Dam. There's absolutely no question from the evidence that on Friday night, February the 1st, Brenda Van Dam and David Westerfield saw each other at Dad's. No issue, no dispute."

Jumping back in time to shortly after Brenda's friends showed up at the Van Dam house that evening, Mr. Feldman said the three women went into the garage to drink a beer and smoke marijuana. "That night, as the women stayed in the garage getting high, drinking, out comes Damon. Hey, give me a hit." Mr. Feldman made an inhaling sound and gesture. "Give me another hit, give me another hit. He's already two beers gone."

Jumping back to the bar, Mr. Feldman continued. "They're not just drinking there, Brenda is putting the moves on people. Meaning, she's behaving in a sexually aggressive manner. So, she doesn't just dance with Mr. Westerfield, which she is going to deny, she doesn't just dance with two or three other men, she dances with women as well! And one of the things she complains strongly about is that Barbara keeps running her had down her breasts while she's dancing publicly. She wishes she'd stop it in public. I know the evidence will show you that the women were dancing with each other and with other men in a manner designed to solicit other men to come to Brenda Van Dam's residence that evening to engage in certain types of behaviors that I need to leave to your imagination."

Mr. Feldman continued to recount the minute by minute activities of Brenda and her friends on the night Danielle disappeared while taking every opportunity to highlight the drinking, dancing, and smoking. When Brenda and her friends returned home in the early hours of Saturday morning, her friend, Barbara, jumped in bed with Damon, "just long enough for Damon to get whatever Damon wanted." Mr. Feldman conceded the encounter lasted only a moment before transitioning his focus to accusations the Van Dams had lied to the police about their nefarious activities.

"Mr. Van Dam then made a conscious decision to withhold relevant evidence concerning the possible disappearance of his daughter from police."

Moving forward, Mr. Feldman stated the person who abducted Danielle must have been familiar with the home because they would not have known otherwise which upstairs bedroom belonged to Danielle. "Who could get past that dog? Who would know where to go? Who would know that door was unlocked? Nobody checked the kids. You'll hear that as evidence. When Brenda came home, she didn't check the kids, you'll hear that evidence. You'll hear no evidence of any kind linking David Westerfield to that residence. Absolutely nothing. There's not a shred of evidence that puts David Westerfield in that residence.

"The next morning, the parents were concerned. In the panic of the fear of the loss of their daughter, what do we tell the cops? What are we going to say about our lifestyle? What are we going to say about our use of drugs? What are we going to say about our relationship with Barbara? We're going to tell them nothing, we're going to lie. We are going to decide what's important."

Mr. Feldman recalled the immediate influx of media attention as well as the massive search that commenced throughout that weekend and noted that while the Van Dams lied to police, in his initial conversations with detectives on Monday morning, Mr. Westerfield had exhibited sincere cooperation and honesty.

"He behaved just like rest of the neighborhood. He behaved just like all the other neighbors did. He did everything they asked him to do. Contrary to the Van Dams, he told them the truth."

Referencing the state's claim that trace evidence had been discovered in the motorhome, Mr. Feldman emphasized the motorhome was often parked on the street where anyone could have entered at any time. He then clarified that an overwhelming majority of the porn found on Mr. Westerfield's computer featured adult women with large breasts. "In virtually every single photo it's adult women. We don't speculate, we prove."

After noting that Mr. Westerfield had been under constant police surveillance between February 5 and his arrest on February 22, Mr. Feldman said, "the science of time of death is going to come to Mr. Westerfield's rescue. You're going to hear the results and, after you hear those results, you're going to be convinced beyond any doubt that it was impossible for David Westerfield to have dumped Danielle Van Dam in that location.

"So, we have doubts. We have doubts as to cause of death. We have doubts as to the identity of Danielle Van Dam's killer. We have doubts as to who left her where she resided, where she remained. And we have doubts as to who took her. Thank you."

Following the conclusion of the defense's opening

statement, the prosecution called their first witness, Julie. Julie lived across the street from the Van Dams with her husband of sixteen years as well as their eight year old daughter and five year old son. They had lived in their Sabre Springs neighborhood home in Poway since the development was originally constructed six years ago.

Although Julie had known Mr. Westerfield by sight, they had never spoken. His home was at the southwest corner of Mountain Pass Road and Briarleaf Way three houses east and across a street from the Van Dams.

"Do you know if the Van Dams have any children?" Mr. Dusek asked.

Julie revealed the Van Dam's had three children; Derrick who was ten, Dannielle who was seven, and Dylan who was five. They and Julie's two kids all attended Creekside Elementary School, which was a little more than half a mile north of their homes.

On the morning of Saturday February 2, 2002, Julie and her husband had a t-ball meeting at Sabre Springs Park, about a mile away, at 9:30. A few minutes before the meeting, Julie walked her kids across the street and left them with Brenda who had previously agreed to watch them for an hour or so.

At about 9:45, Brenda called Julie's cellphone while she was at the baseball field.

"She sounded urgent, upset. She said you need to come back, we can't find Danielle, you need to come home and get your children."

Ten minutes later, Julie and her husband pulled up to the Van Dam's house just as the first police car arrived. Damon jumped in his van looking worried and drove toward the main road, searching for Danielle. Julie reached the front door before the officers.

"She said, 'we still can't find Danielle.' She seemed very urgent and like she was in disbelief and in panic."

Julie took her kids along with Derrick and Dylan Van Dam back across the street to her home. A few minutes later, Brenda and Damon were asked by officers to remain outside while they searched the house. As Brenda and Damon stood in their driveway trying to process the situation, Julie brought them some water and chairs. Another neighbor gave them some food.

"Did you see anybody cleaning the house at that time?" Mr. Dusek asked.

"Absolutely not."

"Did you see anybody vacuuming or destroying evidence at that time?"

"No."

"What was their condition?"

"Damon was in tears. He was sitting down with his head in his hands and he was devastated. He was crying. He said somebody took my baby."

"Objection," Mr. Feldman interrupted. "Hearsay."

"Sustained. Next question."

"How about Brenda? What was her condition?"

"She was more controlled. She was trying to comfort Damon. She was trying to talk with police. She was obviously very distraught."

"Did you see or hear them talk about coming up with a plan to lie to the police about what happened?"

"No."

That night, Brenda and Damon slept at Julie's while detectives and evidence technicians processed the Van Dam's home. The next day, police turned the home back over to the Van Dam's.

"Did you hear any discussion between the police officers and Damon Van Dam regarding the ability to got back into the home?"

"Damon asked specifically are you sure that you collected everything you need and that we can go back in."

"Objection. Hearsay," Mr. Feldman interjected.

"Overruled. It's not for the truth. The answer will stand."

Julie recalled that Damon was very insistent about all the evidence being collected and revealed the first thing he did when reentering the home was place a gate in the doorway of Danielle's bedroom to prevent anyone from entering. At that time, a group of neighbors arrived to clean the numerous areas where finger print power had been used. Damon specifically instructed them not to enter her room.

"How long would you estimate the Van Dams have lived in that neighborhood?"

"Three or four years."

"Have you seen the Van Dam children outside playing?"

Julie stated they were allowed to play in front of the house while supervised and were not allowed to wander.

"Thank you, ma'am," Mr. Dusek said and turned the witness over to the defense.

In his cross examination, Mr. Feldman first established that it had taken Julie and her husband ten to fifteen minutes to reach the Van Dam's home after Brenda called.

"You don't know what Brenda and Damon talked about in that ten or fifteen minute period, do you?"

"I do not."

"Did Brenda ever tell you what she had done the night before?"

"No."

"Did Brenda ever tell you who had been in the house the night before?"

"No."

After confirming that both Julie and Brenda were stay at home moms, Mr. Feldman noted she was not always aware of when the Van Dam kids played outside and could not say definitively that they did not play in the neighborhood by themselves.

"You knew Mr. Westerfield had a motor home, right?"

"Yes."

"You knew that he would park his home from time to time right across the street on Briar Leaf?"

"That's correct."

"No further questions."

In his redirect examination of Julie, Mr. Dusek asked if she had ever seen the Van Dam kids cross the street on their own.

"Absolutely not," Julie answered. "They were not allowed to cross the street."

"Thank you, ma'am."

Judge Mudd dismissed Julie from the witness stand and directed her not to discuss her testimony with anyone until the trial concluded.

Mr. Dusek next called Karsten, a milkman of twenty years who had volunteered to search for Danielle on February 27. He and his friend, Chris, met at the ReMax Real Estate office in Poway along with approximately twenty other volunteers who were instructed on search methods and directed to look for items that might have belonged to Danielle, specifically a blue blanket. If they found a suspicious item, they were directed to call a nearby team leader and tie an orange marker, or dial 911.

The volunteers were split into two separate groups and assigned a specific area of focus. Karsten, Chris, and thirteen other volunteers carpooled to the Singing Hills Golf Course on Dehesa Road, at the eastern edge of El Cajon in an area that was remote, unpopulated and at the base of a desert mountain range. At around noon, the volunteers broke off into smaller groups and started searching the hillside across the street from the golf course. Approximately two hours later, having found nothing suspicious, roughly half the volunteers left the search, several so they could pick up their kids from school.

Karsten, Chris, and three others drove about a mile further east on Dehesa Road where they parked and continued searching. Karsten and Chris walked on the south side of Dehesa between the road and a small parallel body of water as they headed back toward their initial starting point near the golf club entrance. About forty minutes later, they crossed to the north side of the street and walked back along a desert hillside at the base of a mountain.

Along the hillside, Karsten and Chris found numerous large items of junk. Old refrigerators, mattresses, couches and boxes scattered the landscape, which had the appearance of a widely recognized dump site due to its remoteness and accessibility. As they started getting close to their vehicle and the end of their search, Karsten and Chris began smelling a strange scent similar to a dead animal they had encountered earlier, but different. Chris saw the body first and yelled out to Karsten who ran his direction.

"Specifically, can you describe for us what you saw?" Mr. Dusek asked.

"A body laying down on her back, her head facing to her right. There were portions of her body missing, maybe decomposed. Initially, I thought they were burned, but that's because I had never seen a decomposing body before."

"Did you see any clothing on her?"

"No."

"Did you notice any jewelry on her?"

"I noticed the shimmering of her earring."

About one minute after discovering the body, at 2:09pm, Karsten dialed 911. Nearly forty minutes later, officers arrived.

"Thank you, sir," Mr. Dusek said and sat down.

Mr. Boyce led the cross examination.

"The area in which you found the body, people had been dumping their trash, is that correct?"

Karsten confirmed that much of the hillside was littered with trash people had dumped illegally. After showing Karsten eight photographs of the surrounding area, Mr. Boyce ended his questioning.

The state next called Karsten's friend, Chris. Chris recalled that he had decided to volunteer his time that day, "because I was unemployed, I had time, and I saw a lot of other people doing it and I thought it would be a good thing to do."

Chris recounted the events preceding and during the search. He remembered looking in bushes, picking up boxes, and searching beneath various items of junk littering the ground until he picked up the scent of death. A few minutes later, Chris discovered, "a badly decayed young girl on her back. Her head was to the right and she was severely decayed."

Although her skin was dark brown, he knew it was Danielle because the hair was long and blonde, she had a, "shiny earring on her left ear," and looked similar to the missing girl photo.

"Was she missing any parts?"

"She was missing a foot and a lot of flesh on her legs."

Mr. Dusek reconfirmed that none of the volunteers had touched the body before asking what he and the other volunteers were doing while they waited for police.

"We were hugging each other, consoling each other, looking at the body."

"Thank you, sir."

Following the afternoon break, Mr. Boyce began the cross examination by highlighting the large presence of junk surrounding the recovery site that included mattresses, old refrigerators, and other large objects.

"You didn't touch the body, is that correct?"

Chris answered that neither he nor any of the volunteers had touched the body. After a few questions about Chris's previous contact with Mr. Dusek, the cross examination ended.

Judge Mudd excused Chris and the prosecution called Erin Miller, a Supervisor at the Sycuan Casino Resort about two and a half miles east on Dehesa Road from where Danielle's body was found. At the casino, Ms. Miller oversaw the club program, which was a player tracking system that rewarded active players with points they could later redeem for food, merchandise, and hotel room discounts.

Ms. Miller revealed that on October 1, 2001, David Westerfield signed up for and received a club card he used in a slot machine that night at 11:58 and again a few times after midnight. After that night, Mr. Westerfield did not use the card again.

"Is there anything that would prevent an individual from just coming in and gambling, simply not using their cards and you have no record of it?"

"No, they can come in and play whenever. They don't need a card."

Mr. Dusek showed a map of the area around the casino and Ms. Miller informed the court the Singing Hills Golf Course was part of the Sycuan Casino. She discussed the short distance between the location of Danielle's body and where casino property began. She additionally revealed Interstate 8 was just seven miles north.

In his cross examination, Mr. Boyce discussed the casino's location, the various roads in the area, and the fact that a person driving from El Cajon, which was directly west, could reach the casino without driving on I8.

"I have nothing else, your honor."

Ms. Miller was excused.

The prosecution's next witness was Deputy Sheriff Larry Alston. Deputy Alston had worked for the San Diego County Sheriff's Department for eleven years when he received a call at 2:40 on February 27 about the discovery of a small child's body. At about 3:00, Deputy Alston arrived at a scene he described as grassy, deserted and dusty. There was a mining company across the street, but no other nearby businesses or homes.

As the first officer on the scene, Deputy Alston made

contact with the volunteers who were visibly shaken. One was crying. They informed the deputy about the body and led him up a rough path so he could verify their discovery. Approximately fifteen yards up a small embankment, in a grassy area near a tree, Deputy Alston found a small body. The left foot was missing and the flesh on the lower left leg was gone. Bone was exposed in her lower right leg as well as her pelvic and torso area where flesh was also missing. Around the neck was a small choker necklace. The skin appeared black as if it had been burned, but he assumed the person was Caucasian because of the long blonde hair. Deputy Alston contacted his supervisor and secured the scene. Once the homicide investigators arrived, his job was finished.

In his very brief cross examination of the deputy, Mr. Boyce confirmed he had not disturbed the body and noted that the sun was setting fast as additional police personnel arrived.

"I have nothing else, your honor."

After dismissing the witness, Judge Mudd concluded the first day of trial by reminding the jury to leave their notebooks on their chairs and hoped the new secret phone number would be set up the following day. He additionally instructed the jury to, "remember the admonition of the court not to discuss any of the evidence or testimony among yourselves or with any other persons. Don't formulate any impressions or opinions until the matter is turned over to you for decision. Good thoughts toward the Padres. Maybe collectively we can get at least one win against San Francisco. Have a safe and pleasant evening. We will see you all at 9:00am tomorrow."

DAY 2

After a nine minute proceeding not made part of the public record, Judge Mudd welcomed the jury back. "Before we get started this morning, folks, I have to answer the telepoll question from Keokuk, Iowa. No, I'm not wearing makeup and yes, despite what you see on television, I still do have hair although my hairline has changed dramatically since my high school graduation picture in 1962.

"All right, in all seriousness ladies and gentlemen, as the shepherd of this flock, it's my job, among other things, to monitor the media coverage." Judge Mudd again directed jurors to avoid the radio news stations and reminded them not to read any stories in the paper, which they didn't need to read anyway because, "you were here, you know what happened."

Judge Mudd recognized the increased difficulty they would have avoiding television stories and advised them to become Padres fans so they could watch baseball a few hours every night and not worry about self-policing. For those not interested in baseball, he recommended watching movies.

"Self-policing is going to require a good deal of courage on your part. Between radio and television, every lawyer that ever practiced criminal law in this city is an expert. They are giving opinions and they are talking about things you've seen and heard. They are not going to make the decision; you folks are. So, it's very important as to the television coverage, extensive as it is, that you avoid it at all costs. That way, we can guarantee your decision will be based solely on what you see and hear in the courtroom."

Mr. Clarke of the prosecution interjected. "Excuse me, your honor. Was the court also going to bring up the internet?"

"Yes, I didn't cover the internet, frankly, because I don't know my wife's password at our home computer so I have no idea what the internet- but stay off the chat rooms and all of that. Obviously, you can go on the internet and use your computer. Just don't get into the chat rooms and things that are dealing with this particular case."

The first witness on day two was Dr. Skip Sperber, a forensic odontologist. Dr. Sperber had graduated with degrees in chemistry and zoology from Carleton College in Minnesota and earned a doctor of dental surgery degree from New York University College of Dentistry in 1954. After leaving the Navy in 1964, he was hired by the Medical Examiner's office where he used dental records to identify unknown bodies. During his career, Dr. Sperber had worked on approximately four thousand cases, had been consulted by law enforcement organizations all over the country and had worked on several high profile cases including Ted Bundy, Jenny Rojas, Craig Pyor, and Jeffrey Dahmer. He had also helped identify victims who died on 9/11. In addition to his forensic dentistry work, Dr. Sperber owned and operated a family dentistry office.

On February 28, Dr. Sperber received dental records for Danielle Van Dam and took teeth x-rays of the body found near Dehesa Road. The inside of the mouth was very decomposed and there was not much tone left in the tissue. Although all the teeth in the lower jaw were firm and intact, the upper jaw was missing several teeth in the front. Several adjacent teeth still present in the upper jaw were loose.

"Were you able to make a comparison between the known x-rays of Danielle Van Dam and the x-rays you took of this body?"

Dr. Sperber was, "very certain," the body was Danielle Van Dam's. He additionally revealed that four of the six upper front teeth were missing, one of which was an adult tooth that would not have been replaced. He found one of the missing teeth deep inside her mouth. One of the teeth still in place was very loose. Although three missing teeth were never found, Dr.

Sperber explained front teeth often become dislodged during decomposition.

Because there was no evidence of injury in the tissue or bone, Dr. Sperber did not believe she had been struck by a blunt instrument, but he could not explain why the missing teeth were not with the body when it was discovered. "They could have been lost during the transportation of this body to that area or they could have been lost at some time just prior to her death or after her death."

"Based upon your experience, are teeth something that animals take away?"

"Not usually," Dr. Sperber explained scavenging animals wanted tissue and meat, not bone. If an animal had taken the teeth, evidence of their activity would have been visible on her face.

"If the teeth fell out because of decomposition or even trauma and decomposition, where would you expect them to be?"

"I would expect the teeth to be directly under the body or possibly in the oral cavity, in the mouth area."

"Thank you, sir." Mr. Dusek finished.

Mr. Boyce began his cross examination by confirming the body had undergone significant decomposition and animal activity. He pointed out the missing foot and asked how Dr. Sperber knew there was no animal activity in the area of her mouth. Dr. Sperber explained there were no tooth marks in the tissue, but the defense persisted.

"You can't exclude animal activity in this area, can you?"

"Well, going by the lack of trauma to the tissue, I would say I could."

Mr. Boyce reviewed the missing teeth and asked, "any other opinion from you concerning what happened to those teeth would be speculation, is that right?"

Dr. Sperber clarified that any opinion regarding the location of the missing teeth would be speculation, but emphasized animals do not take teeth.

After several questions implying the missing teeth could have naturally fallen out, Mr. Boyce turned Dr. Sperber back over to the state.

"Doctor, can teeth be loosened from trauma, soft trauma, that will lead to their falling out?"

"It's very conceivable that could happen."

"Even without any trauma or signs inside the mouth?"

"Yes, sir."

"Thank you."

Mr. Boyce stood. "You didn't see that in this case, did you, Doctor?"

"I did not, that's correct."

"So, anything based on that would be speculation on your part, is that right?"

In his answer, Dr. Sperber revealed a blow that directly hit a tooth could potentially dislodge the tooth without fracturing the surrounding bone.

When Mr. Boyce asked if he had observed any soft trauma, Dr. Sperber confirmed he had not.

"Thank you, your honor,'" Mr. Boyce finished and Judge Mudd excused the witness.

The prosecution next called Danielle's father, Damon Van Dam. Damon was thirty-six years old and had been married fourteen years. For the previous four years, they had lived in their home on Mountain Pass Road in the Sabre Springs neighborhood in Poway, a pleasant, family oriented suburb in the northeast corner of San Diego. Damon worked as a software engineer at Qualcomm and had two sons in addition to Danielle. Derek was ten and in fourth grade, Dylan was six and in kindergarten.

"Are you nervous?" Mr. Dusek asked.

"Yes."

When asked when Danielle was born, he replied, "September 26th, 1994," and stated she was in second grade. All three of his children attended Creekside Elementary School about half a mile north, down the hill. Brenda Van Dam always drove the kids to and from school, except for a few occasions when they walked.

"Do you have a dog?"

Damon said they had a one year old Weimaraner named Layla who weighed about sixty pounds and was a brownish gray color. She did not usually bark.

"Did you come to know an individual by the name of David Westerfield?"

Damon recalled speaking with Mr. Westerfield once briefly in his driveway shortly after they moved in, but never spoke to him again and did not know his name. During their brief encounter, Mr. Westerfield had talked about his dune buggy, which he called a, "sand rail." Damon had never socialized with Mr. Westerfield, had never been in his home, and had never seen his backyard. Prior to Danielle's disappearance, Mr. Westerfield had never entered the Van Dam's home or their back yard. Damon had never seen him on their side of the intersection that separated their homes.

When asked about Mr. Westerfield's vehicles, Damon recalled seeing a Volkswagon Baja style bug with the engine exposed, an older Porsche Carrera, and a large motorhome that pulled a small white trailer with the sand vehicles. Damon remembered the motorhome well because he and some of the other neighbors had become annoyed by how often it was parked in the street, something the neighborhood prohibited.

Damon and Brenda only allowed their kids to play on their side of the street in front of their house. They were not allowed to cross the street on their own.

On Friday February 1, Damon left his work in Mira Mesa, about seven miles southwest of his home, around 5:30. Originally, he had planned on driving to a friend's cabin in Big Bear with Derek for a weekend of snowboarding, but on Thursday, his friend changed the plans to Saturday instead so Damon planned to spend Friday night at home.

While driving home after work, Brenda called to see how far away he was because she was going to pick up a pizza and didn't want the kids at home alone for more than a few minutes. Since he was almost home, she left. When he arrived at the house, the kids were watching television. Brenda arrived a few minutes later and they all sat down at the kitchen table and ate. It was the last moment they would all spend together.

"Is your backyard fenced in some sort of way?" Mr. Dusek asked.

Damon said they had, "a six foot fence all the way around. It's got a slope in the back that the fence goes up and then at the top of the slope there's a seven or eight foot brick wall. The fence closes off so you can't go through it." Damon further described a small paved walkway at the front right side of the house where there was a gate leading to the back yard.

That night, Brenda planned on going to Dad's Café and Steakhouse with her friends, Barbara and Denise. "Dad's" as they called it, was a popular neighborhood bar about two miles away in Poway. When Barbara and Denise arrived around 8:00 that evening, Damon was playing video games with the boys while Danielle was writing in her journal at the kitchen table.

Brenda, Barbara, and Denise went out to the garage to smoke cigarettes and drink beer. When Damon joined them a few minutes later they were all smoking marijuana. Damon smoked some too.

"Why?" Mr. Dusek asked.

"Because they had it out there."

After a couple of puffs, Damon went back inside and continued playing video games with his boys. A few minutes later, Brenda left with her friends. At around ten, he and all three kids went upstairs and got ready for bed. The kids brushed their teeth and put on their pajamas then Danielle read for Dylan in his room.

A few minutes later, Danielle crawled into her own bed where she was accompanied by her dolls and stuffed animals. A princess like canopy draped her bed and fluffy hearts hanged from the ceiling fan. Damon gave her a hug and kiss goodnight, and turned off the lamp, triggering the nightlight.

Because Derek was older, he was allowed to stay up later as long as he was in his room. Damon left each of their doors cracked a few inches, but closed his door so Layla didn't roam the house and disrupt the kids. Once in his own bed, Damon turned on the television and a few minutes later fell asleep.

After Layla woke him up at around 1:45, Damon walked downstairs and let her out through the sliding glass door by the kitchen. When he returned to bed, he left the bedroom door open because he knew Brenda would return home soon.

Asked by Mr. Dusek about their security system, Damon explained the house was equipped with an alarm that monitored all the doors and windows. When a door or window opened, the system chirped. If the door or window remained open, a red light on the alarm panel would flash. There were alarm panels downstairs near the front door and upstairs near the door to the master bedroom.

A few minutes before 2:00am, Brenda returned home. She parked her Ford Excursion in the driveway and entered through the front door. Damon heard the ladies talking as they entered and heard some male voices as well. A moment later, Barbara and Brenda entered the bedroom; Brenda heading for the bathroom, Barbara for the bed where she laid down next to him. After Brenda walked back downstairs, Damon wrapped his arm around Barbara and rubbed her back. She snuggled into him and they kissed.

"Was she on top of the sheets or underneath the sheets?" Mr. Dusek asked.

Damon recalled she was on top of the sheets, while he

was under. A few minutes later, Brenda asked them to go downstairs because they were being rude to their guests.

"When you reported the situation to law enforcement did you include this part of what happened?"

Damon revealed he had not informed officers about his interaction with Barbara because he did not think it was important. When they emphasized the need for full transparency about everything that happened, Damon disclosed the full story.

Downstairs, Damon found his friend Rich, and Rich's cousin Keith, sitting at the kitchen table eating left over pizza with Brenda and Denise. Approximately twenty minutes later, Barbara, Denise, Rich, and Keith all left.

"Did they have Danielle with them?" Mr. Dusek asked.

"No."

Once back upstairs, Damon put Layla in Derek's room where she could sleep in his bottom bunk. At about 2:30 in the morning, Brenda and Damon got into bed, turned the lights off, and went to sleep.

"When you went to bed that night, did you think the house was secure?"

"Yes."

"Did you think anybody else was in that house besides members of the Van Dam family?"

"No."

Sometime during the three o'clock hour, Damon woke and noticed the red light on the alarm panel flashing. He walked downstairs and noticed a cold draft moving through the home. The sliding glass door by the kitchen was open about eight inches. Narrower than the width of the dog, but wider than an extended hand. Damon closed and locked the door. When he passed the downstairs alarm panel, the flashing red light had stopped.

Judge Mudd intervened. "Ladies and gentleman, you might note that the clock you see in the courtroom is different than the real time. There is a reason for that. This is a County of

San Diego maintained implement. At any rate, let's try and coordinate our watches and times so one or more of you don't hold up the whole group. Have a pleasant lunch."

When the trial resumed at 1:30, Judge Mudd provided jurors the court's new secret number. "For you folks and you folks only. If you're having a problem of any kind, you can feel free to call that number. And, hopefully, I'll stop getting phone calls for pizza and hair transplants and stuff like that."

He then answered a request by Juror 13 to make it colder by assuring everyone they intended on keeping the forty year old building as cool as possible in the summer months, but disclosed the antiquated venting systems sometimes made that task difficult.

"All right. Mr. Dusek."

Mr. Dusek picked up the timeline at about 8:00 on the morning of Saturday, February 2. Damon woke before Brenda and found Derek already downstairs watching television. A few minutes later, Brenda came down and started making eggs and cleaning the kitchen. She told Damon Julie's kids were coming over soon as he took out the garbage before going upstairs and dressing. When Julie's kids arrived, they went into the living room with Derek and Dylan. When Julie's daughter asked about Danielle, Brenda walked upstairs to wake her up. Damon was downstairs when Brenda first called down and asked why Danielle was not in her room.

"It gets very – it got frantic quick after this," Damon recalled.

Damon and Brenda searched the house. They looked in all the rooms, under the beds, under the stairs, in the garage, and in the back yard. The side gate, which was about six feet from the side door in the garage, was open about eight inches.

"How easy is that door to open, that gate?"

"The gate is very hard to open. The wood swells." Damon explained how the wood of the gate door rubbed against the wood of the frame. Opening the gate required lifting the latch and pushing the gate in a particular manner and with strength.

"What was her emotional condition?"

"She was frantic, very upset, pale, shaking." She called 911 as Damon continued searching. After jumping in his car and driving around the block, the first police officer arrived. Damon and Brenda spoke with the officer as neighbors began gathering outside. A few minutes later, the police locked down the house and began their investigation.

"During the time that you discovered Danielle missing, did you use the vacuum cleaner?"

"No."

"Did you clean or destroy any of the physical evidence that might be in the house?"

"No."

That night, Damon, Brenda and the two boys stayed at Julie's house across the street. When informed they could return home the following afternoon, Damon and Brenda were concerned not all of the evidence had been collected. Although assured by detectives, Damon closed Danielle's door and put up a gate.

"Why did you do it?"

"I was worried there was evidence in there because I knew something bad had happened."

"In fact, after officers told you that you could resume occupancy of the house, did they come back looking for more?"

Damon recalled police returning on several different occasions, once for Danielle's closet door and on two other occasions for a door in Damon's office and a chunk of wall from the downstairs entryway. Investigators had also conducted chemical tests in her room.

"Was there a time before Danielle was taken that Layla

started to bleed?"

Damon recounted a time a week or two before Danielle disappeared when Layla scratched her nose and bled inside the house.

"At some point after these events did you repaint the house?"

"Yes. It was pretty much destroyed from the fingerprint dust."

"Did you do anything with regards to the carpeting?"

"All the carpet's been changed in the house. It was also destroyed by fingerprint dust."

"Thank you, sir." Mr. Dusek turned the witness over to the defense.

Mr. Feldman started his cross examination by reminding Damon he had previously testified under oath in a pretrial hearing and by asking if he had read any news articles or watched any television reports related to the case since the trial began. Damon had not engaged in any media coverage and had not spoken with anyone who informed him what the previous witnesses had said.

"The first time the police talked to you, they told you it was very, very important for you to tell them the truth, isn't that right, sir?"

"Yes."

Mr. Feldman then introduced a transcript of an interview of Damon by Detective Thrasher that occurred at 1:42am on Sunday, February 3.

"We haven't seen this before, your honor," Mr. Dusek said.

"That's okay, we just got the tapes last night," Mr. Feldman responded as he gave copies of the transcript to the prosecution and Damon. He again repeated that Damon had been urged to reveal the complete truth when discussing the events surrounding Danielle's disappearance. He asked Damon if he made, "decisions as to what you believed to be relevant as opposed to what they were asking?"

"Yes," Damon answered and confirmed he had decided what was appropriate for disclosure.

"And you lied to the police, isn't that true?"

"Moments before being told the gravity of the situation and how important it was, yes, I did. Moments after that I told the truth."

"Among the details that you left out was your marijuana use the night preceding, isn't that true?"

"Yes."

"The fact that Barbara had gotten in bed with you the night before. That's true, isn't it."

"Yes."

"The fact that your wife had some form of communication from David Westerfield the Wednesday preceding, isn't that right?"

"That doesn't relate at all to anything," Damon answered.

Mr. Feldman revealed police had informed Damon that the person who took Danielle likely knew the layout of their home and was possibly familiar with Layla because they had been in the house earlier that night.

"I don't recall that statement being made," Damon said.

Mr. Feldman pointed his attention to the transcript and Damon confirmed, "Steve Flores apparently made that statement."

"And Steve Flores said that they knew how to get in and out of your house and knew the dog wasn't going to bite him or bark?"

"Objection," Mr. Dusek said. "This is testifying to hearsay, your honor, for improper purposes."

Judge Mudd agreed. "Unless there's some valid reason, sustained."

Mr. Feldman noted the interview that occurred at 1:42am was about fifteen hours after he learned Danielle was missing. It was not the first time officers had stressed the importance of complete transparency.

"True," Damon conceded.

"You told me just a moment ago that it was only a couple of moments between the time you decided it was appropriate not to tell the truth and the time you decided it was appropriate to tell the truth. This is actually a fifteen-hour period of time, is it not?"

Damon stumbled for an adequate explanation. "I answered no. When I was told it was important to tell the truth, I answered yes. It happened that fast."

Mr. Feldman asked if Damon recalled, "telling the police in response to a direct question did you use any drugs, your answer was no?"

"I answered no out of nervousness," Damon responded and stated after being told they were concerned only about Danielle and not his drug use, he admitted he had smoked marijuana.

"But you understood that one of the reasons it was necessary for the officers to know who had been in the house was because of the obvious belief communicated to you that the police believed someone who may have been responsible for the disappearance of your daughter was familiar with the inside of your house?"

Judge Mudd intervened. "Before the witness answers the question, ladies and gentleman, I just want to remind you questions are not evidence. It's only the answers that are meaningful. You may answer, Mr. Van Dam."

"Yes."

Mr. Feldman moved his attention to Brenda's friends Barbara and Denise. "They were your friends also, weren't they?"

"Yes."

"In fact, they were your intimate friends, isn't that true?"

"Yes."

"Isn't it correct that on at least three separate occasions you had sexual intercourse with Barbara prior to February 1st?"

"No."

"How many times?"

"Once," Damon answered and said it had occurred at her house.

"Had you had intimate relations with Denise?"

"If by intimate relations you mean sex, yes."

"Isn't it true your wife communicated to you that she was uncomfortable with Barbara talking to your daughter?"

"Objection, hearsay."

"Sustained."

After revealing Brenda, Barbara, and Denise had also gone to Dad's the week before Danielle's disappearance, Mr. Feldman returned his focus to Friday February 1.

"Did you smoke marijuana with the women?"

"I believe I did have one or two puffs."

"And did you feel the effects of the marijuana?"

"A little bit."

"Rich, you had known him for a while, isn't that correct?"

"Yes."

"He was your supplier of marijuana, wasn't he?"

"Yes," Damon answered.

"You told us that you were eating cookies, do you recall that?"

"Yes."

"Was marijuana in those cookies?"

"No, they were packaged *Chips Ahoy!* cookies."

"Was that before or after you were in bed with Barbara," Mr. Feldman asked.

"After."

Mr. Feldman then asked about the alarm panel status when Damon woke up and let the dog out just before Brenda returned home. At that time, he had not noticed if the light flashing.

"Did you invite any men over that night?"

"No."

"Before your wife went partying that night, did you discuss with her whether it would be appropriate for her to bring back, I don't know, people to party with?"

Damon stated he had not specifically discussed any plans with his wife for after they went out and estimated Barbara had stayed in his bed for only three to five minutes.

"And what were you doing in that three to five minute period of time?"

"Kissed, snuggled a little. I put my arm around her, rubbed her back some."

"And where was your wife?"

"Downstairs."

"At some point in time, Brenda had to come back upstairs and tell you she was getting embarrassed, isn't that true?"

Damon disagreed with the characterization of embarrassed, but confirmed she asked them to go downstairs.

"And when Brenda came in, you were still in the process of hugging and kissing her, is that correct?"

"Not kissing. I believe I kissed once or twice and then just laid there." Damon recalled he had stood out of bed in his underwear and dressed in front of Barbara.

"Isn't it true that on at least three separate occasions either you had sex or you attempted to have sex with Barbara in the presence of your wife?"

"Yes."

"When you had relations with Denise who else was present?"

"Objection. Irrelevant," Mr. Dusek said.

"Overruled."

Damon answered, "my wife and her husband," and stated

it had occurred in his bedroom.

"Within the previous six to eight months were there occasions that you became upset with Danielle for going out and playing outside the gate?"

"No."

Noting the upcoming afternoon break, Mr. Feldman asked if they could start the break early so he could organize his next questions. After dismissing the jury, Judge Mudd addressed the media in the gallery who, he said, had worn good poker faces initially, but had recently become inappropriately animated. He warned if they could not remain stoic, they would be removed.

Judge Mudd then dismissed the gallery so he could speak privately with a juror who was concerned about a person watching from the gallery she knew from her child's daycare. She wanted to remain anonymous and was worried that the individual would recognize her and tell people.

"You know women in day care, we talk about everything, so the last thing I wanted was for her to leave the courtroom, go back to the school, and say this is where I am."

Because the individual was not in the gallery after lunch, Judge Mudd decided against taking action, but if the woman returned, she would be removed. Judge Mudd did not want the names of any jurors leaked to the media and believed precautions were reasonable.

After the break, before the jury returned, Mr. Feldman asked Judge Mudd for guidance. "Your honor, there's a piece of impeachment that I wanted to go to, but before I went there I wanted some guidance as to how to go there. I think this implicates potentially inadmissible evidence, your honor, and so whatever the court wishes with regard to-"

Judge Mudd interrupted. "Turn the cameras and microphones off please. Thank you for bringing that to our attention." After a long proceeding not made part of the public record, the jury returned to their seats.

"Well, I hoped to have a Padre update, but my radio went on the britts so I can't tell you whether we're winning or losing at this point in time. All right. Mr. Feldman."

Mr. Feldman asked, "Mr. Van Dam, is it the case that your children would play outside in the front yard all of the time?"

"I wouldn't say all the time. I would say on occasion."

Reading from the transcript, Mr. Feldman asked, "isn't it true, you told Officer Flores at 1750 hours on the 2nd of February, 'my kids are playing out front all the time?'"

Damon found the page and confirmed.

"In fact, the next morning when you realized your daughter went missing one of the reasons you went into the backyard was because you were concerned your daughter had sleepwalked into the backyard, isn't that true?"

Damon did not recall saying, "sleepwalked," but Mr. Feldman again showed him the transcript which confirmed he had. In the interview, Damon said, "she's done it a couple of times, but only to our room. I don't think she's ever gone outside."

Mr. Feldman then asked Damon, "the reason you were looking in the backyard was on the theory that your daughter may have sleep walked in the backyard?"

"Yes."

When Mr. Feldman asked if Damon and Brenda had discussed withholding information about their, "sexual behaviors" from the police after calling 911, Damon said, "I don't specifically recall agreeing with Brenda to withhold information from the police."

"You specifically indicated to the police that basically it was time for the police to please tell your wife that you had let the cat out of the bag with regard to your sexual behaviors and so it was now okay for her to discuss that, isn't that true?"

"That's true."

"Now, does that mean you, in fact, did agree with Brenda to withhold information from the police?"

"I do not recall."

"No further questions." Mr. Feldman turned the witness back over to the state.

In his redirect, Mr. Dusek quickly addressed multiple nonrelated issues back to back. He clarified that Danielle had sleepwalked on only a couple of occasions and only to her parent's bedroom. The night Damon had sex in his house with Denise, the kids were sleeping at a friend's house. His first conversation with an officer lasted only two or three minutes and he conveyed only a very basic outline of the events that occurred on Friday night and provided the names of everyone who had been in their home that night. Subsequently, Damon supplied investigators, "every detail possible to try and get my daughter back and now get justice for her."

"Thank you, nothing further."

Judge Mudd dismissed Damon Van Dam and informed him that Mr. Dusek would notify him when he could attend the gallery as a spectator.

The prosecution next called Dr. Brian Blackbourne, the San Diego County Medical Examiner. Dr. Blackbourne had earned a medical doctor degree at the University of Alberta in 1962 and had worked at the Vancouver General Hospital before undergoing surgical training. He later focused his interest on pathology, spent a year learning neuropathology at the Barrow Neurological Institute in Phoenix, Arizona, and then worked at the Memorial Hospital in New York City. He was board certified in both anatomic and forensic pathology.

Dr. Blackbourne had worked as an Assistant Medical Examiner for Dade County, Florida for five years, a Deputy Chief Medical Examiner in Washington, DC for ten years, and a Chief Medical Examiner for the state of Massachusetts for seven years. Since 1990, he had worked as the San Diego County

Medical Examiner where he investigated all sudden, unexpected, or violent deaths that occurred in the county including homicides, suicides, and motor vehicle collisions. He had performed approximately seven thousand autopsies and had testified in over four hundred trials.

At about 10:45pm on February 27, Dr. Blackbourne arrived at the location near Dehesa Road where the body was discovered. Sgt. William Holmes briefed him on the history of the case and then led him up an incline to a grassy area where the body was laying. Large lights illuminated the site.

Dr. Blackbourne saw the body of a, "young white female in a state of marked decomposition. In addition to the decomposition, there was extensive animal feeding on the body. A lot of tissue on the body was missing. The face was intact, the skin was mummified, but the features were still quite recognizable."

Dr. Blackbourne recalled her long blond hair and noted that below the colar bone, much of the muscle and tissue on the front of her body had been removed by animals. She was missing muscle and skin from her chest and abdomen, large chunks of flesh were missing from her thighs, exposing bone, her foot was missing below the ankle, and some of the tissue in the upper arms was gone.

"Could you tell the sex of the body?"

Dr. Blackbourne believed the facial features and hair appeared female, but noted that the area of her pelvis had been completely consumed by animals.

A necklace was present and, in both ears, there were blue stone earrings with Micky Mouse designs. The back of one was missing. There was no clothing on the body or on the ground nearby.

"From what you observed there, were you able to detect any insect activity on her?"

"Just looking at the body there were no obvious insects

running around, but it was on the ground so I knew there would be a lot of insects."

After he and his team photographed the scene, they placed white paper bags over her hands, right foot, and head, and wrapped the body in a white sheet before placing it in the body bag. The paper bags and sheet were there to collect any trace evidence, including fibers and hairs, that might fall off during transport.

At 10:00 the following morning, Dr. Blackbourne performed the autopsy. Mr. Dusek showed the court pictures of Danielle's body before the autopsy began. Dr. Blackbourne reported that the body was fifty-one inches long and weighed only thirty-seven pounds. The hair was eight inches long. He did not find any obvious abrasions or bruising, but because the skin was so dry and mummified, such evidence might not have been visible.

Dr. Blackbourne used an enlarged photograph of the body to show the jury what parts of the body were missing. "These are the ribs, all the skin and muscle is gone over the top of them so you see the bare ribs here." Some brown leaves were stuck to the body, both femurs were exposed, and the vaginal area was completely missing. Her hands were intact as was her right foot, but the left foot was gone. The spleen, pancreas, stomach, adrenal gland, and one kidney were also absent. In addition to the significant animal activity, the body demonstrated severe decomposition and mummification.

"Did you examine the body for signs of insects?"

Dr. Blackbourne recalled a large number of insects running across the body and table, all of which were collected by David Faulkner, an entomologist at the Natural History Museum who had been hired to assist the investigation.

"What were the conditions of her eyes?"

"The eyes were really destroyed. The decomposition had pretty much really destroyed the eyes."

Beyond the animal trauma, Dr. Blackbourne did not identify any obvious physical mechanical trauma that might have been caused by force. There were no fractures anywhere on her body including her head, neck, and ribs, but Dr. Blackbourne did confirm four teeth had fallen out of the front, upper jaw, one of which was found inside the back of the mouth. The other three were never recovered.

When asked if he was able to determine a cause of death, Dr. Blackbourne explained that Danielle had no documented natural disease and her toxicology report was negative. There were no penetrating wounds from a gun or knife, no lacerations, and no evidence of blunt force trauma. He had found no signs of hemorrhage in her neck or a larynx injury that would have indicated she had been strangled by hands or something tied around her neck.

"What is suffocation?" Mr. Dusek asked.

Dr. Blackbourne explained that suffocation was a form of asphyxia that resulted when a person's nose and mouth were covered by a hand, pillow or other restrictive object. The process usually took three to five minutes for the brain to become so damaged the person would not wake. Depending on how much a person was able to fight back, a suffocation death might not cause many obvious injuries.

"Did you consider suffocation as a possible cause of death?"

Dr. Blackbourne confirmed he had, but noted the lack of positive findings needed to definitively reach that conclusion.

"Were you able to rule out suffocation as a cause of death?"

"No. I was unable to rule it out." He added that a vast majority of cases involved a clear cause of death such as a gunshot wound, motor vehicle collision, heart attack, or suicide. Only rarely was he not able to determine with certainty how the person died.

Regarding time of death, Dr. Blackbourne discussed how estimating time of death became increasingly difficult the longer a body had been decomposing. Determining the time of death of bodies left outdoors in the elements was even more challenging and imprecise.

At 4:28, Judge Mudd suspended testimony and wished the jury a pleasant evening.

DAY 3

A few minutes after 9:00 on Wednesday morning, Judge Mudd welcomed the jury back to the courtroom. "Little did I know yesterday when I told you how much courage it would take to be a Padre fan, what courage it really is going to take for the rest of the season. But hopefully with their day off it might make a difference, which is a great segue to remind you that tomorrow we will not be in session on this matter so you will be off from this particular case. Also, I wanted to give kudos where kudos are due. Apparently, the maintenance department in this fine building got wind of the fact that I commented about a couple things. We now have a new battery in the clock and maintenance has set the thermostat as low as it will go. With all the bodies in here it has a tendency to warm up a little bit, but at least they're trying to keep the temperature at a nice cool level for you. All right, let's get to Dr. Blackbourne."

Mr. Dusek resumed his questioning where he left off the day before. "Were you able to give us a ballpark estimate on time of death for Danielle?"

"Just looking at the body, it was clear to me she had been dead for a considerable period of time. Just looking at the body alone, not taking any circumstances into consideration, I would say from ten days to possibly six weeks."

Dr. Blackbourne explained it would take at least ten days to reach the extreme mummification present and because her heart and lungs were still identifiable and intact, he concluded she could not have been dead longer than six weeks.

When asked if he could determine if she had been sexually assaulted, Dr. Blackbourne stated he had swabbed the inside of her mouth as well as areas inside what he thought were the remaining sections of her rectum and vagina, though the area was so degraded he was not sure. Given the extreme state of mummification and decay, he did not expect sperm to be found. Therefore, Dr. Blackbourne was not able to definitively determine if Danielle had been sexually attacked.

"Were you able to determine manner of death?"

"I concluded it was homicide."

"Thank you, doctor."

Mr. Feldman started his cross examination by confirming Danielle had not suffered any traumatic injuries or fractures. He asked the doctor to define the words bruise, abrasion, and laceration, then discussed various tools that could cause blunt force trauma.

"And you noted, quote, no definitive traumatic injury is identified, isn't that true?"

Dr. Blackbourne agreed and also confirmed that no knife wounds had been discovered.

Regarding the mummification process, Mr. Feldman noted that Dr. Blackbourne had not examined weather charts for the weeks Danielle was missing and was not in a position to, "render an opinion as to what effect, if any, temperature may have had," when determining the speed of decomposition.

"Now, you just told the jury that you thought ten days to six weeks would be a reasonable estimate for time of death. Assume that there was a Santa Ana condition between the 16th of February and the 27th of February, might the existence of that Santa Ana condition accelerate the decomposition process?"

"That certainly would play a process in the decomposition if the temperatures were exceedingly high."

Mr. Feldman noted that law enforcement had hired forensic entomologist David Faulkner to collect the insects at the autopsy, an unusual request Dr. Blackbourne had not encountered previously. The purpose of collecting insects and larvae was to help narrow the estimated time of death, "because you realized that the time of death might be a very important circumstance in a case where the identified defendant had been on national television from February the 5th, correct?"

"Yes."

Mr. Feldman transitioned back to the lack of injuries found on Danielle's body and how the intact hyoid bone indicated she had not been strangled.

"It either didn't happen," Dr. Blackbourne clarified, "or the individual is so young and the structures are cartilaginous or gristle-like that they didn't fracture."

"You have no evidence to conclude, do you, that Danielle Van Dam was strangled?"

"No."

"Any opinion that you would render about whether or not she had been sexually assaulted is nothing more than speculation, correct?"

"It would be speculation, but I have rendered no opinion."

"You found no skull fracture, correct?"

"Correct."

Mr. Feldman moved back to Danielle's time of death and asked if the weather had been particularly hot could that become eight or seven days instead of ten. Dr. Blackbourne agreed it could, but did not think San Diego had experienced in February the intense heat that would require.

"You weren't provided with the weather reports, were you?"

"I was not."

"Is it your professional opinion that Danielle Van Dam could have been alive on February the 6th, 2002?"

"From just examining the body, she could have been, yes."

"February the 7th?"

"Yes."

"February the 17th?"

"Possibly, yes."

"No further questions, thank you."

In his redirect, Mr. Dusek asked Dr. Blackbourne to define extreme temperature.

"Over a hundred."

Mr. Dusek noted that there had been no days of one hundred degree temperatures in February and definitely not enough to have caused such severe mummification in just ten days. Therefore, Mr. Dusek determined, Danielle could not have been alive on February 17th and any suggestion she was alive at that time was speculation not based on known facts.

Mr. Dusek then showed a picture of the body, focused on the absent soft tissues in the pelvic area, and confirmed that there was no way of knowing if Danielle had been sexually assaulted. Dr. Blackbourne further stated that he did not expect to find any evidence of ejaculation on or in her body due to the significant tissue deterioration present.

"There was really no examination. There was no tissue to examine. There's no way to determine it."

"Thank you, sir."

Dr. Blackbourne was dismissed and directed not to discuss his testimony until the trial concluded.

The prosecutions next called Danielle's mother, Brenda Van Dam.

"Good morning, Mrs. Van Dam."

"Good morning."

"You ready?"

"Yes."

Brenda told the court she was thirty-nine years old and had lived in Sabre Springs the last four years. When not taking care of her three children, she worked from home selling library books to school libraries.

"Who is the oldest?" Mr. Dusek asked.

"Derek is ten. In fourth grade."

"Who is your next child?"

"Danielle."

"How old was she?"

"Seven." Brenda started to cry.

"If you want some time, ma'am. I think once the first cry is over, then usually you're able to go."

Brenda took a moment, composed herself, and continued.

"What grade was she in?"

"Second."

"And the youngest?"

"Dylan. Today is his birthday. He turned six."

"Did you know an individual named David Westerfield before this thing happened?"

"Yes." Brenda recalled seeing Mr. Westerfield on occasion while driving in and out of the neighborhood because she drove past his house on her way out. They would exchange waves as would other neighbors, but she did not meet him until he bought Girl Scout cookies from Danielle in 2001, one year before she disappeared. At that time, Mr. Westerfield invited Brenda and Danielle into his home, which was undergoing a kitchen remodel, while he filled out the order form.

"Would Danielle go out alone selling the cookies?"

"No. I don't allow her to go out alone."

The Tuesday before Danielle disappeared, one year after their initial encounter with Mr. Westerfield, Brenda, Danielle and Dylan again knocked on doors in the neighborhood selling cookies. His was the last house they visited.

Mr. Westerfield again invited them inside his home and showed Brenda the upgraded kitchen. As he filled out the form at the kitchen counter, Danielle and Dylan asked if they could go outside and look at the pool. Brenda asked if that was okay and Mr. Westerfield said yes before Danielle and Dylan walked outside through the sliding glass door in the kitchen.

"Did you know his name at that time?"

"I didn't know his name. I could not read his writing on

the cookie form from the year before."

Once the kids were outside, Mr. Westerfield turned the conversation to the previous Friday night when he had seen Brenda and her friends at Dad's.

"He was very interested in one of my friends. He said, your friends look like a lot of fun."

"What are your friends' names?"

"Denise and Barbara. He said to tell Barbara that I had a rich neighbor that I could introduce him to."

Brenda said her friends wanted to go out again that Friday, but she didn't think she could because her husband was going away on a snowboarding trip. If she was going out, she would need a sitter.

"How did the defendant react?"

"He liked the fact that he might get to meet Barbara. He asked me why I didn't introduce him to my friends. I said I don't even know your name, how could I have introduced you?"

Mr. Westerfield then introduced himself and gave her two of his business cards. "And then he said why don't you write you and your husband's name down on this piece of paper. And he said, I have parties. I have barbecues where the kids come and people bring their own food to cook. And I also have – he has family parties and I have adult parties."

"What did you say?" Mr. Dusek asked.

"I finished writing my name down and gave it to him. I was in the middle of writing it down. I didn't feel like ripping it up and taking it away and being rude."

"How long would you say the kids were out back looking at the pool?"

"Three minutes," Brenda answered and said when they returned they stood with her in the kitchen.

"When did they go upstairs?"

"No one went upstairs."

"How do you know?"

"Because Dylan asked me if he could go upstairs and I told him absolutely not."

"Did you see them go in any other rooms downstairs?"

"No."

"Do you remember any laundry, clothing, loose articles in the family room or living room area?"

"No. The house was very tidy."

On their way out, Mr. Westerfield mentioned a bar called, "In Cahoots" he enjoyed on Wednesday nights.

"He said, don't forget to wear your boots to 'In Cahoots.'"

"Did you know what 'In Cahoots' was?"

"I had no idea."

Mr. Dusek transitioned to the night of Friday, January 25th, one week before Danielle disappeared. Brenda recalled that her friend Denise was moving away for work and they had initially wanted to go out on February 1, but because of Damon's snowboarding trip they went out the previous week instead. On that night, after Barbara and Denise arrived together to the Van Dam house, the three ladies smoked marijuana in the garage before driving to Dad's in Brenda's vehicle. When they arrived, Brenda noticed Mr. Westerfield at the bar.

At that time, Brenda knew he was the neighbor with the motorhome and sand vehicles, but did not know his name or anything else about his life. Mr. Westerfield said hello and bought them drinks; vodka cranberries for Brenda and Denise, a vodka soda for Barbara.

While at Dad's, Brenda danced with her friends, but did not have any further interaction with Mr. Westerfield. When they arrived back at Brenda's house shortly after 1:30, Barbara and Denise left and went home.

"How many guys did you bring home?"

"None."

"Did you invite anybody to come home with you?"

"No."

"Was there a sex party at the house when you got home?"

"There's never been a sex party at my house."

Moving to the night of Friday, February 1, Brenda discussed how Damon's snowboarding plans had changed and how she, Barbara and Denise had decided on another night out.

As Damon drove home from work, Brenda left the kids in the house while picking up Domino's pizza, speaking with Danielle on the phone as she drove. When she returned home, the family ate its last meal together.

When Barbara and Denise arrived at about 8:00. Brenda was cleaning up the kitchen, the boys were playing video games in the living room, and Danielle was sitting at the kitchen table writing in her journal. Brenda, Barbara, and Denise went to the garage where they smoked a cigarette and passed around a joint. Barbara and Denise shared a beer and a few minutes later, Damon joined them for a few hits from the joint. Brenda recalled the side door being opened to released the smoke from the room. A few minutes later they went back inside.

"Do you know if anybody closed that side garage door?"

"No, I don't."

During the short drive to Dad's, Brenda mentioned her conversation with Mr. Westerfield and his interest in Barbara. When they arrived, the parking lot was full and the bar was busy. Upon seeing Mr. Westerfield standing at the left corner of the bar, Barbara approached him and introduced herself. Brenda and Denise sat at the opposite corner where Barbara joined them a moment later followed by Mr. Westerfield who dropped some cash on the bar and bought their first drinks.

After a brief conversation with Mr. Westerfield, Brenda, Barbara and Denise talked together while Mr. Westerfield stood just outside their triangle. Fearing she was being rude, Brenda turned her seat around to face him and apologized. She explained they were there to spend time with each other because Denise was moving away.

A few moments later, their friends Rich and Keith arrived to support a friend of Keith's who was playing in the band. When they saw Brenda, they joined her group and ordered drinks. Mr. Westerfield was a few feet away talking with two friends of his own.

As the bar area became crowded Brenda, Barbara, Denise, and Keith started playing pool in the back of the bar; Barbara and Keith played at one table, Brenda and Denise at the other. Mr. Westerfield's two friends jointed them and as they played Mr. Westerfield stood nearby and watched.

After playing a few games, the band started and Brenda, Barbara, and Denise went outside with Keith and Rich. The ladies sat inside Brenda's SUV and smoked a joint while Keith and Rich stood outside. While talking through the passenger side window, Keith and Barbara kissed.

"Was anything going on with you and Rich?"

"No."

About ten minutes later, they went back inside and headed for the dance floor.

"Did you dance with the other girls?"

"Yes."

"And Rich and Keith, did you dance with them?"

"Yes."

"How about the defendant, did you dance with him?"

"No."

During the night, Brenda recalled drinking three vodka cranberries, a shot of tequila, water, a red bull, and possibly a diet coke. A few minutes after last call, Brenda and her friends left the bar and headed back to Brenda's house, the ladies in her car, the men in their own vehicle.

"As you pulled into your driveway, did you see any vehicles around the defendant's home?"

"No."

"Did you see a motorhome there?"

"No."

Upon walking through the front door, Brenda discovered a red light flashing on the alarm panel, indicating an open door or window. While searching for the source, she walked upstairs to tell Damon that Rich and Keith were there before checking the garage where she found the side door ajar. After closing the door, the red light on the alarm panel stopped flashing.

As Brenda heated up leftover pizza for everyone, Rich and Keith joked about why Barbara and Damon had been upstairs so long. Brenda walked back to the bedroom where Barbara was laying with Damon and requested their presence downstairs because they were being rude.

"Did you check on your children that evening once you got back from Dad's?"

"No, I did not. I went to their doors and closed them. I didn't want them to wake up."

Back downstairs, Denise finished heating up leftover pizza and everyone ate.

"Any alcohol?"

"No alcohol."

"Any marijuana?"

"No."

After about twenty minutes later, Barbara and Denise left. Rich and Keith followed just behind.

"Did they have Danielle with them?" Mr. Dusek asked.

"No."

"Where did you think she was?"

"In her bed."

After locking the front door, Brenda checked the back door by the kitchen, which was already locked, then went to bed and fell asleep. When she woke on Saturday morning, Damon was already downstairs. She showered and changed before heading down and starting breakfast. At around 9:00, Julie dropped off her kids and left. Realizing Danielle was still in bed, she walked upstairs to wake her up and noticed that her bedroom door was open.

"When you walked into the room, what did you see?"

"Just her bed."

"What did you do?"

"I went into the bathroom to see if she was in there and then I asked Damon if she had slept in her own bed and he said yes, she should be in her room, and I said, well, she's not. I started looking around the house and looking at other beds and looking in the closets and Damon came upstairs and started looking with me and we were yelling out her name and then we went downstairs. Damon went out front and I went out back, but we couldn't find her."

"Did you call anybody?"

"I called 911."

After calling 911, Brenda contacted Julie. "I told her Danielle was not in her bed and her two children were getting very upset and I told her she needs to come back and get them."

The first officer arrived fifteen minutes later.

"What were you doing during that time?"

"I was searching for Danielle."

That night, Brenda, Damon, and their boys stayed across the street at Julie's while the house was processed for evidence. When they returned home the following afternoon, black finger print dust covered the inside so she took the kids out back while some neighborhood friends cleaned. A gate was placed in the doorway of Danielle's bedroom to prevent anyone from entering.

"What does Danielle sleep in?" Mr. Dusek asked.

Brenda described her pajamas as baby blue with cascading flowers on the legs and noted that Danielle often played with their dog, Layla, before bed.

"How long was her hair when she disappeared?"

Brenda revealed Danielle's hair was shoulder length and recalled having it cut the last weekend in January. Regarding

Brenda's own blonde hair, Mr. Dusek asked if it was chemically treated and she confirmed it was.

"No further questions, your honor."

After Mr. Dusek returned to his seat, Mr. Feldman carefully began his cross examination.

"Good morning, ma'am."

"Good morning."

"Please tell me if any of this becomes difficult and I'll ask the judge to recess, okay?"

"Okay."

Mr. Feldman's first series of questions focused on the many times Brenda had talked about the case with Mr. Dusek who, Mr. Feldman noted, had previewed many of the questions the defense would likely ask. In preparation for her testimony, Brenda had also reviewed numerous reports, statements, transcripts, and recordings.

"Do you recall at some point in time, at least understanding, that there had been some form of phone trace or phone taps on your telephones?"

"No."

"Directing your attention to approximately the 16th of February 2002, do you recall getting a telephone call, a message concerning your daughter?"

"Objection. Hearsay, beyond the scope, third party."

Judge Mudd invited the counselors to sidebar and after a lengthy discussion not made part of the public record, Mr. Feldman changed subjects.

"Were there times in your neighborhood when you would go for walks with the dog and the children?"

Brenda said they had been on walks with the dog and Danielle a few times, but not often and Layla was always on a leash.

"And the dog was walked past Mr. Westerfield's house?"

"I don't know."

"How frequently would your kids go to the park?"

"Rarely. It wasn't very often."

Mr. Feldman pointed out that sometimes Brenda walked Danielle to school and sometimes she walked to a friend's house directly across the street from Mr. Westerfield.

"Are you aware that Mr. Westerfield had a motorhome?"

"Yes."

"How did you know that?"

"Because he leaves it in front of his house."

"In fact, he left it in front of his house so frequently the neighbors complained about it, isn't that right?"

"Correct."

Mr. Feldman inquired further about the motorhome while doing his best to maximize the amount of time the motorhome had been parked in the neighborhood.

"What is your relationship to Rich?"

"I'm friends with his wife."

"And he's also the source for your marijuana, isn't he?"

"Yes."

At that time, Judge Mudd stepped in and dismissed the jury for lunch.

When the jury returned at 1:30, Juror 13 raised their hand and said, "I'm kind of shaken up about what happened."

"Ladies and gentleman, one of the finer citizens of San Diego has seen fit to come to this courthouse and apparently in some form or some effort protest, make their opinions known, and it was done in front of you intentionally. The only thing I can tell you is it has absolutely nothing to do, number one, with the job you have, number two, it has nothing to do with the lawyers on either side of this, and number three, it has nothing to do with the evidence. It is just one more of the kinds of publicity or bias that you have been selected to overcome. So, everybody take a deep breath, sit back, and relax. We're going to do everything we can to ensure that this is not repeated."

Mr. Feldman restarted his cross examination by returning to the night of Friday January 25. "What was your purpose going to Dad's for that night?"

"We were going for a girls night out because Denise was moving."

"You had other girls nights out, had you not?"

"Objection. Irrelevant, beyond the scope."

"Overruled."

"I had a couple."

"When you say a couple, what number comes to mind?"

Brenda said two or three and recalled a time she went to a ceramic painting café with Denise on the night Denise introduced her to Barbara.

"And approximately when was that, ma'am?"

"August 2001."

"Directing your attention to Halloween of 2001, did you have a party?"

"Yes."

"You told us on direct examination that you, quote, had never, end quote, had a sex party at your house. Do you recall that answer?"

"Yes."

After confirming the Halloween party included Barbara, Skip, Denise, and Denise's husband, Andy, he asked, "the party was risqué, was it not?"

"Objection. Vague as to meaning."

"Overruled. You may answer."

"No," Brenda said.

"Was there alcohol at the party, ma'am?"

"Yes."

"Did you have anything to drink that night?"

"Objection. Irrelevant. Your honor, if it's to impeach this

statement-"

"Let's just get to the statement, counsel," Judge Mudd ordered.

"Isn't it true that on Halloween evening in the year 2000 you engaged in sex with Denise, and Andy, and Damon?"

"Yes."

"So, when you told Mr. Dusek that you had never had a sex party at your house, had you forgotten that?"

"I don't consider that to be a sex party."

"Had you previous to October 2001 engaged in consensual sex with another person other than your husband?" Mr. Feldman asked.

"Objection. Irrelevant, he's changing the years."

"Sustained, sustained, sustained."

Mr. Feldman tried again. "Was October 2001 the first time you had sex with Andy?"

"Objection. Irrelevant."

"Sustained."

"Was October 2001 the first time you had sex with Denise?"

Brenda told him, "you need to repeat that question, you have the dates wrong."

Mr. Feldman apologized and asked, "what date was it that was the first time you had sex with Denise?"

Confused, Brenda stumbled, "I have never, what is he-"

"Okay. Have you had sex with Barbara before?"

"No."

"When was it that you had consensual sexual relationships with Denise?"

"It was October 2000."

"Between October 2000 and October 2002, how many different times, if any, did you engage in consensual sex with Denise?"

"None."

Judge Mudd stepped in, "This is June 2002."

"Did I just misstate my dates?"

"He keeps doing it and it's confusing me," Brenda said.

"Let me redirect your attention to October, 2001, okay? In that time period did you have a relationship with Barbara?"

"Objection. Vague as to relationship."

"Sustained."

"Did you have a sexual relationship with Barbara?"

"No."

Mr. Feldman had a brief discussion with his co-counsel, Mr. Boyce, before moving back to the night of January 25. "At the Dad's bar, you were dancing with the women, is that correct?"

"Yes."

Mr. Feldman proceed with a series of questions regarding their alcohol consumption that night and noted she had been the designated driver. Brenda admitted that Denise had, "drank a little too much," and said she was dancing, "a little on the wild side."

"When you say a little on the wild side, could you please tell us what you mean to communicate?"

"She was kissing the guy she was dancing with."

Mr. Feldman pointed out in addition to Barbara and Denise, Brenda had danced with additional women and possibly other men as well.

"And, do you recall, was that dancing provocative?"

"Objection. Vague."

"Sustained."

"Was that dancing done in a manner to demonstrate, connote, or infer sexual behaviors?

"Objection. Still Vague."

"Overruled, you can answer."

"Yes."

"And you were all hugging each other, isn't that true?"

"Yes."

"And when you were hugging each other, that means that you were embracing in an affectionate manner, does it not?"

"Yes."

"Do you recall when you were dancing together and hugging each other that other people would join in?"

"I wasn't watching what other people were doing," Brenda answered.

"Do you recall one of the women coming up behind you while you were dancing and putting her hands around your waist while you were hugging others?"

"No."

Mr. Feldman admitted a transcript of an interview with Brenda conducted on February 7 and asked her to review the highlighted section.

"Isn't it true, ma'am that you told Detective Labore that while you were dancing she came up behind you and put her hands around your waist?"

"It doesn't say that. I was talking about Denise and Barbara dancing."

After a short and awkward debate about the meaning of Brenda's descriptions, Mr. Feldman moved forward.

"Was Barbara that evening being touchy feely or grabby?"

"Yes."

"Did Barbara grab your breasts?"

"No."

"Did she try to grab your breasts?"

"Yes."

"Did you indicate to Barbara that you didn't appreciate that behavior publicly?"

"No."

"You have engaged in behavior similar to that with Barbara privately, though, isn't that true?"

"Yes."

"So, she was taking something that you had done privately and making it public on the dance floor at Dad's, isn't that true?"

"Objection. Irrelevant."

"Sustained," Jude Mudd decided. "You need not answer, ma'am."

"Do you recall that Mr. Westerfield was present that night?"

"Yes, he was." Brenda confirmed he had bought her, Barbara, and Denise drinks.

"And Mr. Westerfield was being appropriate, was he not?"

"Objection. Vague as to what appropriate is."

"Sustained."

When Mr. Feldman asked if Mr. Westerfield was being polite, Brenda answered, "I didn't have much contact with him, but the contact I did, yes."

"That evening, isn't it true that Denise was sexually dancing with a woman?"

"Yes."

"And is it the case that Denise and Barbara were rubbing their bodies together?"

Mr. Dusek objected again and again disrupted the minimal rhythm the defense had generated. Judge Mudd sustained.

"On both the evening of the 25th and the evening of the 1st, both Barbara and Denise were at your house. That's correct, isn't it?"

"Yes."

"And with regard to each of those women, both you and your husband had engaged in sexual relations with them and their male partners, isn't that true?"

"Objection. Beyond the scope, your honor."

Judge Mudd asked both counselors to approach the bench.

When Mr. Feldman continued, he picked up where he left off. The court reporter read back the previous question and Brenda answered, "yes."

Mr. Feldman then transitioned to the evening Brenda, Danielle, and Dylan had sold Girl Scout Cookies to Mr. Westerfield the week of her disappearance. After spending several minutes inquiring how Brenda knew now the day had been Tuesday when she previously stated she was not sure, Mr. Feldman showed her a copy of the order form and asked what Mr. Westerfield had purchased.

"Two boxes of Samoas and two boxes of Aloha Chips."

Mr. Feldman added that Mr. Westerfield had purchased an additional box that would be sent to soldiers overseas.

"You were inside the residence about fifteen minutes, isn't that true?"

"Approximately," Brenda answered and recalled talking about the cabinets and knobs in his kitchen.

Mr. Feldman asked about Danielle and Dylan going outside through the back door before he spent significant time showing photos of Mr. Westerfield's home and asking redundant questions about the layout. The defense clearly wanted the jury to see that Mr. Westerfield lived in an upscale home that was well decorated and immaculate, the kind of house a highly functional individual would own, not the kind of home where a child murderer would live.

"Is this the backyard area in which your kids played?"

"They didn't play. They looked at the pool."

"So, they could have been in the backyard or accessing the garage or any area and you wouldn't have known it, isn't that true?"

"That's not true. They wouldn't wander off, they would come and ask me first."

Mr. Feldman asked how she knew they were in the backyard and not in the garage and Brenda said she could hear their voices.

"Did you understand that "In Cahoots" was a cowboy bar?"

"I had no idea what it was."

After confirming that Brenda had given Mr. Westerfield her home phone number, Mr. Feldman noted that, "the two of you were talking about going to Dad's the next Friday, isn't that true?"

"I had mentioned that I might be there. He said he wanted to meet my friend Barbara and I told him that I might be there if I could get a babysitter."

"And you indicated to Mr. Westerfield that Denise was like twenty-six years old, right?"

"Yes."

"And Mr. Westerfield said that's too young for me, what about the tall one, isn't that right?"

Brenda answered, "yes," and confirmed Barbara was the tall one.

"Is she older than twenty-six?"

"Yes."

"Older than thirty-six?"

"Yes."

"And it was at that point David Westerfield gave you the Spectrum business card, is that right?"

"Yes."

"When Mr. Westerfield mentioned that he had adult parties, in point of fact that meant something in particular to you, isn't that right?"

"Objection. Calls for speculation."

"Overruled. You can answer that yes or no only ma'am."

Brenda responded, "yes."

"Did you tell your husband that you were surprised that Mr. Westerfield had a common interest with you and your husband?"

"No."

"Didn't you discuss with your husband the matter of Mr. Westerfield's remark concerning adult parties?"

"Yes."

"Objection. Hearsay."

Judge Mudd sustained the objection and Mr. Feldman moved forward.

"Isn't it true that it was your opinion that Mr. Westerfield would mention out of the blue a conversation about adult parties because your friends were really loose with the guys at the bar the week before?"

"I don't understand the question."

Mr. Dusek objected and Judge Mudd sustained. "You need not answer, ma'am."

"Approximately what time did Damon come home from work on the 1st, if you recall?"

"I don't know the exact time."

"Because you weren't home, were you?"

"No."

After reviewing Brenda's activities between the time she came home with the pizza and when Barbara and Denise arrived, Mr. Feldman asked, "and the reason you went into the garage was because you were planning to smoke a joint, isn't that true?"

"Yes."

"You locked the door to conceal your illegal activities from your children, isn't that true?"

"Objection. Argumentative."

"Overruled. You can answer."

Brenda said, "yes," and confirmed Damon jointed them and smoked as well.

"So, the four of you basically went out in the garage and got high together?"

"Yes."

Brenda remembered the side door in the garage partially

open to let the smoke out, but was not sure who actually opened the door.

Mr. Feldman then asked Judge Mudd, "your honor, could we take a break, please?"

"All right. Ladies and gentleman, we will go ahead and take the afternoon break a little bit early. Please be outside at 3:00 o'clock."

After the short break, the jury returned and Mr. Feldman reviewed Brenda's activities at Dad's bar after she arrived.

"And about what time was it that you and the women went out and smoked some more marijuana?"

"Between 9:30 and 10:00."

"When the decision was made to go out and smoke marijuana, you had already had at least one of the vodkas, isn't that correct?"

"Yes."

"The reason you went out to the car in the parking lot was so that you could get high, isn't that right?"

Brenda answered, "yes," and said she had rolled the windows down and turned the music up.

"Kind of dancing and rocking out in the car a little bit, weren't you?"

"Yes."

"And then you were smoking marijuana, right?"

"I don't know if it happened in that order, but-"

"Who supplied the marijuana?"

"We brought it from our house. It was the one we had earlier."

Mr. Feldman asked if it was true that at some point that night, Keith informed Brenda he had taken Viagra, was really excited, and wanted to hook up with Barbara.

"Objection. Hearsay."

Judge Mudd sustained and Mr. Feldman switched gears.

"Were Keith and Barbara kissing?"

"I can't remember."

"Do you remember telling the police that they were French kissing in a very intense manner at that point?"

"No, I don't remember whether or not it happened."

"Do you recall dancing with David Westerfield?"

"No. Didn't happen."

Jumping to when Brenda arrived home, Mr. Feldman asked about the flashing light on the alarm panel and Brenda recounted searching the home for the source of the alert and finding the side door in the garage open. Mr. Feldman then asked how long Barbara was upstairs alone with Damon.

"Did you later notice that your husband not only put his arm around Barbara, but that they were kissing?

"Objection. Misstates the evidence."

"Overruled. You can answer."

"No," Brenda said.

"Do you consider yourself to be kind of a touchy sort of person?"

"Yes."

"When you communicate with people you use your hands and you may touch them from time to time, is that right?"

"Yes."

"With regard to your communications with Mr. Westerfield in the bar on the 1st, do you recall touching him?"

"No."

"The next morning you realized there was a problem. I want to move you through the emotion. I don't want you to go to the emotion if I can keep you out of the emotion, sorry. In that period of time between the 911 call and the time police arrived, did you have conversations with your husband, Damon?"

"We were searching for Danielle."

"Did you specifically discuss with Damon that it would not be a good idea for you to discuss your sexual private life?"

"No."

"So, you and Damon never discussed withholding from the police the fact that you may have had a sexual relationship with Barbara and Denise who had been in your home that evening, correct?"

"No." Brenda answered.

"Nor did you have a conversation with Damon to withhold from the police the fact that you had used marijuana on the evening of February 1st?"

"No, it did not occur."

"You didn't tell the uniformed officer that you had smoked marijuana the evening before?"

"The first initial officer, no."

"Did you tell her that you had intimate relations with the two women that had been in your house?"

"No."

Mr. Feldman walked through her first contacts with police and how her extra marital relationships became part of the discussion. He then asked, "in your house, did you have a computer, ma'am."

Brenda said, "yes."

"Is it correct that you would observe your husband viewing naked twenty year olds?"

"Objection, your honor."

"Sustained."

Mr. Dusek asked that the jury be admonished and Judge Mudd requested the counselors approach. After a brief proceeding not part of the public record, Judge Mudd reminded the jury questions are not evidence and directed them to disregard the question.

"No further questions, your honor."

In his redirect of Brenda Van Dam, Mr. Dusek asked about her initial conversations with police. "What were you trying to convey to that officer?"

"That Danielle was gone."

"When you were asked regarding your activities with any of these people did you provide the answers?"

"Yes."

"And you told them everything you could think of, didn't you?"

"I would have told them anything they needed to get Danielle back."

When asked if Layla, their dog, had ever been inside Mr. Westerfield's house or motorhome, she said, "never."

"Was anything else missing or taken from your house?"

"Not that I know of. I checked jewelry. I checked everything to see if anything else was missing. I wished they had taken everything else but her."

"Thank you, ma'am."

"All right, ma'am," Judge Mudd began, "you're free to leave at this time and Mr. Dusek will keep you posted on when you may return. Thanks for coming in."

Brenda stepped down from the witness box and exited the courtroom before Mr. Dusek called his next witness, Sean. Sean was the bar manager at Dad's Café and Steakhouse where he had worked the previous four years. As the head bartender, Sean was in charge during the weekends and typically worked from 5:00 in the afternoon until close at 2:00.

"Did you become aware of an individual by the name of David Westerfield?"

"Yes, I did."

Sean recalled meeting Mr. Westerfield on January 25 through a regular customer named Garry. That night, Mr. Westerfield drank Bacardi and Coke and sat next to Garry at the left corner of the bar. About an hour later, Brenda arrived with two friends, a tall blonde and a shorter brunette. Sean additionally revealed Mr. Westerfield became upset when he learned the price of drinks increased after 9:00 when the band started.

"Did you see any inappropriate behavior that evening from either Brenda Van Dam or her friends?"

"No."

Moving to Friday February 1, Sean believed Mr. Westerfield had arrived alone around 7:30 and sat again at the corner beside his friend, Garry.

"Did you ever see him play pool?"

"No."

"Did you ever see him dance?"

"No. He would just hang out with Garry."

After Brenda and her friends arrived, Sean remembered they sat at the bar and had a drink while talking to each other. He saw Mr. Westerfield speak with one of the ladies briefly, but did not think he was part of their conversation. When asked about how much Brenda drank, Sean recalled two or three drinks and said she was not acting drunk. At around 10:30, he noticed Mr. Westerfield had left.

"Did you see any inappropriate behavior on the part of Brenda Van Dam at Dad's that evening?

"No, I did not."

"How about with her two girlfriends?"

"No, I did not."

"Regarding Mr. Westerfield's state of sobriety, do you have an opinion about that?"

"I believe David had a couple of drinks and maybe he's feeling good and he has taken the edge off, but I don't think he was drunk by any means."

Mr. Dusek turned the witness over to Mr. Boyce of the defense who pointed out that the bar was busy and Sean could not have possibly seen whether or not Brenda had danced with Mr. Westerfield.

"I believe you noticed that the girls were partying hard regarding drinking and dancing, and were very flirtatious with males in the bar?"

"That statement was fabricated a little bit," Sean responded. He confirmed the officer he spoke to wrote that description, but claimed the statement was an exaggeration of his words.

"Then Detective Roerson is incorrect, is that right?

"Yes. By stating that, yes."

"You told Detective Roerson you noticed that they, referring to David Westerfield and Garry, were in the group and talking with Brenda and her girlfriends, is that right?"

"Yes."

"At the moment Mr. Westerfield left, you aren't aware of his state of intoxication or sobriety, are you?"

"That's very correct."

"Nothing further, thank you."

After dismissing the witness, Judge Mudd informed the jury they would not be starting on Monday until 9:30 and assured them court would end every day at 4:30. He wished the jury, "a pleasant weekend. We'll be in recess until Monday at 9:15."

DAY 4

On Monday June 10, Judge Mudd welcomed the jury back and hoped they had a, "pleasant three days to relax and sort of catch your breath before we start another week of very intense work. I got to tell you, though, that I got discovered this weekend. My wife and I on Friday were at our local PetSmart getting dog food. Our dog, incidentally, is a retired, rescued greyhound. Anyway, I'm getting the Iams food and, all of a sudden, a voice says, 'you're Judge Mudd.' Now, in my business, that's not a good thing. In this case, however, it turned out to be a Padres fan who wanted to let me know they were winning. Taking two out of three is a good start on the road trip so hopefully you'll all be Padres fans by the time you get out of here. All right, Mr. Dusek, next witness."

The state's next witness was Brenda's friend, Denise, who was twenty-eight years old and had known the Van Dam's for five years. Denise worked as a flight attendant and had known Barabara since she became her next door neighbor a little more than a year before. Damon worked with her husband, Andrew, at Qualcomm.

Denise recalled going out with Brenda and Barbara on January 25 because she was moving to Baltimore for work. That evening, before going out, she and Barbara arrived at Brenda's home where they smoked cigarettes and half a joint in the garage, saving the other half for later.

Brenda drove the three to Dad's where they had a few drinks and danced. Denise danced with Brenda and Barbara as well as a blonde haired man who danced well.

"Do you know an individual by the name of David Westerfield?"

Denise confirmed she did and although she had not seen him that night, she knew he had been there.

"Did you dance with Mr. Westerfield that evening?"

"No."

"Did you see whether or not Brenda or Barbara danced with him on the 25th?"

"They did not."

"Describe for us what your believe was your state of intoxication or sobriety."

"I had a bit to drink. I was toasted."

Shortly before Dad's closed, Brenda drove them back to her house and Denise and Barbara went home.

Jumping a week forward to the night of Friday, February 1, Denise said Brenda was cleaning the kitchen when she and Barbara arrived. Denise ordered three boxes of Girl Scout Cookies from Danielle, two for herself and one for the soldiers. Danielle filled in the form.

In the garage with Brenda, Denise and Barbara shared a beer and they all took turns smoking the joint.

When Denise answered a call on her cellphone, the reception was bad so she opened the side door and went outside. Unable to connect with her friend, Denise walked back into the garage and closed the side door behind her.

"Did you lock it?"

"No, I did not."

When they arrived at Dad's, Brenda introduced her to David Westerfield who was standing at the corner of the bar with his friend, Garry, who Denise described as a short and friendly Italian looking guy.

"Once he bought the round of drinks, what did you and your girl friends do?"

"We sat together at the bar talking."

"Was Mr. Westerfield included in that conversation?"

"No."

"What was he doing?"

"He was standing on the side. He was very quiet and

weird. He was creepy. He didn't talk at all."

"Objection, your honor."

"As to the characterization, sustained. The jury is to disregard the characterization."

"Thank you," Mr. Feldman responded.

When Rich and Keith arrived, they joined Denise and her friends. She had met Rich before, but not Keith.

"What about Mr. Westerfield? Was he part of that conversation?"

"No, he was not."

Denise then played pool with Brenda, Garry, and a man named Jeff who also wanted to play. Barbara and Keith played on the other table as Mr. Westerfield watched from a distance. After pool, Denise, Brenda, and Barbara went out to the car with Rich and Keith. They listened to Macy Gray and smoked the rest of the joint Barbara had kept in her cigarette pack.

"Did you see them do any kissing?"

"I didn't."

After they went back inside, Denise went to the bar for another drink and some water while Brenda and Barbara started dancing.

"Did you do any dancing?"

"I didn't dance that night. I stayed at the bar and watched them dance. I wasn't in the mood."

"Were you aware of the defendant being in the bar area?"

"Yes."

"What was he doing?"

"Nothing. Standing there by himself. Just standing there."

"Did you see Mr. Westerfield dance with anybody?"

"I believe he danced with Barb for a minute or two and then he walked off."

"Did you dance with the defendant?"

"No, I did not."

"Did you see Brenda dance with the defendant?"

Denise answered, "no," and recalled that Mr. Westerfield left a short time later, around 11:15.

As the bar closed Brenda drove Denise and Barbara back to her house. Upon encountering the flashing red light on the alarm panel after they entered the front door, Denise helped Brenda find the source and discovered the open side door in the garage.

"Who had last used that side door as far as you knew?"

"I did."

"And how open was it?"

"It was wide open."

They closed the door, went back inside, and ate left over pizza. A few minutes later, Denise and Barbara went home.

"When you left that house, did you take Danielle with you?"

"No, I did not."

"Did Barbara take her with you?"

"No."

On Saturday afternoon, sometime between 2:00 and 3:00, Damon called Denise and told her Danielle was missing. Police officers wanted to speak with her about the side door so she immediately drove to the Van Dam's house. Because the road was barricaded, she parked down the street and walked the remaining few blocks.

"Did you have to go by the Westerfield residence?"

"Yes. As I was walking down the street to Brenda's I saw Dave standing across the street from his house on the sidewalk. He said, 'hey,' and I said, 'hey,' and he said, 'I can't believe what happened.' I said, 'yeah, I know. I'm going there now,' and he said, 'well, I left at 9:00 o'clock,' then I kept walking. I didn't stop, I just kind of talked as I was walking."

"He said he had left at 9:00 o'clock?"

"Yes."

"About what time did you last see him at Dad's?"

"The band didn't start until 10:00 and after that I noticed him leaning on that wall so he couldn't have left at 9:00." Although Mr. Dusek assumed Mr. Westerfield was referencing 9:00 the previous night, Mr. Westerfield was possibly referring to the time he left in his motorhome that morning.

"Thank you, ma'am. I have no further questions."

Mr. Feldman began his cross examination by discussing how the Van Dam's dog, Layla, jumped on Denise when she first arrived. He then directed her attention to Halloween 2000 and asked if she and her husband, Andy had, "engaged in sexual relations with Damon and Brenda Van Dam."

Denise explained, "Andy was with Brenda and I was with Damon. It was more of a swap."

"And is it the case that in fact your divorce became final on or about January 31st?"

"Objection. Irrelevant.

"Sustained. You need not answer."

"In 2001 did you attend a Halloween party at the Van Dam Residence?"

"Yes."

"Was Barbara at that party?"

"Yes."

"Was that party risqué."

"It was a Halloween party. Everybody dresses up and we have a first, second, and third prize. There's nothing risqué about it."

Regarding the night of January 25, Mr. Feldman pointed out that she had split a bottle of wine with Barbara before arriving at Brenda's where she then smoked marijuana in the garage.

"Was it good marijuana?"

"I don't know."

"Did it get you high?"

"Yes."

"That was the reason you were smoking it, to get high, right?"

"It's usually what you do."

"Do you feel as a result of your use of marijuana on the 25th that you may have had short term memory loss?"

"Objections. Calls for speculation."

"Sustained. You need not answer."

"Isn't it true, when you first talked to Detective Grbac you never mentioned your sexual encounter with the Van Dams?"

"Yes, that's true. Our encounter was nearly three years ago. I didn't think that had anything to do with it."

"So, you are telling us then, that you were making judgements as to what would be appropriate to communicate to law enforcement concerning the subject matter of their investigation?"

"Yeah," Danielle answered.

"And is it true that you had a conversation with Brenda Van Dam and Damon Van Dam before you talked to the police where all of you discussed the fact that although you had all had sex together at one time or another, you weren't going to tell that to the police either?"

"I never had that conversation with them, no."

"And, isn't it true, that ever since you introduced Brenda and Damon to Barbara it's like every time you hung out they were hooking up with each other?"

"I believe-"

"Objection. Irrelevant, beyond the scope."

"Overruled. You may answer yes or no."

"I believe they were together twice."

"Objection. Speculation, no foundation."

"Sustained. The jury is to disregard the entire question and answer."

Mr. Feldman refocused on their first night out. "On the

25th, you, Brenda, and Barbara were dancing together, isn't that correct?"

"Yes."

"Were you kissing a guy on the table?"

"No."

"Was Barbara dancing with other girls?"

"Yes."

"And it's also correct that the three of you were quote, pretty loaded, end quote?"

"Yes. Not belligerent, just having a good time."

"While Brenda was dancing, you formed the opinion that she was pretty loaded also, isn't that true?"

"I don't recall saying that but-"

"Is it correct that on the 25th you observed Brenda dancing with other girls?"

"We were all dancing together. There were lots of people on the dance floor.

"The women were dancing in a very provocative manner, isn't that true?"

"Yes."

Moving forward to the night of February 1, Mr. Feldman again focused on the marijuana and alcohol; who brought it, who lit it, who smoked it. After reviewing their arrival at the bar, Mr. Feldman asked, "you continued on the 1st to basically engage in the same kind of provocative behavior you had engaged in on the 25th?"

"No."

"Isn't it true you told detectives that, in fact, Barbara was playing provocative pool with whomever she was playing?"

"I don't think I said it in those words, but I believe she was flirtatious. They both were."

"During your first series of interviews with the police, you never once mentioned anything about seeing David Westerfield at the bar on the 25th, isn't that true?"

"That's true."

"Nor did you ever once mention seeing David Westerfield at the bar on the 1st during the first series of interviews before the media had focused on Mr. Westerfield as a suspect?"

"No, I did." Denise recalled telling Det. Grabac about the neighbor, Dave.

"And did you tell Grbac that Mr. Westerfield had said something about leaving at 9:00 o'clock at the bar on the 1st?"

"Yes, I did."

Mr. Feldman pointed out the detective's report did not match her testimony and pressed her about whether her memory improved with time.

"There's nothing I don't remember about the 2nd."

Mr. Feldman recounted several formal interviews with police during which time she never mentioned seeing Mr. Westerfield on the 1st.

"Do you usually smoke marijuana before 8:30 in the evening?"

"Objection. Irrelevant."

"Sustained."

"When you were at the bar, do you recall who purchased the first round of drinks?"

"Yes. Dave did."

Mr. Feldman pressed Denise on how many drinks she had and how strong they were. He noted in addition to her first drink, which Mr. Westerfield bought, and a couple of others she had bought, the man she played pool with had also purchased a shot for her, all before she went to the car and smoked marijuana.

Mr. Feldman emphasized they were listening to loud music and were dancing and singing while smoking marijuana, eager to characterize Brenda and her friends as reckless drug and sex fiends, which, in 2002, may have actually had an impact on the older jurors.

"And something about Macy Gray?" Mr. Feldman asked. "That's who we were singing."

"I'm sorry, I'm old. Who is Macy Gray? Is it rock music? Is it cowboy music?"

"She's just a singer. I don't know, it's upbeat."

Denise specified they were smoking the rest of the joint Barbara had placed in her cigarette box earlier in the garage and said she did not see Barbara and Keith do anything more than talk.

"You have been asked before whether or not you saw them kissing, that's correct, isn't it?"

"I didn't see them kiss." Denise clarified she was sitting in the middle and talking to Brenda and Rich, not paying attention to Barbara.

"Had you gone to the Van Dam's residence with your husband or other friends and met other people at the Van Dam residence?"

"Objection. Irrelevant."

"Sustained. You need not answer, ma'am."

Mr. Feldman expressed his desire for reconsideration and Judge Mudd said he could present his case at the break.

Once back inside the bar after smoking marijuana in the car, Mr. Feldman noted Denise had another vodka cranberry and a glass of water and repeated the list of drinks she had consumed that night.

"Is it the case that there really wasn't a point that whole night when you were without a drink?"

Denise agreed and Mr. Feldman transitioned to when they arrived back at Brenda's house, spending several exhaustive minutes showing photos of the home's interior layout and asking about her activities immediately after she entered. He then disputed her previously stated claim that Damon had been downstairs eating with everyone by showing her an interview transcript in which she said, "he didn't come down at all."

"Yes, I don't recall seeing him in the kitchen. I was concerned with eating and leaving."

"It's the case things were fuzzy because you had a bit to drink?"

"No, I was hungry and I wanted to eat. I didn't pay attention to what everyone else was doing."

"Okay. So, you're not sure at this moment did he come downstairs or didn't he come downstairs, or you got no memory."

Denise remembered seeing him downstairs after they came in from closing the side door in the garage, but not when she was in the kitchen eating.

"What was Damon wearing when you saw him in the garage?"

"I don't remember what he was wearing."

"Do you remember what Brenda was wearing that night?"

"I think she was wearing a red shirt and black pants."

"No further questions at this time, thank you."

Judge Mudd dismissed the witness and reminded her not to discuss the case with anyone until the trial ended. A few minutes before noon, Judge Mudd dismissed the jury for their lunch break, and offered the defense an opportunity to discuss their issue.

Mr. Feldman explained. "I asked a question concerning other parties and whether or not the Van Dams had been social people and that relates to the issue of access. On further point, I know your honor's very, very diligent about telling them not to talk about the case, but my request is that you also advise them, and you have done so, but not in every instance, don't form or express any opinions. "

Mr. Boyce then recited an incident in which he heard a member of the media loudly sharing his opinions about the case on the phone in the hallway. Judge Mudd agreed such behavior was unacceptable.

"I'm not sure who's doing what, but I don't want to have any media person communicating with anybody in the hallways of this courtroom." He directed his staff and bailiffs to monitor the hallways and stop such incidents when they occurred.

Mr. Boyce additionally raised the fact that two of the witnesses, Rich being one, had hired attorneys before testifying. He believed the defense should know whether or not immunity had been offered to either of those witness.

Mr. Dusek answered, "no one's been given any immunity."

"We'll be in recess till 1:30."

After the lunch break, Mr. Dusek called Rich. Rich was self employed in the field of data communications cabling and had lived in Sabre Springs for over four years. He was married and had two young children. His youngest son was in the same class as Dylan, which was how his wife and Brenda met and became friends. They lived down the street in the same neighborhood and the two families often watched each other's kids.

Rich revealed he had been to Dad's a few times with his son's Little League team and had eaten dinner there once or twice. On the night of Friday February 1st, Rich went to Dad's with his friend, Keith, who had previously been married to the sister of Rich's wife. Keith also lived in Sabre Springs and had a friend in the band. Keith invited Rich because he didn't want to go alone. His wife could not find a sitter so she stayed home with the kids.

They arrived at Dad's sometime after nine, saw Brenda and her friends, and joined them at the bar. Brenda introduced them to David Westerfield who Rich had never seen and did not know. The bar was crowded so Rich went to the pool tables with Keith and started playing. He later danced with Brenda and then another lady. He did not dance with Barbara or Denise. When they went outside to the car, he stood by the driver side window and talked to Brenda.

"Any romance out there?"

"I didn't see that."

When they went back inside, he did not see Mr. Westerfield.

"How much did you have to drink?"

Rich was not certain, but knew he had at least one or two beers and two shots of tequila. After leaving, Keith drove to Brenda's house where they ate some pizza at the kitchen table.

"Do you know if Damon was down there?"

"He did come down eventually."

"Did you guys have anything to drink there?" Mr. Dusek inquired.

"No, we didn't drink there."

"Do you know if anyone went outside through the sliding glass door to the backyard?"

"I didn't see anybody go outside."

"Did you see any drugs being used at the house?"

"No."

A few minutes after they ate, Brenda walked Barbara and Denise to the front door and they left. Rich and Keith followed a moment later.

"Did you have Danielle with you?"

"No."

"Did Keith have Danielle with him?"

"No."

The next morning, Brenda called Rich's wife and told her about Danielle. Law enforcement contacted Rich that afternoon.

"Did you tell them what you could remember from that evening?"

"Yes."

"Did you tell them everybody that was at the Van Dam house that evening?"

"Yes."

"Thank you, sir."

Mr. Dusek sat down and Mr. Boyce took over.

Mr. Boyce spent several minutes reviewing the number of times Rich had met with Mr. Dusek before his testimony before recounting, step by tedious step, Rich's activity on the night of February 1st. Without covering any new ground, Mr. Boyce repeated all the details Rich discussed during direct testimony.

"In going over to Brenda's house, it wasn't your purpose to hook up with any of the girls, was it?"

"No."

"But it was Keith's purpose, wasn't it?"

"Objection. Calls for speculation."

"Sustained."

Mr. Boyce moved on. "That night wasn't the first night you had been over to the Van Dam's house, is it?"

"Objection. Relevancy."

"Overruled. You can say yes or no."

"That wasn't the first time I was there, no."

Mr. Boyce switched his focus to Layla who he claimed Rich had described as a, "big sloppy dog."

Rich denied using those specific words and explained Layla was a high energy puppy. Mr. Boyce showed Rich a transcript of a statement he made to police in which Rich did, in fact, describe Layla as a, "big, sloppy dog."

Mr. Boyce transitioned to what happened after he arrived at the Van Dam house and, with the same methodic redundance he exhibited earlier, reviewed the activities step by step, lulling the room to sleep.

"The marijuana you smoked that night, was that marijuana you provided to Brenda?"

"Yes."

"How much did you provide her?"

Rich said he gave her a small amount that he had placed in an envelope.

Mr. Boyce finished his cross exam by asking if Rich was at the Van Dam's Halloween party.

Rich answered, "no."

Judge Mudd excused Rich and advised him against discussing his testimony with anyone until after the trial ended. After excusing the jury for the afternoon break, Judge Mudd spoke with Juror 16 who had stayed behind. Earlier that day, she had notified the court that the women she knew from her child's daycare had returned. Judge Mudd had reached out to the women who explained she was attending for academic reasons and had agreed not to discuss the case with Juror 16 or tell anyone at their mutual daycare. Therefore, the judge allowed her continued attendance so long as she complied with the conditions. If any problems at the daycare were to arise, Judge Mudd would prohibit her appearance.

"All right, we'll be in recess until 3:15."

Following the break, the state called Mr. Westerfield's friend, Garry. Garry was a truck driver and lived with his friend, Jeff, who was the second man who played pool with Brenda and Denise. He had initially met Mr. Westerfield at Big Stone Lodge in Poway about four years prior. He had visited Mr. Westerfield's home a few times and had seen his motorhome, Volkswagen bug, and dune buggy. Garry had known the owner of Dad's for about six years and had started going there often after the Big Stone Lodge closed in November 2001.

On January 25, Garry was sitting at the bar when Mr. Westerfield arrived.

"Did you know an individual by the name of Brenda Van Dam?"

Garry recalled meeting her that night along with her friends Barbara and Denise.

The following Wednesday at In Cahoots, Garry saw Mr.

Westerfield with some of his work friends.

"What type of place is it?" Mr. Dusek asked.

"Country bar dancing."

Mr. Dusek moved forward to the night of Friday February 1 when Garry had made plans to meet Mr. Westerfield at Dad's between 8:00 and 8:30. He mentioned that his friend and roommate, Jeff, had been talking to Mr. Westerfield about possibly manufacturing some parts for Mr. Westerfield's business. When Garry arrived, he sat at the corner of the bar next to Mr. Westerfield who was already there. Jeff arrived alone in his Mustang a few minutes after nine.

Shortly before the band started playing, Brenda arrived with Barbara and Denise. The two groups exchanged greetings, Garry mentioned something about the way Denise had been dancing the week before, and Mr. Westerfield bought them drinks. Garry was drinking a tall Bacardi and Coke. After the bar area became crowded, he and Jeff played pool with Brenda and Denise.

"How about the defendant, where was he or what was he doing during that time?"

Garry was not sure about what Mr. Westerfield was doing the entire time, but did see him at the bar.

"Was there anything unusual going on in the pool room?"

"No."

"Any provocative actions or people coming on to each other?"

"Not that I saw."

"Were you interested in any of the females there?"

"No."

After playing pool for a while, Garry left Dad's. As he walked out, Mr. Westerfield was standing at the bar.

"Was he with anyone?"

"No."

Garry then drove a few minutes away to a restaurant

called O'Harley's where his friend, Yvette, was a bartender.

"Is she your girlfriend?"

"No, we do this every week."

At O'Harley's, Garry helped Yvette close up the restaurant before she drove them back to Dad's where they arrived sometime after midnight.

"Did you, that evening, ever see Brenda Van Dam dance?"

Garry had not seen Brenda or her friends dance and after last call, noticed Brenda and her friends leave. He and Yvette did the same a few moments later.

"Do you know if the defendant, since you have known him, owned any dogs?"

"I don't know."

When asked if he had ever seen a dog at Mr. Westerfield's house, Garry replied, "no."

Garry then recalled finding out about Danielle's disappearance a few days later and realizing his friend, Dave, was the suspect. During that first week, he spoke several times with police who searched his apartment on two separate occasions, once with dogs.

Mr. Dusek concluded his questions and turned the witness over to the defense.

Mr. Boyce reestablished that Garry's roommate Jeff was a machine operator negotiating with Mr. Westerfield for a job developing parts for his business.

"Were you familiar with Mr. Westerfield's patents?"

"Objection. Irrelevant."

"Sustained, you need not answer."

"You've met his girlfriends haven't you?"

"Yes."

"Objection. Irrelevant."

"Overruled. The answer was yes, it will stand."

Mr. Boyce then asked, "Did you know Susan?"

"Yes."

"That was a girlfriend that was living with Mr. Westerfield?"

"Objection. Irrelevant."

"Sustained."

Mr. Boyce asked Judge Mudd to reconsider because the question was foundational. Judge Mudd was not sure and did not, "want to get into something I'm going to regret." He discussed the issue at sidebar where Mr. Boyce explained Susan owned a dog that had been inside Mr. Westerfield's house and RV.

Mr. Dusek pointed out that Garry already said he had never seen a dog.

Judge Mudd asked if he had never actually seen the dog what was the purpose of him being aware of a dog. "What's the relevance of is he aware of something?"

Mr. Boyce answered, "Mr. Dusek asked did he have a dog, this was Susan's dog."

"All right, you can clear it up. You'll be permitted to ask did he ever see a dog or any indication of a dog at the house, but that's it."

Back in front of the jury, Mr. Boyce asked Garry, "when you were over at Mr. Westerfield's house on these occasions, did you ever see a dog."

"No, I did not."

Mr. Boyce moved on to the night of January 25 and asked if Garry had seen Denise, "dancing in a provocative manner."

Garry agreed she had and noted she was receiving increased attention from people in the bar.

"What was she doing that caused you to believe it was provocative?"

"Probably the closeness, you know, and rubbing up against each other the way they were doing it."

"Was she kissing the person she was dancing with?"

"I'm not sure."

Regarding the night of February 1, Garry recalled Brenda and her friends drinking and dancing, and stated that Mr. Westerfield had stayed at the bar while they were playing pool.

"Nothing further," Mr. Boyce said.

Judge Mudd released the witness and Mr. Dusek called to the stand Yvette. Yvette worked as a nurse's assistant during the week and as a bartender at the restaurant O'Harley's on Friday nights. She had originally met David Westerfield four years prior at the Big Stone Lodge where she was working as a bartender and had originally become friends with Garry.

On Friday September 1st, Yvette recalled, she had closed the restaurant around midnight and then drove with Garry to Dad's where she liked to have a drink after work.

"You can't drink while you're at work?"

"No."

Once at Dad's, Yvette went to the bar and ordered a Crown Royal and Coke.

"Did you see the defendant at Dad's at that time?"

"No."

Yvette did not know who Brenda Van Dam was and did not notice her that evening. After leaving Dad's, Yvette drove Garry to his car, which was parked at O'Harley's and went home.

"Thank you, ma'am."

In his cross examination of Yvette, Mr. Feldman repeated that Garry was just a friend she sometimes drank with after work on Fridays and not a romantic interest. He reviewed her previous statements to police in which she said she, "had seen Brenda Van Dam on the news since the event and recognized her as a group of three women that were partying at the bar."

Yvette said, "that was one of the statements I didn't agree with."

"Don't think that it's accurate?"

"Exactly."

"Is it correct that when you arrived with Garry these girls

were intoxicated and very flirtatious?"

"I didn't notice three girls specifically, I noticed one." Yvette recalled noticing only Barbara, the tall blonde, because she had been sexually aggressive toward her.

"Barbara kept rubbing your back and your buttocks?"

"No, I didn't mention my buttocks."

"Did Barbara ask you to stay and party with her?"

Yvette confirmed she had and said the offer made her uncomfortable.

"At some point did Barbara place her hand inside your blouse?"

"Yes, that was the first thing that happened when I got to the bar." Yvette recalled grabbing Barbara's arm and asking what she was doing. Barbara said, "she just wanted to help."

"Now, you also had a friend at the bar whose name was Cherokee, is that right?"

"Yes."

"Have you talked to Cherokee since this event?"

"Yes."

"Thank you. Nothing further."

In his redirect of Yvette, Mr. Dusek revealed the reason Barbara put her hand down Yvette's shirt was because a bartender had dropped a piece of ice down her shirt while Barbara was standing nearby.

"She reached in to get it out?"

"Yes."

"Thank you, ma'am."

Judge Mudd excused Yvette, directed her not to discuss the case with anyone until the rial ended, and released the jury a few minutes early. "Have a safe and pleasant evening. Hopefully by now the Pads aren't already six runs behind. We'll see you tomorrow morning at 9:00. After the jury left, Judge Mudd disclosed, "I've received a communication from one of the jurors that discloses a little bit about who she is. I need to discuss it with counsel so at this time we're going to clear the courtroom and terminate any broadcast."

After a brief proceeding not part of the public record, Judge Mudd ended the fourth day of trial and closed the first section of the state's case against Mr. Westerfield. Having concluded the events leading up to the morning of Saturday, February 2, the prosecution would focus next on the movements and activities of David Westerfield in the hours and days immediately following Danielle's disappearance.

DAY 5

Before the jury entered the courtroom for the fifth day of trial, Mr. Feldman requested a discussion about an event that had occurred the day prior. He mentioned his objection to Denise's description of Mr. Westerfield as "creepy" and stated that his investigator had later informed him that the very next question had addressed the same issue.

"The defense wasn't quick enough on the trigger to make the objection, apparently, at least if you believe the news media, which I'm not conceding as accurate." Mr. Feldman requested that Judge Mudd strike the remark retroactively. Mr. Boyce further requested the jury be instructed not to consider the remark for any reason.

Judge Mudd provided Mr. Dusek an opportunity to weigh in.

"I'm not sure I've heard of instant replay in court. Objections are supposed to be made when they are occurring and having not been made, we go on." Mr. Dusek then conceded that the second remark had been deliberate. "I don't know why they didn't make it, it was certainly loud enough for everyone to hear. I figured it was tactical for some reason. I don't think there's any basis to go back and bring attention to something that was said yesterday when she's already gone."

"I think that's the primary thing," Judge Mudd started, "it draws unique attention to the issue that the media would have put in irregardless. There's nothing that prohibited them from using the answer she gave prior to that even though I told the jury to disregard it. So, at this time the request to revisit that will be denied. I don't, frankly, see any benefit to anyone to get into that."

Mr. Feldman then requested the court sequester the jury because of the unavoidable deluge of media stories about the trial.

Judge Mudd mentioned he had denied without prejudice the motion previously so it could be revisited, but again denied the request.

Mr. Dusek then asked on behalf of Brenda and Damon Van Dam if they could watch the trial from inside the courtroom as it entered its next phase. Mr. Feldman objected and Judge Mudd clarified they had only been restricted from attending during testimony focusing on the events leading up to Danielle's disappearance. Since the prosecution was moving on to evidence that did not directly involve them, Judge Mudd cleared the Van Dams to watch the remainder of the trial from the gallery.

Once the jury was back in their seats, Judge Mudd informed the jury, "I generally like to start the day on a light note before we start the intense work that awaits each of us, but today, unfortunately I have to talk to you about something serious and, no, it has nothing to do with the Padres' inability to preserve a lead. I have gotten ahold of a memorandum from a county employee that raises some issues that may be of concern to the twelve of you as taxpayers and jurors on this particular case.

"To give you the flavor, let me just read to you the opening paragraph: 'I'm sure it has come to your attention that Judge Mudd from the Westerfield trial has really stuck his foot in it. I've been trying to listen to the trial as much as possible as I am very interested in it, however, Judge Mudd is really making a foul impression on the world about San Diego County.' And she expresses two concerns."

The first concern, Judge Mudd revealed, was his criticism of the pens, clock, and air conditioning and the implications they were small examples of a larger competency problem affecting the county government.

"I have not intentionally in any way, shape, or form intended to make light of county government, however, I do occasionally comment on what the truth is and the truth is that this building is over forty years old and has problems. So, any offense you may have had as a citizen of our community that somehow I am making light of the County of San Diego, I apologize for that. Will I not do it in the future? No, I'll still do it, but, the fact is, this employee took offense.

"Now, the second issue is a little more concerning. This employee speaks about the fact that I attempt to lighten the mood in the courtroom and then goes on to say, 'there have been many complaints from many sources regarding his joking attitude amidst such a crucial case, one where a man's life is at stake."

Judge Mudd informed the jury he had worked cases involving rapes, robberies, murders, and other violent crimes exclusively since 1989. "All of those cases bring enormous human emotion into a courtroom. It is emotional for the victims, the victim's families. It is emotional for the people that are accused. When I set out on my career, one of the things I decided to do was not follow in the footsteps of some of my colleagues who had a morose demeanor about them and treated the courtroom as a dark, dank dungeon.

"What I have hopefully done is make it easier on you to come in in the morning. I am not making light of this trial or the rights of the individuals involved, but I am trying to put you in the frame of mind where you can sit back and absorb the material and work with it, knowing we're all humans. I've used the Padres because it's baseball season." He further explained that he did not want jurors, "going home at night a basket case. So, at the end of trial, when this is all over, you can let me know if I've been successful or not. All right, Mr. Dusek, call your next witness, please."

The prosecution called Detective Johnny Keene. Det. Keene had worked for the San Diego Police Department for sixteen years. For the past three years, he had worked in the Robbery Division which handled commercial robberies, carjackings, extortions, and kidnappings.

At 5:59am on Sunday February 3, Det. Keene was paged

while still in bed sleeping. He dressed quickly and arrived at the command post around 7:00. The command post was a motorhome that could be parked near a crime scene during critical situations. On that day, it was parked at the twelve thousand block of Mountain Pass Road, a few houses down the street from the Van Dam's home. His partner, Detective Maura Parga, arrived at the same time and together they were informed that a little girl was missing and they would be working the case. The command center was full of activity as the search for Danielle had continued through the night.

Their first assignment was to make contact with all of the neighbors, obtain their names and information, record a brief statement about where they were and what they were doing during the weekend, and determine what, if anything, they might have seen or heard. Det. Keene and Det. Parga took turns leading the interviews as they moved through the neighborhood. They started at the first house on the southeast corner of Mountain Pass and Briarleaf Way and worked their way east on the south side of the street before crossing over to the north side and working their way back west.

The detectives made contact at all twelve or so homes they approached until arriving at the last house on their list; Mr. Westerfield's. They reached his home at about 11:45 that morning and noticed that his lawn and front yard were extremely well manicured except for a hose that had been stretched to the sidewalk then haphazardly thrown back on the lawn. Due to the dry climate, it was common knowledge that leaving a hose on the lawn could very quickly kill the grass and leave a noticeable yellow stain an otherwise immaculate lawn. Det. Parga assumed the resident had been in a hurry, which immediately triggered her suspicion. She peaked over the side fence to see the back yard and looked through a window into the garage.

In addition to making contact with the neighbors, Det. Keene and Det. Parga opened several sewer drains and climbed down the ladder with a flashlight to search the dark below. They found nothing in the sewars and none of the neighbors they spoke to reported seeing anything unusual.

After completing their search of the neighborhood, Det. Parga contacted the Chula Vista Mounted Police Unit who searched the canyon areas behind the neighborhood on horseback, but did not find any evidence related to Danielle. Det. Keene did not go home until midnight.

On Monday morning, Det. Keene reported to the northeast substation, about three miles away from the Van Dam's neighborhood, where he was informed that members of the special investigations unit had made contact with Mr. Westerfield at his home. Det. Keene jumped in his vehicle and contacted Det. Parga who was stuck in traffic, but on her way.

When he arrived at Mr. Westerfield's home at approximately 9:25, Det. Keene found Sgt. John Wray, Det. Stetson, and Det. Mark Tallman from the Special Investigations Unit speaking to Mr. Westerfield. Det. Parga arrived a moment later and together they began their interview. It was a cool morning, approximately fifty degrees and Mr. Westerfield was wearing a gray, long sleeved, collarless knit shirt, blue jeans, sneakers, and a jacket.

At the front porch, Det. Keene informed Mr. Westerfield they had spoken with all of his close neighbors the day before and wanted to speak with him as well about where he had been over the weekend and if he had seen anything late Friday night. Mr. Westerfield informed the detectives he had woken up on Saturday morning at about 6:30am, took a shower, and left at about 7:45 to pick up his motorhome, which was parked at a residence approximately eight miles into the high valley northeast of Poway.

At the motorhome, Mr. Westerfield recalled he had moved a box of eating utensils and other supplies from his Toyota 4Runner before driving the motorhome back to his residence where he used the hose to fill the water tank, stocked some food, and left at about 9:50. The hose Det. Keene had noticed the day before remained stretched out across the yard in a haphazard manner that was not consistent with the immaculate condition of everything else around the home.

Mr. Westerfield said he he had originally intended to go to the desert, but then realized he had forgotten his wallet and went to Silver Strand instead. About thirty miles southwest of Poway, Silver Strand was a very thin stretch of land that ran parallel to San Diego on the west end of San Diego Bay. About five miles south of the Hotel del Coronado was the Silver Strand State Beach where Mr. Westerfield reported he had arrived on Saturday morning.

As a state park, the Silver Strand State Beach had areas for motorhomes to stay the night. Mr. Westerfield filled out a registration envelope in which he placed cash to pay for three nights. A short time later, a park ranger knocked on his door and informed him that he had put $54 in the envelop instead of $24. Mr. Westerfield assured the ranger he had not overpaid and assumed the extra thirty belonged to someone else.

Mr. Westerfield recalled that because the temperature was too cold, he decided to leave Silver Strand State Beach around 3:30 in the afternoon. When he arrived home, he immediately noticed the numerous news vans and police vehicles and had to park the motorhome down the street near the park. While walking to his house, his neighbor, Mark, informed him that a little girl was missing.

Mr. Westerfield then told Det. Keene he became worried Danielle might have drowned in his pool. He searched his house and back yard, but found nothing amiss and did not locate his wallet. He drove back up to the residence in the high valley and found the wallet in his 4Runner. From there, Mr. Westerfield drove to the Chevron near Ted Williams Parkway, filled up the motorhome, and drove fifteen miles north to Escondido where he turned east and headed into the desert toward Glamis. Although Glamis was only about one hundred and fifty miles from Poway, less than a three our drive, Mr. Westerfield did not arrive there until 10:00 that night, which left a large, unaccounted for, multi-hour chunk of time.

More of an intersection than a town, Glamis was located on the edge of a vast desert landscape famous for sand dunes and offroad trails where people could drive off road vehicles like four wheelers and dune buggies. Although Mr. Westerfield had a dune-buggy and four-wheeler, he did not bring them. They were in a trailer at the residence where he kept his motorhome.

Running southeast from Glamis was a narrow road that ran parallel to a set of train tracks. Approximately every one hundred yards were small drainage canals that ran beneath the tracks known as "washes." The washes were numbered and were used as markers when turning right off the road and into the desert where people set up camp and from there drove their sand vehicles into the desert. Starting with wash number one, which was just south of Glamis, the wash numbers increased the farther south you travelled.

Mr. Westerfield told Det. Keene he did not find the friends he was looking for between washes three and six, encountered a loud group, and ended up down at wash fourteen where he decided to spend the night. About six or eight hours later he woke up and realized the motorhome was stuck in the sand.

After trying and failing to dig himself free, Mr. Westerfield was forced to seek professional help. When help arrived, the man wanted $150, but Mr. Westerfield only had $80. The man wrote down his info and agreed to help if Mr. Westerfield would send him the rest later. Once free, Mr. Westerfield left Glamis and drove to Superstition Mountain about fifty miles west where he spent about twenty minutes before continuing on to Borrego, which was about an hour and thirty minutes northwest. In Borrego, he drove down a dirt road looking for a good area to camp and again got stuck. This time, he was able to free himself with a shovel and some firewood.

Mr. Westerfield informed Det. Keene that he left Borrego at approximately 6:00pm on Sunday evening. He drove around the mountains, avoiding Julian because of potentially dangerous conditions, and ended up back at the Chevron in Poway where he had filled up the day before. Mr. Westerfield refilled the tank and asked a kid driving a white Thunderbird to go inside and buy him a paper, which he did. From there, Mr. Westerfield drove back to Silver Strand State Beach where he found the gates locked. He parked in the Coronado Cays neighborhood directly across the street and went to sleep.

Still standing on his front porch with detectives, Mr. Westerfield continued recounting his weekend with robust detail the detectives found unusual and suspicious.

Mr. Westerfield recalled that at about 4:00 on Monday morning, he woke up and decided it was time to go home. A few minutes after 7:00, he returned to Poway. Because he did not want to wake anyone at the home where he parked the RV, he stopped in a lot nearby and slept a few minutes more. After leaving the motorhome and picking up the 4Runner, Mr. Westerfield arrived home at about 9:20. At that time, he took a shower and did laundry, drying the load twice because the lint filter was full and the clothes had not fully dried.

Mr. Westerfield did not explain how he could have run a load of laundry through the wash once and the dryer twice if he had not arrived home until 9:20, which was just a few minutes before the detectives arrived. The only way that was possible was if he had returned home at least two hours earlier.

When Det. Keene asked about Friday night, Mr. Westerfield recalled he had grilled a steak at home by himself and then met his friend Garry at Dad's Café and Steakhouse where he stood around the bar while drinking rum and Coke. While at the bar, he had seen Brenda with two female friends. Brenda mentioned something about a father daughter event and stated that Damon was not excited about his girl growing up so fast.

At that moment in his recollection, Mr. Westerfield paused and said he thought Brenda had told him at the bar the kids were home with a babysitter. He had not realized they were home with their father.

Moving on, Mr. Westerfield recalled leaving the bar around 11:00 or 11:30 and noticed when he arrived home that neither Brenda nor Damon's cars were in the driveway. From Dad's, Mr. Westerfield would not have passed on his way home the Van Dam's house, which was two houses farther down the road on the same side of the street and on the other side of an intersection. He would not have known if anyone's cars were in their driveway unless he purposefully looked that direction or drove past their house.

When Det. Keene asked Mr. Westerfield how well he knew Brenda, he recalled seeing her a few times in passing, but had only experienced three actual interactions. The first was at Dad's the previous Friday, the second was the Tuesday before her disappearance when Brenda, Danielle, and her youngest son had stopped by selling Girl Scout Cookies, and the third was the Friday before Danielle disappeared.

Mr. Westerfield additionally stated Danielle and Dylan had run around the ground level of the house and checked out the pool in the back yard. Det. Keene asked if they had gone upstairs, but Mr. Westerfield could not say for certain and emphasized they were only there for ten or fifteen minutes.

Although the temperature was near fifty degrees as the detectives interviewed Mr. Westerfield in front of his home, he was sweating profusely. Sweat had darkened the clothing under his arms.

Recognizing the need for further investigation, Det. Keene asked for permission to search the inside of his home for which Det. Parga handed him consent to search forms for his house, motorhome, and 4Runner. Mr. Westerfield agreed and signed the forms.

The first thing detectives noticed when they entered his home was that it was immaculate. He had very nice furniture and everything was clean and in its place. On a waist high divider wall just inside the front door they found a flier for Danielle. Det. Keene and Det. Parga walked through the living room, dining room, and kitchen, not searching as much as observing. Det. Parga complemented the attractive slate fireplace and Det. Keene found the backyard and pool very well manicured.

Mr. Westerfield revealed he had a twenty-one year old daughter in college and an eighteen year old son. He worked at home and owned multiple patents. Upstairs, the detectives found a room with a couch and television and opened the closet door in his son's room. They then went into the room Mr. Westerfield called his office which had multiple computers and work equipment. He mentioned he had his friend Garry's phone number on the computer, but after a brief search, was unable to find it.

As they moved to the master bedroom, Mr. Westerfield started apologizing profusely for the room being a mess and explained he had stripped the bed before leaving for the desert. The detectives noted that his bedroom, like the rest of his house, was pristine. The only thing slightly off was the lack of a comforter on the bed. In the master bathroom, Det. Keene noticed that the screen in the window was pushed out slightly as if someone had leaned on it. Det. Keene described Mr. Westerfield's behavior as overly cooperative.

Back downstairs, the detectives entered the laundry room where they saw a dirty tan blanket on top of one of the machines. As Det. Parga started to inspect the blanket, Mr. Westerfield dismissed it as laundry from the desert and quickly escorted them through the next door, which led to the garage.

In the garage, the west wall was covered with cabinets and the black Toyota 4Runner was parked on the east side, appearing shiny and clean. Mr. Westerfield opened the automatic garage door to give the space some light and then opened up the back of his vehicle, which appeared and smelled as if it had just been cleaned by a professional car wash. There was not a single spec of dust. In their limited search of Mr. Westerfield's home, the detectives discovered no visible traces of Danielle.

Back outside the front of the house, Det. Keene asked to see his motorhome and clarified he was not obligated. Mr. Westerfield agreed to the search and led the detectives to the address on Sky Ridge Road where the motorhome was parked.

Det. Keen recalled the area as being elevated up winding roads with large houses on spacious properties with horses and livestock. They parked at a dirt shoulder on the north side of the road and walked up the driveway toward two RVs, one about twenty-five feet long that belonged to the property owner, and one about forty feet, which belonged to Mr. Westerfield.

The detectives inspected the exterior of the motorhome and opened all of the compartments, which were unlocked. Inside the RV, both detectives wore gloves and headed opposite directions. Det. Parga checked the front cabin, Det. Keene walked toward the back where he found a bed with only a fitted sheet. Like in Mr. Westerfield's bedroom at home, the comforter was missing.

Once the detectives exited the motorhome, Mr. Westerfield offered to show them what he referred to as his "sand toys." He pointed out a nearby white trailer, which he opened to reveal a dune buggy and two four wheelers. The detectives briefly looked inside before they all returned to Mr. Westerfield's home where officers had been searching with dogs.

After parking his vehicle in the driveway, Mr. Westerfield walked over to a news crew filming his home and gave a brief interview with Mark Matthews of KGTV. Det.

Keene and Det. Parga left the scene, grabbed lunch, and checked in at the command center where Det. Parga then called Mr. Westerfield and asked him to come in for a formal interview.

After Mr. Dusek concluded his direct examination, Judge Mudd broke for lunch.

Following the break, Mr. Feldman started his cross examination. "Was this cases kind of one of the biggest items that was on your plate at the time?"

"I would say so, yes."

"Were you aware that the media had very early on focused on Mr. Westerfield as a suspect?"

"Yes."

"Have you ever seen so much attention paid to any one case?"

"Objection. Irrelevant."

"Sustained. You need not answer."

Mr. Feldman proceeded to review many of the details the prosecution already discussed regarding his investigation on Sunday, February 3. He then pointed out that Det. Keene had never asked Mr. Westerfield about specific routes he drove, where he obtained the cash he used at Silver Strand, how long it took for him to reach Glamis, what the weather conditions were, or if he was looking for friends at Glamis.

Regarding the friends in Glamis, Det. Keene responded that he had not asked, but Mr. Westerfield told him anyway.

"Do you recall there was a hailstorm that left in Scripps Ranch and Sabre Springs a blanket of hail that almost looked like an inch worth of snow, do you remember that in January?"

"Now that you've mentioned it, I do remember, yes."

"Did you check independently what the relevance that hailstorm had on the road at Julian?"

"No."

Mr. Feldman noted that black ice was not visible, was very dangerous, and could have been present at higher elevations near Julian.

Moving on to when Det. Keene arrived at Mr. Westerfield's home on the morning of Monday February 4th, Mr. Feldman noted the presence of numerous officers and asked, "do you think the presence of six officers might cause a person to become a little bit nervous?"

"Objection. Speculation."

"Sustained. You need not answer."

Referencing the sweat Det. Keene had observed underneath Mr. Westerfield's arms, Mr. Feldman asked, "you testified that might be unusual because it wasn't so hot out, is that right?"

"Correct."

"In your experience, don't people sweat when six or seven officers appear to want to talk to them?"

"Not necessarily."

"When you asked Mr. Westerfield a question, he would give you an answer, isn't that true?"

"Not always a specific answer, sometimes he was vague and other times he just answered with I don't know." Det. Keene added that Mr. Westerfield did not answer questions about specific times.

"You did not ask Mr. Westerfield about the dry cleaners, did you?"

"No."

Mr. Feldman also pointed out he had not asked about where Mr. Westerfield parked on Sunday night after finding the gate to Silver Strand locked. Regarding the day Brenda, Danielle, and Dylan were in Mr. Westerfield's home, Mr. Feldman asked, "Mr. Westerfield specifically told you that the two kids were running around the house, correct?"

"Correct."

"Mr. Westerfield specifically told you that the two kids were running and jumping around the house, correct?"

"Correct."

"He specifically told you, you know how kids are, they were kind of jumping on everything?"

"Correct," Det. Keene replied.

"He also said, 'I think they even ran upstairs.' He made those statements to you, did he not?"

"Yes."

"The first time you talked to Mr. Westerfield concerning his encounter with Mrs. Van Dam regarding the cookie sale, he told you that her children were upstairs in his house?"

"Correct."

Mr. Feldman continued. "And his comment was he didn't give it much thought because they're just kids and that's the way some people raise their children, correct?"

"Correct."

Mr. Feldman then asked if the "kids were wild that day?"

"Objection. Calls for speculation."

Judge Mudd sustained the objection and directed the witness not to answer.

"And trace evidence, you're aware based on your training and experience can be moved from one place to another inadvertently, correct?"

"True."

"And so what you're telling us today, one of the precautions you utilized to protect against that was to put on gloves?"

"Correct."

"Did you have any shoe coverings?"

"No."

"At that point had you focused on Mr. Westerfield as being a possible suspect?"

"No."

"And you were aware, because you're trained, that it's possible to move evidence inadvertently, if it's trace evidence, from one location to another, isn't that correct?"

"Objection. Asked and answered."

"Sustained. Next question."

Mr. Feldman moved on to what happened after they looked through the motorhome. Det. Keene recalled he and Det. Parga were briefed at the command center where they decided to ask Mr. Westerfield if he would be willing to talk to detectives at the police station.

"Did you then telephone Mr. Westerfield and ask him to come down to the command center?"

"Detective Parga did."

"Nothing further," Mr. Feldman said.

In his redirect of Det. Keene, Mr. Dusek asked about black ice, snow, and hail, referring to Mr. Westerfield's statement that he had traveled a longer route to avoid potentially dangerous conditions.

"And if someone wanted to go from the desert region out there by Borrego or Glamis and avoid black ice, and snow, and hail, and high altitudes, is there a way to get to San Diego without going the back way through warner springs?

"Sure. Interstate 8," Det. Keene answered, referring to the highway that passed just a few miles north of where Danielle's body was discovered.

When asked why he had not asked Mr. Westerfield about the dry cleaners, he stated he did not know about a dry cleaners at that time because it was never mentioned.

"Did he ever suggest you go to a drycleaners at Pomerado Road and Twin Peaks?"

"No."

Moving back to Det. Keene's search of Mr. Westerfield's home, Mr. Dusek asked, "did he say where the comforter was?"

"No."

"Did you see a comforter in the motorhome?"

"No."

"Nothing further."

After Judge Mudd dismissed Det. Keene, the state called his partner, Detective Maura Parga. Det. Parga had been a police officer for sixteen years, a detective for five, and a detective with the Robbery Division for one.

Det. Parga recalled receiving a page at approximately 6:00 in the morning on Sunday February 3 at which time she responded to the mobile command post where she was informed about a missing girl and was assigned, along with her partner, Det. Keene, the task of knocking on doors in search of witnesses. She reviewed the steps she and Det. Keene took that day and noted that the garden hose laying on the grass in Mr. Westerfield's otherwise pristine front yard, "seemed unusual. It just didn't seem right to me. My gut feeling told me that-"

"Objection."

"As to her gut feeling, sustained."

Det. Parga recalled not getting an answer at the front door before looking into the backyard. She then discussed her involvement with the Chula Vista Mounted Patrol for whom she was a volunteer. On Sunday afternoon, the mounted unit had searched the Penasquitos Reserve and the Sycamore Canyon area.

The following morning, Monday, Det. Keene called and asked her to meet him at Mr. Westerfield's address where she arrived few moments later and assisted him with the interview. She remembers the weather being cold and wearing only a light jacket and jeans.

"How involved were you in that interview?"

Det. Parga said Det. Keene led the interview and recalled leaving the conversation intermittently to provide information to the Special Investigations Unit and to retrieve consent to search forms from her vehicle.

When asked if she noticed anything about Mr.

Westerfield's appearance during the interview, Det. Parge noted his, "extremely sweaty armpit area," and remembered him wearing a long sleeve cotton shirt. After concluding the interview outside, Mr. Westerfield signed a consent to search form and escorted the detectives through his home.

"What condition was the house downstairs?"

"Beautiful. Everything was very neat. Very clean. White leather sofa. It was very nice." Det. Parga described the upstairs as equally impressive.

"Did you see any covering for that bed when you were there?

"No. Just the sheets. He apologized for it being a mess."

Det. Parga then recalled entering the laundry room downstairs where some dirty tan colored laundry was sitting on top of the dryer along with some blankets. She did not look inside the machines, but when she started to touch one of the blankets, Mr. Westerfield ushered them into the garage.

On the east side of the garage, between the workbench and 4Runner, Det. Parga smelled the odor of bleach. Because he had also consented to a search of his car, Mr. Westerfield opened the doors to his black SUV.

"It was absolutely beautiful. Very clean. It looked like it had just been cleaned. Like when you drive through a car wash and they spray that stuff on the inside to clean your windows. It smelled nice."

Once at the motorhome, Det. Parga and her partner checked the exterior compartments before walking through the inside. After searching the motorhome, the detectives left Mr. Westerfield and headed down the steep winding road.

"Thank you, detective. Nothing further."

Following the afternoon break, Mr. Feldman began his cross examination, which was a prolonged series of questions reviewing already discussed details of her investigation and peripheral subjects that had little bearing, if any, on the innocence or guilt of David Westerfield. He asked about her shoes, how many times she had testified, details about the command center, whether police were waiting outside Mr. Westerfield's home until he returned on Monday morning, how she and her partner divided responsibilities, why the word "gloves" never appeared in her reports, and a multitude of other questions that probed potential peripheral weaknesses without ever landing a direct blow. After a long and fruitless cross examination that provided no new information or alternative explanations, Mr. Feldman released the witness.

The prosecution next called interrogation specialist and polygraph expert Paul Redden. Mr. Redden had worked for the San Diego Police Department since 1985 and had worked in law enforcement since 1969. Before taking his current position administering lie detector tests in San Diego, he had worked as a sergeant, lieutenant, and sheriff in Wyoming.

On Monday, February 4, Det. Keene and Det. Parga had escorted Mr. Westerfield into the interview room where Mr. Redden was ready and waiting. A tape recorder was placed on the table between them.

Just as Mr. Redden's testimony started, Judge Mudd interrupted.

"All right, ladies and gentleman, I'm going to have you folks come back at 9:00 o'clock. Have a safe and pleasant evening. If the Padres are leading today, maybe they can hold it. We'll see you all tomorrow morning."

DAY 6

Before Judge Mudd brought the jury in for the sixth day of trial, Mr. Feldman informed the court the defense had not been provided information about a fiber collected at the recovery site the prosecution had referenced in its opening statement.

"It's not possible for us then to confirm or rebut that proposition. We were provided a report which insinuated that there was a match, but much later, Mr. Clarke has advised me, didn't represent a match and so I'm raising this as a potential discovery issue because now we're well into the prosecution's case."

Mr. Clarke, the state's DNA and fiber specialist responded. "I'm not sure what to say other than obviously we have kept the defense apprized I think almost by the hour as to the status of testing. We expect DNA results in the next few days on other items. As to that specific fiber, the defense did receive discovery about the fact that fiber had been discovered I think a few weeks ago. Obviously, the comparison process is ongoing."

Judge Mudd acknowledged the issue and believed both sides were making good faith efforts to cooperate, but Mr. Feldman interjected.

"Given that this is a capital case, your honor, I need to raise objections under the fifth amendment, the due process clause, the fourteenth amendment, and the eighth amendment."

Judge Mudd noted and denied the objection. He did not think a discovery violation had occurred.

Mr. Feldman then requested that the Van Dams not be allowed in the courtroom for that day's testimony which included neighbors who had seen Mr. Westerfield's motorhome during the weekend Danielle disappeared. Judge Mudd restated his position that the victim's parents could attend the trial after the testimonies focusing on the events leading up to her disappearance had concluded, which they had. Judge Mudd denied the request and noted for Mr. Feldman that the television cameras largely blocked any view the jury might have of Danielle's parents.

Mr. Dusek then discussed his concern about an eleven year old witness scheduled for that morning. "Her mother does not want her name nor her face on TV. I've informed defense counsel of that situation, they seem agreeable. I'm looking for some assistance from the court as to how we can question her and have her testify without using her name or her face if at all possible."

Mr. Feldman mentioned the likelihood of additional minor witnesses going forward and agreed a uniform approach was appropriate.

Judge Mudd directed the camera operators to film any juveniles from the neck down only. No head shots. He additionally determined the juveniles would be referred to only by their first name. Mr. Feldman further requested the jury be instructed, "that it's California law and not to draw any adverse inferences against the defense."

Judge Mudd agreed and brought the jury back into the courtroom.

"Ladies and gentleman, welcome back. Before we start today, I've got some good news and some bad news. The good news is I haven't heard from any more county employees since yesterday. The bad news is I'm starting to be contacted by all the soapbox lovers who have great concern about having to set their VCRs at 3:00 in the morning to find out what *The Young And The Restless* are doing today. So, it seems like we've offended a whole new group of people. Okay. The record should reflect Mr. Redden is now with us"

Mr. Dusek resumed his examination of Mr. Redden who confirmed he had obtained consent from Mr. Westerfield after explaining the interview was voluntary.

"During the interview, what topics did you cover?"

"We talked about what he had done the night prior to the Van Dam girl going missing and what he had done that weekend."

"Was there a time that you discussed the events at Superstition Mountain?"

"Yes."

"And did he say something unusual at that point?"

"Yes, sir. During the interview, he had been using the singular I. He changed his tense and said we twice when he was at the Superstition Mountain Area."

Mr. Dusek then submitted as evidence an audiotape recording of Mr. Westerfield's interview with Mr. Redden along with a forty-two page transcript. The recording lasted about forty-one minutes and was played for the jury in full while they read transcripts distributed in advance. After the recording ended, Mr. Dusek concluded his questioning and Mr. Feldman hit back hard.

"How many hours did you spend speaking with Mr. Westerfield?"

"Objection 352, your honor," Mr. Dusek said, siting the balance of probative value and prejudice. Judd Mudd sustained.

"How many different times did Mr. Westerfield ask you for counsel?"

"Objection, your honor, 352."

"Sustained, you need not answer."

"352, your honor?" Mr. Feldman asked.

"A variety of reasons, one of which I'm going to discuss with you at sidebar."

After a brief discussion between Judge Mudd and the attorneys that was never made public, Mr. Feldman moved on.

What the jury never learned was that Mr. Westerfield had been interviewed for over eight hours by Detective Michael Ott and others. During that time, Mr. Westerfield had asked multiple times for a lawyer and requested to go home, but the interrogation continued. Because Mr. Westerfield's rights had been violated, much of that interview had been ruled inadmissible by Judge Mudd before the trial began.

"Did you have a heater going in the room that you were speaking to Mr. Westerfield?"

"Yes, sir, I had a space heater." Mr. Redden explained that he had brought in the heater because he was cold.

As an interrogation expert, Mr. Redden was asked what is the difference between an interview and an interrogation.

"Probably an interrogation at some point becomes accusatory."

"Did you construe your communication with Mr. Westerfield as accusatory?"

"Not at this point that we've just listened to. No, sir, it was still an interview."

Mr. Feldman asked if he was aware that Mr. Westerfield, "had been with law enforcement essentially almost continuously without a break since about 9:00 that morning?"

"Objection. Hearsay."

"Sustained."

"As part of your technique, you try and make the subject comfortable, is that right?"

Mr. Redden agreed.

"And among the ways in which you make the subject comfortable is to engage in kind of conversational tone subjects, is that right?"

"I try to establish a rapport with the individual."

"As part of your training as an interrogation specialist are you permitted to lie to people you are talking to?"

Mr. Redden repeated that he tried to establish rapport to keep the atmosphere relaxed and not adversarial.

"Kind of like a salesman?" Mr. Feldman asked.

"You could use that scenario if you like, sir."

"Except in your specific instance, you've indicated you would go so far as to not tell the truth to establish that rapport?" Mr. Feldman was referring to a moment in which Mr. Redden had stated he had trouble remembering things that occurred yesterday when in fact he had no such trouble.

"Did you provide Mr. Westerfield any food?"

"I did not, no sir."

Mr. Redden recalled that he had asked Mr. Westerfield how much sleep he had the night before and when he had last eaten. Mr. Westerfield answered he had slept for about five hours the night before, but had not eaten.

"No further questions at this time."

Judge Mudd dismissed the witness and excused the jury for their morning break.

When they returned, the prosecution called Christy. Christy lived in the home behind Mr. Westerfield's property at a slightly higher elevation, which gave her a clear view of his back yard. On the night of Friday, February 1, Christy went to bed around 10:30 and noticed that his back porch light was on and slightly shining into her room.

"Was that unusual?"

"Not really for that time."

Christy fell asleep and woke at about 2:00 because her two year old son was crying in his room. She brought him back into her room and noticed the back light at Mr. Westerfield's house was still on.

"Was that unusual at that time?"

"Yes. I thought it was just because it was so late."

Christy additionally noticed all of his windows and blinds were drawn tight as if he had left town. She hoped he didn't go to the desert for the weekend and thought, "that's weird. Why is everything shut down like that? And no, I don't remember seeing it fully shut down before. That's what made me think he had taken off to the desert."

"You had never seen the rear of Mr. Westerfield's house that sealed up before?"

Christy said that she had not and assumed he must have left on vacation.

Regarding the motorhome, Mr. Dusek asked how long it would usually be parked in the neighborhood. She recalled a day or two while he would pack it up with what looked like camping supplies.

"Did you know the Van Dam family?"

"No."

"Had you ever seen Danielle out on the street?"

"No."

"Objection, speculation," Mr. Boyce said.

"Overruled, she said no. Next question."

Mr. Dusek sat down and Mr. Boyce of the defense took over.

"Other than noticing Mr. Westerfield's lights on and the blinds closed, it was a normal Friday night?"

Christy agreed.

"And you thought this was unusual because you noticed all the blinds in the house were closed, is that right?"

"Yes."

Christy recalled she had seen the police in the neighborhood, had heard the helicopter flying overhead with messages about Danielle being missing, and had later watched the investigation on the news where she saw Mr. Westerfield. On Tuesday February 5, Christy drove to the command post and reported the unusual activity she had witnessed.

Regarding the motorhome, Mr. Boyce asked if somedays the motorhome appeared and left on the same day.

"Typically, it was there a day prior, at least."

Mr. Boyce tried again. "But sometimes you would see it there the same day Mr. Westerfield leaves, other times it may be there for two or more days before he leaves?"

"The majority of the time I saw it there at least one day prior."

When asked if she had seen the motorhome at any time on Friday, Saturday, Sunday, or Monday, she stated she had not.

After Christina was excused, the state called Holly, the eleven year old granddaughter of Sherman who owned the residence on Sky Ridge Road where Mr. Westerfield parked his motorhome. On the weekends, Holly stayed at her grandparent's home between Friday evening and Sunday afternoon while her mother worked.

On the morning of Saturday, February 2 at approximately 9:00, Holly exited her grandparent's home and walked up the driveway for the newspaper. That morning, she saw a man she did not know, Mr. Westerfield, standing outside his motorhome wearing a baseball hat, sunglasses, and t-shirt. Mr. Westerfield waved and said hello and Holly returned to her house from where she watched the motorhome leave a few minutes later. When her mother picked her up on Sunday, the motorhome had not returned.

In his cross examination, Mr. Boyce was gentle and careful.

"Did you see anyone else around the motor home?"

"No."

"Did you see anyone inside the motorhome?"

"No, all the doors were closed."

"Thank you, Holly."

"Okay, Holly," Judge Mudd started. "Your time with us is done, however, I have to remind you and your mom that you're not to discuss the case or your testimony until this matter's over, okay?"

Holly agreed and exited the courtroom.

The prosecution next called Sherman, her grandfather. Sherman said he had lived in his home which sat on a little more than four acres for over twenty years. He had met Mr.

Westerfield in November 2001 after his son in-law asked if he would be interested in allowing someone to park their motorhome on his property for $100 per month. He and Mr. Westerfield wrote up a short agreement, which they signed on November 10.

When Mr. Westerfield arrived at his home with the RV, he also had a trailer. Although not part of the original agreement, Sherman allowed him to park it behind his own motorhome. He did not know what was in the trailer and never asked because he did not like prying into other people's business. Sherman recalled Mr. Westerfield warning him about a very sensitive alarm system that might go off if anyone gets too close to the motorhome.

On Saturday morning, February 1, Sherman saw Mr. Westerfield through the kitchen window and wanted to speak with him about parking the trailer in a better spot, but by the time he walked out his front door, Mr. Westerfield had already left. Uncharacteristically, Mr. Westerfield had not taken his SUV with him, something he had never done before. Usually, he picked up the RV with his son who would drive the SUV away. Additionally, Mr. Westerfield had not taken his trailer with the sand vehicles, which also struck Sherman as odd.

Since they had started their arrangement, Mr. Westerfield had picked up the motorhome about six or eight times. Most of the time he appeared neat and wore nice clothes like a golf shirt and upscale jeans. When Mr. Westerfield returned the motor home at 7:30 Monday morning, he was ragged and disheveled.

Sherman clarified that he appeared ragged by Mr. Westerfield's standards which was still more put together than most people. He appeared as if he was fatigued after a long trip, but otherwise acted normal.

"Was your residence ever searched, sir?"

Sherman confirmed police had searched the inside of his

home for Danielle and stated the dogs had waited outside.

"Thank you, sir."

In his cross examination, Mr. Boyce asked Sherman about the six or eight times since early November that Mr. Westerfield had picked up the motorhome. Sherman again stated that Mr. Westerfield usually brought his son who would drive the 4Runner home and then recalled some more specifics about his own activity on Saturday, February 2. Regarding the conversation Sherman had with Mr. Westerfield on Monday, Mr. Boyce asked, "for all other purposes he appeared normal?"

Sherman agreed and said the Mr. Westerfield had always been polite, nice, and courteous. He additionally stated that Mr. Westerfield had returned later that afternoon at around one looking for his cellphone. "I had no reason to mistrust him for anything because he had been really good with us.

"Nothing further, your honor."

Judge Mudd dismissed the witness and broke for lunch.

That afternoon, the prosecution called seven different witnesses who lived in Mr. Westerfield's neighborhood, had seen the motorhome and were familiar with Mr. Westerfield's routine of parking it in front or at the side of his home a day or two before and after he went away on trips. One witness had seen the motorhome leaving the neighborhood on Saturday February 1 and another had seen it return that afternoon. Some were aware of neighbors who complained about the RV in the neighborhood. Several had talked to police that weekend and had their homes searched with dogs. Most of the witnesses worked in high level professions, including an attorney, a photojournalist, and a software engineer.

The defense focused on minor inaccuracies between their statements and the official police reports, while doing their best to maximize the time the motorhome was parked in the neighborhood and available to the many kids running around and playing. Throughout the afternoon, the defense focused on minute details that possessed no real importance to the case, possibly in an attempt to drown the substantive details out with a wave of meaningless information.

After discussing a few minor scheduling arrangements, Judge Mudd reminded jurors not to discuss the case with anyone or form any opinions until their deliberation began. "Have a pleasant evening everyone. We'll see you tomorrow morning."

DAY 7

After welcoming the jury for the seventh day of trial, Judge Mudd directed jurors to avoid the LA Times due to its extensive coverage and advised them to be very careful if they looked at the San Diego Union-Tribune. "Don't even read the headings if you can avoid it because you can obviously know what the case is about simply by looking at the nature of the article.

"Also, it has been brought to my attention, and I have seen, a series of interviews that were done with a family member of one of the participants in the trial. That person is now under a gag order and is not to have any additional public exposure or public interviews. So again, I just give you a heads up. Do the best you can to stay away from the material. All right, Mr. Dusek."

The state's next witness was Greg Sheets, a Senior Customer Service Representative at Verizon who was the Custodian of Record. At the request of Mr. Dusek, Mr. Sheets had collected Mr. Westerfield's cellphone records for the weekend of Danielle's disappearance. The records showed who he called, when, and, most importantly, from which cell tower the call was routed.

The first call Mr. Westerfield made on Saturday February 2 was to 679-8976 at 10:08am. The call was received by the Southport cell tower in San Diego County, but did not go through. The next call was to 679-5767 and occurred at 10:46am.

"You don't have information about the subscribers to those specific numbers, do you?" Mr. Clarke asked.

"No."

The second call connected for forty-two seconds and went through a cell tower on Federal Boulevard in downtown San Diego. At 11:10, Mr. Westerfield redialed 679-8976. The call lasted eighty-three seconds and was routed through a cell tower in downtown Chula Vista, which was located just south of San Diego on the way to the Silver Strand beach on the coast.

At 3:28pm, Mr. Westerfield received a call from 679-8976 that went directly to voicemail. At 5:31pm, he called 679-5767 again and spoke for forty-eight seconds. The call contacted a cell tower near interstate 15 northwest of Poway.

At 6:12 that evening, Mr. Westerfield received a call that went straight to voicemail. When he accessed his voicemail a few moments later, his cellphone contacted a cell tower located in Ramona, about thirteen miles northeast of Poway, a northern route toward the desert that would pass through Julian. At 6:15, Mr. Westerfield returned the call from 679-8976 and spoke for a little more than two minutes. This call also went through a tower in Ramona.

The last call Mr. Westerfield made on Saturday was to 679-5767 at 10:26pm and lasted nearly two minutes. The call was made from Imperial Valley, a large area of desert that included everything between the Salton Sea and the Mexican border, including the small town of Glamis and the nearby sand dunes.

Mr. Westerfield did not make another call until Sunday, February 3 at 7:33pm when he called 679-5767 and spoke for just under two minutes. At that time, his phone made contact with a cell tower in Miramar, about ten miles southwest of Poway.

"I have no further questions, your honor."

In his cross examination, Mr. Feldman reviewed the science of cellphones and cell towers. He asked about how voicemail works, signal strength, dropped calls, and whether he had collected call data from Monday, February 4th. When asked if he knew who Mr. Westerfield was calling, Mr. Sheets said he did not.

"So, you don't know whether or not that's Mr. Westerfield's home number?"

"No."

"Did you know whether or not he was trying to talk to

117

his son?"

"No."

Mr. Feldman proceeded to imply that Mr. Westerfield's call might have been bounced from a busy tower and ended up being processed by a tower further away. Mr. Sheets explained if that occurred, it would generally not be a difference of more than fifteen miles.

"Is it conceivable that a call could be placed from Borrego and it might bounce into Imperial County?"

"Yes."

Mr. Feldman then highlighted ten different calls Mr. Westerfield received on Tuesday, February 5 between 8:30 in the morning and 10:14 at night, all of which went to voicemail. On Wednesday, he received nine calls between 7:34 in the morning and 2:52 in the afternoon, all of which also went to voicemail. Mr. Feldman did not disclose the importance, if any, of the calls received by Mr. Westerfield's phone on Tuesday and Wednesday.

Mr. Clarke started his redirect examination by asking about when a congested cell tower will bounce a call to another tower. Mr. Sheets revealed that weekdays are when towers become the most busy and stated that calls made during the weekend were much more likely to successfully contact the nearest tower.

After revealing Mr. Westerfield had two phone numbers on his cellphone plan, presumably one for him and another for one of his children, Mr. Clarke asked if the second number on his plan had been called at any time between February 2 and 4.

Mr. Sheets answered, "no."

"Nothing further."

Mr. Sheets was dismissed and after the morning break the state moved on to Mr. Westerfield's activities at Silver Stand State Beach. The next witness was Nicole, the wife of a traffic division sergeant at the Chula Vista Police Department. At around noon on Saturday February 2, she and her husband arrived in their motorhome for a party they were having for two of her husband's colleagues who had recently been promoted. His entire unit and their families had been invited. Although most of the people attending were only there for the day, Nicole and her husband brought their motorhome so they could spend the night.

Upon their arrival, she and her husband noticed a large and beautiful motorhome parked nearby. About ten police officers and their families attended the party, which took place about one hundred feet from Mr. Westerfield's vehicle. At about 2:00 or 3:00 in the afternoon she, her husband, and several of the officers watched the motorhome drive away. Nicole had not seen the driver.

In his cross examination, Mr. Boyce focused on the time the motorhome left. After confirming the existence of a northern exit, Mr. Boyce ended his exam.

Following the lunch break, before trial resumed, Judge Mudd reminded the court about the, "email from that very disgruntled county employee," and said he was hesitant to open further mail and email, "so, you can well image what my thoughts are when I got this note. This shows what a world class operation the Padres are. 'Dear Judge Mudd, we, in the executive offices at the Padres, have been watching the Westerfield trial. I think everybody is. Admittedly, we get a kick out of each time you mention the club. We are honored you are able to create some humor at our expense in spite of the somber circumstances.' Maybe there's some county employees out there that ought to think along the same lines. They also sent some memorabilia which my staff will thoroughly enjoy. I wanted to let you know there's a positive note out there as well and, of course, what the TV is not picking up is that a couple of our jurors are in Padre blue today. All right, Mr. Dusek."

The prosecution's next witness was Jimmy, an inventory analyst and planner who drove his twenty-seven foot motorhome with his wife, daughter, son in-law, and three grandsons to Silver Strand State Beach on Friday February 1. They parked in spot sixty-six and set up their area with astroturf, chairs, and toys for the kids. That night, while he and his wife slept in the motorhome, his daughter and her family slept in a tent trailer.

On Saturday morning while cleaning up after breakfast around 10:30, they noticed a large motorhome park three spots away close the front curtain. The curtains in all of the other windows were already closed.

"When you drive, do you leave the curtains open or closed?"

"Usually, the curtains are open. It gives me a better chance to look out side windows to see traffic."

"What did the motorhome do after it parked?"

"It basically parked, pulled all the drapes and just sat there."

"Do you remember what kind of day it was?"

Jimmy recalled the day was sunny and comfortable and said people were out walking and riding bikes. His kids were out playing.

"Did you see anyone get out of the motorhome at any time?"

"No, I did not," Jimmy answered and said he and his wife joked that maybe the driver never came out because he had a girlfriend in the back.

A few hours later, his wife saw a park ranger knock on the door of the RV and speak briefly to the driver. Several minutes after their conversation, the windshield curtains opened and the motorhome drove away.

"How long would you say he was there before he left?"

"No more than five minutes,"

"Thank you."

Mr. Boyce led his cross examination with questions about whether he had seen the motorhome on TV and then focused on photographs of the vehicle he may or may not have been shown.

"Between February 1st and February 5th, were you aware that a young girl named Danielle Van Dam had disappeared?"

"We were not aware of it until the detectives called on Tuesday morning."

"And you say, when you're driving down the road you open your curtains, correct?"

"That's correct."

"Are there occasions when you want some privacy and you close your curtains?"

"Not while driving, no."

"When it's parked?"

"At night when you are going to bed or changing clothes. During the day, we don't."

Mr. Boyce moved on to his first conversation with detectives and if his wife had been present when he was shown a photograph of Mr. Westerfield's motorhome.

"Thank you. I have nothing further."

"Sir, your time with us is done," Judge Mudd said before excusing the witness with instructions not to discuss the case.

The prosecution next called Brian Neill, a State Park Ranger for the California Department of Parks and Recreation who had just started working as a ranger and was still being trained by Ranger Olen Golden on February 2. Ranger Neill informed the jury the primary responsibilities of park rangers included campground operations and security as well as endangered species protection.

During the winter months, a visitor would drive through the campground entrance and check in with the camp host who greets guests, writes down their information and license plate, and informs them about the registration process. Guests then pick a campsite and park their RV. To register, they fill out their information on a registration envelope that records their name, campsite number, the number of nights they are staying, if they have dogs, and the amount of cash enclosed. Visitors then leave the envelope in a metal deposit box at the campground office.

At about 2:00 on Saturday afternoon Ranger Neill collected the envelopes from the metal box they called the "Iron Ranger." He and Ranger Golden split the stack and started going through each envelope. They counted the cash in each, confirmed the balance was correct, then marked the finished envelopes with a red pen.

In Mr. Westerfield's envelope, Ranger Neill found a fifty dollar bill and four ones. He only owed $24. Ranger Neill set the envelope and cash aside and noted the campsite number. After the rangers finished processing all the envelopes, Ranger Neill put the fifty dollar bill in with the rest of the cash and took back $30 to give to Mr. Westerfield. At about 3:15, he walked to campsite seventy-two and knocked on the door, noticing the curtains fully closed and that nothing had been set up outside. After a long moment, Ranger Neill thought maybe the guest was not there and started walking away. Then he saw a curtain move and heard the door open. Mr. Westerfield stepped outside and closed the door behind him.

When Ranger Neill informed him he had overpaid by $30, Mr. Westerfield insisted he had not. Ranger Neill said he had used a fifty dollar bill instead of a twenty and informed him that two rangers had been present when the envelope was opened and checked.

Ranger Neill handed the cash to Mr. Westerfield who accepted the bills and said nothing further. After a short, awkward silence, the ranger walked away. Mr. Westerfield did not reenter his motorhome until after Ranger Neill had left.

"Did you have any further contact with the defendant that day?"

"No, sir."

"Thank you."

Mr. Feldman focused his cross examination first on the substantial media coverage the case had attracted and when Ranger Neill realized he possessed relevant information. Ranger Neill recalled he had been contacted in person by a detective on February 4 or 5 who asked about the campsite number system, showed the ranger some photos, and asked him to circle with a green pen a light post in the photo. Then Mr. Feldman asked about the process of visitor check in which had already been covered by the prosecution.

When Mr. Feldman eventually asked about Ranger Neill's encounter with Mr. Westerfield, it was only to confirm that Mr. Westerfield had exited the vehicle and accepted the cash.

"Ultimately, he kind of made a joke, didn't he? He said something about winning the lottery. Do you remember that?"

"No, I don't."

Mr. Feldman then asked why they were called campsites instead of parking spaces and exhaustively reviewed the layout of the park, and the registration process. He pointed out an error in the date on Mr. Westerfield's envelope and discussed Ranger Neill's training. After a long, seemingly directionless cross examination, Mr. Feldman finally concluded his exam.

The prosecution's next witness was Donald, the camp host. Donald was an Army veteran who had worked as an assistant school superintendent before retiring. For a few weeks every year for the past thirteen years, he and his wife had volunteered as camp host at Silver Strand State Beach.

At about 4:00 on Saturday afternoon, Mr. Westerfield had approached him regarding money a ranger had given him that he did not think he deserved. He explained he had just received twenty dollar bills from an ATM and showed additional twenties in his wallet. Mr. Westerfield insisted that the ATM did not give fifty dollar bills.

In his thirteen years of volunteering as camp host,

Donald had never encountered an individual agitated about receiving too much change. He called the ranger office on the intercom for guidance and was told they did not want the money back. Mr. Westerfield informed Donald he was leaving and walked back to his motorhome. As the vehicle drove away, Donald wrote down the license plate.

Mr. Feldman focused his cross examination on the conversation Donald had with a detective the following week.

"And isn't it true you told the detective quote, you did not think Westerfield was the same person? Isn't that what you told them?

"No, I don't recall ever saying that, sir. I remember saying something about I don't know whether I could identify him or not. That's a misquote."

Mr. Feldman tried figuring out what time he had spoken to Mr. Westerfield and Donald thought it was between four and five.

"Thank you. Nothing further."

Judge Mudd dismissed Donald and the prosecution moved forward to Mr. Westerfield's activities in Glamis by calling Dan Conklin.

Dan had lived in Glamis in the Imperial County desert for two years and owned a towing business that also repaired off road vehicles. Dan described Glamis as a small town near a unique spot in the desert where there were lots of sand dunes as well as a large, flat, open areas where people camped and drove four wheelers, dune buggies, and exotic off road vehicles. Dan's shop was just behind the Glamis Store which was near the only intersection in town.

At 10:00 in the morning on Sunday, February 3, someone stopped by his store and informed him about a motorhome that was stuck in the sand and needed help. Dan and his Australian Sheppard Lab mix jumped in his Ford F-150, which was set up for towing.

Dan explained that washes were a system of small bridges placed beneath the railroad tracks approximately every quarter of a mile. The bridges were designed to control the flow of water and prevent flooding. Each wash was numbered, the first of which was just south of the primary intersection in Glamis. The numbers increased the farther south one travelled away from the tiny town.

Dan drove nearly three miles southeast from Glamis to wash fourteen and turned right into the desert. About a half mile in, he discovered a motorhome stuck in very soft sand. He noted the vehicle was about a quarter mile past the area motorhomes could safely drive without getting stuck. The nearest vehicle was several hundred yards away. Although people often get stuck in the sand when entering the desert at night, the RV had travelled much farther into the desert than expected, especially for a weekend that was not crowded. The driver could have stopped in a safer area close to the road and be no less isolated.

The back end of the motorhome was sunk in sand all the way up to the metal panels and all the curtains were closed. Mr. Westerfield was standing outside the vehicle, aggravated by his predicament and in a hurry. He questioned if Dan's F150 could pull the motorhome out and asked how much it would cost. Dan said his truck was capable of pulling out large vehicles, but it would cost $150. With no other choice, Mr. Westerfield agreed.

Dan and Mr. Westerfield began digging the back wheels out with shovels as the dog ran around. At one point while digging, Dan thought he heard Mr. Westerfield say something, but when he asked him to repeat what he said, Mr. Westerfield claimed he had not said anything. After nearly forty minutes of digging, Dan put down some wooden planks and Mr. Westerfield discussed if they should pull the RV forward or backward.

Dan informed him they could not tow it forward because newer motorhomes had a cowling underneath the front end that would break. Mr. Westerfield told Dan another vehicle had tried earlier that morning to pull him out and had used the front end. When Dan crawled under the front end, he discovered the cowling had broken. Mr. Westerfield directed Dan to hook up in the front anyway.

Mr. Westerfield adjusted the hydraulic jacks and put the motorhome in drive while giving it a little gas as Dan pulled. With one strong pull, the motorhome was free. They drove back toward the road to an area where the sand was hard, and stopped. Dan unhooked the RV and Mr. Westerfield asked if he accepted credit cards because he only had $80.

Dan explained he had just opened the business and had not yet set up card processing. He accepted the $80, wrote down his information, and asked Mr. Westerfield to send him the rest when he returned home. Dan then told Mr. Westerfield he would go back for the shovels and Mr. Westerfield's leveling ramps and would meet him back at the main road. After collecting the equipment from the original site Dan headed back to the road, but Mr. Westerfield was already gone.

During his cross examination, Mr. Feldman noted that Mr. Westerfield did not need the wooden levelers he left behind because the motorhome was equipped with hydraulic levelers. He then asked if people ever drove their motorhomes out to wash fourteen.

Dan replied, "some people do, yes."

Mr. Feldman mentioned there were actually two other motorhomes at wash fourteen and when asked to estimate the distance between those vehicles and Mr. Westerfield, Dan said, "several hundred yards."

"At night do people tend to party at Glamis?"

"Yes."

"The people that go out in their RVs tend to distance themselves to have some privacy, isn't that right?"

"Yes."

"There's nothing unusual about that, is there?"

"No."

Mr. Feldman asked and Dan confirmed that Mr. Westerfield was aggravated more than nervous and did not seem more upset than others in the same situation. He had helped Dan dig the wheels out and even offered him a cold drink.

"After you pulled Mr. Westerfield free, it's the case, isn't it, that Mr. Westerfield offered to go back with you to help pick up the wood that had been used under the tires?"

"No," Dan replied. "I offered to get the wood and bring his part of it back to him."

"Isn't it true that you did not think Mr. Westerfield seemed inpatient to leave?"

"He seemed to be in a hurry."

"Out in your neck of the woods, it gets pretty dark at night, doesn't it?"

Dan confirmed that it did.

"And many times, people, even experienced drivers, find themselves stuck and you have to come get them out, is that right?"

"Yes."

"No further questions."

Mr. Dusek began his redirect by asking Dan, "is it unusual for him to be where he was stuck in that motorhome?"

Dan answered, "yes," and explained that it was very far from the road and the sand was very soft.

"Were there other locations out there where you could be away from a noisy crowd but still be on hard sand?"

"It was a light weekend for a crowd, yes."

Mr. Dusek reviewed Mr. Westerfield's hurried behavior and quick exit, and noted Mr. Westerfield had not brought any sand vehicles with him to the desert, which was the primary reason people stayed in the desert outside of Glamis. Mr. Dusek then asked about a conversation Dan had with an investigator working for the defense in which he stated he would only answer the defense's questions if they paid the $70 Mr. Westerfield still owed.

After Mr. Dusek finished, Mr. Feldman had one last question.

"You didn't see anything that made you think anybody else was in the motor home, did you?"

"No."

"Nothing further."

Judge Mudd excused Dan and concluded the day.

"We'll be able to start right at 9:00 o'clock on Monday morning so have a safe and pleasant weekend. A lot of good baseball teams coming to town, so enjoy yourselves. We'll see you Monday morning."

At 4:20, the jury went home.

DAY 8

At 9:03 on Monday, June 17, Judge Mudd welcomed the jury back into the courtroom for the eighth day of trial. "I hope you all got a lot of rest and relaxation this weekend getting you ready for a full week of testimony. Obviously, the Padres started off the home stand real well and the American team is still in the world cup. Who would have thought of that?"

After spending the morning interviewing several witnesses who encountered Mr. Westerfield while his motorhome was stuck in the desert near Glamis, the prosecution followed up on Mr. Westerfield's claim he had spent the night of Sunday, February 3 across the street from the Silver Strand State Beach after finding the gates closed. Officer Mike Britton was an employee of the Coronado Police Department who patrolled the Silver Strand area. At approximately 2:34 in the early morning of Monday February 4, Officer Britton had received a call about a motorhome illegally parked in a lot near Coronado Cays, a private and affluent residential neighborhood across the street from Silver Strand State Beach. Although the lot was open during the day, it was a tow away zone at night.

When Officer Britton arrived at the lot, he found the motorhome and knocked on the door several times without a response. Eventually, the inside lights turned on and an individual stepped out. Officer Britton described the person as in his fifties and between six feet and six feet two. He was wearing glasses and had balding gray hair. The individual gave the officer an ID that said his name was Cecil Halterman and his license plates were from Iowa.

Officer Britton informed the individual he was not allowed to park there and warned if he did not move, he would cite him and/or tow his vehicle. The individual apologized and said he had arrived at the park after it closed. The individual then drove away.

"The individual that you asked to move there in the cays, was that the defendant in this case, David Westerfield?"

"No, sir."

"Are you sure?"

"I'm positive."

In his cross examination, Mr. Feldman emphasized that the call about an illegally parked motorhome only mentioned one vehicle, not two or more. He noted that in Officer Britton's report, he had written that the only other motor homes observed in the Coronado Cays belonged to the residents. When asked how he knew which vehicles belonged to the residents and which did not, the officer conceded he did not know.

In his redirect, Mr. Dusek revealed the Coronado Cays neighborhood had a guard gate at the entrance that allowed entry only to residents of the neighborhood. They also had security patrols.

Continuing their progression of Mr. Westerfield's activities immediately following Danielle's abduction, the state next called Julie, an employee at Twin Peaks Dry Cleaners where she had worked for twelve years. Twin Peaks Dry Cleaners was located in a Poway strip mall about four miles from Mr. Westerfield's home alongside multiple restaurants, a grocery store, and a Target.

Sometime between 7:00 and 7:30 on the morning of Monday February 4, Mr. Westerfield parked his motorhome in front of the cleaners and entered wearing only a t-shirt and very thin boxer shorts that made Julie uncomfortable. It was very cold that morning and he was not wearing shoes, socks, or pants. Mr. Westerfield had been a customer for approximately eight years and had never stopped by wearing only underwear and a t-shirt.

Normally, she saw him in the afternoon and he had always been polite, smiling, and talkative. On that morning, however, Mr. Westerfield appeared tired, distant, and not engaged. He did not say much, looked down, and avoided eye contact. Mr. Westerfield dropped off two pillow cases, two blankets, and a sport jacket.

In his cross examination, Mr. Feldman asked about the other businesses in the strip mall, a time discrepancy on the receipt, when she first spoke to a detective, and her awareness of the case. An explanation for why Mr. Westerfield had arrived at a cleaners at 7:00 in the morning wearing only an undershirt and boxers was not offered.

"If any of the items had blood on it, you would have spotted it, wouldn't you?"

Julie answered, "yes."

Mr. Dusek started his redirect by asking Julie, "did you have a packet of blood from Danielle Van Dam at the drycleaners?"

"Objection."

"Sustained."

"Nothing further."

Judge Mudd excused the witness and the stated called Julie's coworker, Kelly. Kelly worked the second front counter shift at the Twin Peaks Drycleaners, from noon to 7:00 when they closed. On the afternoon of Monday, February 4, Kelly recalled Mr. Westerfield returning at approximately 1:40 with a black sweater, black pants, and black t-shirt. Because he was a regular customer, Kelly just wrote down his name, the number of items, and when he wanted to pick them up.

Mr. Westerfield asked if he could pick them up that afternoon and was informed the items had to arrive by 10:00 in the morning for same day pick up. Kelly recalled that Mr. Westerfield was usually talkative and smiling, but on that day had been curt and distant. When asked if Mr. Westerfield returned for the clothes, Kelly answered he had not and revealed detectives had picked them up a few days later.

When Mr. Feldman cross examined Kelly, he focused

first on inaccurate time stamps on the receipt then asked if there was anything unusual about Mr. Westerfield bringing in those items of clothes. She answered, "no."

"It just kind of seemed like he had a bad weekend, huh?"

"It could have, yes."

"No further questions."

Homicide Detective Neal Torgersen was called next. Det. Torgersen reported he had been asked to locate a dry cleaners related to a receipt found in Mr. Westerfield's 4Runner. Because the receipt did not show the name or address of the business, Det. Torgersen started at Mr. Westerfield's home address and began searching outward. On Tuesday, he tried four different drycleaners without success. At 2:00 in the afternoon on Wednesday, Det. Torgersen showed the receipt to Julie who confirmed he was in the right place. Julie said she knew Mr. Westerfield and revealed she had taken his order Monday morning.

Det. Torgersen went back to the police station, obtained a warrant, and returned to Twin Peaks Drycleaners the following day. He collected two pillow covers and a comforter from the same floral patterned set as well as one striped comforter, a black t-shirt, a black sweater, black wrangler pants, and a sports jacket. He in turn delivered them to Forensic Specialist Karen LeAlcala, at the San Diego Police Department crime lab.

In his cross examination of Det. Torgersen following the afternoon break, Mr. Boyce reviewed his interaction with Julie and noted she had brought out several items of clothes after she received the receipt.

"And at that point you terminated the interview?"

"Yes."

"Nothing further, your honor."

Judge Mudd released the witness and the state called Rosalyn Youngblood, a Custodian of Records at Chevron Credit Bank. Ms. Youngblood was asked to discuss purchases Mr.

Westerfield had made with his Chevron credit card the weekend Danielle disappeared.

On Saturday, February 2 at 5:26pm, Mr. Westerfield purchased $65.20 of gas at 11030 Rancho Carmel Drive, which was at the entrance to Interstate 15 just a few miles from Mr. Westerfield's home in Poway. Mr. Westerfield returned to the same station the following day, Sunday at 7:12pm when he purchased $83.91 worth of fuel. On Monday February 4 at 1:23pm, Mr. Westerfield made a purchase of $14.92 at the 12410 Poway Road station, two miles northeast of his home.

The defense had no questions for Ms. Youngblood.

At 3:37, Judge Mudd dismissed the jury early and reminded them to return by 9:00 the next morning. "All right, we'll be in recess."

DAY 9

At 9:00 on Tuesday morning, Judge Mudd welcomed the jury and said, "now, I don't want this to be taken as a criticism of any county department or employee, however, it's very obvious to all of you that we are in the middle of a fire and it's coming into this courtroom. Right now, as we speak, the maintenance department is meeting to determine why all of that outside air is coming in here. The good news is the air conditioning is still working, so hopefully it will stay cool even though it's going to smell like we're right on the fringes of that fire.

"The other thing I have left to tell you is we are being invaded. Yesterday, we noticed a number of ants. Again, this is not a critique of anything, but if you start noticing ants in the jury box, please let me know. I urge you also to be very careful with your drinks and everything so you don't spill them. All right, Mr. Dusek."

"Mr. Clarke today."

"All right, Mr. Clarke."

Having completed their review of Mr. Westerfield's activities in the hours and days immediately following Danielle's abduction, the prosecution entered the third and final stage of their case; the evidence. Leading the state's presentation was George "Woody" Clarke who had become famous during the OJ Simpson trial where he presented the DNA evidence and, in turn, introduced the country to the ground breaking new technology. Mr. Clarke's first witness was Forensic Specialist Dorie Savage.

Ms. Savage had earned a degree in evidence technology from Grossmont College and had worked the previous three years at the San Diego Police Department crime laboratory where she had initially received extensive, closely supervised training. Her responsibilities included photographing crime scenes, finding and collecting finger prints, recovering finger nail clippings, and taking hair samples and DNA swabs from victims, suspects, and other persons of interest.

On Saturday February 2, Ms. Savage arrived at the Van Dam house at approximately 4:20pm. At that time, the area was active with numerous police officers and detectives as well as search and rescue personnel. The sun was setting fast so she checked in at the command post and began taking photos of the exterior home.

When Forensic Specialist Ruben Inzunza arrived, they performed an initial walkthrough of the home before identifying, photographing and collecting items of interest. Using a strong flashlight, Ms. Savage also searched for fingerprints upon which she would apply black powder before collecting.

That night, Ms. Savage collected prints from Danielle's door, door frame, and desk. She additionally collected seven prints from the stairway banister. From the floor of Danielle's room, Ms. Savage collected Power Puff Girls pajamas that were inside out, socks, a purple shirt, and a pair of jeans. In the garage, she swabbed a red stain on the floor and on the side gate outside she collected a small hair. At 5:30 the next morning, Ms. Savage and Mr. Inzunza finished processing the Van Dam home and transported all the evidence to the police station.

On Sunday morning at about 10:00, Ms. Savage returned with detectives and collected more evidence and fingerprints. During her second trip, Ms. Savage noticed the black powder had been cleaned, the downstairs floor had been vacuumed, and a gate had been placed in front of Danielle's door. She collected a bean bag from Danielle's room for possible blood stains and found additional spots of blood on the stairwell wall near the landing. She collected carpet fibers from Danielle's bedroom as well as hair from the Van Dam's dog, Layla, a medium sized gray Weimaraner.

On Tuesday, February 5 at 10:00am, Ms. Savage and Mr. Inzunza processed Mr. Westerfield's 4Rnner at the impound lot.

That night, Ms. Savage searched the inside of the 4Runner using a strong light that utilized different wave lengths which, in conjunction with special goggles, could reveal biological trace evidence such as stains, hairs, and fibers that were not visible with the naked eye. Ms. Savage also used a Cyanoacrylate superglue packet that adheres to and exposes hidden fingerprints that can then be photographed. In total, Ms. Savage lifted five prints from the vehicle's exterior as well as one from the interior driver side door and one from the interior passenger door.

A few days later she collected mouth swabs and hair from Brenda and Damon Van Dam, and their two sons. On February 13, Ms. Savage returned to the Van Dam's home where they used Ninydrin in several locations. Ninydrin was a chemical spray used to illuminate prints that were then photographed. With the Ninydrin, Ms. Savage discovered several more prints in the upstairs hall as well as on a wall between the kitchen and the door to the garage. A portion of wall between the garage and kitchen was extracted and taken back to the lab for further study.

On February 27, Ms. Savage accompanied Forensic Specialist Karen LeAlcala to the scene off Dehesa Road where Danielle's body was found. She examined bushes that had been cut away as well as vegetation, leaves, grass, and sticks in the area surrounding the body. She collected vegetation from beneath the body, took swabs of Danielle's neck, and used tape lifts on the bottom of her right foot.

The following day, Ms. Savage attended the autopsy where she collected the white sheet that had been used to wrap the body, scraped under the finger nails, swabbed her neck in multiple spots, and plucked some of Danielle's hair for their root before the doctor cut the rest off and gave it to her. Ms. Savage also collected hair that was tangled in Danielle's right hand and a short dark hair stuck to her skin beneath her arm. From Danielle's necklace, Ms. Savage collected hair, sticks and dirt.

"To your knowledge, did another collection specialist

whom you've referred to earlier as Karen LeAlcala also collect items in this case?"

"Yes, she did."

"Were you ever inside the house of David Westerfield?"

"No, I was not."

"Were you ever inside a motorhome identified as belonging to David Westerfield?"

"No, I was not."

Concluding his direct examination, Mr. Clarke handed Ms. Savage an envelope of evidence he asked her to open. She opened the brown envelop and took out a transparent plastic bag. Inside the bag was the necklace Danielle was wearing when she died.

"Your honor, I would ask the court's permission for the witness to hold that up so the jury can view it."

Judge Mudd answered, "certainly."

Ms. Savage held the necklace up for the jury to see.

"Thank you, Ms. Savage. No further questions, your honor."

Mr. Feldman started his cross examination of the state's first forensic witness with questions about the size of the Van Dam's dog, Layla. He then asked for the definition of cross contamination, which Ms. Savage described as the process of inadvertently removing an item from one location and transporting it to a second. Mr. Feldman noted she had previously mentioned the large amount of evidence in the Van Dam case and how Ms. Savage alone had been responsible for collecting approximately one hundred separate items.

Regarding the bean bag in Danielle's room, Ms. Savage recalled that a presumptive blood test called a Hemastix she had applied to several dark stains confirmed the presence of blood.

Implementing a strategy he would use throughout the evidence segment of the trial, Mr. Feldman followed a relatively short and simple direct examination with a long, exhaustive cross that focused on a variety of adjacent subjects with little, if any, relevance. Mr. Feldman asked numerous questions about why her photos were not time stamped and reviewed in detail her process of labeling and organizing crime scene photos. He asked why she wore gloves at crime scenes and inquired about theoretical causes of crime scene contamination. He discussed the seven finger prints found on the banister and asked her to point out in photos where each print was found before reviewing in detail the process of collecting finger prints. Although the accusation lingered, he never directly accused Ms. Savage contaminating evidence nor did he ever question the legitimacy of the fingerprints collected.

Moving forward, Mr. Feldman inquired about the piece of wall that had been removed on February 13. She recalled using Ninhydrin and taking forty-seven photographs before removing the section. She explained the process of using a variety of exposure and lighting combinations in hopes of finding the algorithm that revealed the print best. Mr. Feldman speculated the print might have been left by an intruder entering from the garage.

Ms. Savage also revealed that she had found a print on a desk near Danielle's bed and another forensic specialist had found prints on the sliding glass door in the kitchen.

"Your honor, is this an appropriate time to recess?"

Judge Mudd said it was and told the jury, "ladies and gentleman, we are going to take the lunch break. Take some deep breaths, walk, get your motors going here again. I think we've put half the country to sleep this morning. Have a pleasant lunch and remember not to formulate or discuss any opinions regarding the case till the matter's submitted to you for decision."

Following the lunch break, Mr. Feldman asked Ms. Savage about her interactions with the Van Dams.

"Were they cooperative?"

"Yes, they were."

"You didn't draw any adverse inference from the fact that somebody might be cooperative, did you?"

"Objection, argumentative."

"Sustained. You need not answer."

After reviewing more of her activities within the Van Dam home, Mr. Feldman asked whether she was briefed before going to the Van Dam house the second time, who was at the briefing, what time she arrived at the house, and how long she was outside the motorhome at its Skyridge location. After confirming Ms. Savage had searched the Van Dam's laundry room, he revealed there were clothes in the washer and dryer.

Mr. Feldman then moved on to the body recovery site. "Was your job, one of your primary responsibilities, to preserve the scene to make sure it could not be contaminated?"

"No." Ms. Savage explained that was not her responsibility and noted the scene was roped off and secured by numerous officers while she was there.

"Do you recall a helicopter?"

"It wasn't there when I was there."

Mr. Feldman asked multiple questions about what the patrol officer and detectives were wearing that night and how close to the body she was when collecting evidence. He then showed a large image of the recovery site that unnecessarily included Danielle's body. Mrs. Van Dam started crying and immediately left the room.

Without losing a beat, Mr. Feldman asked Ms. Savage to point out where the bushes that had been collected were located. Every time he seemed close to uncovering a significant revelation, Mr. Feldman began a new series of questions that again led nowhere.

Although Mr. Dusek's direct examination lasted only a little more than an hour, Mr. Feldman's cross examination endured for nearly three and contained very little relevant substance. Well into the afternoon, Ms. Savage was finally dismissed.

Mr. Clarke next called Detective James Tomsovic. Det. Tomsovic had worked as a police officer for thirty-two years. He had been a detective for fifteen, and a homicide detective for four. At 11:00pm on Monday February 4, Det. Tomsovic was contacted by Sgt. William Holmes who requested that he report to the Rancho Penasquitos police station to assist the investigation of a missing child.

Shortly after midnight, Det. Tomsovic attended a briefing led by Sgt. Muren that included about twenty different officers and detectives from multiple investigative units as well as several FBI agents. For the next hour, Sgt. Muren discussed the known details that had been collected by the already extensive investigation.

At about 2:15 in the morning of Tuesday, February 5, Det. Tomsovic delivered a search warrant to Mr. Westerfeild at his home. He then entered the residence with Forensic Specialist Karen LeAlcala and together they walked through the home room by room, taking photos and identifying evidence with numbered placards. After completing the walkthrough, Ms. LeAlcala photographed and collected the evidence. Det. Tomsovic additionally drew rough sketches of each room that included the dimensions, furniture, and location of evidence. Ms. LeAlcala took approximately one thousand photos.

On the kitchen counter, they found gas station receipts from Chevron dated February 2 and 3, a note containing the name "Dan" along with an address in Glamis, mail that included an ad from Linens 'N Things depicting a four post bed with lace-like drapes that was very similar to Danielle's bed, a notepad that had Brenda and Damon's names and phone number, a drycleaner receipt, and a shopping list that included Mountain Dew, Pepsi, rum, dryer sheets, eggs, mouthwash, and bleach.

Upstairs, they took photos of Mr. Westerfield's son's

room, which was a little messy, as well as a den that looked onto the street. The first location that attracted increased attention was an upstairs office where they found a desk, two computers, a fax machine, a copy machine, and a bookcase filled with binders, computer related books, and computer software. Det. Tomsovic and Ms. LeAlcala did not examine the office beyond taking photos because two agents from the Regional Computer Forensic Labs were on their way.

In Mr. Westerfield's bedroom, the bed was covered with a fitted bottom sheet and a flat top sheet. Two pillows with pillowcases and an unmade comforter were on top and on the floor beside the bed were two pillows, without cases, near a laundry basket. Other than the bed, the room was immaculate. The closet was filled with clothes that were well organized and neat.

In the master bathroom, Det. Tomsovic noticed the window screen had been pushed out. When he leaned forward through the window frame he could see a portion of the Van Dam's back yard a few houses away. When Mr. Dusek asked if he had found any binoculars upstairs, Det. Tomsovic revealed he had found a set in the top drawer in the dresser adjacent to the bathroom door. Another set had been found on the kitchen counter.

"How long were you at the Westerfield residence?" Mr. Dusek asked.

Det. Tomsovic recalled they had worked until 3:00 the next afternoon.

"Had you been into the Van Dam residence before you went into the Westerfield residence?"

"No."

From Mr. Westerfield's home, Det. Tomsovic, Sgt. Holmes, Forensic Specialist Karen LeAlcala, and Criminalist Annette Peer drove out to the property where the motorhome was parked. They searched the exterior and collected a few items before the vehicle was towed to the impound facilities where it was searched the following day.

Mr. Dusek displayed a series of photos showing the interior of the motorhome for the jury and noted a small bath towel that was laying on the floor outside the bathroom. He then focused on a cabinet above the left side of the bed where black fingerprint powder was present.

"Who lifted the prints?"

"Karen LeAlcala"

Finger prints had also been lifted from several locations inside the bathroom including the sink, toilet lid, and floor.

"Did you go to the recovery site down on Dehesa Road?"

Det. Tomsovic recalled he and his team arrived at the scene at around 6:00 as the sunset was turning into night. He remembered the location was, "just east of the Singing Hills Golf Course across the road from the Sloan Canyon Sand and Gravel Pits approximately 1.5 miles east of Willow Glen Road and approximately a half mile west of Sloan Canyon Road."

"Do you know where Sycuan Casino is?"

Det. Tomsovic revealed the casino was about three miles east of where Danielle's body was found. Because the sun had set and the scene was secure, Det. Tomsovic and his team left the site and returned the following morning. Mr. Dusek asked him to describe the scene.

"The area where the body was found is like a little pocket valley. There's a high ridge of mountains to the north. It's isolated, there are no homes along that particular stretch. On the south side of Dehesa Road is a series of interconnected ponds that belong to the sand quarry. There are no habited dwellings along that part of the road and it's fairly isolated. There's some low shrubbery, Sumac bushes, grass, meadow grass, and as it proceeds up the hill it becomes a predominantly grassy area."

Mr. Dusek showed a picture of where the body was found, which was near the only oak tree along that stretch of road amid a thicket of Sumac bushes. On the ground around her body were leaves, dirt and grass.

In the area immediately surrounding where Danielle's body was discovered, criminalists David Cornacchia and Annette Peer had searched on hands and knees for trace evidence such as hairs and fibers, and looked for missing body parts as well. Beyond a five foot radius to about fifty feet Det. Tomsovic and Ms. LeAlcala searched on foot for items that might have been used to wrap the body like clothing, blankets, or trash bags. They also looked for missing body parts. Beyond about one hundred yards, a group of additional detectives formed a search line and moved up the hill. South of Dehesa Road, a search and rescue team with the Sheriff's Department searched the quarry with dogs.

"When Danielle was found did she have any clothes on?"

"No, she didn't."

"Did you find any clothing?"

"No, we didn't."

"Did you find any teeth?" Mr. Dusek asked.

"No, we did not."

"Did you find any blankets or pajamas?"

"No."

"Did you see any signs that would indicate parts had been dragged away?"

"Not immediately around the body, but some distance away we found a trail that appeared like possibly a body part had been drug and left this greasy brownish stain on the ground."

"Why do you say it appeared to be?"

"The appearance was similar to stains that were found close to the body. It had a distinct odor of decomposing flesh."

"Did you ever find the missing foot?"

"No. I believe there were also probably entrails that were missing. There had been some animal activity on the body."

Mr. Dusek transitioned to questions about the Van

Dam's dog, who Det. Tomsovic described as very friendly.

"How many times did she bark?"

"She never barked."

"How many times did she bite you?"

"She never did."

"Have you been in both the Van Dam and the Westerfield home?"

"Yes, I have."

"Can you describe the carpeting?"

When asked if the carpeting in the Van Dame's house was the similar to the carpeting in Mr. Westerfield's, Det. Tomsovic answered, "no" and said they were a different material and color.

"Thank you, sir."

Mr. Boyce started the defense's cross examination of Det. Tomsovic by noting the mail flier found in Mr. Westerfield's kitchen showing a canopy over a four post bed was junk mail and therefore just a coincidence that it was the same style bed as Danielle's. He then revealed that the view of the Van Dam's backyard from the upstairs bathroom window was only of a very small area in the center of the yard, not the entire yard.

"Yeah, where the play area is located," Det. Tomsovic responded.

"In fact, from the bathroom window you had to lean out, didn't you?"

"Yes."

"Did you see a poster bed in the back yard?"

Det. Tomsovic said, "no," and confirmed that he did not see a canopy in the back yard either.

"And this junk mail flier that Mr. Dusek showed you, that's a junk mail flier that was mailed to every house in the neighborhood, isn't it?"

Det. Tomsovic did not know.

Mr. Boyce moved on to his prepared questions starting

with the night Det. Tomsovic and his team had first been called. He focused on the large number of police personnel who had worked the neighborhood and who had also stepped inside the Van Dam house. Mr. Boyce did his best to place as many officers as possible in the briefing room within direct proximity to Det. Tomsovic.

"About how many people were in this room?"

"About twenty maybe."

Mr. Boyce reviewed the briefing which had lasted about an hour, ending at around 2:00am. Multiple evidence technicians had also attended, including Karen LeAlcala.

After leaving the briefing, Det. Tomsovic recalled driving to the Sabre Springs neighborhood. Continuing his cross contamination innuendo, Mr. Boyce discussed the mobile command post that had been parked down the street from the Van Dams and without directly accusing anyone of cross contaminating trace evidence, implied that either Det. Tomsovic or members of his team had come into contact with individuals who had been inside the Van Dam house earlier that day.

Det. Tomsovic recalled that when he arrived at Mr. Westerfield's home with the warrant, Mr. Westerfield was sitting at his dining room table with Det. Keyser and Det. Ott who had interviewed him earlier that day.

Det. Tomsovic again recalled walking through the house with Karen LeAlcala. Starting their search around 3:00am in the living room, they walked through the entire downstairs including the laundry room and garage before heading upstairs.

At that time, Judge Mudd paused the testimony. "All right, ladies and gentleman, we are going to break for the evening. Hopefully the Pads can keep their American League tour going. Have a safe evening, we'll see you tomorrow at 9:00."

DAY 10

After a short proceeding not made part of the public record, Judge Mudd invited the jury back into the courtroom for the tenth day of trial. "Good morning ladies and gentleman, and welcome back. Early on in this trial I basically told you that my function obviously is to ensure that both sides get a fair trial, but in addition to that I basically describe myself as the shepherd and you as my flock. I use that analogy primarily to let you know that my job is to create an environment in this courtroom for citizen jurors that is conducive to your doing the work, the very difficult work, we ask of you and at the same time maintain your normal life and your normal well being."

Judge Mudd proceeded to discuss the importance of avoiding media stories about the trial whether they are newspaper, television, or radio. He then mentioned that one of the jurors incidentally knows a regular visitor in the gallery. The juror and the spectator had been advised not to communicate at the courthouse because the media may assume they were discussing the case. Although Judge Mudd was confident they would not discuss the case, he did not want to provide the media an impression of impropriety. The spectator was additionally warned not to disclose the name or information of the juror to anyone in the media or in the courtroom.

Judge Mudd additionally discussed negative publicity he had received regarding, "some of the things and some of the actions that I have taken and I am going to say right now I make no apologies. I am leaving that strictly up to your critique of me at the end of this case as I have indicated before. Hopefully, the environment I'm seeking to create will indeed be the environment that you find yourselves in and, when this experience is over, you will have found it to be number one rewarding, but number two, a pleasant or a good experience as a citizen in the community in a very, very serious case. All right. Mr. Boyce, you may continue your cross examination."

"Thank you, your honor."

Mr. Boyce returned to the Linens 'n Things flier found on Mr. Westerfield's kitchen counter and noted that it was addressed to "Our Neighbor At." When asked how he learned Danielle's bed had a similar canopy, Det. Tomsovic revealed he had been told by another detective.

Regarding Mr. Westerfield's upstairs office, Det. Tomsovic recalled they had photographed and searched the room out of order so when computer specialist Officer Watkins arrived he could immediately begin his work.

Although not discussed during the state's direct examination, Mr. Boyce asked Det. Tomsovic about a brown paper envelop discovered behind some books in the top left corner of the bookcase behind the desk in Mr. Westerfield's office. Inside the envelope, Det. Tomsovic had found several CDs and small zip drives he placed on the desk for Ms. LeAlcala to photograph.

Mr. Boyce asked if he had looked at the contents of the disks.

"I did not see their content, I just saw the disks themselves."

"Approximately what time was it that you finished processing Mr. Westerfield's house?"

"We left the house at about 3:00pm," Det. Tomsovic answered and stated that all the evidence boxes were placed in Karen LeAlcala's van.

After concluding his questions about the search of Mr. Westerfield's home, Mr. Boyce moved on to the search of Mr. Westerfield's RV.

"Who was the first person into the motorhome?"

Det. Tomsovic recalled that the Sheriff's Department had search dogs that entered before they began processing the inside, which took a total of three days.

"When you first entered the motor home, you noted a layer of dust throughout the inside?" The detective agreed and Mr. Boyce added it, "didn't appear anybody had attempted to remove the dust inside the motor home recently?"

"It was not a heavy layer of dust. It wasn't like something that accumulated over a long period of time. It was a light coating. The motorhome was very clean, and neat, and orderly. But it doesn't look like it had been wiped down if that's the point you're making."

"Approximately how many latent fingerprints were recovered from inside the motorhome while you were present?"

"As I recall, Karen LeAlcala took six fingerprint lifts, some of which may have contained more than one individual print."

Moving on to the detective's activities at the recovery site, Mr. Boyce asked what time Dr. Blackbourne had examined the body.

"Approximately 10:00pm that night," Det. Tomsovic recalled and noted the body had been wrapped in a white sheet after paper bags were placed over her hands, feet, and head.

"And in your investigation, I believe you determined that the last precipitation in that area was on February 17th of 2002?"

"Based on meteorological records, yes."

"What did you mean to communicate by the last precipitation?"

"Rain, heavy dew, anything that could have altered the scene due to weather activity."

"I don't have anything further, your honor," Mr. Boyce concluded.

In his redirect examination, Mr. Dusek noted that Danielle's bedroom was in the front of the house and her bed was potentially visible from the street.

"You talked about the envelope that came from the Westerfield office as being hidden back in the bookshelf. What type of items were around the area where the envelope came from?"

Det. Tomsovic recalled that the envelope had been in the extreme top left corner of the bookshelf behind a three ring binder, cardboard box, and some computer related books.

"Do they generally appear to be computer books for work?"

"I would think so."

"When seizing items from the house, from the laundry, from the garage, did you make any efforts to keep them separate from each other?"

Det. Tomsovic stated they separated each item of evidence in their own sealed bag to prevent any kind of cross contamination.

"Questions were asked about the sheet at the recovery site," Mr. Dusek began. "What is the sheet for?"

"To wrap the body in and contain any possible trace evidence that may adhere to the body and could fall off in transport."

"Do you guys reuse those sheets?"

"No."

"Was a brand new one used on this occasion?"

"Yes."

Regarding the dogs used to inspect the motorhome, Mr. Dusek asked if hair samples were ever obtained from the animals and Det. Tomsovic confirmed samples had been collected.

In his recross, Mr. Boyce returned again to the flier and Det. Tomsovic clarified that Officer Labore had informed him about the flier before he had started processing the home. Mr.

Boyce mentioned that a dog bed had been found in one of the motorhome's exterior compartments and asked what he had been wearing the night Danielle was found.

Det. Tomsovic was not sure what he or anyone else had been wearing.

"Nothing further."

After Judge Mudd excused Det. Tomsovic, the state called Forensic Specialist Karen LeAlcala. Ms. LeAlcala had graduated from Pennsylvania State University before earning a degree in evidence technology from Grossmont College. She had worked for the San Diego Police Department in the crime lab for two years.

At a few minutes after 2:00 in the morning on Tuesday, February 5, Ms. LeAlcala arrived at Mr. Westerfield's home where she was directed to take photos and collect evidence. Ms. LeAlcala recalled that she and Det. Tomsovic walked through the house and identified items of interest before she marked them and took pictures. She did not start actually collecting evidence until 8:23 that morning.

"Do you use gloves at all as part of that collection method?"

"I always wear gloves when I collect evidence, yes."

Focusing on the laundry room, Ms. LeAlcala revealed she had collected from the washing machine a white bath towel, multiple pillow cases, and two off white bedspreads. The items in the wash were wet and one of them had a grass like material clinging to the inside. From the dryer, she collected a long sleeved, gray, extra-large shirt, medium sized black and gray boxer shorts, socks, pillowcases, and towels. On top of the dryer, she found a white large Eddie Bauer t-shirt, a white XXXL t-shirt, black extra large sweat paints, grey medium sized boxer shorts, and three pairs of white size 36 briefs. She additionally found a box of linens in the garage.

"What is a criminalist?" Mr. Clarke asked.

Ms. LeAlcala explained criminalists were trained to analyze evidence and usually had a specialty such as trace evidence or gun shots.

"Did your search of the residence also include the master bedroom area?"

"Yes."

"Did your collection of evidence include retrieving any items from the headboard area in that room?"

"Yes. I collected video cassette tapes and a bottle of what was labeled as *Juicy Lube.*" Mr. Clarke showed the courtroom pictures of the *Juicy Lube* bottle found by the headboard of Mr. Westerfield's bed.

"Did you also collect any evidence from the actual bed in the master bedroom?"

"Yes, I did. I collected pillowcases, a fitted sheet, and a flat sheet."

"Did those items appear to have a pattern to them?"

"Yes. They appeared to all match."

"In your search, did you also collect items from the garage area of the Westerfield residence?"

Ms. LeAlcala recalled finding in the garbage located in the garage a black trash bag containing lint from the dryer, food items, dryer sheets, an empty bottle of bleach, an empty bottle of rum, a post-it note, and other trash items.

From Mr. Westerfield's motorhome, Ms. LeAlcala seized numerous items, including a comforter that was on the bed, a blue bath matt from the bathroom, fibers from multiple locations, and a hair from the sink drain in the bathroom. She additionally recovered fingerprints from several locations, including two that were on a cabinet located over the head of the bed. She found four additional prints in other locations.

A few days later, Ms. LeAlcala received four clothing items seized from the drycleaner that included a floral patterned comforter. She additionally received hair samples from Layla, the

Van Dam's dogs, a scent dog, Hopi, and mouth swabs from Mr. Westerfield.

At the recovery site at approximately 5:40pm on February 27, Ms. LeAlcala first took photos and then collected evidence from the area immediately surrounding the body.

"Did you observe at any time any teeth outside the body of Danielle Van Dam?"

"No."

"Were you ever inside the residence of the Van Dams?" Mr. Clarke asked.

"No, I was not," she answered.

"I have nothing further, your honor."

For the defense, Mr. Feldman led the cross examination. He started by discussing in detail the concept of cross contamination, without actually claiming that cross contamination had occurred, and provided several hypothetical situations in which trace evidence could be transported from one location to another.

"Can evidence be transferred even though you use gloves?"

"Objection."

"Sustained."

After confirming that Mr. Westerfield was speaking to Det. Ott and Sgt. Holmes when she arrived at his home, Mr. Feldman referenced the shopping list found in the kitchen and asked, "is it uncommon for people to go shopping after a short trip?"

The state objected and Judge Mudd sustained.

Switching to the recovery site, Mr. Feldman noted the large number of officers and detectives present at the scene and asked if she had collected insects at the site. Ms. LeAlcala said she had taken all the insects she could find and placed them in two different containers, one of which containing rubbing alcohol. She subsequently turned the containers over to Forensic

Entomologist David Faulkner.

When Mr. Feldman moved to show a photograph of Danielle's body at the recovery site, Mr. Dusek asked for a side bar, which Judge Mudd thought was appropriate. Out of the jury's hearing range, Mr. Dusek suggested that the Van Dam's leave the room because the day before Mrs. Van Dam had left court in tears after the defense unexpectedly showed a photo of Danielle's body. Because, in part, the media had reacted strongly to her exit, Judge Mudd agreed.

After the Van Dams left the room, Mr. Feldman showed a picture of Danielle's body at the recovery site and asked Ms. LeAlcala what she had done to avoid touching the Poison Oak in the area. Ms. LeAlcala recalled wearing a black jumpsuit.

Because the defense had no real purpose in showing the picture of Danielle's body at that time or the day before, the objective might have been to upset the Van Dam's to the point they would leave the courtroom crying in front of the jury, an issue that could later be used in appeal to argue that jurors had been emotionally tainted.

"Did you notice any trash in the area?"

"Yes. In the surrounding area I remember there being mattresses and old sofas, things like that."

Moving on to Mr. Westerfield's home, Mr. Feldman reviewed the items she had collected in the laundry room and wondered which of the underwear, if any, belonged to Mr. Westerfield's son, Neal. When asked why she had not inspected Neal's room, Ms. LeAlcala explained the homicide detectives had not asked for an inspection of his room. Mr. Feldman pointed out that zip disks and compact discs were found in Neal's room also.

"Did you alter any of the evidence?"

"No."

"Did you change the position of any of the evidence?"

Ms. LeAlcala recalled she had placed the CDs and zip drives found in the brown envelope on the desk for a photo and

Mr. Feldman noted that no effort had been made to lift any fingerprints from the CDs or zip drives.

"Counsel, we are going to break for lunch," Judge Mudd addressed the jury. "I watch you folks and I watch the audience very carefully, and some of the pundits in the courtroom indicated that when Mrs. Van Dam left the courtroom yesterday that a number of you appeared quite concerned. I disagree wholeheartedly in their observations, but I want to publicly remind you that if at any time any of you see any person in this courtroom that you feel in any way is intimidating to you or in any way interfering with your objectivity and the job you have to do, please let me know and I will correct the situation. If you become concerned for any reason that you're being compromised, please let me know and we will deal with it. Have a pleasant lunch, we'll see you at 1:30."

After the lunch break, Mr. Dusek asked if the Van Dams could return and watch the remainder of the trial. The defense again objected based on what had occurred the previous day. Judge Mudd responded.

"I don't see a problem. What causes me a little bit of concern, Mr. Dusek, and since they are in the courtroom I'm going to let them know, I observed you go to them, let them know what board Mr. Feldman was going to use, and I observed them basically say something to you that caused you to come back inside the rail and they remained in the courtroom. I didn't know what decisions they made, but as a parent, I can't imagine sitting through that. I don't want any problems and I haven't seen any problems. And, Mr. and Mrs. Van Dam, you shouldn't think you have caused any because, in my humble opinion, you haven't. The media picked up on something that I obviously never saw, but they are welcome to remain. If they are not going to exercise judgment as to some of the boards, I'll exercise it for them, because I just don't want any problems. They are welcome to remain."

Mr. Feldman then discussed his concern the jury was being negatively impacted by seeing the officers escorting Mr. Westerfield through the halls, which were essentially shut down in the process. He requested that Judge Mudd instruct the jury not to draw any adverse conclusions based on standard courtroom procedures. Judge Mudd found the request appropriate and agreed.

Once the jury returned, Ms. LeAlcala's cross examination continued. Mr. Feldman inquired about the collecting process then transitioned to the motorhome. He asked about the small shovel found in one of the exterior compartments and noted the presence of soil, leaves, and sand on the rear of the vehicle.

"Law enforcement collected vegetation apparently for the purpose of comparing any vegetation at the recovery scene against potentially anything found on the motorhome?"

"I do remember collecting grass at the recovery scene, yes."

"Did you compare or ask anyone to compare any vegetation that may have been located at the recovery scene against any of the vegetation that was found on the motorhome?"

Ms. LeAlcala said she had taken grass found on the rear and passenger side of the motor home to a botanist named John Rebman. Without exploring the botanist's findings, Mr. Feldman switched his focus to the fingerprints found in the motorhome. He discussed chain of custody and confirmed she had collected six latent prints. Regarding the items found in the laundry room, Mr. Feldman asked, "you can't tell us how it got there can you?"

"No."

"No further questions."

After Ms. LeAlcala exited the courtroom, the state called Jeffrey Graham, a latent print examiner at the San Diego Police Department crime laboratory. Mr. Graham had earned a degree in evidence technology at Grossmont College, had worked for the SDPD for eight years, and had received hundreds of hours of training from the California Department of Justice, the California Criminalistics Institute, and the FBI. He had reviewed tens of thousands of prints during his career and had passed annual proficiency tests. Mr. Graham then explained all fingerprint matches were checked by a verifier who independently reached their own conclusions.

On February 28, Mr. Graham attended Danielle's autopsy for the purpose of acquiring her fingerprints. Because her hands were extremely mummified, dried out, wrinkled, and shriveled, the detail was compressed and he was not able to obtain a useable print. Dr. Blackbourne ultimately cut her hands off and gave them to Mr. Graham so he could take them back to his office and perform a rehydration procedure in an attempt to attain a print usable for comparison purposes.

Mr. Graham first submerged the hands in chemicals, but without sufficient improvement after a week, he decided to remove sections of skin from the left middle finger and ring fingers. He laid them on paper, held them down with some wooden swabs, and applied silver powder. He then photographed the prints using a three times enlarging polaroid camera with increased contrast. On March 7, Mr. Graham compared Danielle's prints to the two prints found on the cabinet over the bed in the motorhome.

"What did you find?"

"That these two prints were made by Danielle Van Dam."

"How certain are you?"

"Absolutely certain."

Of four finger prints left on the cabinet, Mr. Graham was able to match two, her left middle and ring fingers. The quality of the other two prints was not strong enough for a definitive comparison. Mr. Graham showed the jury how Danielle's left hand was placed straight up on the cabinet with the thumb likely off the right edge, as if she was being pushed up against the wall or trying to get away.

Mr. Graham additionally determined that prints lifted from the bedroom windows in the motorhome matched the teenage daughter of Mr. Westerfield's ex-girlfriend, Susan, and her friend, Jennifer. Several remaining prints collected from the motorhome were not clear enough for a positive identification.

On April 17, Mr. Graham went back to the motorhome where he collected sixteen additional prints from various interior locations.

"Did you find any of David Westerfield's fingerprints in the motorhome?"

"No."

"Does that mean he's never been there?"

Mr. Graham said, "no" and explained that he might just not have touched the surfaces examined or maybe had very clean hands.

From the Van Dam home, Mr. Graham evaluated over three hundred prints. With prints of all Van Dam family members as well as Barbara, Denise, Rich, Keith, and all the officers and investigators, Mr. Graham matched one hundred and twenty-two. Unknown prints were found on the downstairs sliding glass door, the stairway railing, and the upstairs banister knob. None of the prints collected from the Van Dam home belonged to David Westerfield.

"What happens if you wear a glove? Is that going to cause you to leave a print?"

"No."

"Thank you, sir."

Mr. Feldman began the most important cross examination up to that point by asking Mr. Graham if fingerprints were "an art or a science?"

Mr. Graham explained how fingerprint matching was a

science with one hundred years of research.

"In order to become a fingerprint examiner, there's no specific test that you can take, is there?"

Mr. Graham confirmed there was not a specific test and stated that qualifications for employment varied by department. After doubting the legitimacy of fingerprint science as well as Mr. Graham's qualifications and competency, Mr. Graham discussed the differences in comparison methods and prodded Mr. Graham about slight inconsistencies in his statements regarding the field of fingerprint analysis.

"You discussed the orientation and you discussed your theory as to that, but you weren't there and didn't see it, right? You are just drawing inferences as best you can?"

"The print has been identified as Danielle Van Dam's, which means she touched that cabinet."

Conceding the most crucial piece of evidence yet presented was valid and true, Mr. Feldman then asked," You can't tell me when she touched it, can you?"

"No, I can't."

"You can't tell me exactly how she touched it, can you?"

"No, I can't."

Regarding the palm print on the stairway railing at the Van Dam house, Mr. Feldman asked if, "David Westerfield is excluded as the maker of that print?"

"Yes, he is."

Mr. Westerfield was also excluded as the source of a print found on the inside of the side door in the garage and the sliding patio door by the kitchen.

"If a person was wearing gloves and they had moved their hand over an existing print might you see some evidence of smudging?"

"Yes."

"You didn't identify them to any of the known people, is that right?"

"Yes."

"Therefore, one reasonable inference is that somebody else might have been there, correct?"

Mr. Dusek objected. Judge Mudd overruled. "You may answer."

"From what I've heard, other people have been in there, yes."

"Did you compare any of the unknown latents that you found in the motorhome against any of the unidentified latents you found in the Van Dam residence?"

"No, I didn't."

"I have no further questions at this time."

Mr. Dusek started his redirect by assuring Mr. Graham had passed annual proficiency tests and that his laboratory was certified and accredited. He then clarified that the process of comparing prints did not destroy the print and asked, "the defense would be allowed to look at those fingerprints?"

"Objection. Relevance."

"Overruled."

"Your honor, I want a sidebar."

"I'll give you an opportunity."

Mr. Graham confirmed the defense could independently examine the fingerprints and make their own comparison.

"In the chain of custody, would it indicate whether or not that happened?"

"Yes.

Mr. Dusek presented the chain of custody form for Mr. Graham and asked if the defense had made their own comparison.

"Continuing objection, your honor."

"Duly noted."

Mr. Graham revealed the defense had taken the prints to a private latent print examiner who, "does defense work. He is a former San Diego PD latent print examiner, a former police officer." Overall, the individual had examined roughly a dozen different prints related to the Van Dam case.

After the conclusion of Mr. Graham's testimony, Mr. Feldman requested and was granted a sidebar where he expressed his concern about the questions implying the defense had hired an expert to independently examine the prints. "By asking the questions that have been asked, it now raises the inference that the defense is provided essentially confirmation of this witness' conclusions, which I don't think is a fair inference."

Judge Mudd asked the prosecution for a response.

Because Mr. Feldman had attacked Mr. Graham's credibility and competency, doubted the science, and questioned the chain of custody, Mr. Dusek believed he had an obligation to reveal the defense had hired an independent print analyst who had confirmed the results.

Judge Mudd agreed with the state primarily because the chain of custody had been questioned. "So, it's relevant. You've made your record. I abide by my ruling."

Before dismissing the jury for the day, Judge Mudd discussed the process of moving defendants in and out of court. Because the building was old and not up to current logistical standards, "it requires that he move in public corridors. Obviously, because of the nature of the case, it's required that those corridors be, for a lack of a better word, sealed off momentarily while he is taken from one portion to another. There are a couple things we need to talk about this situation. His custodial status has absolutely nothing to do with this case or his guilt or innocence of the charged offense. It is just simply a fact. He is in custody. It has nothing to do with the decision you have to make. It has nothing to do with the determinations of fact that you're going to have to make. I am going to assume that you just know and understand this is the reality of where we're at and it has nothing to do with this case."

"Okay, tomorrow we are going to be able to put in a full day. Hopefully, we'll be even up with Boston by tomorrow. I commend to you the ball game, last night was real exciting until the home run in the eighth inning. We'll see you all tomorrow morning at 9:00am."

DAY 11

On Thursday June 20, the eleventh day of trial, Judge Mudd started the day by encouraging the jury to jump on the Padres bandwagon because, "last night was a great ball game and a great series coming up this weekend."

The first witness of the day for the state was Criminalist Sean Soriano. Mr. Soriano had obtained a bachelor of science degree in biology from San Diego State University and had worked as a laboratory technician, process group chemist, and research technician before moving to the San Diego Police Department crime lab where he was responsible for examining evidence for the presence of biological materials such as blood and saliva.

When Mr. Soriano was initially assigned the Van Dam case, the number of items that required processing was so substantial a meeting including crime lab personnel, police investigators, and attorneys from the prosecutor's office was called to prioritize and distribute the evidence. Within the crime lab, two separate rooms were designated for processing evidence to prevent the possibility of cross contamination. All the evidence discovered in Mr. Westerfield's house and motorhome were analyzed in one room. All the evidence associated to Danielle Van Dam was analyzed in a different room. At no time was evidence related to the defendant in the same room as evidence taken from the victim.

Mr. Soriano started with the clothing Mr. Westerfield had left at the drycleaners; one pair of pants, a sweater, a t-shirt, and a green jacket with some blue areas on the collar, back, and button areas. On the jacket, Mr. Soriano discovered blood like stains on the front right middle outside the lapel, the front right shoulder, and the back of the collar on the left side.

"Did you test those areas for blood?"

Mr. Soriano explained he performed a chemical presumptive test, which confirmed the presence of blood in all three locations.

From Danielle's room Mr. Soriano identified seven blood stains on the bean bag and discovered a blood stain on her multicolored blanket as well. On the multicolored striped comforter seized from the drycleaner, Mr. Soriano did not find any blood stains, but did collect a number of hairs and fibers using tape lifts. On the clothing taken from Mr. Westerfield's dryer, Mr. Soriano collected multiple blond hairs, one of which was on a pair of his boxer shorts. He collected additional hairs and fibers from the pillowcases and sheets that were taken from Mr. Westerfield's bedroom. Long brown, black, and white hairs were found along with short black hairs and white featherlike blue green fibers. All blood stains were photographed, cut out, wrapped in paper, and placed in separate envelopes for DNA analysis.

"Were you ever inside the home of David Westerfield?"

"No, I was not."

"Were you ever inside the motorhome of David Westerfield?"

"No, I was not."

"Thank you. I don't have any more questions, your honor."

In his cross examination, Mr. Feldman discussed the special procedures implemented to handle the mass volume of evidence and inquired about how the lab prevented cross contamination.

"If the evidence has already been cross contaminated, you have no control over that before it gets to the laboratory, correct?"

"Objection. Assumes facts not in evidence."

"Sustained."

Mr. Feldman moved to questions about how Mr. Soriano handled the jacket and what kind of camera he used when taking pictures of the stains. He asked Mr. Soriano to circle on a photo the locations of where the stains on the jacket were found and reviewed their measurements.

"About how many different items did you test?"

"Approximately ninety-seven items."

Mr. Soriano recalled he had tested Mr. Westerfield's clothing and bedding for semen and had not found any positive results. Vaginal and rectal swabs taken from Danielle were also negative for semen.

Regarding the blood found on Mr. Westerfield's jacket, Mr. Feldman asked if Mr. Soriano could, "tell me how the blood got there?"

"No, I cannot."

In his redirect, Mr. Clarke asked Mr. Soriano if he had tested, "every single inch on every item identified as coming from Mr. Westerfield's home?

"No, I did not."

"Did you ever have a sample of Danielle Van Dam's blood?"

"No, I did not." Mr. Soriano responded.

"To your knowledge, did law enforcement ever have a sample of her blood?"

"No, not that I am aware of."

"Thank you, I have nothing further."

The state next called Criminalist Annette Peer. Ms. Peer worked in the biology unit of the SDPD crime laboratory and had earned a bachelor of science degree in criminalistics from California State University Long Beach before attending postgraduate courses at San Diego State University in genetics, biochemistry, and molecular biology. She specialized in analyzing and comparing biological evidence like saliva, blood, and hair. She was a member of the California Association of Criminalists and was certified by the American Board of Criminalists. Ms. Peer had first been hired as a criminalist in 1983 and when, in 1990, the SDPD was provided funding for a DNA laboratory, she and Dr. Patrick O'Donnell were chosen to lead the effort.

Late in the evening on Monday, February 4, Ms. Peer had been directed by Sgt. Holmes to assist in the search of Mr. Westerfield's home. That night, she searched the home for biological materials while also looking for anything unusual or potentially significant. She additionally assisted Forensic Specialist Karen LeAlcala.

"Did you locate any evidence in this examination of interest to you?"

"No, I did not."

On February 6, Ms. Peer searched Mr. Westerfield's motorhome and tested nineteen different stains for blood. Three presumptive tests returned positive results; one on the topside of the bedspread near the foot end on the passenger side of the bed, one on the carpet floor between the bathroom and closet, and one on the curtain to the left of the driver's seat. Ms. Peer extracted each blood stain using a scalpel before securing them in an envelope she labeled, signed, and dated.

"Were you ever inside the home of Danielle Van Dam?"

"No, I was not."

When asked what bleach does to DNA, Ms. Peer said, "bleach effectively destroys DNA."

"Did you perform DNA testing in this case?"

Ms. Peer confirmed she had and noted that samples had been taken from Danielle, her parents, and Mr. Westerfield for comparison. Because her body contained no blood, Danielle's DNA had been extracted from the inside of one of her ribs, which had been removed during the autopsy.

Moving on to the DNA results, Ms. Peer revealed one of the blood stains found on the green jacket seized from the drycleaners matched Mr. Westerfield. The other blood stain did not.

"The profile you obtained from the carpet in the motorhome, did you compare that with the profile you obtained from the shoulder of that green jacket?" Mr. Clarke asked.

"Yes, I did."

"Were they the same or different?"

"The same."

"Could those stains have come from David Westerfield?"

"No, they could not."

"Could they have been from Danielle Van Dam?"

"Yes, they could," Ms. Peer answered, confirming Danielle's blood had been found both on the floor outside the bathroom in Mr. Westerfield's motorhome and on the shoulder of his jacket.

"What's the approximate likelihood of selecting someone at random having that same genetic profile found in both the carpet stain and Danielle Van Dam?"

"One in 1.7 quadrillion."

"How many zeros are in a quadrillion?"

"Fifteen."

Regarding the additional blood stains, no DNA results were acquired from the curtain in the motorhome or the from the neck of Mr. Westerfield's jacket. Blood on the comforter taken from the bed in the motorhome belonged to Mr. Westerfield, and three stains found in the stairwell of the Van Dam housed were not human. A swab taken from a red stain on the floor of Mr. Westerfield's garage was positive for blood, but the DNA was too degraded for a DNA match. From Danielle's fingernails, no foreign DNA was discovered.

Mr. Clarke concluded his examination by noting that Ms. Peer had additionally sent a portion of the jacket shoulder stain to a private laboratory for an independent study.

After the lunch break, Mr. Feldman began his cross

examination by asking why she had not photographed all the stains found in the motorhome and then repeated the fact that Mr. Westerfield's DNA had not been found on Danielle's fingernails.

"Can you tell me when the blood got there?"

"I cannot tell you that."

"Can you tell me how long it was there?"

"No, I cannot."

"Can you tell me how it got there?"

"No, I cannot."

"No further questions." Without disputing the DNA findings, Mr. Feldman finished his brief exam.

The prosecution next called Dr. Lewis Maddox Ph.D., director of Orchid Cellmark, one of the first private DNA labs in the world and the first accredited by the American Society of Crime Laboratory Directors. Dr. Maddox had graduated from Clemson University with a bachelor of science degree in microbiology, earned a Ph.D. in medical genetics from the University of Alabama, and was a postdoctoral fellow at Duke University Medical Center.

Dr. Maddox reported he had examined a portion of the blood stain extracted from Mr. Westerfield's green jacket along with a mouth swab from Mr. Westerfield and a piece of Danielle's rib.

"We determined that the DNA which was obtained from the jacket stain was from a female," Dr. Maddox started. "The DNA profile which was obtained from this sample matches the DNA profile obtained from the rib sample from Danielle Van Dam. We also concluded that David Westerfield was excluded as the source."

"Thank you very much."

In his cross examination, Mr. Feldman repeated the only minimal defense he could offer in the face of catastrophic evidence.

"Sir, with regard to the bloodstain that you evaluated, can you tell when it got to whatever location it came from?"

"No, we cannot."

"Can you tell how it got to whatever location it came from?"

"No, I cannot."

"Can you tell me how long it could stay in the location it came from?"

"Not specifically, I cannot."

"No further questions."

Judge Mudd wished the witness a good trip back east and asked him not to discuss his testimony until the trial reached its conclusion.

The state's next witness was Dr. Catherine Theisen Ph.D. Dr. Theisen worked in the mitochondrial DNA unit of the FBI laboratory in Washington D.C. and had earned a bachelor's degree in biology from the University of Virginia before obtaining a Ph.D. from Johns Hopkins University in molecular genetics. She had worked at the FBI for fourteen years and was a certified inspector who assessed forensic laboratories around the country and graded their proficiency based on how well they adhered to nationally recognized quality assurance standards. She also served on the American Society of Crime Laboratory Directors proficiency review committee where she evaluated DNA analysts all across the country.

Dr. Theisen explained that nuclear DNA was inherited from both the mother and father, which made comparisons very precise and explained how the source of a mitochondrial DNA sample was identical to the source's mother and her mother's siblings as well as the source's siblings. Although not as specific as nuclear DNA, which was used for the stains on Mr. Westerfield's jacket and on the floor of the motorhome, mitochondrial DNA could identify a family lineage and was useful when testing evidence that did not possess large quantities of nuclear DNA such as hair, bones, and teeth. When a hair falls out and does not have the root attached, there is not enough nuclear DNA, but there is enough mitochondrial DNA. While mitochondrial DNA cannot ascertain a definitive match, it can exclude an individual as being the source or can narrow the potential group of possible matches.

"What year did the FBI begin actually using mitochondrial DNA in its case work?"

"In 1996, six years ago."

On February 14, 2002, Dr. Theisen received a number of items for examination; a blonde hair found in the motorhome's vacuum cleaner, a blonde hair collected from the motorhome's bathroom rug, a blond hair discovered on the rear driver side seat in the SUV, hairs from Danielle's hairbrush, and a saliva sample from Brenda Van Dam. She additionally received hairs from David's ex-girlfriend, Susan, and her daughter.

When testing evidence, Dr. Theisen examined only one item at a time and always analyzed the unknown samples first. The known samples were never touched until examinations of the unknown samples were complete.

Dr. Theisen determined that multiple hairs discovered in the motorhome's vacuum cleaner and in Mr. Westerfield's SUV did not match Danielle Van Dam or her mother, but were consistent with Mr. Westerfield's ex-girlfriend and her daughter who were each of Asian descent.

Regarding the hair found on the bathroom rug in the motorhome, Dr. Theisen determined Danielle, her mother, and her siblings could have been the source.

"Thank you very much."

Following the afternoon break, Mr. Feldman began his cross examination by pointing out that some of the hairs in Danielle's brush precluded meaningful microscopic comparison. He focused on the hairs that did not match Danielle while highlighting some of the details Dr. Theisen did not know such as the length and color of each hair tested.

Mr. Feldman wondered why she had not taken photographs of the hairs studied and revealed she had conducted testing with the help of colleagues and not on her own. He walked her through the DNA process in detail, asked about the other members of her team, and emphasized that the blonde hair in Mr. Westerfield's 4Runner had not come from Danielle. He concluded his cross examination by asking about hair that had been bleached, dyed, or otherwise treated. At no point in his examination of Dr. Theisen did Mr. Feldman dispute the conclusion that Danielle's hair had been found on the bathroom rug in Mr. Westerfield's motorhome.

At the conclusion of Dr. Theisen's testimony, Judge Mudd asked the jury, "have you had enough biology and genetics today?" and rewarded their dedication by letting them go home an hour early. "I hope you don't mind. I see you're all very disappointed. Great baseball weekend coming up. If you don't have anything else to do, I recommend it very highly 'cause we may not see these teams for quite some time." He reminded the jury they had Friday off and directed them to return at 9:00am on Monday.

DAY 12

On Monday June 24, Judge Mudd welcomed the jury back. "Hope you got a lot of rest and relaxation over the past three days. Certainly, the Padres hitters got a lot of rest and relaxation. They weren't very productive, but it was exciting to see some teams in town we don't normally see. Now Barry Bonds is coming to town, so we better really hold onto our hats."

Judge Mudd informed the jury the prosecution was reaching the end of their case and that they may receive an additional day off before the defense's case began. He also revealed his approval of an in person visit to Mr. Westerfield's motorhome that would take place later in the week and noted the following Monday had been set aside for a hearing for which they would not be needed. "So, you can let your employers know that you can go to work next Monday. All right, Mr. Clarke."

"Thank you, your honor."

Mr. Clarke called to the stand Criminalist David Cornacchia. Mr. Cornacchia worked for the San Diego Police Department crime lab in the forensic biology unit where he was responsible for testing biological fluids. Mr. Cornacchia had earned a bachelor of science degree from Michigan State University before working for the Oklahoma State Bureau of Investigation for nearly five years and the San Diego Sheriff's Department for two years.

On February 14, Mr. Cornacchia was ordered to examine a pair of blue and white Power Puff Girls pajamas and a purple and blue long sleeve shirt collected from the floor of Danielle's bedroom. Small red stains on the left pajama sleeve and the left shirt sleeve tested positive for blood. He cut out each stain and placed them in separate envelopes and then swabbed seven different blood stains found on the bean bag in Danielle's room.

"Were you ever inside the residence of the Van Dam's?"

"No, I was not."

"Were you ever inside a residence identified as belonging to David Westerfield?"

"No, I was not."

"Were you ever inside a motorhome identified as belonging to Mr. Westerfield?"

"No, I was not."

Of the stains collected from the bean bag, four did not provide enough DNA to construct a profile. Of the other three, one belonged to Danielle's brother Derek, one was a mix of Derek and another individual who was possibly Danielle, Dylan, or Brenda, and one was a mix of Derek and an unknown individual who was not a Van Dam and was not Mr. Westerfield.

From the items taken from Mr. Westerfield's washing machine and the top of the dryer, Mr. Cornacchia collected numerous hairs from multiple items, labeling each with their place of origin. Items taken from the 4Runner yielded no biological or trace evidence.

Mr. Feldman focused his cross examination on the size and nature of the stains as well as the process of separating multiple sources within the same stain.

"Specifically directing your attention to the area of the bean bag chair from which the stain was sourced, you cannot tell me whether or not that was Danielle Van Dam's blood?"

"That's correct."

"You can't rule it out, correct?"

"I could not rule it out."

Mr. Feldman discussed the method of comparing DNA profiles and asked multiple questions about Danielle's pajamas and where they were found. He revealed the blood stains on the pajamas had been sent to an outside lab. When asked if he found any biological evidence in the 4Runner, Mr. Cornacchia replied he had not.

"Based on the conclusion that you didn't find any

biological evidence, we can exclude Danielle Van Dam from being in the SUV, isn't that true?"

"Objection. Argumentative, lack of foundation."

"Sustained."

Mr. Feldman proceeded to ask a series of questions about Mr. Cornacchia's activity at the body recovery site which he again noted was littered with trash. "And you concluded, did you not, that whether parked on the dirt road or on the side of Dehesa Road, it appeared to you that the perpetrator would have had to enter the grouping of the trees from the north side?"

"Correct."

Without explaining why this detail was important, Mr. Feldman concluded his exam.

The state's next witness was Criminalist Tanya Dulaney. Ms. Dulaney had graduated from San Diego State University with a bachelor of science degree in biology and since 1995 had worked as a criminalist in the trace evidence unit of the SDPD crime laboratory where she specialized in fiber analysis. She had attended the California Criminalistics Institute as well as numerous classes covering the analysis of hair, fibers, shoes, paint, and other sources of trace evidence frequently encountered during police investigations. She had additionally completed a course in hair and fiber analysis at the FBI Academy in Quantico, Virginia. Since February 3, Ms. Dulaney had worked exclusively on the Danielle Van Dam investigation.

Ms. Dulaney's investigative process began by using tape lifts on a variety of items seized from Mr. Wesrterfield's home. She then examined the extracted material under a microscope, searching for hair and fibers that stood out or were otherwise not consistent with the environment in which they were found.

From the items collected from Mr. Westerfield's laundry room, Ms. Dulaney found blue fibers and orange fibers on items taken from the washing machine as well as dog hair, blue fibers, and orange fibers on items inside and on top of the dryer. On items seized from the master bedroom, Ms. Dulaney collected multiple orange fibers on both pillowcases, one blonde hair on the fitted sheet, and two blonde hairs on the flat sheet. In the dryer lint recovered from the trash in the garage, Ms. Dulaney discovered three blonde human hairs as well as eighteen short animal hairs.

From the motorhome, Ms. Dulaney recovered multiple items of interest, including a light colored carpet fiber from the carpet beneath the bedroom nightstand on the driver's side, one blonde human hair, three light colored fibers from the carpet between the bathroom and bed, one blonde hair from the bathroom sink, one light colored carpet fiber, two dog hairs, and one dog hair from the bathmat. From the comforter seized at the drycleaners, she collected numerous dog hairs.

"When you were conducting your hair comparison in this case what were you looking for?"

"I was looking for characteristics in the hair that were similar to Danielle Van Dam's hair. Blonde hairs, possibly long hairs, hairs that hadn't been color treated, hairs that may have been cut recently, and those types of characteristics." When Ms. Dulaney found hairs that fit those specifications, she packaged them and sent them to several laboratories, including the FBI, for mitochondrial DNA testing.

Mr. Clarke presented a large chart for the jury that showed the location where each group of hairs had been found, the number of hairs in that group, if the root had been recovered, and a description of their color and length. At the bottom of the chart was a separate area that noted the length of the hair taken from Danielle's body at autopsy ranged between roughly one to eight inches.

Mr. Clarke moved on to the process of examining fibers. Ms. Dulaney explained she first used a high powered microscope to identify fibers she thought were relevant and then extracted those fibers and analyzed them using an infrared spectrometer that determined their chemical composition which was considered a fiber's unique fingerprint. She then used a comparison microscope to compare the unknown fibers side by side with fibers taken from the carpet in Danielle's bedroom. When examining the fibers, she analyzed color, length, diameter, cross sections, and optical properties visible with lighting changes.

Ms. Dulaney then showed the jury photographs taken through the comparison microscope of the fibers found in the motorhome next to a fiber taken from Danielle's bedroom. She revealed that a majority of carpets in existence were nylon while polypropylene was the second most common and polyester was the third. Acrylic fibers were the most common fibers found in clothing. The light colored fibers found in the motorhome and the fibers in Danielle's bedroom carpet were polyester.

After testing the fibers found in the motorhome on the carpet by the nightstand, hallway, and bathmat, Ms. Dulaney determined, "all these fibers were consistent with the carpet fibers from Danielle Van Dam's bedroom."

For further analysis, Ms. Dulaney took the fibers to a laboratory in Sacramento where they were examined using a unique spectrophotometer microscope that was capable of identifying the color components of fibers. The spectrophotometer confirmed the unknown fibers found in the motorhome could have come from Danielle's bedroom.

"Are these fibers available for further examination if anyone believes your results are incorrect?"

"Yes, they are."

Mr. Clarke then switched to the animal hairs she had discovered. Ms. Dulaney recalled she had compared the unknown animal hairs to hairs plucked from the Van Dam's Weimaraner, Layla, as well as the search dog, Hopi. In her examination, Ms. Dulaney noted the unknown hairs were short and gray before examining them under a microscope where she studied their pigment, size, and composition. She used several different magnifications and multiple lighting arrangements. The hairs from Layla were also short and gray.

"As a result of your comparison of these hairs, did you reach any conclusion when you compared them to the known samples you were provided?"

"Yes," Ms. Dulaney answered. "All of the hairs from the evidence items were similar in all the areas I've looked at to the hairs from the Van Dam's dog, Layla." She further revealed, "they were not similar to the hairs from Hopi."

Ms. Dulaney showed the jury side by side comparisons of the hairs taken from Layla next to the hairs found in Mr. Westerfield's home and RV and stated that their length, color, and size were consistent. For DNA analysis, Ms. Dulaney sent some of the dog hairs to a veterinary genetics laboratory at the University of California Davis near Sacramento.

When asked why samples of Layla's hair were not taken at the beginning of her analysis, Ms. Dulaney explained the lab did not want comparison hairs in their possession until the initial analysis was finished as an extra layer of protection against potential cross examination.

"Thank you. I don't have any more, your honor."

Mr. Feldman started his cross examination by focusing on the dog hairs. "With regard to human hairs, there's not sufficient individualization short of DNA for you to be comfortable to make a match, is that a fair statement?"

"Yes."

"You got the same problem with dog hairs, don't you?"

"Yes."

"You're not telling the jury you've matched any hairs, you're just saying hairs could have come from that dog, correct?"

"That's correct."

"Of course, they could have come from another dog, too, isn't that true?"

"That's true."

"How many dogs are you aware of that have gray brown hair?"

"I don't know."

With no grounds on which he could credibly question the validity of her findings, Mr. Feldman lead the court through a long, meandering trail of irrelevant and repetitive questions that focused on pointless details like the various lengths of people's hair, how much hair can grow in a month, how many hairs people typically shed in a day, how many different times she had analyzed dog hairs, how many tape lifts she had used inside the motorhome, and the meaning of 'a few.' He additionally pointed out she had also found animal hairs in the motorhome that were not consistent with Layla.

After a dense, information heavy morning mixed with several explosive findings and dull, tedious ramblings from the defense, Judge Mudd dismissed the jury for a much needed lunch break.

After a short proceeding not made part of the public record, the jury returned at 1:30.

"Okay, welcome back ladies and gentleman."

Judge Mudd mentioned his intent to keep the room as cool as possible due to increasing summer heat and large crowds in the gallery. "There's a lot of body heat in this courtroom and, as a result, that causes the fluctuation in temperature. We are just going to keep it as cold as the coolers will allow it so you may want to dress with the layered look because hopefully it will stay nice and cool throughout the trial. Okay, Mr. Feldman."

Mr. Feldman restarted his cross examination by focusing on evidence that had been collected and not tested, including a grey pubic hair found on the floor between the driver's seat and door of the SUV.

"Did you have that DNA'd?"

"I don't believe so."

He revealed numerous animal hairs had been found in the motorhome, but only the ones Ms. Dulaney decided were relevant had been tested. He listed the multiple areas in the motorhome where additional animal hairs were found and confirmed they were not similar to Layla's. He asked if she was a scientist and if guessing was consistent with the scientific method.

"Did you do any study of the dog hairs that you found for the purpose of discerning how many different dogs had been inside that vehicle based upon differences in the hairs?"

Ms. Dulaney answered, "no, I didn't."

Mr. Feldman then discussed a number of hairs collected from the motor home that did not match Danielle including a blonde hair found in the shower drain. He asked if she had compared the hair to Brenda Van Dam and she said, "no, I did not."

"So, that's another circumstance where you identified a hair that you thought may have been similar or may have some evidentiary value based on what you were screening for was sent off to a DNA lab and you were wrong?"

"Yes."

Mr. Clarke stood. "Excuse me, the counsel is arguing with the witness."

Judge Mudd agreed. "He is. The jury is to disregard the last answer."

Mr. Feldman pointed out that a hair found in the bathroom was also not similar to Danielle's and explained the difference between treated and untreated hair.

Regarding a blonde hair found on the blanket in the motorhome that was treated and therefore not Danielle's, Mr. Feldman asked, "did you compare that hair against the known hair standard of Brenda Van Dam?"

"No, I did not."

When Mr. Feldman suggested there were three or four different possible sources for the blonde hair, the state objected and Judge Mudd sustained.

The defense discussed the specific differences between Danielle's hair and the other blonde hairs found in the motorhome that were not Danielle's, reviewed with intense precision the process of visually comparing hairs, and noted that a number of additional hairs found in the motorhome did not belong to Danielle including a collection of hairs found on a pillow on the driver's side of the bed and a hair found on the floor of the shower that was 9cm long, dyed, and brown.

"Is that now five or six or seven distinct hair types that you've identified within the motorhome as we have gone through this list?"

"Certainly, a number of different hairs in the motorhome, yes."

Mr. Feldman returned to discussing the characteristics of multiple hairs that did not match Danielle until he noticed he was losing the jury. "Your honor, I'm concerned about boring, as your honor put it last week- Maybe this would be an appropriate time to recess."

"Judging from the eyelids in the group over here it looks like they need a stretch break. All right, ladies and gentlemen, I'll give you a little extra time to stretch your legs. Let's be back at 3:00 o'clock, okay?"

After the break, Mr. Feldman focused his attention on evidence collected from Mr. Westerfield's home, starting with the numerous hairs found that did not belong to Danielle. He discussed each hair's characteristics and the locations where each was found until moving on to the fibers.

Ms. Dulaney explained the definition of a fiber and the manufacturing process that created fibers. A company typically makes one extremely long string of fiber that is later cut up into tiny strands which are then used to make a carpet. About four or five different companies produced nearly all carpet fibers and one spool of fiber could be multiple miles long and source thousands of carpets.

Mr. Feldman noted that the Sabre Springs neighborhood where the Van Dams and Mr. Westerfield lived was relatively new. "A number of houses in the very same housing development could therefore theoretically have the same carpet?"

"Theoretically, yes."

Mr. Feldman highlighted the very small number of carpet fibers that had been found and asked Ms. Dulaney to explain Locard's Transfer Principle, which stated that contact between two items will result in the exchange of microscopic material. He then discussed hypothetical scenarios in which a fiber could move from one person to another and end up in a new location.

"What if I was behaving in a wild manner, if I was playing around with my brother and we were running all over the house, might that cause more of a potential transfer of physiology?"

Mr. Clarke objected. "Assumes facts not in evidence, also calls for speculation."

"Sustained."

When asked how many shoes she examined from Mr. Westerfield's closet with tape lifts, Ms. Dulaney answered, "twenty-five."

"And in each of those instances your purpose was to try and locate something that might prove David Westerfield was in Danielle Van Dam's house, is that correct?"

Ms. Dulaney answered, "that's correct," and revealed that no fibers from Danielle's bedroom were found on Mr. Westerfield's shoes.

"And you recall that your written conclusion was six tan carpet fibers found in the motorhome were similar to the victim's carpet and could share a common source with that carpet?"

"Yes."

"You told Mr. Clarke that the fibers were consistent with a particular carpet. They were also consistent with any number of other carpets, isn't that true?"

"That's true."

"So, in other words, your opinion with regard to carpet fibers is not an individualized opinion like the DNA numbers, for instance."

Ms. Dulaney answered, "oh, absolutely."

"Did you microscopically compare an orange fiber against other orange fibers that you may have located?"

"No, I did not.'"

Mr. Dusek then interrupted and asked for a sidebar regarding scheduling. His next witness was scheduled for that day and would not be able to return the following day. He had assumed the defense would have finished with Ms. Dulaney already and although his next witness would be brief, "I'm concerned about what the word brief means now."

Mr. Dusek asked if he could put his next witness on at that time and continue with Ms. Dulaney later. Judge Mudd agreed.

Mr. Clarke called to the stand Dr. Holly Ernest, director of the forensics unit and the wildlife research unit at the veterinary genetics lab at the University of California Davis. Dr. Ernest had earned a bachelor's degree in biology at Cornell University, a master's degree in veterinary physiology and pharmacology, and a doctor of veterinary medicine degree from Ohio State University. After working as a vet for six years, she acquired a Ph.D. in ecological genetics. Dr. Ernest specialized in evaluating the genetics of purebred horses, dogs, cats, and other animals. She also consulted for the California Department of Fish and Game and a variety of other state and federal agencies.

Dr. Ernest recalled that on April 18, she had received from Criminalist Tanya Dulaney a packet of hair samples for the purpose of nuclear microsatellite DNA testing. On April 29, she had received a cheek swab from the Van Dam's dog, Layla. Unfortunately, Dr. Ernest was unable to extract any DNA from the samples provided and explained it was not unusual to fail in such attempts.

Mr. Clarke had no further questions and the defense did not cross examine.

Once Ms. Dulaney was back on the stand, Mr. Feldman noted that fibers and animal hairs found on a towel were not from Danielle's bedroom or dog and mentioned that the motorhome had not been recently cleaned.

"With regard to the carpet fibers, is it true that the carpet fibers could have come from a different carpet than the Van Dams', but one that had common properties?"

"Yes, that's true."

"Thank you, no further questions."

In his redirect examination, Mr. Clarke asked about the significance of multiple sources of trace evidence being found in one location.

Ms. Dulaney explained the more transfer items discovered, the higher the likelihood they all came from the same source. Rug fibers consistent with Danielle's bedroom, animal hairs consistent with Danielle's dog, and human hair consistent with Danielle had all been found in Mr. Westerfield's motorhome and animal hair consistent with Danielle's dog and human hairs consistent with Danielle had been found in his house. If any one item had been found in just one location, the possibility of a coincidence was reasonable. The fact that multiple sources of trace evidence had been discovered in two separate locations associated to David Westerfield made the weight of that evidence much more profound.

When asked if the hair and fiber evidence had been available for the defense to independently analyze, Ms. Dulaney answered, "yes."

Regarding the blond hair found on the hallway carpet in the motorhome, Mr. Clarke asked if she had sent it out for mitochondrial DNA testing.

"Objection. Hearsay."

"Overruled."

"To your knowledge, did mitochondrial DNA testing establish that it could have come from Danielle Van Dam."

Mr. Feldman objected and again and again was overruled.

Ms. Dulaney answered, "yes."

"How many hairs came from the master bedroom bedding in Mr. Westerfield's home?"

"Six hairs."

"Are you familiar with whether or not mitochondrial DNA testing established whether those hairs could or could not have come from Danielle Van Dam?"

"Yes. They all could have come from Danielle"

"One or more of them?" Mr. Clarke asked.

"All six of them."

"Thank you, I have no further questions."

Mr. Feldman ended his questioning and warned he might recall her at a later date. Mr. Dusek then asked Judge Mudd if he could approach the bench where he requested an additional warning to the jury about avoiding the television because Damon Van Dam had threatened to go to the media after being excluded from the courtroom.

After reports had surfaced accusing Damon of studying Mr. Westerfield's security protocols and threatening to kill the defendant, Judge Mudd had decided that morning to remove Damon from the trial.

Judge Mudd responded to Mr. Dusek's request. "It's a very short rope, but I will emphasize the admonition."

"Ladies and gentleman, looks like we've reached the end of the day. Tonight, we are going to see some hitting, it only depends on how many times we pitch to Bobby Bonds, I think, who does the hitting, but hopefully we'll have good news tomorrow. I've made a couple of rulings today that may or may not hit the press tonight. I just want to reemphasize that it's very important you not look at the news, read your newspapers, or anything along those lines. In other words, just self-police the way you've been doing all along and we shouldn't have any problems. Have a safe and pleasant evening, go Pads. We'll see you at nine o'clock tomorrow morning."

DAY 13

Judge Mudd started the morning by correcting a mistake he made the day before. "Good morning ladies and gentleman. Apparently, I misspoke yesterday. I said watch out for Bobby Bonds. I'm afraid my age and upbringing in the bay area shows a little bit. I'm sure the Pads had wished it was Bobby Bonds hitting yesterday instead of Barry. It's amazing how everybody that watched the ballgame knew what he was going to do but the manager didn't. So, I haven't figured that out yet. All right, Mr. Clarke."

The state next called Criminalist Melvyn Kong. Mr. Kong had graduated with a bachelor's degree in chemistry from Occidental College in Los Angeles before working seven years for the Orange County Sheriff's Department where he handled alcohol analysis, antemortem toxicology, crime scene investigation, drug analysis, gunshot residue, and trace evidence. After stints at the Santa Ana Police Department and Los Angeles County Sheriff's Department, Mr. Kong began working as a supervising criminalist in the trace evidence unit at the San Diego Police Department crime lab. In total, Mr. Kong had worked as a criminalist for twenty-four years.

Mr. Kong first recalled examining the hair collected from the side gate at the Van Dam house, which, "I determined it to be animal hair. Probably a cat or dog."

Mr. Kong also examined bedding taken from Danielle's bedroom that included a fitted sheet, blanket, purple comforter, and pillows.

From your examination of those items, were you able to determine the presence or absence of any orange acrylic fibers?"

"Yes. I didn't find any."

In his very limited cross examination, Mr. Feldman asked a few questions about Mr. Kong's role in the investigation and revealed he had not succeeded in finding the missing back of Danielle's earring.

After Judge Mudd dismissed Mr. Kong, the state called Criminalist Jennifer Shen. Ms. Shen had graduated from the University of California San Diego with a degree in biology before earning a master's degree in forensic science from National University. She had worked as a toxicologist for the San Diego Sheriff's Department before moving to the trace evidence unit at the SDPD crime lab where she specialized in fibers and hairs.

Mr. Clarke began his questions about her role in the Van Dam case by asking about the fingernail clippings taken from Danielle's body during the autopsy. Ms. Shen recalled examining the fingernails under a microscope and collecting several very small fibers and chips of what looked like blue paint. She used a toothpick to scrape the fingernails, packaged the scrapings along with a small piece of skin tissue, and sent them to an outside lab for DNA testing.

Ms. Shen next examined a clump of hair found in Danielle's hand as well as a single hair collected from Danielle's body and determined they were consistent with Danielle's hair.

"In your experience, is it unusual to find a victim's own hairs in her hand after she's been killed? Or on the victim's body itself?"

"No, that's fairly common."

When asked about her overall strategy when examining items taken from the recovery site and Danielle's body, Ms. Shen explained how she focused first on hairs and fibers that were foreign to the victim and her environment. In particular, she looked for carpet fibers consistent with those in Mr. Westerfield's house and motorhome.

At the recovery scene, Ms. Shen used tape lifts on Danielle's body and later searched vegetation and soil that had been taken from the area beneath her body. After that, she focused on items taken during her autopsy including her earrings and necklace as well as the white paper bags that had been placed on her hands, foot, and head, and the white sheet used to wrap her body.

After starting with her focused approach, Ms. Shen began noticing specific fiber patterns; some with unusual color, others with unusual quantity. Once she constructed an inventory of the fibers found with Danielle's body, she examined tape lifts taken at Mr. Westerfield's house.

On tape lifts taken from folded laundry found on top of Mr. Westerfield's dryer that included a tan blanket, Ms. Shen discovered numerous long, bright orange fibers that were not like any of the other fibers collected in his home.

"Were they significant to you for any reason?"

"Yes. They were significant to me because I had seen a bright orange fiber somewhere else and that triggered my memory."

"Where was that?" Mr. Clarke asked.

Ms. Shen recalled finding a clump of hair tangled in the chain of Danielle's necklace. Within that clump of hair, she had discovered a long orange fiber. After finding the long orange fiber, she studied and became familiar with its characteristics knowing she might encounter the fiber again during her investigation.

On some of the other items seized from the laundry room, Ms. Shen also found short blue fibers that had a unique shape and grayish tint. Although the tape lifts had collected hundreds of different fibers, the short blue fibers stood out because she had observed them before as well.

Ms. Shen examined the blue fibers and the orange fibers under a microscope and used an infrared light to determine their chemical fingerprint. After completing her own analysis of the fibers, Ms. Shen took them to Criminalist Faye Springer at the Sacramento County Crime Laboratory where they were further examined using the microspectrophotometer.

Ms. Shen determined, "based upon the tests conducted that the fiber taken from the victim's necklace could share a common source with the fibers taken from the laundry and the bedding."

Mr. Clarke presented the jury with photos taken through a comparison microscope of the orange fiber found on Danielle's necklace side by side with an orange fiber found on the tan blanket in Mr. Westerfield's laundry room. Ms. Shen pointed out the color, diameter, width, and cross section were all similar.

Mr. Clarke then showed comparison photos of the orange fiber found on the necklace side by side with an orange fiber found on a pillowcase in Mr. Westerfield's bedroom. Ms. Shen concluded, "the fiber from the necklace is microscopically similar to the fibers taken from the pillowcase from the bedding."

At Mr. Clarke's request, Ms. Shen showed the jury Danielle's necklace and pointed to where the hair and orange fiber had been found. After explaining the hair and fiber had been covered in debris from the recovery site, Ms. Shen revealed it was reasonable to believe, "the fiber came in contact with the body and the necklace at or near the time of her death."

"Objection, your honor. I don't believe that last portion of the expert's opinion was subject to expert testimony."

"Duly noted," Judge Mudd responded. "Overruled, the answer stands."

"Ms. Shen, based on your comparison of the fiber from the necklace and the fibers from Mr. Westerfield's laundry room and the bedding, did they share the same type of fiber?"

"They were the same fiber type. Acrylic fiber."

Mr. Clarke asked how many orange fibers found in Mr. Westerfield's laundry room were similar to the orange fiber found on her necklace.

Ms. Shen revealed she had recovered approximately twenty-five orange fibers from the clothes in the washing machine, between fifty and one hundred from the items on top of the dryer, and about fifty to one hundred from laundry found inside the dryer. From Mr. Westerfield's bedroom, she found between ten and twenty orange fibers on a pillowcase.

Mr. Clarke asked, "in this case does that represent a relatively large number of fibers?"

"Yes."

Mr. Clarke moved forward to the blue fibers. Ms. Shen recalled the first place she had noticed the blue fibers was in the vegetation collected from under the back and pelvis of Danielle's body. She then found nineteen blue fibers on the sheet used to wrap her body and found one blue fiber in her hair. Once she had established the presence of the blue fibers, Ms. Shen searched Mr. Westerfield's laundry where she found approximately ten similar blue fibers.

For the blue nylon fibers, Ms. Shen performed a microscopic comparison as well as a chemical comparison using the infrared spectroscope. She did not utilize the microspectrophotometer at the lab in Sacramento. Mr. Clarke showed the jury a magnified photo of a blue fiber collected from the white sheet side by side with a blue fiber found on clothing that was in Mr. Westerfield's laundry room. The fibers were similar in length, diameter, width, contour, and color.

"What conclusions could you reach in making those comparisons?"

"I concluded that those fibers were similar macroscopically and microscopically and they're similar chemically and, therefore, they could share a common source."

"As a trace analyst, in your examination of evidence, is there any significance to the fact that there are multiple colors and types of fibers that you found shared that similarity in this case?"

"Yes, there is. One of the things that makes a fiber comparison more significant is if you have more than one distinctly different type of fiber that you find in each location." Ms. Shen explained the presence of multiple orange fibers and blue fibers on Danielle's body and in Mr. Westerfield's laundry strengthened the significance of both findings.

"Does the presence of additional evidence, namely hair evidence, add any significance to the fiber evidence?"

"Yes." Ms. Shen emphasized the more individual items of trace evidence found in multiple locations the more impactful their significance became. "In this particular case we have the presence of twenty to thirty of these orange fibers, plus we have seven of the distinctively different colored and type of blue-gray nylon fibers, and then in addition to that, there is one hair that is consistent with the victim's hair, so when you add those three things together, those comparisons become more significant."

Ms. Shen continued. "The significance here is that in this particular environment, the defendant's home, we have the orange fibers, the blue fibers, hair consistent with the victim's, and dog hair consistent with the victim's dog. So, you have all four of those things in this environment. It's an additive effect."

"Thank you very much. I have no further questions, your honor."

Mr. Feldman started his cross examination of Criminalist Shen by asking her to define what she meant by "environment," which she explained was the place where a person of interest spent most of their time such as their home.

"Is a dance floor an environment?"

"I suppose it could be."

"And if an individual and another individual had shared a common environment from time to time, might that explain how one or the other individuals might have similar trace evidence?"

"Yes."

Mr. Feldman proposed, "if I went to your house, and I walked through your house with my children, and my children jumped up and down, and they came back to my house and you came in as an evidence tech, might you find some of your environment in my house?"

"It's possible."

"Even though you and I have virtually no relationship other than that one encounter, correct?"

"Yes."

"If then I saw you, we'll say, twenty-four hours before one of my children disappeared and I danced with you and in the process of the dance you touched me, might I get some of your trace evidence that was on you attached to me?"

"Objection. Assumes facts not in evidence."

"Sustained."

Mr. Feldman then asked her to assume hypothetically they had danced on a dance floor and touched while dancing. If his clothes were later washed would evidence from her environment still be on his clothes?"

"Objection, speculation."

Judge Mudd sustained before Mr. Feldman asked to approach the bench. After a long proceeding not made part of the public record, Mr. Feldman was allowed to continue his line of questioning as long as he kept his questions within a hypothetical frame.

"I'd like you to assume hypothetically that you and I are neighbors, and I'd like you to further assume hypothetically that I have two children. I'd like you to further assume hypothetically that one of my children may disappear on February 1st or 2nd. I'd like you to further assume hypothetically that you and I were dancing on February 1st at about 10:30pm. I'd like you to assume further hypothetically that within two or three days of February 1st I brought my children to your house, they ran around your house, and we left. Under that hypothetical scenario, would there be transference from my environment to yourself or from your environment to mine?"

"There certainly could be," Ms. Shen answered.

"Are there particular garments that are more receptive to acceptance of transfer of fibers than others?"

Ms. Shen discussed how easily shedable garments like sweaters are more likely to leave fibers behind while garments with tackiness or texturing hold fibers most efficiently.

Mr. Feldman then noted how the significance of fibers decreases if legitimate contact occurred between two individuals.

"If individuals were together socially in a particular environment, take a bar, a steakhouse, or a café, and they were closely together, might that increase the likelihood of a fiber transference?"

"If there was contact between these two individuals, yes, there is an increase in possibility of transfer."

Regarding the, "fibers that you've testified about, what's their source?"

"I don't have a source for either the blue fibers or the orange fibers."

"Isn't it true, that with regard to the absence of a source the value of the evidentiary findings is reduced?"

"I would certainly agree with that in the case of the blue nylon fibers. The lack of a source is less significant in the case of the orange fibers because there are so many of them in one environment."

Mr. Feldman then pointed out Ms. Shen had not concluded the fibers had come from the exact same source, only that they were similar. "In other words, they could have come from a common source, correct?"

"That is correct."

"But they could not have come from a common source as well?"

"It is possible they did not come from a common source, yes."

Mr. Feldman then moved his focus to a three inch brown

hair discovered on Danielle's body that did not belong to her or Mr. Westerfield.

"Did you compare it against anybody else?"

"No."

Mr. Feldman revealed that Ms. Shen had also found numerous colored fibers on and around Danielle at the recovery scene that included red fibers, blue fibers, green fibers, white fibers, and purple fibers. Ms. Shen suspected that Danielle had contracted the fibers in her last environment, but admitted she had not found similar fibers anywhere else.

"How do you account for the existence of the red fibers?"

"I cannot account for them."

"Did you go to the Van Dam environment?"

"No."

"So, you don't have anything in specific to compare against the Van Dams, is that a fair statement?"

"That's correct."

Ms. Shen noted that five of the different colored fibers found on Danielle were polyester and had possibly originated from a multicolored blanket.

Mr. Feldman finished his cross by asking if, while searching Mr. Weserfield's shoes for trace evidence, she had discovered any evidence from the Van Dam environment.

"No, I did not."

In his redirect, Mr. Clarke asked first about where she thought the orange fibers might have originated.

"The most likely source for that type of fiber would have been a blanket or maybe a fuzzy sweater or something." She additionally stated that acrylic fibers of that kind shed and transferred easily, and described orange fibers as uncommon.

Mr. Clarke clarified that the unknown hair found at the recovery site was located in the debris and vegetation underneath Danielle. The hair was not on her body.

When asked which color fiber she encountered the most,

Ms. Shen answered, "the orange acrylic fiber found in the laundry in the defendant's home."

Regarding Mr. Westerfield's shoes, he asked, "whether those tape lifts included the shoes Mr. Westerfield was wearing the evening of February 1st?" Ms. Shen did not know and confirmed that walking resulted in the loss of fibers stuck to the bottom of a shoe.

"Thank you, I have no more questions, your honor."

During a short recross examination, Mr. Feldman noted the many unique and colorful fibers found in Danielle's bedroom that were not found in Mr. Westerfield's home.

"Thank you very much."

At 12:08pm, Judge Mudd broke for lunch. He reminded the jury not to discuss the case and asked them to return at 1:30.

After lunch, before the jury returned, Judge Mudd informed the counselors that media had, "contacted the court in a variety of ways to inform us that they have confirmed that Mr. Van Dam has been precluded from attending the balance of the trial. In addition to that, they have requested a copy of the transcript of the proceedings that led to that result."

Judge Mudd did not see a reason to keep the transcript sealed and acknowledged that the information was now public. "I don't know if it was confirmed with Mr. Van Dam or what. I have heard of no press conferences."

Mr. Feldman stepped in and stated that his investigator had told him during lunch that Mr. Van Dam had been barred from the third floor. The investigator additionally recounted a segment on the television news reporting that Brenda Van Dam had said, "there goes Satan," as Mr. Westerfield was being moved through the hallway. "We find this troubling," he said.

Judge Mudd agreed and asked if it was in the presence of any jurors. Mr. Feldman said he did not know the details, just that the report had been on television. Judge Mudd asked Mr. Dusek to respond.

"I know nothing at all about that, your honor. My belief is only as I have been with Brenda Van Dam yesterday and today and she's been on her best behavior."

"She has in this courtroom, certainly," Judge Mudd responded. "I have not seen anything and I don't believe any staff members have had any problems."

Mr. Dusek said he had more faith in what the staff said than what the media reported.

Judge Mudd agreed and stated that he was not, "inclined to exclude her from the courtroom unless and until her conduct, quite frankly, gets to the level of her husband, which actually was commencing to interfere with the security arrangements." Judge Mudd again warned that the media would likely acquire a transcript of the decision to exclude Mr. Van Dam from the trial.

When Mr. Clarke informed the court that his next witness was the forensic computer expert, Mr. Feldman interjected. He first asked to pursue questions about pornography on the Van Dams' computer and then stated in reference to Mr. Westerfield's computer, "in our view, there's no relevance to the introduction of the pornography. We renew our objection because I think counsel had indicated originally that it was offered for motive."

"As to the renewed motion to strike the alleged pornographic materials," Judge Mudd started, "the motion will be denied for the reasons previously stated. As to the checking of the Van Dam household computers and what it may or may not contain, I don't find it to be relevant or probative on any issue this jury is to decide. So, any questioning in that area is denied."

At that time, the state called Forensic Examiner James Watkins. Mr. Watkins worked at the Regional Computer Forensics Laboratory (RCFL), a cooperative hub for more than thirty southern California law enforcement agencies including the San Diego Police Department. The lab had been constructed three years prior and was the first of its kind in America. Mr. Watkins had received approximately eight hundred hours of computer forensic training from multiple sources including the FBI, the National White Collar Crime Center, and the International Association of Computer Investigative Specialists.

In the early morning of Tuesday February 5, Mr. Watkins arrived at David Westerfield's home along with computer specialist and FBI Agent, Lee Youngflesh. In Mr. Westerfield's second floor office, there were two computers, a printer, a copy machine, a fax machine, and a highspeed modem. Mr. Watkins set up his portable computer, known as a field imaging kit, which he connected to Mr. Westerfield's computers.

The imaging kit, nicknamed the "lunchbox," copied every tiny bit of data from each of the computers, including data that was old, hidden, deleted, or otherwise not visible. The process took several hours and created mirror copies of the computers which gave Mr. Watkins the ability to search and analyze Mr. Westerfield's computers without ever having to access or alter the actual evidence.

While the hard drives were being copied, Mr. Watkins searched the desk area for passwords and additional evidence. In the bookshelf, behind a book in the top left corner, he discovered a medium sized manilla envelope containing two CDs and three zip drives. Mr. Watkins immediately reviewed the contents of each in search of information that might help locate Danielle as well as any pornographic images featuring children.

Mr. Clarke asked, "did you observe any images that appeared questionable to you?"

Mr. Watkins answered, "yes."

After finding images he thought included underage girls while at the house, Mr. Watkins contacted Sgt. Holmes and showed him what he had found. At that time, copies of the CDs and zip drives were made for further examination and the items were turned over to the homicide detectives.

Mr. Clarke then reviewed in detail a number of mundane, but necessary details about how computers and the internet worked. In 2002, the internet was still very new and somewhat limited. Most people, especially middle aged and older, had no use for the internet, had never been on the internet, and did not know how to access the internet. Mr. Clarke explained how modems worked, how a DSL cable was faster than dial up, what it meant to download an image, and how zip drives and CDs worked.

Judge Mudd noticed the jury's attention drifting. "I want everybody in the room, open those eyes, breathe. I thought DNA was putting you to sleep, folks, but this has got a couple of you having a hard, hard time with this. You're a few minutes away from a stretch break, ladies and gentleman, so hang in there. Okay, they are back with you, Mr. Clarke."

Mr. Watkins began his formal search of Mr. Westerfield's computer hard drives, as well as the CDs and zip drives, several days after they were seized from the office. He reported the CDs and zip drives were very well organized with folders, folders within folders, and files with descriptive labels. For example, one folder was titled "Cartoons," and had multiple folders inside separating different types of cartoons.

Both CDs were digitally titled "Spectrum 01." When asked if he became familiar with the word "Spectrum," Mr. Watkins replied, "there was some different materials that spoke of a company called *Spectrum Design*. I was informed that was the name of Mr. Westerfield's business. On both CDs and two of the zip drives Mr. Watkins found questionable still images and movies, the term he used for content he believed contained underage girls.

"With regard to these still images and, I think you've described questionable movies as well, are they in a format we can play them in court here?"

"Yes, sir, they are."

Judge Mudd recognized his queue and stepped in. "Ladies and gentleman, I think we've come to a point where all of you need a nice stretch break. We are going to set up the equipment so are going to give you a little extra time so you can come back wide eyed and bushy tailed."

After the afternoon break, a five minute proceeding not made part of the public record was conducted before the jury was invited back to their seats.

"Welcome back ladies and gentleman. It's interesting, the media has given up their prime front row seats to move into the corner so they can see the TV monitor. I won't comment on that move. All right, Mr. Clarke, you can proceed."

"All right, your honor. With the court's permission, this will be done in about four or five segments. Can we lower the lights?"

The lights were dimmed and Mr. Watson began his first segment, which showed a number of photos taken from one of the zip drives. The second segment displayed multiple pornographic animated still images Mr. Watson referred to as "Anime," that had been found on the second zip drive. The third group also featured animated still images, but from one of the CDs.

In the final segment, Mr. Watson played a video found on the second CD that depicted a girl who appeared underage being raped by two adult men as she screamed and cried. After the movie was stopped and the lights were raised, two jurors were crying.

"Thank you," Mr. Clarke said. "I have no more questions, your honor."

In his cross examination, Mr. Feldman asked about additional computers found at Mr. Westerfield's home. Mr. Watson recalled he had found two computers in the office and one in an upstairs bedroom. He had subsequently received a fourth computer which was a laptop, as well as a Palm Pilot.

Mr. Feldman discussed the meaning of various extensions attached to file names such as AVIs, MPEGs, MOVs, JPGs, and GIFs. He then asked what kind of computers Mr. Westerfield used. Mr. Watson said there was a Hewlitt Packard and a Gateway in the office, and stated that the laptop and the computer in the bedroom were also Gateways.

When asked, "how many nudes" were found on all the computers combined, Mr. Watson answered, "a total of between eight and ten thousand."

"And that included what looks like about seventeen stills the jury just saw, is that right?"

"Yes, sir."

"So, apparently out of eight to ten thousand, you spotted fourteen or so that the jury just saw?"

"Yes, sir."

When asked how many videos were found, Mr. Watson answered, "I determined there were several hundred digital movies."

"And did you notice that most of them, there was kind of a common theme?"

"Yes, sir."

"The common theme seemed to be intercourse with mature women, didn't it?"

"Objection, best evidence."

"Well, I'm going to allow it because we are going to need to discuss this matter. You may answer that, sir." Judge Mudd answered.

"In fact, most of the movies with a couple of rare exceptions involved adults engaged in various consensual acts, is that right?"

"Most of them, yes, sir."

"With regard to the eight to ten thousands still images, there was a theme to those, too, right? Large breasted women, correct?"

"Objection. Best evidence, your honor. Let's look."

"Overruled. We are going to be discussing this, I suspect, at length. You may answer."

When asked again if, "a large amount of pictures," featured, "large breasted women," Mr. Watkins answered, "yes, sir."

Mr. Feldman then discussed the difference between allocated and unallocated space on a hard drive. Mr. Watkins explained that allocated space contained all the items a user can see and interact with on the desktop. When a file is deleted, the file moved to the unallocated space where it was no longer visible, but had not yet been fully removed. Only as additional space was needed on the hard drive did the computer permanently erase the deleted files. If additional space was never requested, deleted files would remain in the unallocated space indefinitely, making them subject to recovery.

Mr. Feldman then disclosed that on Monday February 4 between 4:00 and 5:00 in the afternoon, while Mr. Westerfield was answering questions at the police station, someone was using the computer.

"Do you have the capability to look into the computer to identify the person that downloaded a particular photo?"

"No, sir."

At Mr. Feldman's request, Mr. Watkins explained the concept of temporary internet files. When viewing a page on the internet, the computer will download various images and text files associated with that page so when a user returns, the page loads faster. The images are temporarily stored on the computer and can serve as a record of what the user had recently viewed.

After asking Mr. Watson to explain the meaning of internet surfing, Mr. Feldman asked, "is there something called porn surfing?"

"I haven't heard the term before, but I can image what the notation is."

Mr. Feldman showed a screen capture of a pornographic JPG downloaded from "TeenDream.com" on February 4 at 4:47pm.

Regarding the CDs and zip drives, Mr. Feldman asked if he had considered, "fingerprinting the disks to determine who last touched them?"

"No, sir."

"No effort was made to preserve the evidence for fingerprint purposes, correct?"

Mr. Watkins recalled he had handled the CDs by the edges while initially checking their contents before placing them in an evidence bag.

Mr. Feldman then revealed that five of the images shown to the jury had been found on the computer in the bedroom and transitioned his focus toward email. On February 4 at 6:51pm, an email from "PinkForFree.com" was sent to dnwest@hotmail.com.

He then discussed the names of some of the folders on the computers, which included, "Simpsons, Star Trek, Superman." Others were called, "Babes and Celebs." Another folder was called, "Neil's Music."

"In your forensic experience you've seen lots of Anime, haven't you?"

"Yes, sir."

Mr. Feldman stated that Anime was popular and often featured Asian women engaging in sex. "Did you ever hear of Anime.com?"

After saying he was not familiar, Mr. Watkins was shown several animated still photos that had been found on one of the zip drives.

"You specifically indicated in one of the reports that you were unable to link the questionable images to the Westerfield office computers. Those were your words, isn't that correct?"

"Yes, sir."

Without ever disputing the claim that the images and video showed underage girls, the defense concluded its cross examination. "I have no further questions at this time."

Mr. Dusek was ready. "Your honor, I have two binders I'd like to have marked in this case."

Judge Mudd approved. "I think it's appropriate."

Mr. Feldman was caught off guard. "Your honor, can we sidebar this?"

"No. We're going to have a full discussion regarding this." Judge Mudd informed the jury he was sending them home early and warned, "we know Barry Bonds is going to get up at least four times. If we can do something about it, maybe we'll be winners." He wished the jury a pleasant evening and directed them to return by 9:00 the next morning.

After the jury left, Mr. Watkins was asked to have a seat in the gallery. With Judge Mudd clearly irritated, the defense requested and was granted a ten minute recess, but when they returned, Mr. Feldman's confused posture persisted. "Are we discussing evidentiary matters concerning admissibility?"

Judge Mudd answered, "No. We're discussing the alleged images in this matter that are now a matter of public record, Mr. Feldman."

"I don't understand that one."

"You've represented to this jury, Mr. Feldman, that out of eight thousand images, there are only thirteen that are such that the district attorney can find against your client. You know, I know, that is not true."

"Your honor, I asked-"

Judge Mudd interrupted and said he had done, "everything humanly possible to structure this particular issue out of the presence of the media and the public. Over your objection I made findings that this is relevant material. I realize you disagree with that. I asked the district attorney to pare it down so we can see the images they wanted to use in trial apart from all of the images they could have used. I pared it down to minimize your client's exposure to minimize the prejudicial impact. And the very first thing you do on cross examination is say how many images were there. And we get down to thirteen. Now, this is the search for the truth, believe it or not, and the truth is there are more than thirteen images. Now, you tell me, Mr. Feldman, why you have not opened the door to every single image that is on every disk that was confiscated from that house. I'd be interested in hearing it."

Mr. Feldman sheepishly claimed he had not intended to, "end run any of your rulings. I didn't do it to front your honor off in any way. I intend to be respectful and I think I have been."

Judge Mudd was frustrated Mr. Feldman had given the jury the impression there were only thirteen images and one video of questionable content when the number was much larger.

"Your honor," Mr. Feldman attempted a recovery. "The police report of Mr. Watkins plainly indicates no more than I think it may be eighty total questionable images. If you rule that those are admissible, so be it, but I want the record explicitly clear I did not intend to open any doors. If I did so it was inadvertent. I am doing the best I can for my client."

Judge Mudd asked Mr. Clarke about their intentions.

"I think, at this point, the jury has been clearly misled as a result of cross examination and at this point, as the court knows, we have hundreds and hundreds of pornographic photos and I think the jury is now in a position that it needs to hear that due to their being misled during cross examination."

"I concur," Judge Mudd responded before Mr. Feldman persisted his objection and the manner in which the process was being conducted. "You're honor, first of all, there is no best evidence rule. There is no best evidence law. Nobody said let's sidebar. That never happened here. That would have been an appropriate way to address the issue. Had I realized it was raising the court's blood pressure- We raised federal due process and eighth amendment as well and submit it."

"I've ruled on those motions," Judge Mudd continued. "I did it all in the friendly confines of this courtroom without any members of the media or public present in an effort to structure this case in a way that would minimize the prejudicial impact of this information. Had there been any doubt, Mr. Feldman, you could have approached the bench just as easily as the people, but you immediately went for the jugular and you left no room for doubt as to where you're going. Let's mark these things for the record then call it a day."

Mr. Clarke introduced two large binders packed with thousands of pornographic images. In addition to the approximately eighty questionable images, the prosecution was admitting every single pornographic image found on the computers in Mr. Westerfield's home, all eight to ten thousand of them.

"Your honor, I just want to be sure if the court's ruling now that's all admissible, which is how I'm reading the court, I just want the opportunity to-"

"You're welcome to mark it, Mr. Feldman. If the jury wants to look at all of this material, they're going to be welcome to do it. This door has been open like a barn yard."

Mr. Feldman questioned the logic. "Of course, there's no rule of law about opening the door."

"There may not be any rule of law regarding opening the door, there may not be a best evidence rule, although we all know what is on these images and on these tapes. And the one thing I will ensure in this courtroom is that there be no distortions to the people of this community that are going to make this decision. They are now going to know everything."

The state admitted one large white binder labeled "Pornographic Images Westerfield Hard Drives" and another white binder labeled, "Pornographic Westerfield Loose Media."

Mr. Boyce pointed out that the admitted collection

included photos that had been placed under seal during the preliminary hearing.

"I think they were images of a-"

"Well, they're all marked now at this point it time. We'll deal with them when and if the people seek to introduce them. All right, we're in recess."

DAY 14

"Welcome back, ladies and gentleman. I hope none of you turned off the ballgame too early last night. It was an exciting game." He then informed them that CBS had, "elected to do a series of shows or at least news segments on 'Anime,' the kinds of things you saw yesterday, cartoon animations of individuals engaged in various sex acts. They are doing it as a kind of commentary. It has nothing to do with this case, but obviously their timing is something that causes me some concern. If you see something on that particular subject, please disregard it because, again, those are going to be impressions from people that are talking about it from a completely different perspective than the way you're going to be called upon to look at it."

In 2002, the internet was still a very new phenomenon that many people, particularly those over the age of forty, knew very little about and never accessed. Even less knew or understood the shadowy underworld of internet porn. Because web pages and processing speeds were still very limited, most porn on the internet were still images. The only videos available were low resolution clips users could download, but not stream. Within the already obfuscated world of internet porn was a very niche genre of Japanese animated porn called Hentai. Hentai was and still is a cartoonish style of animation that often features forbidden themes like rape and sex with underage girls.

Anime, however, was a genre of gritty Japanese animation movies that became popular in the 1990s with films like *Ghost In The Shell*. Anime movies were stylish action films that often portrayed good versus evil battles in futuristic or otherwise alternative realities. Anime was popular with school aged kids who liked the unique stories and sharp style. Anime was not pornography.

On Mr. Westerfield's computers, investigators identified

numerous Hentai images with themes that included violent sex with young, underage girls. Meanwhile, Mr. Westerfield's son, Neal, enjoyed Anime and often visited a website called Anime.com, which was not pornographic. Because the Hentai images were animated, they were not considered child pornography even when they featured young girls and were therefore not considered, "questionable."

When Judge Mudd turned the court over to the prosecution, Mr. Clarke immediately addressed the two white binders he had introduced the day before. Mr. Watkins informed the jury that the binders contained all the pornographic images he had found on Mr. Westerfield's devices. Each page contained about sixteen images.

"Is there any way to estimate the number of photographs or images?"

"I believe there's going to be approximately eight thousand."

One of the binders contained all the images found on Mr. Westerfield's computer, the other contained all the images found on the two CDs and three zip drives.

Mr. Clarke asked, "do those images include images of children?"

"Yes, they do."

"Do those include images of children who are either nude or partially clothed?"

"Yes, sir."

"Do these images include images beyond or in addition to those that were shown to the jury yesterday?"

"Yes, sir, they do."

Mr. Clarke highlighted a series of pages and asked Mr. Watkins to describe the images. Mr. Watkins stated that there was a series of animated images depicting, "what appears to be a young girl who is assaulted, bound, and then ultimately raped."

"The images appear to be of a child," Mr. Clarke noted.

Mr. Feldman stood. "Your honor, can you note a continuing objection?"

"I will note that for the record."

Mr. Clarke continued. "Do they depict the tying and binding of a child?"

"Yes."

"And the sexual assault of that child?"

"Yes, sir."

Mr. Clarke then asked Mr. Watkins to summarize the associated text, which depicted a girl first being surprised by a man behind her before telling the person about all the sexual acts she wanted him to perform on her.

When asked where the images were found, Mr. Watkins surprisingly revealed these images had been found on the bedroom computer and not any of the devices taken from the office. Mr. Clarke moved on to the next series of images and asked Mr. Watkins to describe their content.

"It depicts several digital photographs of bestiality." Asked to define bestiality, Mr. Watkins said, "the act of a person having sexual acts with animals.

The next series of images Mr. Clarke showed had been found on one of the office computers and had not been downloaded from the internet. The images had been downloaded from a camera that likely belonged to Mr. Westerfield. The first photo showed an adult woman with a juvenile girl. The next series of images depicted the female juvenile outside in a bikini. The photos had been taken from multiple positions and angles; some from close up, others at a distance. A few photos focused on her legs, a few other showed her face. In one, her legs were spread. Mr. Clarke revealed the young girl in the photos, which were found among the large stash of pornography, was the daughter of Mr. Westerfield's ex-girlfriend, Susan, whose name was also Danielle.

Mr. Clarke then turned his attention to the computer

found in the bedroom of Mr. Westerfield's son, Neal. He noted that five of the questionable images shown to the jury the day before had been found in the unallocated area within the computer found in Neal's bedroom, which was an older model that had been handed down to him by his father. Before giving Neal the computer, Mr. Westerfield had deleted all the pornographic images, which ended up in the hidden unallocated storage space where Mr. Watkins found them during his search. The laptop Mr. Watkins had examined had numerous games on it, did not access the internet, and had zero porn files on its hard drive.

Regarding Mr. Westerfield's method of organizing the images and videos on the CDs and zip drives, Mr. Watkins revealed they were organized into folders based on the sex act or theme they depicted. One folder titled "Jetsons" showed images depicting *The Jetsons* cartoons in which Mr. Jetson was having sex with his teenage daughter, Judy.

A majority of the images shown in court the day before came from the folder titled, "Young Ones."

All of the images shared the prefix "IEA" followed by a unique number; something the user would have done manually to every single file. Mr. Watkins did not know what "IEA" referred to and noted that the files were all, "very orderly and very organized."

"Did you also see in your examination of these computers images relating to the business *Spectrum Design*?"

"Yes. Several files had the same naming convention."

After again noting the CDs were labeled, "Spectrum 01," Mr. Clarke asked, "can you determine when the CDs were last accessed?"

"No, sir, I cannot."

"Could they have been accessed as recently as February 1st, 2002?"

"Objection. Speculation."

"Overruled. You can answer."

"It's possible," Mr. Watkins responded.

"Thank you. I don't have any more questions."

Mr. Feldman started his recross examination by clarifying for the jury that in his search of Mr. Westerfield's computers, CDs, and zip drives, Mr. Watkins had discovered a total of eighty-five questionable images that may have depicted an underage girl.

"That was out of the eight to ten thousand?"

"Yes."

"So, you thought there might have been a complete total of eight-five images that may have depicted images of, I'm sorry, boys and girls, girls, under the age of eighteen?"

"Mostly girls. There were several that were borderline and in those I kind of give to the benefit of the defendant."

"You're aware that the sellers of porn hire women to dress and pretend as though they're younger than they really are, isn't that right?"

"Some do, yes."

Although the process of determining age was subjective, Mr. Watkins explained he approached the task as if he was an independent, reasonable person viewing the image.

"You would concede that reasonable minds might differ on the age of the subject depicted?"

"I'm looking at what has that appearance of under eighteen. And again, I try and use, I guess, just a reasonable person standard." In his opinion, the eighty-five specifically identified images depicted girls that clearly appeared younger than eighteen. The unknown number of borderline images were not included in that number.

"You and I could might look at the same picture and form different opinions as to what age is depicted?"

"Yes, sir. That's possible."

"And you utilized that subjectivity in evaluating the total

number of eighty-five questionable images, is that correct?"

"Yes, sir."

"What percentage is eight-five of, I think you told us, eight to ten thousand."

"About one percent," Mr. Watkins guessed.

"Would you agree then, that two police officers might look at the same image and form different opinions?"

"Yes, sir."

"And you have no evidence to support the speculation, correct?"

"That is correct."

Mr. Feldman shifted his focus. "What was the total number of digital movies that you were able to remove from all of the computers?"

"I think about twenty-six hundred digital movies."

"And how many were questionable?"

Mr. Watkins answered, "thirty-nine," which Mr. Feldman noted was only 2% of the total videos found. Mr. Feldman also revealed that some of the videos were just one clip in a series of five or more additional files that were all part of the same scene.

"Now, you told us you couldn't identify who was on the computer at a particular time, is that right?"

"That's correct."

Regarding the photos of Susan's daughter, Danielle, Mr. Feldman pointed out they appeared like home photos and did not contain anything lewd. "In those photos, the girl seemed to be sunbathing, didn't she?"

"Yes, sir."

"Can you tell me, with regard to the seventeen or so files that we saw yesterday, what the dates of download were?"

"No, sir, I can't determine that."

"Can you tell me what was the date of the last access on those files that came from the zip disks?"

Although he could not determine the last time the images and movies on the CDs had been viewed, the files on the zip drives had not been accessed since March 11, 2001, and some of the files had not been viewed since June 2000. Many of the files were initially downloaded in July 1999, which for the internet in 2002 was equivalent of the early renaissance, an entirely different age with none of the current technological benefits.

"So, you cannot rule out that the file was only downloaded and never viewed?"

"That is correct."

"No further questions."

Judge Mudd dismissed the witness with directions not to discuss his testimony until the trial finished.

The state then called Dr. Mitchell Holland, the Laboratory Director at Bode Technology Group, a private forensic DNA laboratory. Dr. Holland had earned a bachelor's degree in chemistry from Hobart College and a Ph.D. in biochemistry from the University of Maryland before completing a postdoctoral fellowship in human genetics at John Hopkins University. At the Armed Forces DNA identification laboratory, Dr. Holland had helped develop the use of mitochondrial DNA testing to identify unknown soldiers who had died in Vietnam. He later assisted the FBI in establishing methods and standards for mitochondrial DNA testing. His lab in New York was accredited by the American Society of Crime Laboratory Directors and was certified by the National Forensic Science Technology Center. Following 9/11, his lab helped identify the sources of more than thirteen thousand skeletal fragments that belonged to people who had died at the World Trade Center.

Bode Technology Group was a forensic DNA laboratory that performed forensic case work and data banking research, and had a convicted offender data bank. They worked on thousands of forensic cases annually and performed both traditional nuclear

DNA testing, which achieves identical matches, as well as mitochondrial DNA testing that identifies only the mother's line.

For the case of Danielle Van Dam, Dr. Holland was provided a number of items for testing along with a mouth swab from Mr. Westerfield and a piece of rib bone from Danielle.

On pajamas found in Danielle's room Dr. Holland was unable to obtain a DNA profile. On a blanket taken from Danielle's room, two DNA profiles were found, one belonging to Danielle, the other to an unknown source that was not Mr. Westerfield. From the left fingernail scrapings and the flake of skin tissue, no results were obtained, and from the right fingernails a partial profile that matched Danielle was recovered.

Regarding the blond hair found in the sink drain in Mr. Westerfield's motorhome, Dr. Holland was able to identify from the root twelve of thirteen DNA markers for a near complete profile.

"With what results?" Mr. Clarke asked.

"The profile obtained from Danielle Van Dam matches the DNA profile from the hair from the sink."

The last item Dr. Holland examined was the blood stain found on the hallway carpet between the bathroom and bedroom inside the motorhome.

"Were you able to determine whether or not either of the individuals from whom you received known samples could or couldn't be the donor of that particular stain?"

"The profile matches Danielle Van Dam. Mr. Westerfield can be excluded as the source of that item."

In addition to the items examined for nuclear DNA, Dr. Holland was sent a number of hairs for mitochondrial DNA analysis. Swabs taken from Brenda Van Dam were also provided for comparison.

Dr. Holland analyzed three hairs found in the dryer lint collected from the garbage in Mr. Westerfield's garage. From the laundry room, he analyzed one hair found on boxer shorts in the dryer and one from the bedding in the washing machine. From the master bedroom, Dr. Holland analyzed one hair taken from the pillow case, two hairs from the fitted sheet, and three hairs from the flat sheet.

All eleven of these hairs matched Danielle and her mother.

"Thank you. I don't have any more questions."

In his cross examination, Mr. Feldman first asked if Dr. Holland had analyzed two dark hairs for comparison to profiles in their convicted criminal database without specifying to which dark hairs he was referring. Dr. Holland revealed he had never received any dark hairs.

After noting that Dr. Holland's services had cost more than $45,000 up to that point, Mr. Feldman focused on multiple hairs not discussed by the prosecution which did not match Danielle. Hairs found on a comforter, in the garage, and down the motorhome's shower drain did not match Danielle or Mr. Westerfield.

"With regard to any of the hairs, can you tell me how long they had been in the location that they were in?"

"No."

"Can you tell me how they had gotten to the location that they were in?"

"No."

Without casting any doubt about the validity of the evidence Dr. Holland had presented, Mr. Feldman ended his exam.

After the lunch break, the state called Jim Frazee, a volunteer canine handler for the San Diego Sheriff's Department. For ten years, he had worked as a canine handler primarily searching for missing people. He had two Vizslas, Hopi and Cielo, medium sized dogs with short, tan hair he had owned since they were puppies and had trained extensively.

Hopi and Cielo were certified by the California Rescue Dog Association (CARDA), a group of volunteer handlers recognized by the California Governor's Office of Emergency Services. Handlers were required to undergo annual evaluations that included fitness tests, and were certified in first aid and CPR. Cielo was a search dog that specialized in finding missing people by following a scent. When a search dog located the missing person it was looking for, the dog would then return to its handler, perform an alert, and lead the handler to the subject.

While also a search dog, Hopi was additionally a certified cadaver dog. To become a cadaver dog, after completing search training, a dog undergoes six months of extensive training that specializes in finding dead bodies. The dog is exposed to the scent, which is then hidden in various locations and circumstances. The training takes significant practice and time. In 2000, Cielo was certified as a cadaver dog and had since worked on numerous cases, discovering cadavers on two separate occasions, once in water.

On February 6, Mr. Frazee arrived at the San Diego Police impound lot with both of his dogs. Hopi briefly searched the inside of the motorhome while Mr. Frazee stood on the second step of the doorway. Hopi walked about halfway down the center aisle toward the back and returned to Mr. Frazee in approximately five seconds.

"Once the dog came back to you, what did you do?" Mr. Dusek asked.

"Well, he appeared that he wanted to-"

"Objection. Relevance."

Judge Mudd responded. "Yes. You've answered the question. Next question."

Mr. Feldman asked him to strike the comment.

"The jury is to disregard the last portion of the answer there. Next question."

Mr. Frazee continued his recollection. A couple of minutes after exiting the motorhome, Mr. Frazee returned with Hopi for a second search.

"Where did Hopi go?"

Mr. Frazee revealed that Hopi had jumped on the sofa behind the driver seat where he stood for about five seconds before they left. Mr. Frazee returned Hopi to his vehicle and then worked the outside of the motorhome with Cielo. After initiating his cadaver command, "bones," Mr. Frazee walked Cielo around the outside of the motorhome, focusing his attention on areas where a scent might escape like the door seams and storage compartments.

When they reached the area of the passenger side door and the first storage compartment, the intensity of his sniffing increased. Hopi then sat, made eye contact, and barked.

"Which means what?" Mr. Dusek asked.

"It means that he has detected a cadaver scent."

Mr. Frazee continued his search of the RV's perimeter, but Hopi did not alert at any other locations. At that time, the compartment door beside the passenger door was opened. Cielo sniffed intensely on a shovel and some lawn furniture that were inside.

"Is this where he had alerted the first time?"

"Yes."

"By sniffing at that location, does that mean to you as its handler, as Cielo's handler, that a body had been in that compartment?"

Mr. Frazee explained the scent might have originated from inside the cabinet, but might also have come from the inside the motorhome and just exited at that location.

"Thank you, sir."

After confirming that police officers were present at the impound while he searched the motorhome, Mr. Boyce asked, "after Cielo was run around the motorhome on February 6th, you told the police officers Cielo showed no positive reaction during his search, didn't you?"

"I don't recall saying that."

"You don't recall? Do you mean to tell this jury that you didn't do it or you don't remember?"

"Objection, argumentative."

Judge Mudd advised Mr. Boyce to calm down and take a deep breath.

Mr. Boyce apologized and continued. He pointed out that Mr. Frazee had never testified in court before and discussed handler bias, the potential for a dog to give a false alert in an attempt to please the handler.

"Instead of releasing Cielo and letting Cielo to search freely, you showed Cielo specific locations around that motorhome, is that correct?"

"That's correct."

Mr. Boyce then revealed that although detectives and officers were nearby, Mr. Frazee did not inform anyone that Cielo had made a positive alert.

"The first time you told anyone Cielo made an alert on the storage compartment of the motorhome was three weeks after February 6th, wasn't it?"

"It could have been."

"And at that time weeks later when you claim you reported your observations of Cielo's behavior, you didn't report them to law enforcement, but you reported them to Cielo's breeder in New Mexico, didn't you?"

Mr. Frazee answered, "yes," and confessed he had emailed the breeder because he thought she would be proud. He additionally revealed he had assumed his unit lieutenant had informed detectives of the positive alert because she had watched Hopi search the motorhome's perimeter and saw him alert by the storage container and passenger door.

"So, you didn't tell your lieutenant that there was an alert either then, did you?"

"I didn't feel it was necessary."

Mr. Boyce thanked and dismissed the witness.

Judge Mudd proceeded to inform the jury they were going to view the motorhome at that time. They were allowed to bring a notebook and pen, and advised they would be released for the day after the inspection finished. Judge Mudd discussed the method of showing the jury the vehicle, which was parked by the loading dock outside the Hall of Justice. Judge Mudd determined that each juror would be given the opportunity to independently enter the RV and walk around freely, and that they would go in order of their number.

When Judge Mudd asked Mr. Feldman if they could proceed without the defendant for the sake of time and simplicity, Mr. Westerfield decided he wanted to attended, possibly to see his beloved motorhome one last time.

Before leaving for the motorhome, Judge Mudd discussed his plan to hear motions the following day in advance of the defense starting its case. Because there would be no testimony, the jury was not needed. He additionally reminded the jury they would not be needed on Monday either due to a separate hearing. Therefore, the jurors would not be needed again until next Tuesday.

MOTIONS

On Thursday, June 27, without the jury present, several motions were discussed. Mr. Feldman raised several objections regarding photos the prosecution was admitting before re-objecting to the photos of Susan's daughter which had been admitted with the two binders of pornography found on Mr. Westerfield's computer. Mr. Feldman asked that her face be blocked out for the jury and that the photos not be released publicly. Judge Mudd agreed.

Mr. Feldman additionally expressed his frustration about the media reporting there were eight to ten thousand questionable images and not just eight-five, and referred to a California appellate decision that had determined "open the gates arguments were nothing more than popular fallacy." He further clarified that, "there was never a tactical decision made by me or any member of the defense team that contemplated what the court ultimately did. That was completely unforeseen. If some appellate lawyer construes I made that as a tactical judgement, which I did not, that would defeat any issue that may arise as a result of the court's ruling."

Regarding the "photos which depict behaviors with animals, there was absolutely nothing in my cross examination which implicated or suggested that there was any relevance to any of that."

Judge Mudd agreed and decided the bestiality images would not be admitted. Mr. Feldman then requested, "the court to direct the jury that with regard to any testimony concerning that subject manner, they are to disregard it for all purposes. Furthermore, based upon the court's ruling, I have to renew my motion for a mistrial based upon all the reasons that were articulated previously and those incorporated by reference today.

"Because of the nature of the publicity on this particular issue, which your honor commented on by virtue of the sudden attendance of vast numbers of media where it appeared during the DNA they were less interested, we renew our request for sequestration. I'm not trying to segue into a different issue, your honor, maybe I should defer on the sequestration. Please just give me direction."

"Get it all out and then I will hear from the people."

Mr. Feldman recalled seeing a news report the previous night featuring an interview with a psychiatrist who compared Mr. Westerfield to Ted Bundy and Jeffrey Dahmer. Mr. Feldman was additionally concerned that the statements Mr. Westerfield gave in his formal police interview, which had been ruled "constitutionally inadmissible by virtue of the illegal behaviors of law enforcement which the court has concluded were involuntarily taken in violation of Mr. Westerfield's fifth and sixth amendment rights, that those are now going to be broadcast on the evening news and adversely influence the jury." Even if the jury was self-policing, "the media is inescapable. Virtually everything we are doing is under a microscope and I think that is implicating the press and the jury."

Mr. Feldman again objected to the binders of pornographic images and stated, "there's no such thing as opening the door. It's not fair to punish Mr. Westerfield because it was not done in bad faith, and the court knows that."

Judge Mudd allowed the state to respond.

Mr. Clarke expressed his frustration about revisiting a subject that had already been discussed and decided. He started by refuting Mr. Feldman's claim that he made an innocent mistake. "Everyone was aware this was obviously a tactical decision to try to minimize the impact of these various photographs involving child pornography. The bottom line is the jury was badly misled, the court noted they were misled. I think everyone in this courtroom knew they were misled because of the actual extent of the pornographic material that was present."

Mr. Clarke believed the jury should have access to everything they found. He further believed the pictures of Susan's daughter were appropriate because her hair was blonde in the photos even though she was Asian. He requested the jury have access to the binders during their deliberation. "They may very well and, I suspect, not want to see it, but nonetheless, I think that should be part of the record."

Regarding sequestration, Mr. Clarke referred to his previous arguments against and noted that the attention given the case by the media was not as significant as in some other cases.

Mr. Feldman interjected. "He's specifically referring to Simpson, your honor."

"I understand that," Judge Mudd before weighing in on the issues.

Judge Mudd started his decision by stating first that the accuracy of media stories was not his responsibility or within his control. Although he did not believe Mr. Feldman had acted in bad faith, he did conclude that his intent was a clear, strategic move not just in one question but during the entire sequence of questions in which his intent was to convince the jury there were only thirteen or so questionable images. "And that is what got the court's ire and blood up."

Before the trial began, they had spent an entire day debating how many images the jury should see before a compromise was reached that determined only a small number would be shown. Because the defense misled the jury about the number of images found, the jury was then informed that the actual number was eighty-five. "Still a small percentage, but they are not going to go away without complete knowledge."

Judge Mudd decided the binders would remain out of the jury room during deliberation, but would make them available if requested. With no evidence the jury was not following the order to avoid media stories about the trial, Judge Mudd denied the request for sequestration.

Judge Mudd planned to continue withholding the last name of Susan's daughter, whose father had expressed his concern in multiple calls to the court, but he deferred a decision about allowing the photos until the defense had presented their case. If the defense did not involve the girl, the pictures would not be made available for the jury during deliberation. The bestiality photos would remain a part of the record, but be removed from the binders.

When asked if there were any additional issues, Mr. Feldman asked for more information about the prosecution's remaining witnesses. He mentioned an entomologist on their list of witnesses and noted if the state ultimately decided not to call him, the defense would need him added to their own list.

When pressed, Mr. Feldman admitted they had not disclosed their computer expert witness, Marcus Lawson, until immediately after Mr. Watkin's testimony, "out of an abundance of caution." He did not want a potential witness writing a report that would be revealed in discovery unless he knew for certain that witness would be called.

"We have provided over seven hundred and fifty pages of discovery to the prosecution. We have provided a list of potential witnesses. It's not as though Mr. Dusek is in the dark."

Judge Mudd asked, "Do you have any other experts that are not disclosed to the people at this point in time?"

Mr. Feldman requested more time to finalize his witness list and hoped he could explain his decision making process in private, "so you see that we're not playing games."

Mr. Dusek responded. "I don't care about the decision making process, we are on the eve of trial. He's given us a name that has not surfaced before. Now we get a CV without any reports. He's hiding behind the no report rule that does not exist. That's the concern. And that there will be other experts we don't know about."

Mr. Feldman explained that Mr. Watkins had not provided some of the information he expected, which was why he was calling his own witness.

"That's why we need discovery, your honor," Mr. Dusek responded.

Judge Mudd reminded Mr. Feldman that prior to the start of trial, he repeatedly requested, and had been given, more time to prepare for the state's witnesses. Now, he was requesting to proceed without extending the prosecution the same courtesy. Judge Mudd agreed to discuss in private why there were no reports ready for discovery and what, if any, witnesses had not yet been disclosed, but directed the defense to be ready to start their case on Tuesday morning.

At that time, Judge Mudd cleared the courtroom for a private discussion with the counselors.

DAY 15

On the morning of Tuesday July 2, Judge Mudd welcomed the jury back and compared some of his responsibilities to herding cats. "Little did I know after watching the Padres for the last couple of days that it might actually be harmful to your mental health mandating you watch them. Hopefully, the road trip will get better. And for those of you who want an option other than that, I'm a golf fan myself, love playing the game and love watching it, although my wife thinks it's the greatest cure for insomnia. But anyway, there's a great golf match on tonight."

Judge Mudd warned the jury about the abundance of wrong and misleading information in the media and encouraged vigorous self-policing so their final decision would result only from information they learned inside the courtroom.

"It's hot, Judge," Juror 12 stated.

"Okay. We will get maintenance on it as quickly as we can."

Mr. Dusek then recalled Jim Frazee, the cadaver dog handler.

"Mr. Frazee, I think when you were here last week you were asked questions by the defense regarding an email you had sent someone. Do you recall that?"

Mr. Frazee remembered sending an email to Cielo's breeder on February 22.

"Would you read the first paragraph for us?"

"I could get in trouble for telling you this, but I'm kind of bursting with pride over Cielo and I have to tell somebody besides Jan (his wife) what he did. She'd certainly admonish me if she knew I was writing you about this."

"Did you also indicate in that email what Cielo did when he was going around the motorhome?"

"Yes, I did."

"He reacted as you testified here in court?"

"Yes."

"Did you write any reports regarding the incident?"

"It was very limited because in keeping with the fact that we're not supposed to discuss the case, all I reported was what I was asked to do and my miles and hours."

"How did the word get to you that you were supposed to write a report?"

"That came through our unit lieutenant, Rosemary Redditt."

"Thank you."

In his cross examination, Mr. Boyce noted that Mr. Frazee had been aware of the extensive search for the missing seven year old as well as the abundant news coverage and public interest in finding Danielle. Despite understanding the importance of the case, after his dog had supposedly alerted, Mr. Frazee had not informed a single police officer or detective.

"You didn't tell anyone until February 22nd that your dog alerted, did you?"

"No."

"You didn't tell anyone until you learned there was blood in the motorhome, did you?"

"That's correct."

Mr. Boyce then revealed that the email had been sent to not one, but three individuals with the subject, "Secret Message."

"And you told them in that email, 'I wasn't sure, but I thought Cielo was giving me his cadaver alert.'"

Mr. Frazee agreed he had made the statement.

"And then you stated in the very next sentence, 'I thought he might be doing these behaviors just to please me,' is that correct?"

"Yes."

Mr. Boyce read more of the email. "I didn't know what to make of what Cielo did and had to leave the scene wondering.

Today, however, came news of the suspect's arrest and it was revealed they had found a body in the motorhome."

Mr. Boyce asked if he had sent the email because he, "thought it was pretty cool?"

Mr. Frazee agreed and Mr. Boyce moved his attention to a report Mr. Frazee wrote on February 19 that stated, "I was also asked to keep the results of any searching I did at the request of the San Diego Police Department confidential."

"I said that, yes."

Mr. Boyce then informed the court that the president of the local chapter of CARDA, the California Rescue Dog Association, the organization that had certified Cielo, was his wife, Jan. "Your wife essentially certified Cielo as a tracking dog or an area search dog, is that correct?"

Mr. Frazee disagreed. "That's a bit of a stretch."

"Your dogs actually went to that motor home on one earlier occasion, didn't they?"

Mr. Frazee confirmed they had searched the outside of the RV while it was parked at the high valley residence. And you ran the dogs around the motorhome and they did not detect a scent, isn't that correct?"

"Yes."

Mr. Boyce passed the witness back to Mr. Dusek who asked Mr. Frazee to read another section of the email in which he recalls that Cielo had shown a particular interest in the area of the door and adjacent storage container on the night they inspected the motorhome while it was still at the High Valley residence. At that time, he was not entirely confident that the alert was authentic. Not until blood was found in the motorhome, was he convinced the alert was real.

"Did you then go on to say how proud you were of the dog?"

"Yes."

"I don't have anything further, your honor."

After Judge Mudd dismissed Mr. Frazee with instructions not to discuss his testimony with anyone, Mr. Dusek called his direct supervisor, Volunteer Reserve Lieutenant Rosemary Redditt. Lt. Redditt was a retired school teacher who had volunteered for the Sheriff's search and rescue bureau as well as the canine unit for the past twenty-four years. A few times every month, Lt. Redditt was called out to search for missing people, mostly hikers, sometimes abducted children. She worked with a number of handlers and dogs including Jim Frazee. Lt. Redditt also had a search and rescue dog of her own.

At the SDPD impound lot on February 6, Lt. Redditt watched from about fifteen feet away as Mr. Frazee escorted Hopi into the motorhome and then again when he walked Cielo around the perimeter of the vehicle. Lt. Redditt recalled that Cielo exhibited a visible response near the storage container adjacent to the passenger side door.

"What did you see Cielo do?"

Lt. Redditt stated that he sat, looked at Mr. Frazee, and barked. After another lap around the motorhome, the storage compartment was opened at which time Cielo put his paws up on the ledge of the container and stiffed intensely.

"Did you have any trouble reading the dog's alert there at the motorhome?

"No."

"Was that an alert?"

"Yes."

"Thank you."

Mr. Feldman focused his cross examination first on details in the report submitted by Mr. Frazee and then on her own training and experience. "If your dog was trained in a particular way to alert, and that particular way to alert was to sit down, make eye contact, and bark, and the dog did that, would there be any question in your mind as to whether or not the dog was alerting?"

"There would not be a question in my mind."

After Mr. Feldman asked a series of questions about who was present when Cielo searched the motorhome at the impound, Lt. Redditt recalled seeing Cielo alert at the storage compartment adjacent to the passenger side door. Mr. Feldman noted that the dog did not perform his alert when the storage container was opened.

Lt. Redditt was dismissed and after the morning break, the state called Dr. Joy Halverson of Quest-Gen Forensics in Davis, California. Dr. Halverson had graduated with a degree in biology from the University of California San Diego in 1976 before earning a doctorate of veterinary medicine, a master's degree in epidemiology, which is the study of how diseases travel in populations, and a master's degree in preventative veterinary medicine. She later started a genetic laboratory that was bought by a large biosystems corporation where she became the head of research.

After leaving the corporation, she started Quest-Gen, which specialized in dog DNA. Dr. Halverson was a member of the International Society of Animal Genetics and had published numerous papers about the genetic testing of animals that included analyzing mitochondrial DNA in dogs. In one of her cases, Dr. Halverson had analyzed dog blood found on the shirt of a suspect and determined that the DNA matched the victim's dog who had also been killed.

Dr. Halverson recalled she had been contacted by a colleague at the UC Davis veterinary genetic lab about samples they had analyzed unsuccessfully for nuclear DNA. Dr. Halverson was asked if she could try obtaining the mitochondrial DNA and she agreed to try before driving over to the lab and picking up five different collections of unknown dog hair. She did not want the sample from Layla until her analysis of the unknown hairs was complete.

"Did you obtain mitochondrial DNA results for all five

evidence items?"

Dr. Halverson stated she had not obtained any results from one sample and only partial results with two samples, but revealed she had achieved full results with the last two.

"Did you make comparisons between the four evidence items that you obtained mitochondrial DNA results from?"

Dr. Halverson concluded that Layla could have been the source of all four samples.

When asked if any of the results excluded Layla, Dr. Halverson answered, "no."

Mr. Feldman spent the first large chunk of his cross examination focused on a typo in one of the reports regarding the number of dogs in her company's database. She was asked to explain the simple typo in detail as well as the amended report she subsequently submitted, which had fixed the mistake. After spending significant time needling Dr. Halverson on her minor and irrelevant error, Judge Mudd instructed Mr. Feldman to approach the bench.

After a short conversation not made part of the public record, Mr. Feldman broadened his focus by emphasizing the importance of accuracy in the scientific process. He then discussed her fees which she estimated would be about $3,000 and explained was calculated by the number of samples analyzed, not the time involved.

Mr. Feldman then moved his attention to her publications, which focused primarily on birds. He asked for the definition of, "peer review," and continued his attempts at chipping away her credibility without ever directly questioning the legitimacy of the evidence she had presented.

"The hairs could have come from Layla, correct?"

"That's correct."

"That means logically that they could not have come from Layla as well, true?"

"Well, yes, of course."

Dr. Halverson was dismissed and after a brief meeting between the judge and the attorneys, Judge Mudd updated the jury on where the case stood. Due to the rapid speed of the investigation and trial, the prosecution still had one more witness, but because their investigation had not finished, they were not yet ready to testify. The state was therefore resting its case except for the additional witness who would testify when ready. Judge Mudd gave the jury their standard hour and a half hour lunch break and confirmed that the defense was ready to begin presenting its case when court resumed that afternoon.

At 1:30 in the afternoon of Tuesday July 2, the defense of David Westerfield began. Mr. Boyce first recalled Detective James Tomsovic who had watched Jim Frazee and Cielo search the exterior of the motorhome.

"You stated in your report the dog showed no positive reaction during the search?"

"Objection, hearsay."

"Overruled, you may answer."

"Yes, I did write that in my report, Det. Tomsovic confirmed.

Mr. Boyce turned the witness over to Mr. Dusek who pointed out that the Detective had arrived some time after Mr. Frazee and Lt. Redditt. Standing about twenty feet away, Det. Tomsovic had been talking about dogs with Lt. Redditt and was not focused on the search or trained to recognize an alert.

"Did you ever get a report from either Frazee or Redditt?"
"No."

Mr. Dusek ended his questions and Mr. Boyce asked one more.

"You didn't see the dog bark or wag its tail, did you?"
"No."

"I don't have anything further, your honor."

Mr. Boyce's next witness was Mark, a software engineer who lived with his wife and three kids across the street from Mr. Westerfield. Mark initially met Mr. Westerfield when they moved in four years prior and had been inside his home on approximately five occasions.

"Did he have girlfriends?"

"Yes."

Mark recalled meeting Susan as well as David's son and daughter. Mr. Boyce asked about the motorhome, which Mark revealed was not always parked by the house for long periods before a trip.

"Do you see a lot of children on the streets?"

Mark stated there were many kids in the neighborhood of various ages and knew the motorhome was not always locked.

On the night of Friday February 1, Mark and his family had been in Coronado and did not return home until 3:30 Saturday afternoon. When they arrived, they saw numerous police cars, taped off areas, news media, and neighbors in the street. While out talking to people about what had happened, Dave drove past in his motorhome. They looked at each other briefly before Dave parked down the street and walked back. Mark spoke with him a moment later and informed him the little girl a couple of houses up the street was missing.

In his cross examination, Mr. Dusek confirmed Mark had not seen the motorhome in the several months leading up to Danielle's disappearance and noted that when parked before a trip, the vehicle was three houses down the street from the Van Dam's house. Mr. Dusek additionally noted the passenger side door was a good distance from the ground and had steps that automatically dropped when the door opened.

"Did you ever see any kids inside the motorhome, little kids, elementary school kids?"

"No."

Mr. Dusek then discussed Mr. Westerfield's routine of

parking the motorhome by his house a day or more before a trip so he could clean the inside and pack supplies.

"When he would go on these trips, he would go with his girlfriend, his son, or other people?"

"From what I am aware of, yes."

When asked about Susan, Mark revealed she had dark hair and stated that the recent breakup had been difficult for Mr. Westerfield whose home he described as very neat, orderly, and clean. He recalled Mr. Westerfield at one point having a small dog with short black hair.

Following the afternoon break, the defense called another friend of Mr. Westerfield's, Paul, a senior engineering manager at Nokia. Paul lived one house west of Mr. Westerfield and had known him since he moved in about six years prior. They shared a backyard fence where they often spoke. Mr. Westerfield was a friend of his colleague, Glenn, who also worked at Nokia.

"Did you have occasion to ever see a hose in Mr. Westerfield's yard?" Mr. Boyce asked.

Paul confirmed he had seen the hose left out on the lawn and driveway on previous occasions and recalled the time Mr. Westerfield had shown him the inside of his motorhome.

"Do you see a lot of children in that neighborhood?"

Paul confirmed he did.

"Would it be uncommon for him to leave his back light on at night?"

"No. Actually, I have even seen the lights on during the daytime."

With his final series of questions, Mr. Boyce attempted to show the jury that Mr. Westerfield's actions the weekend Danielle was abducted were within the range of normal.

In his cross examination, Mr. Dusek asked about the school in their neighborhood which was within walking distance, and confirmed the Van Dams would head the opposite direction from the defendant's house when walking to school. Mr. Dusek then revealed that although Mr. Westerfield did sometimes leave the hose out, he would always put it away a short time later. On the morning of February 2, he had seen the motorhome parked at the end of the driveway, but had not seen anyone loading the vehicle and did not see any of Mr. Westerfield's friends or family.

After Paul's testimony concluded, Mr. Feldman questioned Detective Johnny Keene about the specific times he had been with Mr. Westerfield on Monday February 4. Det. Keene recalled they had been together between 9:30 and 12:00 that morning and again between 3:00 in the afternoon until after 11:00 that night.

In his cross examination, Mr. Dusek asked Det. Keene if he had been wearing gloves on the morning of February 4. Mr. Feldman objected and Judge Mudd requested they meet at sidebar. After a lengthy discussion not made part of the public record, Mr. Dusek continued by showing a photo of Det. Keene wearing gloves at Mr. Westerfield's home that morning.

"What is going on when this photograph was being taken."

"Objection, relevance."

Judge Mudd overruled and Mr. Dusek continued.

Det. Keene recalled that he and Det. Parga were searching the garage.

"Thank you, sir.

Judge Mudd released the witness and said, "All right, ladies and gentleman, we are going to break for the evening. Hopefully things will be better in St. Louis tonight. We'll see you all at 9:00 o'clock tomorrow morning."

DAY 16

"Good morning, ladies and gentleman. My extended family in St. Louis has indicated they would love to have the Padres spend the rest of the summer back there and solidify their position as number one in the central division. I don't know what to tell you, but, you know, at least it is a diversion. All right, Mr. Feldman."

The defense started their first full day by calling the witness they had hidden from the prosecution until the last possible moment, Marcus Lawson. Mr. Lawson was the president of Global Compusearch, a computer forensics firm located in Spokane, Washington. He had earned a degree in justice administration at Portland State University and a JD degree from Pepperdine University School of Law in Malibu, California. After law school, he worked for the Secret Service and then the DEA before spending twelve years as an agent for the Customs and Border Protection Agency. As a customs agent, he had specialized in child pornography and had implemented an undercover program targeting child pornography crimes similar to how the DEA pursued drug crimes. He had taught training classes for over a dozen different law organizations and in 2000, had started Global Compusearch.

In his digital investigations, Mr. Lawson used a forensic software program called EnCase, which allowed investigators to search computers and associated devices without altering the original data. EnCase provided investigators the ability to view the contents of a hard drive as if the investigator was accessing the actual computer.

Mr. Lawson recalled being contacted approximately one month ago to review computer discovery related to the defense of David Westerfield. He was supplied copies of the computer hard drives as well as the CDs and zip drives seized from Mr.

Westerfield's home that had been created by the San Diego Regional Forensics Laboratory. Mr. Lawson initially reviewed the contents at Mr. Feldman's office in San Diego and determined that most of the media did not contain questionable images. He then sent the hard drives to his office in Spokane for a complete analysis, which took approximately 150 hours.

Mr. Lawson started his search with the hard drive recovered from the bedroom. Upon finding school related files, he realized the computer belonged to Mr. Westerfield's son, Neal. In the recycling bin of Neal's computer, Mr. Lawson discovered two images of interest. The first was a naked woman sitting on a motorcycle that was deleted on September 26, 2001. The second was a naked woman with her legs spread apart that Mr. Lawson described as pornographic and lascivious.

Mr. Feldman then asked about Anime, which Mr. Lawson defined as a style of animation that was particularly popular.

"Is there a style of Anime that appears frequently on the internet?"

"Most Anime is oriental related. It's referred to as Japanese Anime, and I can't pronounce the Japanese word. It's Hentai or along those lines that refers to specifically Japanese animated."

Mr. Feldman asked if any Anime of a sexual nature had been discovered on Neal's computer.

Mr. Lawson answered, "yes," and referenced a collection of twenty-six images that depicted various animated sexual images.

"Is there a theme that you were able to associate with this particular series of screen prints?"

"A considerable number of these screen prints involve bondage scenarios where women are tied in ropes and things like that." Mr. Lawson added that most of the animated images he encountered on the computer from Neal's bedroom featured bondage scenarios.

Moving on, Mr. Feldman provided evidence that Neal had frequently checked his email on Mr. Westerfield's office computer, the only computer in the home connected to the internet. He showed a screen capture of an email sent to dnwest@hotmail.com that wrote, "Thanks For Joining Anime.com." Mr. Lawson revealed that "Anime.com" was a website that contained links to various Anime related sites.

Of the two office computers, Mr. Lawson discovered pornographic images on one of the hard drives and revealed all of the images had been created and last accessed before December 17, 2001. On Neal's laptop, Mr. Lawson did not find any activity relevant to the case.

Moving back to the first hard drive from the office, Mr. Feldman stated it was a Western Digital thirty gigabyte hard drive. When asked if the computer had been used to visit a pornographic web site on February 4, Mr. Lawson answered, "yes," and explained both "Anime sites and teen sex sites" had been accessed. Based on the temporary internet files, Mr. Lawson determined a site called "Teen Dreamer" had been visited at 4:47 on the afternoon of Monday, February 4, while Mr. Westerfield was at the police station giving his statement. At roughly the same time, "Lesbian Bordello" was accessed and Neal had viewed an email received from "PinkForFree.com."

Mr. Feldman provided additional examples of Neal using the office computer to look at porn, but the instances were brief, mild, and did not involve content that might have featured underage girls. On one occasion he visited a Hentai website and on another he viewed, "Extreme Asian Bondage. Totally Uncensored." The page claimed it was the, "Most Sexually Perverted Site Online."

While playing up the extreme nature of the content Neal had viewed, Mr. Feldman simultaneously clarified that just because a website said it featured teen content, didn't mean the actresses were actual teenagers. Mr. Lawson recalled that "Lolita.com" specifically stated in its banner that none of its models were under the age of eighteen.

On January 7, 2002, near the time Neal's Hotmail account was accessed, a website was visited featuring, "Hardcore Beast Action; Donkeys, Snakes, Horses, Dogs." One picture showed an innocuous picture of a naked woman with a horse.

Moving back to the computer activity on the afternoon of February 4, Mr. Feldman noted that Neal's Hotmail account was accessed and that he had read messages from "JoinForFree.com" and "PinkForFree.com" at 4:45. At 4:48, a page with "Hot Hentai Cartoons" was visited, and at 4:49 it was "Teens.com."

"You were requested by my office to see whether or not you could determine the date of file creation of a series of MPEGs called 'Attack' that depicted a young Asian woman allegedly being raped by individuals. Do you recall that we asked you to do that?"

Referring to the video shown in court depicting an underage girl being raped, Mr. Lawson recalled reviewing approximately six video files labeled "Attack" that had been found on the loose media. The six video clips were all part of a larger scene that had been cut into parts.

"They were downloaded, or their file creation dates show, August 5, 2001 at 3:42pm in the afternoon with the last access date of November 18, 2001."

When Mr. Feldman asked Mr. Lawson if he had determined who was using the computer when the "Attack" videos were downloaded, Mr. Lawson answered, "the only thing I was able to find that was still available that offered any kind of clue to that at all is an Anime file created on August 5, 2001 at 1:34pm." Mr. Feldman showed the jury the single, nonpornographic, Anime image that was viewed on Mr. Westerfield's office computer a full two hours before the rape video was downloaded.

On October 28, 2001, around the time Neal's Hotmail account was accessed, a site was visited that referred to itself as "The Hottest Preteen Site Out There," and said, "Meet Young Girls Here For Free." Mr. Lawson stated that some of the images viewed included "bondage and Anime porn."

Mr. Feldman next showed a series of twenty-three images found on the CDs and zip drives. Mr. Lawson informed the court that none of the images had been accessed since December 17, 2001. When asked why that date was relevant, Mr. Lawson revealed that it was the same date "the majority of the images on the Gateway computer in Neal Westerfield's room had also been created."

"Based on your review of all of the computer hard drives, based on your review of all of the screen prints, based on your years of expertise, are you able to form an opinion as to whether or not the movies and images on the loose media were downloaded from a particular computer?"

"Objection, no foundation, calls for speculation."

"Overruled."

Mr. Lawson reported that he was not able to determine who downloaded the images found on the loose media.

"Without actually being there you don't really know, correct?"

"That's correct."

"No further questions at this time, thank you."

Mr. Clarke started the cross examination by informing the jury that Mr. Lawson was not an attorney and did not practice law. He then reviewed Mr. Lawson's resume, which listed his membership in the National Association of Criminal Defense Lawyers and included ten legal references, all of whom were defense attorneys. Mr. Clarke noted that his company specialized in assisting lawyers representing defendants charged with crimes involving child pornography.

"What constitutes child pornography?"

"A lascivious exhibition of the child genitals or sexual acts of children."

"So, it has to be a person under eighteen. Doesn't have to be involved in a sex act, does it?"

"Objection, relevance."

After a short conference at the bench, Mr. Clarke moved on and requested any hand written notes Mr. Lawson had made while performing his investigation. Mr. Lawson reported that the only hand written notes he made were summaries of the questionable content he initially viewed while in San Diego. Mr. Clarke believed there were more.

"You left some things out in the final report that were in the summary, didn't you?"

Mr. Feldman objected and asked for a side bar because, "this implicates the attorney-client privilege."

Judge Mudd overruled and Mr. Lawson conceded that he likely left details out of his final report.

"Isn't it correct, that in the preliminary report, you noted that there were obviously individuals in the loose media that were under the age of eighteen?"

"Yes."

"You didn't include that in your final report, did you?"

"No."

"Did you view those movies?" Mr. Clarke asked.

"Yes."

"Did you listen to them?"

"No."

"You never heard the sound?"

"Objection. Irrelevant."

"Overruled. The answer is no."

Moving on to the computer taken from Neal's bedroom, Mr. Clarke asked, "are you aware of whether or not computers are handed down, let's say, from a parent to a child?"

"Yes."

"This term Anime. Does Anime mean sexual in nature?"

"Not necessarily."

"When you go to Anime.com do you immediately see dirty pictures or pornography?"

After Mr. Lawson conceded there were no pornographic images on "Anime.com," Mr. Clarke addressed the twenty-six pornographic images shown earlier that had been linked to Neal.

"When were they downloaded from the internet?"

"This particular file, I just picked one at random, and I don't know if it's Anime, but it's referred to as a cartoon file called big red, was created on January 14, 1999."

"Three and a half years ago, correct?"

"Correct."

Jumping forward, Mr. Clarke then asked, "are you aware of whether or not in the office computers there were business files that had the same prefix IEA?"

"I don't know that. I don't remember that."

"Objection. Argumentative."

"Overruled."

Mr. Clarke pressed harder. "But you didn't look at that?"

"I didn't notice."

Mr. Clarke showed a screen capture of an image shown with the group of twenty-six along with its creation date and asked, "when was it created?"

"April 22, 1999."

"Over three years ago?"

"Correct."

After showing the jury that the porn images found on Neal's hard drive had been likely downloaded while the computer was still in Mr. Westerfield's possession, Mr. Clarke moved on to the emails.

After pointing out that the email from "PinkForFree.com" opened on December 13 was spam, Mr. Clarke asked, "how many of those sites did that person click on when they got that piece of mail?"

"I know on this date I didn't have any screen prints showing any."

"So, it is correct that it appears from your examination that no one even clicked on any of those web sites?"

"On this particular day? I didn't find any examples of clicking on any of these links on December 13th."

Judge Mudd intervened and dismissed the jury for the lunch break. Once the jury had exited the room, Mr. Clarke formally requested discovery they had not received, specifically, the hand written notes Mr. Lawson made while reviewing the questionable content on the CDs and zip drives while he was in Mr. Feldman's San Diego office.

Mr. Feldman disagreed with the assertion and believed the implication in front of the jury was misleading. He insisted that two pages of raw notes had been provided, but Mr. Clarke thought there should have been more. Judge Mudd directed the defense to consult Mr. Lawson, determine whether more pages existed, and provide any missing pages to the state immediately.

"Okay, we'll be in recess till 1:30."

Following the lunch break, Mr. Clarke continued his cross with questions about the computer activity that occurred on the Afternoon of February 4, while Mr. Westerfield was being interviewed by police.

"Isn't it correct that there's no demonstration in any of the records in that machine that any porn sites were actually visited that day?"

Mr. Lawson looked through his report. "The websites that were visited appear to be Pink For Free, The Daily Toon, and possibly Teens.com."

Regarding Pink For Free, Mr. Clarke noted that it was just an email Neal had been sent and asked, "isn't it correct that there is no indication that web site was actually visited?"

"In Hotmail when you receive an email such as this from a pornographic site or from any site that wants you to visit you have to click on the link to go there."

"That didn't happen on that date, correct?"

Mr. Lawson disagreed. "Yes, it did."

"Your honor," Mr. Clarke began, "I have marked as court's exhibit 158 what appears to be a three page document labeled 'Internet Explorer History.' Mr. Lawson can you take a look at that?"

The witness complied as Mr. Clarke asked first about the activity between 3:50 and 8:29 in the afternoon and evening of Monday, February 4.

"In this three page document can you indicate for us where there is an entry regarding PinkForFree.com as a website visit?"

"No, not on this document," Lawson answered, conceding his assertion that Neal had visited porn sites that afternoon was dead wrong.

Mr. Clarke then discussed the websites Neal did access that afternoon, which included a banking site, a gaming site, and numerous visits to the *San Diego Union-Tribute*.

"In your experience, have people received spam type emails from pornographic websites without ever having made a visit?"

"Yes, that can definitely happen."

Switching gears again, Mr. Clarke said, "now, I would like to ask you about the 'Attack' videos,"

After reconfirming Mr. Lawson had watched, but not listened to the videos, Mr. Clarke asked, "have you described them as allegedly showing the rape of a young Asian woman?"

"Yes."

"Do those videos show a rape?"

"Objection."

"Overruled, you can answer that," Judge Mudd decided.

"I don't know whether they do or not."

"Do they involve a girl under the age of eighteen?"

"I don't know," Mr. Lawson answered.

"Do they involve two attackers?"

"Yes."

"You don't know who downloaded those 'Attack' videos, do you?"

"No. No, sir."

Mr. Clarke then noted there was no way of knowing when the 'Attack' videos on the CDs were last viewed because the CDs did not track that information.

"As far as the viewing of those 'Attack' videos, could that have been viewed on February 1st, 2002?"

"Objection. Speculation."

"Overruled."

"Could they have been? Certainly."

"Is that true with each of the movies contained in the loose media?"

"Yes."

"Is that true with respect to all of the still images contained in the loose media?"

"Could they have been viewed? Yes."

Mr. Clarke moved his focus to when Mr. Lawson examined the questionable content on the CDs and zip drives at Mr. Feldman's office in San Diego. "Did you take those back to your home in Washington?"

"No. I don't accept any media that contains anything that is alleged to be child pornography in our office unless it's accompanied by a federal court order for both its transportation and its possession."

"You didn't take those hard drives copied from the loose media to Washington because you were afraid you might be committing a crime in doing so, correct?"

"That's correct."

Regarding the zip disks, Mr. Clarke asked, "do you recall one of those zip disks having stills of young children?"

"Yes."

"Undressed?"

"Yes."

"Was there another zip disk that had still Animes of a young girl?"

"Yes."

"Can you tell us when it was created?"

"Yes. March 18, 1999."

"Do you recall a CD that contained both still images of young girls plus a video?"

Mr. Lawson remembered the images, but did not have screen captures showing their content.

"You don't know who downloaded the images and/or movies as part of the loose media on any of the zip disks, correct?"

"That's correct."

Mr. Clarke noted that the CDs and zip disks had been found in Mr. Westerfield's office and asked, "Is it important to know where they were found in trying to determine who's responsible for them?"

"That can be helpful, yes."

Mr. Clarke discussed the numerous details that indicated Mr. Westerfield had download the child pornography that was found on the CDs and zip drives, including the fact his business name was on the labels, the contents were highly organized and used the prefix IEA which had been used for many of his work files, and the material was found in the bookcase in his office behind books related to his work.

Moving on, Mr. Clarke entered a new territory. "Were you asked or did you otherwise review transcripts of any statements made by Neal Westerfield?"

Mr. Lawson confirmed he had read a transcript of an

interview with Neal by two detectives.

"Did those statements play a role in any conclusions you reached in this case?"

"No."

"Can you tell us, let's say up to and including today, approximately how much you either have billed or will bill in total in this case?"

"We probably spent between 125 and 150 hours. My company's rate for court appointed cases is $135 an hour."

"So, that could be almost $20,000?"

"I'll take your word for it."

"Thank you. No further questions."

In his redirect, Mr. Feldman emphasized that Neal had access to the office computers and asked if Mr. Lawson, "as an investigator, as a forensic consultant, have you investigated cases of what appear to be the patriarch of the family accessing the internet or porn surfing and it actually turned out to be a younger member of the family?"

Mr. Lawson confirmed he had seen such cases previously.

"With regard to the screen prints that you showed us on direct examination, did they represent a particular pattern of pornography access?"

Mr. Lawson stated that the images he was referring to were either Anime or teen pornography and had been viewed around the time Neal's email was checked.

"Were you able to tell if David Westerfield, my client, ever accessed any pornography sites?"

"I'm certain that he did. There were a great number of pornographic sites that had been accessed on both of the office computers."

"And did those sites show a particular pattern?"

"Adult women in nude context," Mr. Lawson answered before revealing the site Mr. Westerfield had accessed most was ProjectVoyeur.com, a site, he explained, where people posted images of their naked girlfriends and wives, many of them in their thirties with large breasts.

"Concerning an alleged rape scene," Mr. Feldman started, "you can't tell whether something's real or not on the internet?"

"That's correct."

"People are paid to fake, aren't they?"

"That's correct."

"Just because you hear sounds or see lights doesn't mean what you're seeing or hearing is real, isn't that true?"

"That's correct," Mr. Lawson responded.

"They're actors and actresses, right? Whether it's in a video depicting a rape scene or a video depicting straight intercourse?"

"Correct."

"So merely because a video looks a particular way doesn't mean what it's depicting is actually occurring, is that right?"

After characterizing the video of an underaged girl being raped as a typical piece of professionally produced pornography starring consenting adults, Mr. Feldman moved back to distancing Mr. Westerfield from the CDs and zip drives.

"It is impossible to tell merely on the basis of the name on the CD who the creator of the CD is?"

"That's correct."

"No further questions, your honor."

Judge Mudd excused Mr. Lawson who was instructed to contact Mr. Feldman if he discovered any additional information that had not been originally provided.

Following the afternoon break, the state called Cherokee. On the night of Friday, February 1, Cherokee went out for dinner with her mother, Patricia. After enjoying a nice dinner and bottle of wine, they went to O'Harley's where they found her friend, Yvette, closing up. Cherokee and Yvette hung out often on Friday and Saturday nights and, on that night, decided to drive over to Dad's Café & Steakhouse. Cherokee recalled that she,

Patricia, and Yvette arrived at Dad's sometime close to 11:30.

At that time, Brenda Van Dam and her friends, Barbara and Denise, were dancing, drinking, and having a good time. Cherokee did not know Brenda or her friends, but at some point, Barbara took an interest in Cherokee.

"Did anybody engage in any kind of sexually aggressive behaviors in the bar?"

Cherokee recalled Barbara grabbing her hands and trying to dance with her, but Cherokee, who was in her early twenties, was not interested. Instead of accepting Barbara's advances, Cherokee found a nearby man named Ryan who was her age and informed him that he was her "official boyfriend for the night" as a way of escaping Barbara's advances. Later in the night, Cherokee and Ryan encountered Brenda and Barbara.

"What did Brenda say when you were with your friend, Ryan?" Mr. Feldman asked.

"Brenda made a comment saying I'd like to take these two home."

"Was that an invitation to go home?"

"Objection. Speculation."

"Sustained."

Later that night, near closing time, Cherokee and Ryan were sitting at a table on the outside smoking patio. Brenda, Barbara, and Denise were sitting at a different table nearby. Cherokee told the court that Brenda had asked her if she and her friend wanted to go back to her house after the bar closed. Cherokee declined.

"Did you see Brenda Van Dam dancing with David Westerfield that evening?"

"I saw her dancing on the dancefloor. I saw someone that could have looked like him, but I don't know for sure if it was him."

When Mr. Feldman asked Cherokee what Brenda was wearing that night, Cherokee recalled she had been wearing a tight red shirt.

"How was she dancing?"

"I wasn't really paying too close attention. She was just dancing."

Regarding an interview she had with a Detective Lucious Mobley at Dad's the following week on Friday, February 8, Mr. Feldman asked, "do you remember telling the police officer that later in the evening you saw Brenda dancing with Dave Westerfield? Do you remember making that statement?"

Cherokee firmly answered, "I did not make that statement."

Cherokee did not know Mr. Westerfield well, but they had played pool together at O'Harley's a few months prior and Yvette knew his friend Garry.

"With regard to Brenda, that evening, did it appear to you that she was quote, buzzed, unquote?"

"Yes."

"No further questions."

Mr. Dusek started his cross examination by asking Cherokee, "were you buzzed?"

"Yeah, I was feeling buzzed."

When asked multiple questions about her arrival time at Dad's, Cherokee could not say for sure what time she had arrived and stressed she had not been paying attention to the time. She and her mother had enjoyed a leisurely dinner while drinking a bottle of wine, then they met up with Yvette at O'Harleys, and a short time later they went to Dad's.

"At Dad's, when you first got there that evening, did you see Mr. Westerfield?"

"I might have seen him on the dance floor. I don't know for sure. I didn't pay attention to him."

"If he had left between 10:00 and 10:30, that would have been before you even got to Dad's based upon your memory?"

"Right."

Referencing a report written by a defense team investigator, Cherokee revealed, "it said later that night I saw Brenda dancing with Dave Westerfield and I didn't see them dancing later that evening. I assume it was someone that could have looked like him." Cherokee further noted a, "majority of the men in Poway look like Mr. Westerfield."

When asked what physical characteristics she was referring to, Cherokee answered, "receding hairline or balding and goatee."

"And you told Mr. Feldman that?"

"Yes."

"Thank you, ma'am."

After Judge Mudd dismissed the witness, the defense called Detective Lucious Mobley. A twenty-one year officer, Det. Mobley had been assigned the task of interviewing people at Dad's who had been at the bar on February 1. He went to the bar the following Friday and spoke to multiple witnesses.

"When you were talking with Cherokee, she specifically told you that she saw Brenda Van Dam dancing with David Westerfield at Dad's on the first, isn't that right?"

"Yes."

"And she told you that at about 1:30, at last call, Brenda and Barbara invited her and a male friend of hers to come over to Brenda's house and party with them, correct?"

"Yes."

"No further questions."

After noting the detective had started interviewing people at Dad's after 10:00 when people were already drinking alcohol, Mr. Dusek asked, "how long had she been at the bar the night you spoke with her?"

"Objection. No foundation, speculation."

"Overruled, you may answer."

"I do not know that one."

"Did you ask her how much she had been drinking the

time you interviewed her?"

Det. Mobley said he did not and revealed she had not been drinking during their conversation.

"Did you make any inquiries to determine whether or not the information she was giving you was based upon a sober recollection or influenced by alcohol?"

"I did do that. On the following Monday, which was two days later, I called her at her house and had her verify the entire statement."

"Did you try to determine whether or not, when she was doing things on the 1st of February she was impaired?"

"I did not."

"Thank you."

"Detective, thank you very much for coming in. You're free to leave."

Keeping their focus on the night at Dad's, the defense next called Glennie. Glennie was originally from Denmark and had met Mr. Westerfield four years prior at the Stone Lodge Bar in Poway. They had become friends and she knew his ex-girlfriend, Susan, as well.

On Friday February 1, Glennie arrived at Dad's with her girlfriend Beverly around 10:00 and saw Mr. Westerfield, Garry, and Jeff at the bar speaking to Brenda and her friends. Mr. Westerfield introduced her to Brenda who he described as his neighbor.

"Did you see Mr. Westerfield dancing at all that evening?" Mr. Feldman asked.

"Yes."

"Do you know who he was dancing with?"

"Denise."

"Did you see Mr. Westerfield dancing with anyone else that evening?"

"Brenda was on his right side dancing and he turned around and danced for a few seconds with her and he turned around and carried on dancing with Denise.

When asked how they were dancing, Glennie recalled that he was "dancing normal," and stated that Denise "was dancing kind of flirtatious."

"When you say flirtatious, how do you mean?"

"Rubbing herself up against him."

"What part of her body was she rubbing against Mr. Westerfield?"

"Her bottom," Glennie answered.

"What about Brenda, was she dancing in a similar or same manner?"

"Not that I recall, no."

"Was she close to Mr. Westerfield when she was dancing?"

"Not too close."

After several unsuccessful attempts at placing Brenda and Mr. Westerfield in close contact, Mr. Boyce moved forward.

"Did you have a conversation with Brenda and Denise later that night?"

"Yes."

"How did that conversation make you feel?"

"Very uncomfortable."

"Objection, irrelevant."

Judge Mudd sustained the objection and directed the jury to disregard.

"Did Brenda make any sexual remarks to you?"

"Yes. She said something about a-"

"Objection. Irrelevant."

"Sustained. Ladies and gentleman of the jury you're to disregard the last answer."

"Were you getting any sexual looks from Brenda?"

"Objection. Vague."

"Sustained."

After several failed attempts, Mr. Boyce was ultimately

able to reveal Glennie had walked away from Brenda and Denise because their advances made her uncomfortable.

"Did you see Mr. Westerfield leave the bar that evening?"

"Yes."

"What was his state of sobriety when he left?"

"He was drunk."

"I don't have anything further, your honor."

In his cross examination, Mr. Dusek asked Glennie, "you're very good friends with David Westerfield, aren't you?"

"Yes."

"In fact, you smiled at him with a big smile when you got here in court?"

"Objection."

"Overruled."

"Yes."

"You consider him a real good friend, don't you? In fact, you've been calling him since these events occurred?"

"I called him once."

"How much were you drinking on the 1st of February?"

Glennie recalled having two Sex on The Beaches.

"When did the defendant leave?"

"Just before midnight. I went with him to the door and said goodbye to him when he left."

Mr. Dusek reviewed what Glennie saw on the dance floor and confirmed David had been near Brenda at one point.

"And Brenda just happened to be out on the dance floor at the same time?"

Glennie answered, "yes," and agreed there were numerous people dancing in the same area.

"How far away was she from the defendant when you saw them dancing? Forget about feet or centimeters, do you see something in here that would be approximately the same distance?"

Glennie pointed to the court reporter which Mr. Dusek guessed was about three feet away."

When asked if Brenda had rubbed against Mr. Westerfield the way Denise had, Gleenie answered, "no."

"They did not touch?"

"No."

"They did not get next to each other and touch or play with her hair or anything like that?"

"No."

"In fact, she wasn't even close enough to drop any of her hair on Mr. Westerfield, was she?"

"Objection. Speculation, your honor."

"Overruled."

"No."

Mr. Dusek confirmed that Mr. Westerfield's ex-girlfriend was Asian and had black hair then asked her what Mr. Westerfield was wearing that night.

Glennie remembered he was wearing a black hat, black jacket, black shirt, black jeans, and black cowboy boots, which was what he always wore when she saw him at the bars.

"Did he talk about a break up he had just gone through with his girlfriend?"

Glennie answered, "yes," and recalled Mr. Westerfield feeling sad and upset.

Judge Mudd intervened.

"Obviously, we're not going to conclude today so we'll start Monday with this witness. Ladies and gentleman, I want to remind you, obviously tomorrow is a holiday which I hope you will enjoy and rejoice in as a citizen." Judge Mudd confirmed they would be off the rest of the week for July 4th and warned about possible shorter breaks the following week, "to get as much accomplished as we possibly can. Have a pleasant four days off. We'll see you Monday and maybe by then the Padres will have won another ball game."

DAY 17

Following the long Independence Day break, the jury returned on Monday, July 8. "Little did I know on Wednesday when I said I hope they win a game the Padres would only win a game. At least they can rest, hopefully, during the All-Star break." Judge Mudd turned the court over to Mr. Dusek who continued his cross examination of Glennie.

"You went up to Mr. Westerfield as he was leaving?"

Glennie recalled that she had met him near the door and said goodbye.

"You were interested in him, weren't you?"

"No, he's my friend."

Mr. Dusek proceeded to questions about the layout of the bar and the overall atmosphere on the night of February 1 then asked her how long Brenda Van Dam and Mr. Westerfield had danced together.

"Maybe twenty seconds, that's all." After that, Glennie said Brenda turned away and Mr. Westerfield turned back toward Denise.

Mr. Dusek showed Glennie a picture of the black Wrangler jeans and the black shirt that had been collected from the drycleaners. Glennie confirmed they looked like the clothes he had worn that night.

"You talked about your friend, Susan. This was the girlfriend of David Westerfield, is that correct?"

Glennie agreed and Mr. Dusek showed the jury a picture of Susan.

"What color is her hair?"

"Black."

"Thank you, ma'am."

In his redirect of Glennie, Mr. Boyce noted she was not watching the dance floor the entire night before asking, "do you recall Mr. Westerfield taking off his jacket and leaving it on his bar stool when he danced?"

"No. He had his jacket on," Glennie countered.

"You've described Mr. Westerfield as a good friend. Did you have a romantic relationship with him?"

"No."

"Did you ever date him?"

"No."

"The girlfriend of Mr. Westerfield that you know, does she have a dog?"

"I don't know.

"Thank you."

After Judge Mudd dismissed the witness, the defense called Patricia, Cherokee's mother. Patricia entered the room with the assistance of a cane. Anxious and slightly hyper, Patricia recounted her activity on the night of Friday, February 1 when she ate dinner and went to Dad's with her daughter. After Patricia interrupted the questions several times, Judge Mudd intervened.

"Ma'am, I know you want to answer, but let Mr. Feldman ask the question and then he'll-"

"I ask the questions?"

"No. You're interrupting. You're anticipating."

"I'm terrible about that. I will slow down, I'm sorry."

"Thank you, ma'am."

Mr. Feldman continued. "What caused your attention to be drawn to a woman you later learned was Brenda Van Dam?"

"Her behavior."

"What about her behavior?"

"Well, she's a flamboyant person. I do not wish to defame Mrs. Van Dam. I don't know her age, maybe this is how younger people act."

Mr. Feldman tried focusing her description on specifics, but Patricia only offered that Brenda had been, "frisky" and "all over the place." Patricia then recalled that Brenda had invited Cherokee to go home with her while they were all sitting at separate tables in the smoking area outside. She had also asked Cherokee, "if she liked girls." Cherokee had answered no. Although Patricia did not know Mr. Westerfield, she had seen him on previous occasions.

"Did you notice whether or not there was any interaction between Mr. Westerfield and Brenda Van Dam?"

"Yes," Patricia said. "Dancing."

"Did you notice whether or not she appeared to be rubbing herself all over him?"

"Yes."

"Those were your words, weren't they?"

"Yes."

When asked to elaborate on what she witnessed, Patricia recalled Brenda had rubbed her, "hip bones and bosom," against Mr. Westerfield.

"Is there a manner in which you would characterize their dancing?"

"Well, it was a movie they called *Dirty Dancing*, so I guess I would have to say that. I'm not really familiar with the way young people dance today."

When Mr. Feldman asked Patricia about Brenda's friends, she described Denise as "exotic," and thought she was "perhaps Asiatic or had Asiatic blood." She also recalled that Denise and Barbara had been dancing together.

"With regard to Brenda's drinking, do you have a-"

"I did not say anything about her drinking."

Judge Mudd interjected. "Ma'am, you're starting to do it again. Please wait until he finishes his question."

"I'm sorry."

Regarding her interview with police, Mr. Feldman asked, "do you recall telling the officer that she had been drinking heavily that evening?"

"I did not say that to him."

"No further questions at this time."

Before dissecting her observations, Mr. Dusek established she had been drinking 7 and 7s that night.

"My father called them highballs, but it's like Seagram's and 7-Up or ginger ale."

After drinking two 7 and 7s in addition to the wine she had at dinner Patricia conceded she had stopped drinking because she had reached her limit and it was getting late.

"How many times did you see Mr. Westerfield dance with Brenda Van Dam?"

"Oh, a couple of times."

"So, while she was pressing against him, he was pressing against her, right?"

"He was kind of giggling I think a little bit. I don't know if he was embarrassed or what."

"He had a smile on his face?" Mr. Dusek proposed.

"If I was a guy and had a beautiful woman like that, I would smile too."

"And he continued to dance with her?"

"Yes."

"Over and over?"

"Several times."

"Did you see him dance with anybody else in there?"

Patricia answered she had not because, "I spent most of my time in the smoking lounge."

Following the morning break, Mr. Dusek switched his focus to Patricia. During the break here it looked like your back kind of twinged up a little bit."

"Yes."

"Do you take any medication for your back?"

"I take Vicodin, yes, but I do not take it if I'm going to have wine and I do not take it if I have to drive. That's why I'm in the pain I'm in."

"Did you take some today?"

"No."

"Thank you ma'am."

Judge Mudd dismissed Patricia and directed her not to discuss her testimony with anyone until after the trial concluded. "You're out of here. Have a good day."

The defense next called Duane, a fisherman who had spent some time with Brenda, Barbara, and Denise at Dad's on January 25.

"Do you volunteer service with regard to the VFW or veterans?"

"Objection. Irrelevant."

"Overruled. You can answer."

Duane confirmed he volunteered for the VFW before discussing the night of January 25. He characterized Brenda as very polite and quiet and said that Barbara and Denise were, "feeling no pain, you know, basically having a good time."

Duane saw Brenda and her friends again the following week on Friday February 1 and thought Barbara and Denise had been, "looking for a man."

Mr. Feldman asked Duane to describe how, "Mr. Westerfield was dancing with Brenda Van Dam."

"Just kind of huggie-huggie from what I seen, just like maybe anyone else would be dancing that's had some cocktails."

"Based on your life experience, are you able to form opinions on whether or not people are under the influence of alcohol and marijuana?"

Duane confirmed he was so qualified and stated that Keith and Rich were, "loaded and stoned."

"Thank you very much. Nothing further."

During his cross, Mr. Dusek confirmed Duane had not seen anyone actually smoke marijuana and could not possibly know how much Rich, Keith, or anyone else had drank. When Mr. Dusek asked when the last time Duane had smoked marijuana the defense objected and Judge Mudd sustained. Mr. Dusek then pointed out that Duane did not know Mr. Westerfield and could not actually recall ever seeing him before despite his previous claims to the contrary.

"Did you form an opinion that the defendant was under the influence of alcohol and marijuana?"

"I didn't form any kind of opinion about the defendant at all."

"Did you see the defendant dance?"

"Yes."

"Just a matter of seconds, is that right?"

"Probably five seconds or so, yes."

Mr. Dusek referenced an interview with the district attorney's investigator in which Duane had described seeing Mr. Westerfield trying to pick up Brenda.

"What did you see that caused you to form that opinion?"

"Maybe the hugging. When you're dancing with a woman and you're kind of huggie, then someone's gonna get the opinion that well maybe they're going to get together."

"Did you see the defendant with Brenda Van Dam at any other time that evening?"

"Not that I recall."

"Thank you, sir."

Judge Mudd excused the witness and broke for lunch.

After lunch, the defense called Glen, a work associate of Mr. Westerfield's who was an Engineering Manager at Nokia. For the previous year and a half, he had contracted Mr. Westerfield for design work on text fixtures. Coincidentally, he was a neighbor of Sherman, the man who owned the property where Mr. Westerfield stored his motorhome.

Glen reported that Mr. Westerfield had contacted him on the morning of February 1 when Mr. Westerfield dropped off some parts at his office and invited him to go off roading in the desert that weekend.

Judge Mudd intervened at that time with directions for the jury. "Ladies and gentlemen, the purpose of the court allowing the last question and the last answer is limited. It is limited to show an intent or a plan. It is not intended for the truth of the statement. So, it's a limited purpose."

Glen recalled Mr. Westerfield could not find anyone to go with him that weekend.

"Did you tell him that you would do anything in that regard?"

"No, actually I had somebody in my office and I had to cut the conversation short."

"Did you tell Mr. Westerfield you would call him back later?" Glen said he would call him back, but never did.

With his cross examination, Mr. Dusek asked if he saw the motorhome on the evening of February 1. Glen confirmed he had and stated that it was not there the following morning.

"Did he say he wanted to go to Silver Strand?"

"No, he did not."

After dismissing Glen, the defense called Donna, an Operations Assistant at Union Bank of California where Mr. Westerfield had an account. Mr. Boyce asked her what denomination of bills the bank ATM gives.

Donna responded, "twenties."

"Can you get a fifty through the ATM?"

"No."

Mr. Dusek did not ask any questions.

Moving forward quickly, the defense next called Dave L., who had been friends with Mr. Westerfield for fifteen years and had travelled to Glamis together with their families on many occasions. Sometimes they planned to go at the same time and camp out with each other, other occasions they met up spontaneously.

"So, it wouldn't be unusual for Mr. Westerfield to go to the desert and look for you even though you hadn't prearranged to meet?"

"No."

When asked if Mr. Westerfield ever arrived in the desert without his sand vehicles, Dave said that had happened once about five years ago. Asked if Mr. Westerfield ever visited the desert by himself, Dave confirmed that he had two or three times, most recently in April 2001. When they had originally started going to Glamis, Dave revealed they had usually camped at wash three, but as the area had become more crowded, they had moved farther out to washes eleven and twelve.

Dave enjoyed going to Glamis on Superbowl weekend because it was less crowded and recalled seeing Mr. Westerfield get his motorhome stuck in the sand on at least three occasions. He additionally confessed he had been stuck in the sand many times as well. Dave informed that court that freeing a motorhome from the sand involved digging the wheels out and usually required the help of another vehicle pulling. Once free, the driver of the motorhome would drive back toward the road where the sand was hard before stopping.

Mr. Feldman then asked Dave if Mr. Westerfield had a problem sweating. Dave confirmed that was true.

"If you were to see him with we'll say sweat rings under his armpits, would that strike you as unusual?"

"No."

In his cross examination, Mr. Dusek discussed the route Dave usually took to Glamis which avoided the small town of Julian because the direct root was precarious in a motorhome due to the steep inclines and potential for black ice during the winter months.

"How good a friend are you with David Westerfield?"

"I consider myself a good friend."

"You winked at him when you took the stand, didn't

you?"

"Yes. I haven't seen the guy in six months."

Mr. Dusek discussed the routes in and out of Glamis and asked, "if someone wanted to go from Glamis to the South Bay area, what's the most direct route?"

Dave answered, "interstate 8," probably not realizing he was placing Mr. Westerfield within a few miles of where Danielle's body was discovered.

When Mr. Dusek asked about how Mr. Westerfield typically spent his time in the desert, Dave revealed that Mr. Westerfield enjoyed sitting out in the sun and spending time outdoors. He would usually set up some chairs outside and had a large artificial turf carpet he would place on the ground.

"And if there's nobody there with sand toys what do you do all day long?"

"I don't know, hang in the sun. Every time I go I've taken my things."

"Did you speak with the defendant before Superbowl Sunday this weekend?"

Dave stated that they had not spoken since last October.

"When was the last time you'd been to the desert on Superbowl Sunday with the defendant?"

"I'd say three years ago."

"Did he call to ask you if you'd be there?"

"No, he did not."

Mr. Dusek then asked who Mr. Westerfield usually brought with him to the desert. Dave said he brought his wife and kids initially, but after the divorce it was mostly just his son and sometimes his girlfriend.

"What was the shortest time he spent with you in the desert?"

"Like a day and a half, I believe."

"Have you ever been with him at the Silver Strand, Glamis, Superstition Mountain, Borrego, and the Strand on the same weekend?"

"No."

Mr. Dusek transitioned to the levelers and whether Dave would just leave wooden levelers in the desert if he had used them to help free his vehicle from the sand. Dave said he would take them so he would have them next time he got stuck.

Regarding the washes, Mr. Dusek noted it was odd and unusual for Mr. Westerfield to drive all the way out to wash fourteen, particularly on a weekend that was not crowded.

Dave countered by saying he primarily chose wash eleven or twelve because that was where his friends go.

"So, he would not expect to find you at wash fourteen?"

"I wouldn't think so, no."

Judge Mudd dismissed the witness and wished the jury, "a safe and pleasant evening."

DAY 18

"Good morning, ladies and gentleman, welcome back. In an effort to take my mind off the trial last night I had to do some channel surfing since there wasn't any baseball on and I hit this movie that is an old classic called *16 Candles*. It's a great movie and it takes your mind off of just about everything including reality. But I was drawn back at 9:00 o'clock because one of my duties as your shepherd is to watch the shows that start recapping what we're doing and as I was watching it last night, I thought to myself this is probably a great segue for me to remind you once again of the need to self-police.

"There is so much out there right now that it's almost inconceivable where it's coming from, what people believe, what they think, short of just about, you know, the rag newspapers in the grocery stores. There are all kinds of theories out there. It's very, very important, ladies and gentleman, that you continue to avoid at all costs synopsis shows, call in shows, reading the articles. That's the only way we're going to be able to get a verdict from twelve individuals that hear and see just the evidence in this courtroom."

Mr. Feldman called to the stand Detective Mark Tallman with the Special Investigations Unit. A fifteen year veteran of the San Diego Police Department, Det. Tallman had been directed on Tuesday February 5 to establish contact with Donald, the camp host volunteer at Silver Strand State Beach who had spoken with Mr. Westerfield about the overpayment.

Det. Tallman showed Donald a photo of Mr. Westerfield and asked if "he recognized him as the individual who had contacted him in connection with an overpayment."

Det. Tallman recalled that Donald, "said that the picture of Mr. Westerfield did not look like the person who inquired about the overpayment."

"No further questions. Thank you."

In his cross examination, Mr. Dusek noted that Det. Tallman was one of several detectives assigned to conduct interviews with people who had been at the Silver Strand beach and had knowledge of Mr. Westerfield and his motorhome. During that trip, he had learned about Jimmy and Joyce who had been parked in space 66, the closest filled spot to Mr. Westerfield who had been parked in 72. Donald informed Det. Tallman that he had advised Mr. Westerfield to keep the money.

After Det. Tallman was dismissed, Mr. Boyce of the defense called Detective Frank Gerbac. On Saturday, February 2 at about 5:00pm, Det. Gerbac interviewed Denise at the northeastern substation. During their conversation, Denise recalled the events of the previous night.

"Did you ask her if she had noticed anything suspicious at Dad's Café?"

"Objection. Hearsay. Not inconsistent."

Judge Mudd invited the counselors to discuss the issue at side bar where he wondered if the purpose of the testimony was to cover areas of inconsistency.

Mr. Boyce discussed two inconsistent statements made by Denise. The first was that Denise had never mentioned Mr. Westerfield during her first interview, the second was that Damon Van Dam had never come back downstairs after everyone arrived at the Van Dam house after Dad's.

Mr. Dusek said, "the fact that she failed to mention anything is not inconsistent."

The defense focused on the fact that Denise had described in her testimony Mr. Westerfield's behavior on February 1 as "creepy," but never said so in her multiple interviews with detectives." To further paint Denise as an unreliable witness, Mr. Boyce insisted he be able to show that she had not been telling the entire truth when she said Damon had not come downstairs while everyone was eating.

Judge Mudd thought she might not have known Mr. Westerfield's name in her initial interview and allowed the defense to proceed on those two subjects only.

Following the morning break, instead of recalling Det. Gerbac, the defense called Detective James Fisher, a different interrogation specialist who had interviewed Denise on Sunday, February 3, at about 1:00 in the afternoon. After establishing that Det. Fisher had interviewed Denise, Mr. Boyce asked if Denise knew whether or not Damon had come downstairs.

"She could not recall seeing him downstairs, no."

"Did you ask her did Damon come downstairs and did she answer, no, he didn't come down at all?" Mr. Boyce asked.

"Yes. I think she also at one time characterized it as not being able to remember him being downstairs."

Mr. Boyce turned the witness over to Mr. Dusek who revealed that the purpose of Det. Fisher's interview with Denise was identifying the events that preceded Danielle's disappearance and identifying potential suspects.

"Did she withhold or appear to be hesitant at all giving those names?"

"No, she was helpful."

Mr. Dusek asked if she had made two statements regarding Damon downstairs. Det. Fisher replied, "yes, one time she said she didn't see him come down and then she drew questions of whether or not he did. In other words, questioning her own memory."

After Mr. Dusek returned the witness back to the defense, Mr. Boyce asked, "she didn't mention anybody by the name of David or David Westerfield did she?"

"She did not."

"During your two hour interview in which you were trying to determine suspects?"

"Yes, sir.

"Nothing further."

After dismissing Det. Fisher, the defense recalled latent print examiner Jeffrey Graham who had previously testified for the prosecution and had revealed that Danielle's fingerprints had been found on a cabinet over the bed in the motorhome.

When asked about the prints lifted with Ninhydrin from the Van Dam's home on February 14, Mr. Graham recalled receiving seven total finger prints from Forensic Specialist Dorie Savage whohad performed the procedure. Mr. Feldman then asked about a palm print found on the wall in the upstairs hallway next to Danielle's bedroom.

"Does that lift depict a particular portion of the palm?"

Mr. Graham confirmed it did and described the palm print as either a small section of an adult's palm or a large portion of a child's palm. Based on the incomplete evidence, he could not say definitively if it was an adult or a child.

"Did you compare that surface against the known latent palm prints of David Westerfield?"

Mr. Graham said he had compared the prints and excluded Mr. Westerfield as the source. Mr. Feldman moved on to a print found on the stairway banister and asked if he had compared the print from the wall to the banister print. Mr. Graham had not.

On the patio table just beyond the sliding kitchen door, three palm prints were discovered and compared to Mr. Westerfield who was excluded as a possible source.

"Did you compare them against the banister print?"

"No, I did not."

"Thank you very much, nothing further."

Mr. Dusek jumped right in by asking about the size of the prints lifted from the table, which Mr. Graham described as "very small. It would have to be a smaller adult, female, young man, small man, but it is very small."

Regarding the print found on the wall, Mr. Graham believed the source was a child, small man, or a woman. Mr.

Dusek additionally pointed out that the prints were not obtained until two weeks after Danielle disappeared and after an unknown number of individuals had entered the home. Mr. Graham reported that six adults other than Danielle's parents were at the house just on the day the Ninhydrin process was performed.

In his redirect, referencing the prints on the wall outside Danielle's room, Mr. Feldman asked, "the print could have come from a large man with small hands, correct?"

"Yeah, it could have, sure."

Mr. Feldman confirmed that Mr. Graham had the prints of twenty-six individuals for this case and asked if any of those twenty six individuals had been excluded as possible sources of the print on the wall outside Danielle's bedroom. For time reasons, Mr. Graham had not compared the print with anyone other than Mr. Westerfield.

After finishing with Mr. Graham, the defense moved on to Christina, one of the daughters of Mr. Westerfield's ex-girlfriend, Susan.

Christina revealed she and her young child had lived with her mother at Mr. Westerfield's home for a few months in the fall of 2000 after she left an abusive relationship. During that time, Christina helped them load and unload the motorhome before and after camping trips she sometimes attended. Mr. Feldman highlighted the fact that the motorhome was parked on the street, possibly unlocked, overnight.

"Would the motorhome be locked or unlocked when you were loading and unloading it?"

"It would be unlocked."

"How long would the motorhome be in that location while you were loading and unloading it?"

"It would be there the day before we left and the day after."

One night, while she was assisting David with a small project on the motorhome, it was near the park down the street.

"While the motor home was parked at the park did you see any children in the park?"

"I remember seeing one child there with their mom."

"Thank you. I have nothing further."

Mr. Feldman passed the witness to the prosecution who pointed out the night the motorhome was left by the park had occurred nearly two years ago. He then discussed the process of preparing the motorhome before a trip and cleaning it up afterward, a procedure that was routinely implemented. When asked what else Mr. Westerfield brought to the desert on his trips, Christina said his trailer and sand vehicles.

"You never, in your experience, have seen any little child around that motor home, have you, except for your kids?"

"Right."

After showing a picture of her mother, Susan, Mr. Dusek asked, "She broke up with the defendant several times, didn't she?"

"Yes."

"And moved out?"

"Yes."

"When was the most recent?" Mr. Dusek asked.

"Maybe December 2001, I'm not sure."

"Was there a dog at the house when you were living there?"

Christina confirmed there was a small, black, curly haired dog at the house while she was staying there, but Mr. Dusek did not ask who it belonged to or how long it lived in there.

"Do you know where Neal, the son, was living full time?"

"I think at his mom's. I never saw Neal outside of-"

"Okay, thank you ma'am."

"Ladies and gentleman, we'll go ahead and break for lunch. We'll see you at 1:30."

Following lunch, before the jury returned, Mr. Feldman notified the court that his next witness was a minor whose father had requested her last name not be used and asked that she not be photographed in any manner. Mr. Feldman asked Judge Mudd on behalf of the witness's father to, "direct the media to cut their head off or do whatever your honor thinks is appropriate. And I think Mr. Dusek would agree with me that this has been somewhat problematic."

Judge Mudd agreed and ordered the witness not to be filmed or photographed and referred to only with their first name and the first initial of their last name.

"Thank you very much, your honor."

Judge Mudd welcomed the jury back to their seats and Mr. Boyce called the defense's next witness, Susan's teenage daughter, Danielle.

"How old are you, Danielle?"

Danielle was sixteen and had just finished her junior year in high school. She had known Mr. Westerfield for approximately three years and had stayed at his house with her mother on frequent occasions. She had also gone camping in the motorhome with Mr. Westerfield and her mother at least five times.

"Do you recall when the last time was that you went camping in Mr. Westerfield's motorhome?"

"I don't recall."

"Was it more than six months ago?"

Danielle was not sure, but said it was definitely before July 2001.

"Did you ever go camping to Glamis?"
"Yes."

"Did you ever go camping at the Strand?"
"Yes."

"Did you ever go camping to Borrego?"
"Yes."

When asked if she had ever taken a friend camping, she said she had once brought her friend, Jennifer.

"Do you recall an occasion when you went to the Silver Strand and it was too cold and then your family decided to go to Glamis?"

"Yes, sir. Actually, it was Borrego."

"You don't recall the toys or the trailer with you at that time, do you?"

"No."

"Thank you, Danielle. I don't have anything further."

Mr. Dusek started his cross examination by asking Danielle how long her mother had been in a relationship with Mr. Westerfield.

"Approximately three years. My freshman year on."

"Do you remember about when it was when you became aware that she broke up with the defendant?"

"I don't recall."

"You never did live with the defendant, did you?"

Danielle confirmed she had always lived with her father.

"The times you went to the desert, did you take the sand toys, the things to ride around in the sand dunes?"

"Yes."

"Every time?"

Danielle answered, "yes," before discussing the setup procedure in the desert which included putting out an Astroturf rug, lights, chairs, and an awning. When asked if the curtains would be open during the day, she said, "yes."

Regarding the day they arrived at the Strand and then drove to Borrego, Mr. Dusek noted they had not gone to Glamis, which was an additional eighty miles east.

After Mr. Dusek asked if Mr. Westerfield had suggested Danielle bring a friend with her on one of their trips, the defense objected and asked for a sidebar. After a brief discussion not made part of the public record, Mr. Dusek moved on to an occasion while driving to the desert when she and her friend, Jennifer, opened a bedroom window.

"When you were at the Westerfield residence, did you ever see his son, Neal there?"

"Yes."

"On how many occasions?"

"I couldn't recall."

"What color is your hair?"

"Blonde."

"Have you treated it a little bit?"

"Yes."

"Thank you, ma'am."

After dismissing the witness, Judge Mudd addressed the jury. "All right, ladies and gentleman, you'll remember that the people had some remaining evidence they were going to put in before they formally rested, but it wasn't quite ready. They allowed the defense to begin its case. You're now going to hear their last two witnesses. So, we're shifting back to the prosecution's case. Mr. Clarke."

"Thank you, your honor. People recall Tanya Dulaney."

Criminalist Dulaney was the analyst in the Trace Evidence Unit who had previously testified about hairs and fibers found in Mr. Westerfield's home and RV.

"Did you examine fibers taken from tape lifts from the motorhome in this case?"

Ms. Dulaney confirmed that on February 6 she had applied tape lifts to multiple areas inside the motorhome including the driver's cabin, the couch, an upholstered chair across from the couch, upholstered bench seats in the kitchen area, and the upholstered headboard in the bedroom.

"Why upholstered surfaces?"

"Those types of fabrics tend to hold trace evidence better than smooth surfaces so I focused mostly on those fabric surfaces."

On July 2, Ms. Dulaney reviewed the fibers she had collected from the motorhome, specifically searching for orange acrylic fibers and blue nylon fibers that were consistent with fibers previously found in Mr. Westerfield's home.

"Can you tell us what, if anything, of significance did you find when you began looking at these tape lifts from the motorhome?"

"I found a number of blue nylon fibers on tape lifts from the various areas of the upholstered fabrics in the motorhome."

Ms. Dulaney reported that she had found a total of forty-six blue nylon fibers; eleven on the headboard, thirty-one on the kitchen bench seats, three on the couch, and one on the front driver seat.

Ms. Dulaney also examined nineteen blue fibers found on the white sheet investigators had used to wrap Danielle's body, one blue fiber found in her hair during the autopsy, and one blue fiber found in the debris beneath her body.

"As a result of the various examinations you conducted, both visually and by the infrared method, did you note any similarities or consistencies between those forty-six fibers and the blue fibers taken from the sheet covering Danielle Van Dam's body?"

"Yes, I did. In all the ways that I measured and compared the fibers, the fibers from the motor home were the same as the fibers on the sheet."

"As far as the comparison that you most recently conducted, was your work and conclusions revealed by anyone in the laboratory?"

"Yes. Criminalist Jennifer Shen."

"Did she concur in your results?"

"Yes, she did."

"Objection. Hearsay, move to strike."

"Overruled. The answer will stand."

Mr. Clarke then showed the jury a series of images

showing fibers taken from the sheet side by side under microscope with fibers found in the motorhome. The fibers appeared identical.

"Thank you. I have no further questions."

Mr. Feldman began his cross examination by questioning whether Ms. Dulaney had arranged the photo exhibits presented by Mr. Dusek herself, which she had not. He noted some inconsistencies in the reports about the fibers, which she described as blue and Ms. Shen described as blue/grey.

"Do you have the slides with you?"

"I do."

"Could we see, please, see what slides you've got?"

Mr. Feldman asked Ms. Dulaney to open the sealed package containing the slides with the fibers. After a difficult and tense moment in which she carefully removed the slides from their box, Ms. Dulaney held up a slide at Mr. Feldman's request.

"So, if we hold the slide up to the light, we can't really see any fibers, is that right?"

"I can see them because I know they're there, but it may be difficult for the average person, yes."

Mr. Feldman asked the court for permission to pass the slides to the jury. Judge Mudd denied his request.

Unable to dispute, invalidate, or refute the damning fiber evidence Ms. Dulaney had presented, Mr. Feldman drowned the court in a long and tedious series of questions that focused on irrelevant details, possibly hoping the jury would forget the evidence directly linking Danielle to Mr. Westerfield's RV. He asked about the differences between various nylons, their melting points, and how she could identify one from another. He asked, how many millimeters are in an inch, how many millimeters are in a centimeter, how she numbered the slides, and how many slides fit inside the boxes in which they were stored.

The prosecution objected due to lack of relevence, but Judge Mudd allowed the defense significant leeway. Following the afternoon break, Mr. Feldman continued his strategy of monotonous overload. He asked about the number of fibers subjected to infrared testing, who prepared the charts shown by the prosecution, how long it took to complete a fiber test, how many chemicals make up a fiber, and numerous other questions that had little, if anything, to do with the substance of the evidence Ms. Dulaney had presented. In his long and purposefully convoluted and exhausting cross examination, Mr. Feldman never disputed the validity of the fiber evidence. Nor did he explain how fibers found in Mr. Westerfield's motorhome ended up on Danielle's dead body.

Following Criminalist Tanya Dulaney, the prosecution recalled Criminalist Jennifer Shen who had previously testified about the hairs found in Mr. Westerfield's bed, laundry room, and motorhome.

Ms. Shen recalled searching Mr. Westerfield's home on February 13 in search of hairs and fibers from Danielle's environment. In his bedroom closet, Ms. Shen had applied tape lifts to twenty-five pairs of shoes including a pair of brown boots. She did not find a pair of black cowboy boots. She also used tape lifts inside his Toyota 4Runner where she additionally collected and processed a blue towel that was inside a laundry bag.

Mr. Clarke asked, "In examining the tape lifts from that towel, did you discover any fibers of note to you?"

"Objection," Mr. Feldman said. "Foundation, and chain."

"Overruled."

Ms. Shen continued. "I noted on my examination of the tape lifts taken from the towel that there were several long, orange, brightly colored fibers." She explained they were notable because they were similar to the orange fibers she had found in other locations. She had originally collected the orange fibers in February before Danielle was recovered and reexamined the tape lifts the first week of July at which time she discovered the connection.

In addition to the orange fibers found on the towel, Ms. Shen discovered seventeen orange fibers from several locations inside the vehicle including on the front passenger seat, the rear seat, and the rear passenger armrest.

"Where had you seen them before?"

"They looked similar to the fibers I had found on the necklace from the victim's neck, the orange fibers I had seen in the defendant's laundry, both in the washing machine, on top of the dryer, and in the dryer, and also looked similar to the orange fibers I had found on the pillowcase from the bedding taken from the defendant's bedroom."

Using a microscope and the infrared process, Ms. Shen compared the orange fiber found in Danielle's necklace to the orange fibers collected from the pillowcase in Mr. Westerfield's bedroom at home and the orange fibers discovered in his SUV.

"With what results?"

"I found that the fibers removed from the blue towel taken out of the SUV were similar in all the ways that I tested to the fibers taken from the defendant's bedding and to the fiber taken from the necklace from around the victim's neck."

"Were your results such that the fibers you obtained from the towel were or were not consistent with the fibers taken from the necklace and the bedding."

"They were consistent."

Ms. Shen additionally tested the other orange fibers found in the SUV and found they also matched the orange fiber found on Danielle's necklace and the orange fibers collected from the pillowcase. Of the twelve orange fibers collected from the interior of the SUV, only two were not consistent with the fiber found with Danielle's necklace.

Mr. Clarke showed the jury multiple images displaying side by side comparisons under microscope of the orange fiber taken from the necklace to orange fibers found inside the SUV. In the images, the jury could see that the diameter, width, and color were the same.

"As far as your data and conclusions in this case, were they verified by a second analyst?"

"Object to the term verification as a conclusion, your honor."

"Overruled. You may answer."

Ms. Shen confirmed that Criminalist Delaney had verified her work.

"In terms of the motorhome, are you familiar with whether or not there was blood which has been identified as coming from Danielle Van Dam in that motorhome."

"Objection. Asked and answered."

After Mr. Clarke claimed it was foundational, Judge Mudd overruled.

"Yes."

"Are you familiar with the fact that hair consistent with Danielle DNA typing was also found in the motorhome?"

"Your honor, same objection."

"We'll show it as a continuing objection. Duly noted. You may answer."

"Yes," Ms. Shen responded.

"Are you familiar with the fact that carpet fibers which could have come from the victim's home were also found in the motorhome?"

"Yes."

"Are you familiar with the fact that dog hairs which were consistent with and could have come from the victim's family dog, Layla, were found in the motor home?"

"Yes."

"Are you also familiar with the fact that finger prints from Danielle Van Dam were found in the motor home?"

"Yes."

"Are you familiar with the fact that forty-six blue fibers were found in the motor home which were consistent with and could have come from the same source as fibers found on a sheet that covered the body of Danielle Van Dam?"

"Yes."

"As a trace analyst, is there any significance to the numbers of different types of samples just described?"

"The fact that you have so many different types of physical evidence that can relate the victim to this environment, that makes the significance of all those pieces of evidence greater."

"I have no further questions, your honor."

Trapped in a web of damning evidence Mr. Feldman threw a Hail Mary.

"Did you take into consideration among all the hypotheticals that Mr. Clarke gave you that David Westerfield and Brenda Van Dam, within a short period of time, were dancing in what appears to have been described as a dirty dancing manner? Did you take that into consideration?"

Mr. Clarke objected and Judge Mudd ordered the defense to lay a foundation, which he did and then tried the question again.

"If Mr. Westerfield had been dancing with someone from Danielle Van Dam's environment, that the two of them were dancing in a manner that's been described as dirty dancing and huggie-huggie, would that affect your opinion as to the import of the aggregate of similarity of trace evidence?"

"Yes, that certainly would impact my evaluation of the evidence."

"Because that would explain, wouldn't it, or potentially explain, how items in one environment might transfer to another environment, correct?"

"That would certainly be important, yes."

When asked if she had performed any fiber analysis on Brenda Van Dam's clothing, Ms. Shen answered, "no."

"So, you did not evaluate her orange sweater?"

Mr. Clarke objected. "Assumes facts not in evidence."

Judge Mudd sustained the objection, squashing Mr. Feldman's underhanded attempt to mislead the jury about the color of Brenda's shirt, which had actually been red.

Like he had done with Ms. Dulaney, Mr. Feldman asked Ms. Shen to take out some of the slides holding the fibers.

"Can you hold it up so the jury can see it please?"

Ms. Shen complied.

"In looking at it can we see a fiber with the naked eye?"

"If you look carefully."

Mr. Feldman proceeded to wade through a number of peripheral topics including inconsistencies in the description of orange, differences in fiber length, the crime lab's process of double verifying conclusions, the number of blue nylon fibers in existence in the world, why melting point tests were not performed, and her process of examining the white sheet. At every step, Mr. Feldman persisted with numerous questions that served little purpose beyond flooding the zone with meaningless details.

"Can you tell us approximately how many fibers you actually collected or were collected in the case, if you know?"

"I couldn't tell you. It was thousands and thousands of fibers."

Mr. Feldman ended his exam by asking if it was true the fibers, "could have come from a common source, but they could also not have come from a common source?"

"This is correct."

"No further questions."

In his redirect examination, Mr. Clarke asked, "was your conclusion with regard to the blue nylon fibers found in Mr. Westerfield's laundry room that they were consistent and could have come from the same source as the fibers found in the body bag?"

Ms. Shen answered, "yes."

Mr. Clarke discussed how slight variations in the length and shade of fibers did not automatically exclude the possibility that they shared the same source. Regarding the fiber found in Danielle's necklace, he asked, "did it fit within the range of color observed in all the orange fibers that you recovered from Mr. Westerfield's house as well as from the Toyota?"

"Yes.

"Thank you. No further questions your honor."

After dismissing the witness, Judge Mudd said, "ladies and gentleman, we're going to break for the evening. Hopefully you'll get home in time for the first pitch of the All-Star break. At the rate the players and owners are going this may be the last year we have an All-Star game or baseball for that matter. At any rate, we've got something that is a great diversion for tonight."

Judge Mudd reminded the jurors not to discuss the case or form any opinions, and informed them they would have Thursday that week and the entire next week off. "Have a safe and pleasant evening. We'll see you at 9:00am tomorrow morning."

After the jury left the courtroom Mr. Dusek confirmed the prosecution had finished presenting their case and Mr. Boyce introduced a motion for acquittal.

"I don't believe there is sufficient evidence to prove the special circumstance of a murder during the course of a kidnapping. Also, I don't believe there's sufficient evidence to show with a sufficient degree of certainty that there's any child pornography in this case."

Judge Mudd offered the people a chance to respond.

Mr. Dusek strenuously disagreed with Mr. Boyce's assertion. "The evidence is overwhelming that Danielle Van Dam was kidnapped from her home, that she was killed during that kidnapping. At any point from the time she was taken until she was killed, she was being kidnapped. And she turned up dead down at Dehesa. It's unbelievable that there would be any concern that this was not a kidnapping or a murder and all of the physical evidence, all of the statements point directly at the defendant."

Judge Mudd responded by saying the motion, "brings to the court the question of whether or not in the best light possible given to the prosecution's evidence is there sufficient evidence to go to the jury on the question of the guilt or innocence of Mr. Westerfield on the charges he is facing. The answer to that question is yes. The motion is denied. We'll be in recess until 9:00."

DAY 19

On Wednesday July 10, Judge Mudd welcomed the jury back to court. "The sorry state of professional baseball in our country was sure on display last night, wasn't it?" Tens of thousands of fans in the stadium, millions of young and old fans throughout the world watching the game, and they call it a tie so that none of our high priced ball players get hurt. It sure lets you know where the fans fit into the scheme of things, doesn't it?

"Well, anyway, ladies and gentleman, I know you haven't been watching television, reading the papers regarding the story, but apparently there's quite a tsunami out there about me taking my vacation. Apparently, a whole lot of people don't have anything to do next week without watching this trial, but I just want to remind you in case you happened to be concerned about that, number one, I advised you of this long ago and the lawyers knew about it a long time ago. My lovely wife paid for a vacation and I've told you that you're going to have a week off.

"The pundits are telling me that you are all a bunch of idiots and you are going to lose everything, you're not going to remember anything, you're going to be left with the impression that the last person that testified is the best witness that you've ever heard. Ladies and gentleman, I'm hoping you'll be able to use the time if you are going back to work to, you know, get back to know your boss and your coworkers, spend some time with your family, take a vacation. This actually, I think, is going to work out to your benefit because it allows a little bit of a break before the end of the trial. And the end of the trial will be very intense as you can well imagine. All right. Mr. Boyce."

The defense resumed its case with Detective Johanna Thrasher who recalled being at the northeastern substation on Monday February 4 while Mr. Westerfield was being questioned. At about 7:00 that evening, she was directed to return to Mr.

Westerfield's home and surveil the residence until a search warrant could be obtained. She learned from detectives on the scene that Neal Westerfield was inside and observed lights on upstairs.

"And although Neal Westerfield was in the house, you were permitting him to stay, but if he left, you would not allow him back into the house. Is that correct?"

"Yes."

At around 11:30pm Mr. Westerfield returned home and was not allowed inside. Neal exited the home a short time later.

"Thank you, Det. Thrasher."

In his cross examination, Mr. Dusek asked about the events leading up to the search warrant being served. "And your assignment was to go to the Westerfield residence and do what?"

"Secure, it, surveil it, make sure nobody came in or out without our knowledge. To secure the residence for the search warrant."

"You wanted to make sure no evidence or potential evidence in the residence was disturbed or destroyed?"

"That's correct."

"Describe how Neal Westerfield left the residence."

Det. Thrasher recalled knocking on the front door and asking Neal to come outside, which he did. After allowing a search of his vehicle, Neal drove away.

"Thank you, ma'am."

Judge Mudd dismissed the witness and following the morning break, Mr. Boyce called Mr. Westerfield's ex-girlfriend, Susan.

Susan discussed meeting Mr. Westerfield approximately four years prior through her friend, Glennie, at the Big Stone Lodge, a country western bar. They started dating a few weeks later and she moved into his home not long after that. She had camped with Mr. Westerfield in his motorhome on many occasions, sometimes with one or both of her daughters.

"Were there times that Mr. Westerfield would go camping in the motorhome alone?"

"Objection. Speculation, hearsay."

"Sustained. Lay the foundation and I'll allow the area of inquiry."

"Did you ever see Mr. Westerfield get in the motorhome and leave and not come back for a day or two days?"

"Not that I recall."

"Well, when you said you knew he would go camping alone, how did you know this?"

Mr. Dusek objected. "Assumes facts not in evidence, speculation."

"Sustained. Rephrase."

"Did you have knowledge that Mr. Westerfield went camping alone?"

"Yes."

"Objection. No foundation, hearsay, speculation."

Judge Mudd intervened. "Ladies and gentleman, you're to disregard this entire line of questioning. Either lay the foundation or move on, Mr. Boyce."

Mr. Boyce switched gears. "The times you went camping with Mr. Westerfield, where did you go?"

Susan recalled they usually visited either Silver Strand, Borrego, or Glamis, and remembered leaving the beach on one occasion and driving to Borrego because it was too cold.

"The time that you went to the Silver Strand, did he have the trailer with him?"

"No."

"When you went camping in the desert was there ever a time when you would arrive at night?"

Susan confirmed they sometimes arrived at night and sometimes met his friend, Dave, and his wife.

"When was the last time you went camping with Mr. Westerfield.

Susan recalled going to Glamis in October 2001 and discussed the process of preparing the motorhome before a trip.

"Where would the motorhome be parked when you were preparing to go camping?"

Susan said the motorhome was usually parked across the street or in front of his driveway and would remain there for up to two days before their trip.

"On occasion would you see children walking on the sidewalks?"

"Yes."

Mr. Boyce asked her what they would do with the hose after filling up the motorhome and she said they would just throw it on the yard, leaving it out.

"Do you recall the back light being left on?"

"Yes."

Prior to leaving for a trip, she remembered that Mr. Westerfield, would close the blinds in his house and stopped at the ATM.

"When you returned from camping in the desert would you do the laundry?"

"Yes."

"After the last camping trip that you went on with Mr. Westerfield do you know whether or not you cleaned the comforters in the motorhome?"

Susan said, "no," but mentioned they were planning to clean them during the winter offseason.

"While you were living with Mr. Westerfield did you meet his son?"

"Yes, I did. He was there every two weeks."

"His son was somewhat of a computer nerd?"

"Yes."

When asked about Mr. Westerfield's black cowboy boots, Susan clarified he only had a pair of brown cowboy boots.

"Did he have a problem with sweating?"

"Yes. He was always be sweating under the armpits and his head and face."

"Even when it was cold?"

"Yeah."

"Thank you, Susan."

Mr. Boyce turned the witness over to Mr. Dusek who asked Susan when she first broke up with Mr. Westerfield and moved out.

"Approximately after, I think, a year, maybe less."

"When was the second time you moved out?"

"I don't remember."

"When you were living with him, was your daughter Danielle living there?"

Susan revealed that Danielle did not visit in the beginning, but said she later started visiting every other weekend. She had never lived at Mr. Westerfield's house full time.

"Was there ever a time that you went to the Strand and never went outside?"

Susan said, "no," but clarified if it was cold outside, sometimes they would stay in and watch movies.

"Did you ever go from the Strand to Glamis to Superstition Mountain to Borrego on one weekend?"

"No."

Mr. Dusek continued moving forward with examples of Mr. Westerfield's typical behavior, which contrasted with his actions on the weekend Danielle disappeared.

"How many nights would be the shortest amount of time you spent at Glamis?"

"I think there was an occasion where we spent one night."

Mr. Dusek pressed. "Do you even remember a time when you spent one night out there?"

"I do, but I don't remember exactly when it was."

"Was there ever an occasion when you showed up out there shortly before midnight and left around noon or 1:00 the next day?

"No."

With Mr. Dusek's direction, Susan discussed how Mr. Westerfield, after arriving in the desert, would set up his chairs and grass rug, relax in the sun, and enjoy driving the sand vehicles in the desert with friends and family. Mr. Dusek additionally noted that when picking up the motorhome from its storage location, Susan or Neal would always drop him off and drive their vehicle back to the house.

Asked if she could remember a time when Mr. Westerfield woke up on Saturday morning and, with no previous plan, drove away in the motorhome a few hours later, Susan answered, "no."

"That is totally out of character for the David Westerfield that you know?"

"Objection. Speculation."

"Overruled. You may answer."

Susan disagreed. "I wouldn't say that."

"You've never seen him do it, have you?"

"Objection. Argumentative."

"Overruled."

"I didn't see him do it, but I was aware of a time that he did do it."

Mr. Dusek looked to Judge Mudd for assistance. "Your honor-"

"The jury is to disregard the last answer."

"You still like him, don't you?"

"I care about him."

"When was the last time you saw him in person?"

Susan recalled seeing Mr. Westerfield a few weeks before Danielle disappeared and revealed she had learned in the news he was a suspect.

Mr. Dusek then transitioned into new territory. "Were you seeing other people at that time?"

Susan answered, "no," and proceeded to discuss a night she had gone out with a male she described as a plutonic friend.

"You were living separately from the defendant?"

"Yes."

After a night out, her friend dropped her off, walked her to the door, and kissed her on the cheek.

"Did you see David Westerfield at that time?"

"No, I didn't."

"Do you know if he was there?"

"Objection. Hearsay."

"Sustained as to what she knew."

Mr. Dusek moved forward. "Did you speak with him the next day?"

"Yes, I did."

"Did he tell you whether or not he was there that night?"

"Objection. 352." Mr. Feldman sited the balance of probative value and prejudice against the defendant.

Mr. Dusek asked for a sidebar, which Judge Mudd granted. After a lengthy discussion not made part of the public record, Mr. Feldman asked for a five minute recess. Judge Mudd made it fifteen.

When court resumed, Mr. Dusek referred to a police report he had shown Susan during the break in which she reported a phone call she had received from Mr. Westerfield the day after her night out with the plutonic friend. During their conversation, Mr. Westerfield stated he had watched her return home with the man.

"You didn't feel comfortable with the defendant at that time, correct?"

"At that time, yes."

Mr. Dusek returned his focus to Mr. Westerfield's standard tendencies.

"The defendant is an orderly type of person, isn't he?"

"Objection. Vague."

"Overruled. You may answer."

"Yes."

"Kind of a routine type of guy?"

"Most of the time."

"Place for everything and everything in its place?"

Susan resisted. "Not always."

"Most of the time?"

"I guess you could say that."

Mr. Dusek specifically focused on Mr. Westerfield's office, which was very organized. Susan rarely entered his office and noted the phone in the office was for business only.

Moving forward, Mr. Dusek discussed the motorhome's alarm system, which Susan said he activated most of the time. She further revealed that at 5'1" tall, the door handle to the motorhome was at the top of her head.

"How easy is it to open?"

"It's not real easy, but it's not hard."

"It requires some strength, doesn't it?"

"A little bit, yes."

"Did you see any change in attitude or personality when he would drink?"

"Objection. 352."

"Overruled."

"Character objection."

"Overruled."

Susan revealed that when drinking, Mr. Westerfield became quiet, depressed, and upset.

"Basically, you'd see a change in character when he would drink, wouldn't you?"

"Objection 352."

"Overruled."

Susan answered, "yes," and conceded Mr. Westerfield was a much different person when he drank.

"When the defendant was drinking, would he become

more forceful?"

"I remember an occasion that he did."

"Is that one of the reasons you left? Because of the drinking?"

"Yes."

"Thank you, ma'am."

Judge Mudd excused the witness and directed her not to discuss the case with anyone until the trial ended.

Mr. Feldman next called Detective Sergeant William Holmes, the supervisor in charge of homicide team four, which included Det. Tomsovic and Forensic Specialist Karen LeAlcala. Sgt. Holmes recounted his initial involvement in the case starting on Monday, February 4.

"To your knowledge, from February 5th until the time Mr. Westerfield was arrested, was Mr. Westerfield continuously surveilled by one or more law enforcement officers?"

Sgt. Holmes answered, "yes," and confirmed he had been under direct visual surveillance the entire time. Additionally, detectives had placed a GPS tracker on his vehicle.

"Did any of Mr. Westerfield's activities take him to the area of the Singing Hills Country Club while he was being surveilled?"

"No, Sir."

"While he was being surveilled, did he go to the area of Dehesa Road?"

"No, Sir."

"No further questions."

Mr. Dusek started his cross examination by pointing out that Mr. Westerfield had not been under surveillance until the early morning of Tuesday, February 5. After discussing the protocol of how and when homicide detectives are summoned to a case, Mr. Dusek noted that Sgt. Holmes and his homicide team had been brought in late Monday night after Mr. Westerfield's long interview with other detectives.

"That was before even Danielle was found?"

"Yes, sir."

After noting that both Mr. Westerfield and the Van Dams had been under constant surveillance by both police and media, Mr. Dusek concluded his interview.

In his redirect of Sgt. Holmes, Mr. Feldman asked if, "this was if not the biggest, one of the biggest investigations you've ever participated in. Is that a fair statement?"

"Not the biggest, but one of the biggest."

"Nothing further, sir."

"All right, folks, we'll take our lunch break. We'll see you at 1:30."

After the jury left the courtroom, Judge Mudd said, "I just want to verify that both of you have received a copy of Mr. Van Dam's motion to be readmitted so both of you will be prepared to argue that tomorrow. We'll be in recess until 1:30."

Following the lunch break, the defense called their most important witness yet, the witness they hoped would prove Mr. Westerfield could not have killed Danielle Van Dam, entomologist David Faulkner.

Mr. Faulkner was a forensic entomologist who applied his extensive knowledge of insects and related invertebrates to criminal investigations. He had earned master of science degrees in biology and zoology from California State University and was certified through the institute of criminal investigations to teach forensic sciences. He had taught at multiple universities and junior colleges and was a research associate in the entomology department at the San Diego Natural History Museum where he served on the editorial board and had published a number of papers in peer reviewed journals on the subject of forensic entomology. He was a member of the Entomological Society of America, the Lepidopterist Society, and the Xerxes Society. Mr.

Faulkner had participated in numerous research expeditions in a variety of locations around the world including Mexico, Central America, and southern Africa, and had consulted a variety of law enforcement organizations, district attorney offices, and law firms. He had also previously testified for Deputy District Attorney Jeff Dusek. His specialty was in time of death, post-mortem interval, and insect development.

Mr. Faulkner recalled that his involvement in the investigation of the murder of Danielle Van Dam had started on the morning of February 28 when he was asked by the San Diego Police Department to attend the autopsy and help determine time of death. At the autopsy, he collected a large and diverse community of insects in various stages of development including adult Hister beetles, rove beetles, and red legged ham beetles as well as blow flies and bottle flies.

Following the autopsy, at approximately 4:00 in the afternoon, Mr. Faulkner examined the site where Danielle's body had been found while it was still closed off and secured. He searched the area for insect activity and dug in the soil beneath where the body was placed as well as the surrounding area, trying to collect as much material as possible in order to obtain the largest sample possible.

"Have you ever had as complete an opportunity to work a crime scene up or do as extensive work as you were provided in this case?" Mr. Feldman asked.

"Not as extensive as in this case. I was there for the autopsy, and then the crime scene, and then allowed to evaluate other materials later on. So, it was a pretty complete effort on my part to try to assemble material."

In a detailed lesson about the lifespan of insects, Mr. Faukner described their developmental stages as more circular than linear. The process starts when eggs are deposited directly on a source that maggots or larvae can eat. Once the eggs mature, they hatch as a larva that then feeds on the source while they grow and develop. Upon reaching a certain size, the larva sheds its skin and increases its size, a process called molting that happens on two occasions during its development.

After completing three stages of growth called instars, the larva reaches its maximum size and no longer requires a food source. At that time, the larva moves away from the host and finds a safe place to pupate. The maggot shrinks, darkens in color, hardens, and develops a protective layer. A short period later, an adult fly hatches and flies away, ready to mate, lay eggs, and restart the process.

Ova position is the moment an insect egg is laid and when development begins. The duration of each instar stage depends on a number of factors including temperature, humidity, and food supply. Postmortem interval is the time between when eggs are laid on a dead body and the time the dead body is recovered. Postmortem interval was the established method of determining an approximate time of death for a body that had been outdoors exposed to the elements for an unknown period of time.

"What insects do you look for when determining time of death?" Mr. Feldman inquired.

"Flies are the insects that provide the most information," Mr. Faulkner responded and explained there were three families of flies commonly found with animal remains; house flies, which were not usually found on animal remains, flesh flies, which were found primarily in warm months, and blow and bottle flies, which were the most common and most crucial when determining the postmortem interval. If there are just eggs on a body when it is discovered, the body had likely only been there between eight and fourteen hours. If pupal stages are present, the remains have been in that location for two weeks or longer. By determining the stages of larva present, the time of death can be approximated. The longer a body remains available to insects, the more types of insects will inhabit the body and the more complex the community of insects becomes.

Mr. Faulkner identified fourteen different species of insects on Danielle's body and collected multiple fly species including black blow flies, blue blow flies, green bottle flies, and cheese skipper flies, which arrive at a later stage of decomposition when the fatty acids in the body degrade, become cheese like, and emit a unique odor. After identifying the species present, Mr. Faulkner determined the developmental stages present and reviewed the weather conditions in the area during the period between when Danielle disappeared and when her body was discovered. By determining the longest larva stages present, Mr. Faulkner could estimate Danielle's time of death.

"After you got the weather conditions and after you did your tests and evaluations, were you able to form an opinion as to when ova position could have occurred?" Mr. Feldman asked, referring to the moment eggs were first laid.

"Yes. Based on all of that and the known temperature regimes of that time, along with the weather conditions, I came up with between about ten and twelve days is when the first time the body was actually infested by insects."

"You concluded, didn't you, that ova position earliest could have occurred between the 16th and 18th?"

"Yes," Mr. Faulkner answered.

"How long does it take once a person is outdoors and dead for the flies to arrive?"

Mr. Faulkner explained if the weather conditions were suitable, insects and flies could begin laying eggs within twenty minutes. Based on the weather at the recovery site in the month of February, Mr. Faulkner concluded that insects could have laid eggs on her body shortly after she was dropped, but clarified that only the daytime temperatures were conducive. The nights had been too cold.

"Is it the case, based on all of your training and experience, that it's your opinion that based upon your entomologic findings that time of death could have been between the 16th and 18th of February?"

"Objection. Misstated the evidence for time of death."

Judge Mudd agreed and differentiated between the moment Danielle died and the moment insect activity began. "You keep using the term time of death. Use a different terminology and I will allow the question."

"Is it your conclusion that the post-mortem interval could have been between the 16th and 18th?"

"Yes."

"As we described before, the postmortem interval communicates into time of death, isn't that right?"

"Yes."

"After you arrived at this conclusion you recognized that it was creating or might create a problem for law enforcement, isn't that right?"

Mr. Faulkner agreed and recalled contacting forensic investigators and discussing whether the body might have been covered or moved from an indoor location. He was informed no evidence had been discovered indicating such circumstances.

Mr. Faulkner further revealed he had found a large number of adult beetles on the remains, but did not find any beetle larvae. Because beetles are not attracted to decomposition until the second week, the lack of beetle larvae suggested Danielle's body had not been there a full two weeks.

"So, the absence of beetle larvae supports the conclusion that the body was first available on or about the 16th to 18th of February?"

Based primarily on the maggots, Mr. Faulkner confirmed the estimation.

"You discussed with law enforcement and Mr. Dusek each of the issues you've discussed with the jury today."

"Yes."

Mr. Faulkner then discussed the weather in and around

the recovery site during the month of February, which he described as extremely abnormal.

"With regard to that abnormality, did that factor into your calculations on ova position or postmortem interval?"

"It did not figure into the determination of how long the body was available to the insects. What it did bring up questions as whether or not adult insects would have been able to find the body."

Mr. Faulkner revealed that the weather during the month of February was unusually warm and the entire winter had been exceptionally dry. Additionally, the insect population in the area was notably lower than normal.

Despite the low insect activity, Mr. Faulkner did not believe a body could go without insect activity for over a week and was certain insect activity would have started in the hours after the body was initially exposed. "It would be hard to totally exclude fly activity for that amount of time given those weather conditions."

"If, hypothetically, the body had been out, say, on February 2nd and hadn't been discovered until February 28th, you have no explanation for that?"

"No, I don't."

"So, it would be nothing more than speculation or guess on your part to conclude that the body was available any time sooner than the 16th of February?"

"Objection. Leading, speculation."

"Overruled, you can answer that."

"I can't exclude the fact that the insects could have gotten to the body earlier, but based again on the immature stages of the flies, they did not."

"And with regard to your work in this case, is it your opinion that this is at least the best opportunity and the best job you've ever had to do the forensic evaluation that you were called upon to do?"

"Yes."

"Even better than when you testified for Mr. Dusek?"

"Yes."

After spending significant time and effort claiming Mr. Westerfield's unusual behavior in the hours following Danielle's abduction was not evidence of guilt, Mr. Feldman hinged his case on the premise that abnormal insect activity was absolute evidence of Mr. Westerfield's innocence.

"No further questions."

Before wading into the science, Mr. Dusek clarified for the Jury that Mr. Faulkner had also previously worked for Mr. Feldman and had testified in trials on both sides.

"In your report, you indicate that you are providing estimations?"

"Yes."

"You're not providing any hard and fast dates, are you?"

"I'm providing a range," Mr. Faulkner confirmed.

"Basically, you are telling us the latest day that body could be available for fly infestation, is that correct?"

Mr. Faulkner agreed that he was providing a range and that the day the eggs were laid on Danielle's body could not have been after February 16 to 18.

"So, that's the minimum amount of time from the body was recovered to when the eggs were laid on the body."

"Yes."

"You did not provide us a maximum amount of time in your report, did you?"

"No," Mr. Faulkner said.

"You cannot tell us with any degree of scientific certainty when was the maximum amount of time, is that correct?"

"That is correct."

"The science just isn't that good, is it?"

"Again, the length of time other than the fastest time, it's difficult to quantify that with insects."

"So, the best you can do in any situation is to give us the least amount of time," Mr. Dusek asked, again referring to the time between when the eggs were laid and the body was found; the postmortem interval.

"That's what the maggots were showing in this particular case."

Mr. Dusek moved on to the weather.

"Have you checked the weather situation?"

"Yes, I have."

When asked about the extreme heat in February, Mr. Faulkner answered, "it wouldn't throw off the calculations as much with the larvae, but it would perhaps throw off what time the flies could actually find a body."

"And that would affect the maximum amount of time the body could have been exposed to the elements and to the insects?"

"Yes."

Mr. Faulkner then discussed how flies required for their eggs a dark, moist place, preferably hidden from sunlight and safe from insects and small animals, typically the nose, ears, and mouth.

Regarding his observations at the autopsy, Mr. Faulkner was asked, "did you see bug infestation as you would expect in a normal situation in the head region?"

"In this particular instance in looking at the decomposition, I would have expected a lot of insect activity in the head area."

"Did you see any?"

"No."

"Does that mean that this is not a normal situation, an expected situation?"

"For me it was atypical."

Mr. Faulkner recalled he at first suspected that her head had been covered. "It made me question the availability of that part of the body to insects."

"You talked about decomposing. Is there also a condition referred to as mummification?"

"Yes." Mr. Faulkner explained that mummification was the process when a body dries out before insect activity fully takes hold. Mummification can delay the availability of parts of the body they would otherwise target. A mummified body also resulted in a less diverse insect community.

"If the body begins to decompose or dry out, does that mean that it is not an attractive site for these bugs that you've been talking about?

"Objection. Vague. Decompose and dry out are different, your honor."

"Overruled," Judge Mudd said. "You can answer."

"With desiccating or drying out, again, you're reducing the water content, the moisture content, and that is not as attractive particularly to flies as it would be if there was more moisture."

When asked if mummification would, "extend the maximum amount of time the body was exposed," Mr. Faulkner answered, "yes."

"Was this body mummified?"

"I'm not a pathologist, but in my experience, the body was rather dry, particularly the exterior surface, the skin."

Mr. Dusek pointed out that flies were not attracted to dry areas and Mr. Faulkner agreed, "they would be looking for something that they could respond to more readily, perhaps something that had more moisture available to them."

Regarding the body's abdomen where a large mass of maggots was discovered, Mr. Faulkner agreed that the area had first been open by a scavenging animal at a time unknown. Once the moisture underneath was exposed, the area became attractive to flies who then deposited their eggs.

"And it was in these chewed areas where you saw the maggot activity primarily?"

"The maggot mass and most of the larval stages of the flies were restricted to the abdominal cavity."

"If we're trying to set a time line, first of all, we would have to wait for however long it took for animals to create that opening in the body before the flies would then show up, and then the flies would begin their activity."

"Objection. Misstates the testimony."

"Overruled. You can answer."

Mr. Faulkner continued. "You may have flies there, but for that particular area of the body where they were located, you would obviously have to have an opening for them to get in."

After discussing the abnormally low number of flies present that winter, Mr. Dusek referred to Mr. Faulkner's inspection of the site the body was found. Typically, the ground beneath a body would contain a complex community of insects attracted to the moisture seeping down into the soil. In this situation, the ground was very dry and insect activity was nearly nonexistent.

"Would that indicate mummification rather than decomposition?"

"When you have a lot of moisture you tend to get a lot of rotting and there wasn't a lot of rotting found underneath the remains."

"Does that then contribute to an inability to set a maximum amount of time the body had been in that location?"

"It would mean that actually the body had been there maybe a lot longer, but because it was dry there was no resource for these insects to remain there."

Moving on to the impact weather had on insect activity, Mr. Faulkner first noted the ideal temperature for insect activity is above 50 degrees.

When researching the weather in the area of the recovery site, Mr. Faulkner reviewed temperature logs from nearby air fields and ultimately settled on temperature data from Lindberg

Field, later renamed San Diego International Airport, which was located on the coast about twenty-five miles west of the recovery site.

Before asking about specific temperatures, Mr. Dusek noted that the temperature and conditions on the coast, although only twenty-five miles away, differed substantially from those found in the desert canyons where Danielle's body was found.

On the coast, the temperatures were cooler during the day and the humidity was higher. In the area where the body was recovered, the temperatures at night were colder, the days were warmer, and the conditions were much dryer.

When asked how weather affects cold blooded creatures, Mr. Faulkner explained, "they're totally dependent on the weather for their activity period. If it's too cold they can't function. They just wait until it warms up."

Mr. Faulkner said the ideal temperature for insect rearing was around 74 degrees at 50% humidity. Between 75 and 90 degrees insect activity increases. Below 45 or 50 degrees, "insects will cease their activity."

In addition to the weather data from Lindberg Field, which showed hourly temperatures, Mr. Faulkner also reviewed the daily high and low temperatures in El Cajon, just a few miles west of where the body was found. While not able to ascertain the exact difference in temperature, Mr. Faulkner noticed that the high in El Cajon was three or four degrees higher. On the day he inspected the recovery site, on February 28, the temperature was 55 degrees at 5:00pm.

"Did you take any cold temperatures at Dehesa to see how much colder it was there to Lindberg field?"

"No."

"If a body is dropped at a location at night when it's cold, is that going to delay insect activity?"

"Yes. Flies are not active after sundown. They're not able to negotiate the environment when it's dark."

"If there's no rainfall, is that going to delay the insect activity around the body?"

"It could," Mr. Faulkner said. "They're not going to come out when it's not suitable to either find food, find mates, and deposit eggs."

"How much rainfall have we had this weather year?"

Mr. Faulkner answered it had only rained about three and a half inches that winter, the lowest amount since 1951. Although there was no research data on flies in droughts, Mr. Faulkner said that extreme weather of any kind disrupts insect behavior.

"Based upon the weather data you had, were there factors that would impact the insect activity on this body?"

Mr. Faulkner answered, "yes," and explained the weather in February had been unusual as a result of two Sana Ana conditions, one that occurred the first two weeks in the month, the second occurred the last two weeks of the month. Santa Ana winds, he explained, were an unusual phenomenon in which strong, dry and hot winds blow through the western parts of southern California. As a result, the temperatures during February were very high and could have suppressed insect activity. The intense winds could also have made it more difficult for the flies to smell the body.

"You cannot tell us the furthest they could be from the time the body was recovered, can you?"

"Objection. Asked and answered."

"Overruled. You can answer."

"No." Mr. Faulkner explained he could only measure the time the largest maggots had been on her body. "If the victim was dead longer, and there was something to exclude the insects from getting at it, of course the body could have been there longer. I can't rule that out."

"Thank you, sir."

Mr. Dusek returned the witness to Mr. Feldman who asked, "your conclusion hasn't changed as a result of Mr. Dusek's cross examination, has it?"

"Not based on the fly larvae, no. The absence of beetle larvae and the presence of the flies that were identified, their stage and development, it still remains the same."

"Therefore, that finding is consistent with your conclusion that ova position occurred between the 16th and 18th of February and not sooner?"

Mr. Faulkner agreed.

"Is it reasonable that one could look at this evidence and form the opinion that the postmortem interval was between the 16th and 18th of February?"

"Basing it on the fly larvae, the species involved in the stage of development, that is the timeframe I came up with the body being available to these insects."

"Sir, do you think that a body could have been laying out for, say, since the 4th of February without attracting any flies?"

"I would find that unusual."

"Based on your training and experience, would you expect that the body could have been out there for three weeks?"

"Nothing shows that it was longer than the timeframe I indicated."

"Thank you very much, nothing further."

"Okay, ladies and gentleman, I want to remind you that the shepherd's going to be away from the flock for a while and what I need for you to do is to guard against, in the utmost way possible, reading or listening to, because I suspect, based on my experience over the 4th of July, that next week when there's nothing live there will be something contrived. They're going to have synopses, all of the talking heads will be out there just to keep the interest up until we start again on Monday the 22nd.

"I've been getting phone calls for the last two days congratulating me on my anniversary because one of the shows happened to say Judge Mudd's been married for thirty years. It's thirty-four actually. I've been getting phone calls from friends that I haven't heard from in years throughout the country.

"You can rest assured that whether you're making your best efforts or not, things are going to pop up. You can be watching a television show on a national network and you're going to see this case. So, it's very, very important that in the interim while we're away from each other that you self-police. I anticipate things will start moving very rapidly when we get back together on the 22nd. So have a pleasant and a safe period off. We'll see you July 22nd at 9:00."

After the jury left the room, Judge Mudd discussed the motion of Damon Van Damon, which they planned to discuss the following morning along with an outline of what each side was planning once the trial resumed.

DAY 20

Following a twelve day break, Judge Mudd returned from vacation on Monday, July 22. "Good morning, ladies and gentleman, and welcome back. Looks like the Padres had a better than five hundred winning average while I was gone. I had no idea while I was gone how many office pools and bets there were as to where I was going on vacation. I got discovered within five minutes of arriving at the docks. My wife and I and family took a cruise so there is a very happy guy that runs the home depot here in San Diego that won his office pool and there were a lot of men and women that came up to me in the cruise and said you lost the bet or I won the bet. So that's what that was all about.

"Ladies and gentleman, of course, as I came back and reviewed the papers over the last week, there is a matter pending in Orange County that bears no relationship whatsoever to this case in terms of its facts or anything else and I simply want to remind you of something that I reminded you of way back when we started. Your obligation is to make your decisions in this case solely based on the evidence you see and hear in this courtroom. Other matters in other locations are of no relevance to this case. All right. Mr. Feldman."

The defense called Forensic Entomologist Dr. Neal Haskell Ph.D. Dr. Haskell had earned a bachelor's degree in entomology from Purdue University in 1969 and a master of science degree in forensic entomology in 1989. He had taught forensic entomology extensively, primarily to law enforcement, coroners, and medical examiners. Dr. Haskell had also studied decomposition and the insects it involves at the University of Tennessee anthropological research facility. He had written numerous peer-reviewed books as well as chapters in several reference books and training manuals. He was a member of the American Board of Forensic Entomology and had worked for various law enforcement agencies including the FBI and police departments as well as medical examiners and coroners. He had also worked on cases in Canada, Germany, Mexico, and Belize.

In preparing his report for the case of Danielle Van Dam, Dr. Haskell studied the insect evidence David Faulkner had collected at Danielle's autopsy and the recovery site, the climatological data from Brown Field, the autopsy report, and photographs of the scene.

"As a result of your investigation and evaluation in the case, were you able to form an opinion as to what the postmortem interval was?" Mr. Feldman asked, referring to the time between when insect eggs were laid and the body was recovered.

"With a reasonable degree of scientific certainty, I concluded that the time of colonization for the decedent would be from the 14th of February through the 21st." By colonization, Dr. Haskell clarified, he meant the moment flies found the remains and laid their eggs.

"In my opinion," Dr. Haskell continued, "the body would not have been there on those dates prior."

Having personally examined the insects and larvae collected at the autopsy, Dr. Haskell showed the jury a chart listing all the insects and larvae found along with their stages of growth. With great detail, he discussed each insect while reviewing the lifecycle of insects as previously discussed by Mr. Faulkner.

"How did you use the life cycle of the flies to make determinations as to postmortem interval?"

Dr. Haskell explained the process of identifying the oldest insect evidence present and counting backwards from the date of discovery.

"Is there a difference between time of death and time of insect colonization?"

"Absolutely," Dr. Haskell answered and explained that normally insects will colonize between a few minutes to a day or two after death, unless temperatures are below freezing when they do not come out at all.

When asked if Danielle's body could have been available to insects as a food source before February 14, Dr. Haskell said, "no" and pointed out that temperatures before that day had exceeded the minimum threshold for insect activity.

After a question regarding the loss of mass in a decaying body, Dr. Haskell initiated a long, wandering ramble about the decay process that frequently drifted into references to his home in Indiana that were not necessarily relevant to the questions asked. Throughout his testimony, Dr. Haskell was long winded, needlessly specific, and lacking focus. Mr. Feldman reigned him in on numerous occasions.

"Whoa, whoa, whoa. I'm sorry. Does that mean, say, hypothetically, a body's mummified – let me back up. Before a body mummifies, hypothetically, the blowflies would get to it, right?"

"When it's fresh."

"Then, hypothetically, it gets hot and somehow the body mummifies?"

Dr. Haskell agreed and said once mummification occurs, blow flies will search for something more fresh.

Moving on to the weather, Dr. Haskell was asked to explain accumulated degree hours or ADH, which he described as a quantification of time and temperature into a unit of energy. ADH quantified hourly temperatures over a period of time.

"Sir, if the skin is mummified, does that mummification create a barrier for blow flies?"

Dr. Haskell agreed that mummification creates a barrier, but noted that mummification did not always occur throughout an entire body all at once. Just because one area was not accessible, did not mean all areas were unavailable.

"With regard to the climate, if it's dry, would you expect that the climate could cause or affect the total number of insects in a given habitat?"

After agreeing, Dr. Haskell proceeded down another long explanation that roamed into stories about his research in Indiana.

Following the morning break, Dr. Haskell was asked again, "based on the insect colonization that you observed, was it your opinion that the decedent was laying out exposed from approximately the 14th of February onward?"

"That's correct."

"In your view, it's not really possible that the body could have been lying out for greater than two weeks and a few days?"

Dr. Haskell agreed. "That's based upon the condition of the body as it was found, fully exposed, the insect specimens that David Faulkner collected and preserved, and the temperatures that we have relating to this period of time."

"You also include, do you not, in your opinion, your professional training in the areas of decomposition?"

"Absolutely."

"Thank you very much, sir. No further questions."

Mr. Dusek began his cross examination by showing that Dr. Haskell was not a medical doctor, was not a pathologist, and had never conducted an autopsy. He then pointed out that he and Mr. Faulkner had reached slightly different dates. Dr. Haskell countered that his dates casted a wider range, but the core aspects overlapped.

"If we have two entomologists with two beginning and ending periods, what would happen if we got a third entomologist? Would we get different numbers?"

Dr. Haskell said he had used a slightly different method and if a third entomologist also used a slightly different method than yes, they might get a third set of dates. Although Mr. Faulkner had reached a narrower time window, Dr. Haskell believed it was still within his own window of estimation.

Mr. Dusek asked if two different entomologists

examined the same evidence and reached two separate conclusions, if a third could form yet another opinion. Dr. Haskell stated that additional variations were possible with alternative approaches. He referred to his approach as the "accumulated degree, hour degree, day method." He did not know which method Mr. Faulkner had used.

"So even though you used the same bugs, if he used a different method, you would get different beginning and ending periods?"

Dr. Haskell said that was possible, which was why he preferred using a wider range.

"And if you use different temperatures you would expect to get different periods?"

"Well, if you use different temperatures there would certainly be a shift one way or the other."

Regarding the weather data used by Mr. Faulkner, Mr. Dusek asked Dr. Haskell if he had determined whether the data he had applied was the most accurate. The defense objected and was overruled. Dr. Haskell explained he chose the data station he thought was most accurate and best represented the area of focus. Dr. Haskell recalled that he had applied the data from Brown Field because its elevation and proximity to the coast were similar. Brown Field was approximately thirty miles southeast on the edge of the desert, not near the coast like Lindberg field. Mr. Dusek noted that Dr. Haskell lived in Indiana, had only visited San Diego a few times, and had not visited the recovery site until just the day before.

"At Brown Field, you can actually see the ocean on a clear day, can't you?"

"I have never been-"

"Objection. Speculation, no foundation."

"Sustained."

Mr. Dusek asked Dr. Haskell why he had not chosen the data from Gillepsie Field, which was less than ten miles away on the east side of the hills separating El Cajon from La Mesa. Although closer than Brown Field, Dr. Haskell said the data from Gillepsie field only included daytime temperatures.

Mr. Dusek explored wind patterns and the effect cool ocean breezes have on the temperature inland except in places blocked off by mountains. Dr. Haskell confirmed the valley east of the mountains facing the desert would have been warmer than one on the ocean side of the mountains.

"Picking the location of temperatures that you're going to use will cause the greatest variance?"

"Yes, it can, and the way to get around that variance is if the investigators, and this is in my book *Entomology And Death*, if there's a question regarding differences between a weather station and the death scene, or where the body's recovered, we can do statistical analyses to quantify and calibrate similarities and/or differences between the recovery site and the weather station." Because the weather in February 2002 had been particularly unique, comparisons of multiple data sets with the recovery site would not have necessarily achieved accurate or reliable results and that data was never collected by police investigators.

Mr. Dusek reviewed the high and low temperatures from multiple days in February. He noted with the data Dr. Haskell used from Brown Field, the low was 36 degrees on February 1st, 38 on the 6th, and 48 on the 11th. He compared the temperatures from El Cajon, which showed 32 degrees on February 1st and 34 on February 6th.

"What happens to the bugs and their eggs when you get to freezing temperatures?"

"They don't grow," Dr. Haskell answered.

"And they grow when it's above freezing?"

"No. They grow above about 50 degrees. So, all these low temperatures they are not growing."

"Anything below 50 and the bugs aren't growing, correct?"

"Correct."

"If we get down below freezing or at freezing, it takes a while for bugs to thaw out doesn't it?"

Dr. Haskell explained insects had an antifreeze defense that prevented them from freezing, but conceded that it took some time for insects to warm up and become active.

"Your primary experience is with flies in Indiana, correct?"

"No, I've had primary experience with a number of flies all over the country because of the research that I've done and the training that I've done."

"You've never lived in California to study the flies out here, have you?"

"No."

"Do you have Santa Ana conditions in Indiana?"

"We have windy conditions all the time, but I don't think we call them Santa Anas, I think we call them just high winds. They're not necessarily drying winds, but we have a lot of wind in Indiana." When asked if Indiana had ever had only three and a half inches of rain in a year in Indiana, Dr. Haskell recalled that had never happened in his experience.

"That would be totally foreign to your personal experience, correct?"

Dr. Haskell disagreed and sited with great pride his participation in decomposition studies that occurred in New Mexico and west Texas where the conditions were very dry and similar to the conditions present in San Diego.

"In those situations bodies dry out fast, don't they."

"Very fast."

"Mummify real fast, don't they."

"Very fast."

"How quickly do those bodies dry out in those areas that you're talking about?"

"Within a few days," Dr. Haskell answered.

"And once the bodies mummify, the flies don't like them, do they?"

Dr. Haskell confirmed flies would not lay eggs on a mummified body.

"Did we have those hot, dry, windy, low humid conditions in February of this year?"

"Yes, you did."

"The body will dry with low humidity and wind, won't it? You don't even need the 80s and 90s to dry out, do you?"

"That's correct. You can have cool dehydrations and you can have hot weather dehydration."

"You made several assumptions in determining the time periods you've given us, haven't you?"

Although Dr. Haskell had just verified on numerous points the likelihood that Danielle's body had mummified within a couple of days, which would have made her body not accessible to insects, he continued to support the belief her body could not have been left in the desert earlier than the middle of February.

Noting that the autopsy had found no trauma to the body that could have caused an open wound along with the fact no larvae had been recovered from the mouth, nose, or ears, Mr. Dusek asked where the flies went.

"I think it was reported by the investigators that there was some maggot activity in the head area and by the time David Faulkner got to the body it had been in a cooler and was subjected to cooler temperatures." The maggots he claimed had been present in her head despite evidence otherwise, he believed, had, "most likely migrated down to the area where the maggot mass and the heat was."

Given that Dr. Haskell had previously stated insects stopped moving in near freezing temperatures, Mr. Dusek wondered how a large number of maggots supposedly in the head area moved to the maggot mass in the abdomen after the body had been placed in the freezer.

"I'm going on the observations and report of the investigator at the scene that recovered the body."

Mr. Dusek pressed. "Give me the name of the investigator, please."

"I'm not sure."

"These individual maggots that were in the head region. How did they migrate after the temperature dropped down to the 30s?"

"They started migrating when they felt the temperature going down. When I open body bags up with a body infested with maggot, maggots are crawling all over the place. You have no idea necessarily the definite location where those maggots originated."

Moving forward, Mr. Dusek discussed whether or not flies could cut through mummified skin.

"No, flies don't eat through anything and maggots are not capable of penetrating human adult skin until advanced decomposition."

Mr. Dusek proceeded to show Dr. Haskell a number of photos of Danielle's body. When asked if the appeared mummified, Dr. Haskell again started to wander.

"Yeah, in most cases I worked, the hands are mummified, the feet and hands and legs are mummified-"

"These hands are mummified?"

Mr. Feldman interrupted, "your honor, counsel's yelling at the witness."

"Calm down," Judge Mudd answered before turning to the witness. "Just answer the question, doctor. We'll get through this a lot faster if you'll just answer the questions."

"All right, your honor."

Referencing the photos of Danielle's hands, Mr. Dusek asked, "how mummified is it?"

"It's mummified."

Noting the dark color of her hands, he asked, "this is the

end stage of mummification, isn't it?"

"This is exactly what I see on bodies in Indiana and Tennessee."

Judge Mudd intervened. "Doctor? The question you were just asked can be answered yes or no."

"All right. No." Dr. Haskell answered before explaining how the mummification process could continue further from that point.

"Are you able to estimate how long it would take for a girl who is a blonde haired, light skinned girl to turn this color? How long does that take?"

"In my opinion, we could see this in a week to two weeks."

Judge Mudd suspended the action and dismissed the jury for lunch before addressing Dr. Haskell. "Doctor, you have a great tendency to get involved way too often in this. Your job here, at least from my perception, is to be an expert witness and tell this jury what you know and what you base it on, not to give war stories and not to get involved in arguments with the lawyers. So, they'll ask you the questions, you do the answering, and don't get involved any further than that, okay."

"Yes sir."

When testimony resumed ninety minutes later, Mr. Dusek picked up where he left off. "How long does it take for internal organs to mummify?"

"A week or two."

"How long does it remain that way?"

"With the environmental conditions we have, I've seen that last for weeks or months," Dr. Haskell answered before clarifying that, "for my postmortem interval, I'm using the insects to make that determination, not the appearance of the tissues."

When asked if he was excluding from his consideration the appearance of the exterior and interior of the body when determining postmortem interval, Dr. Haskell answered, "that's correct."

Mr. Dusek transitioned to the areas on Danielle's body that had been disrupted by animal activity. He noted the findings of Dr. Blackbourne and Mr. Faulkner who had determined the maggot mass in the abdomen was located in an area previously opened by a scavenging animal. Dr. Haskell pushed back on that conclusion, believing the maggots had entered a natural orifice and dug their way up and out.

"In my opinion, I do reject the possibility that the flies came in after the coyotes opened that area. I think the flies were there, the maggots were there, before the coyotes came in."

"Then if the coyotes were eating in the area where the maggot mass was, that would be removing one or two generations of maggots, wouldn't it?"

Dr. Haskell vehemently disagreed, realizing if the original generation of maggots had been removed by scavengers, his estimated time of death would have been completely wrong. Dr. Haskell emphasized he had never examined a case in which more than one generation of maggots were on a body and he had done, "almost five hundred, maybe over five hundred cases, plus research at the body farm plus a thousand, fifteen hundred dead animals that I've worked with over the eighteen years."

"The coyote could remove the maggots when he fed on the body, couldn't it?"

"Some of them, but not all of them."

Noting that multiple organs were missing, Mr. Dusek wondered, "when the animals are chewing that area, is there anything to prevent them from eating all the maggots that are there at that time?"

"They will get out of the way of a coyote trying to eat them up."

"Then if they were to eat some of those maggots, then the next generation, the next flies, would come back and have moist areas to lay their eggs?"

Obviously irritated, Dr. Haskell explained a second generation meant the first eggs had fully reached adulthood, became flies, mated, and then laid eggs on the same body.

"Whether it is a generation or just a second wave of flies, a second wave could come and infest the body after the first wave laid their eggs, correct?"

Dr. Haskell agreed.

"And we have no way of knowing, based upon what you've seen, whether or not the flies sent to you by David Faulkner were from the first wave of flies or the second wave of flies after the animal was chewing on the body, do you?"

"Objection. Assumes facts not in evidence."

"Overruled. You can answer."

"We might have a day or two difference in the initial colonization. The way these blow flies survive is by completing the life cycle. If coyotes are eating them all up then we are not going to have blow flies."

"Or the blow flies came in after the coyotes had their last meal."

"In my opinion, that's not what happened."

Having struck a significant blow to the reliability of the insect evidence as a whole, Mr. Dusek moved his focus to the postmortem interval.

"Basically, entomologists give us the minimum period of time, don't they?"

Dr. Haskell agreed, but said a maximum time could also be approximated.

Mr. Dusek presented a large poster board with excerpts from some of Dr. Haskell's writings and asked him to read a segment.

"Nowhere in that article do you talk about determining

the maximum postmortem interval, do you?"

Dr. Haskell had not read that particular article in some time, was not sure if the rest of the article excluded maximum estimations, and was sure that other articles he had written did.

"The best way of using your work in flies is to determine the minimum amount of time the body was exposed?"

"Well, that's the way we do it."

"When you try to determine a maximum, you have to assume that the body was killed as soon as the flies get there, right?

"That's our basic assumption. If you'll check the *Entomology And Death* procedural guide you will see that's our basis right there. We assume the flies hit almost immediately upon death. What I'm calculating is the postmortem interval based on the insects that are found on the remains and then dealing with the temperatures that drive that growth and development."

"Thank you, sir."

"All right. Thank you for coming in, Doctor, you're free to leave these proceedings, however, you're under an admonition not to discuss your testimony with anyone until the matter's concluded, all right?"

"Yes, your honor, thank you very much."

Following the afternoon break, Mr. Boyce asked Judge Mudd if they could recall Det. Tomsovic. Judge Mudd agreed.

Mr. Boyce referenced the site where Danielle's body was found and asked, "when you were there did you notice a serpentine drag trail that was about forty-five feet long through the grass?"

Det. Tomsovic confirmed he had investigated the trail, which was located approximately ninety feet from the body, and discovered several blonde human hairs as well as a greasy smear across grass that appeared trampled down.

"Did you notice any odor connected with this trail?"

317

"Yes, there was an odor of decomposing flesh," the detective answered and said he thought the trail had been created when an animal had dragged away a body part.

"I have nothing further."

After reviewing the greasy drag marks, Mr. Dusek turned his attention to Det. Tomsovic's observations of Danielle's body.

"Did you get a chance to examine Danielle that first evening?"

"Yes."

"How close did you get to her?"

"Inches."

"Objection. Scope, you're honor."

"It's beyond, but I'll try to keep the detective from coming back again. Go ahead, counsel. Overruled."

"Did you get a chance to examine her head or face region?"

Det. Tomsovic confirmed he spent several minutes searching Danielle's body for insects.

"Have you been trained to identify bug activity on corpses?"

"Yes," he answered and explained he was looking for maggots because they could help determine time of death.

"Did you see some maggots on this body?"

"Not externally, no. The eye orbits were vacant, there was a gelatinous mass inside the head and we could see with the flashlight some movement inside that mass."

"How many maggots did you see?"

"I remember seeing one. Forensic Specialist Karen LeAlcala collected it."

"Did you see any maggots in the mouth?"

"No."

"Did you see any maggots in the ears?"

"No."

"Did you see any maggots in or around the nose?"

"No."

"Did you see any maggot mass near the head of this child?"

"No."

"Do you know whether or not these maggots move when it's dark out?"

"Objection. Lack of foundation."

"Overruled. You can answer."

Det. Tomsovic continued. "It's my experience they're not as active at night."

"Thank you, sir."

"All right," Judge Mudd said. "Any redirect, Mr. Boyce, I'll give you wide latitude on cross."

"Thank you, your honor."

Mr. Boyce started his redirect/cross of Det. Tomsovic by focusing on the single maggot observed in the eye socket of Danielle's body. When asked if he had searched deeper inside the area for additional maggots, Det. Tomsovic said he had not.

"You don't know whether it was a mass of maggots or not, do you?"

"No, I don't."

Regarding the drag marks, Mr. Boyce asked, "were they consistent with a foot being dragged away?"

"It seemed like they were probably, in my estimation, too large an area for a small foot to have caused that kind of a mark. I had envisioned more along the lines of possibly entrails."

"In your report you stated the torso and head were infested with maggots and tiny flies?"

"Yes."

"Nothing further, your honor."

After a lengthy sidebar at Mr. Feldman's request, Judge Mudd informed the jury he and the counselors had issues to discuss the following day, which meant they would have the day off.

"As I indicated before I left for vacation, things will start moving very rapidly when you get to the end of the trial. And, as you are well aware, we are approaching the end. Have a pleasant evening and day off tomorrow. We'll see you Wednesday at 9:00am and maybe the Pads can beat up on LA a little bit more."

Once the jury left, Judge Mudd discussed his plans for the following day, which included planning and scheduling the end of the trial and rebuttal witnesses the state was preparing. He additionally revealed he had received, "a letter from an individual who identifies himself in the letter, but leaves no other information, commenting on his observations of a particular juror in this case. It was Juror 1. I've been watching the entire panel throughout, I don't find a whole lot of credence in his observations, but he includes some additional materials. I'm just alerting you to the fact that this may or may not be of relevance to the two sides so I'll make it available so you could both review it."

After making sure there were no additional issues that required attention at that time, Judge Mudd concluded the twentieth day of trial.

DAY 21

On Wednesday July 24, Judge Mudd resumed trial at 9:00am. "All right, where are we at, Mr. Feldman? Are you prepared to rest today?"

"We are," Mr. Feldman answered and said they planned only one more witness.

After a brief discussion regarding scheduling for rebuttal witnesses, Judge Mudd brought the jury back in. "Good morning, ladies and gentleman, welcome back. Too bad the Padres couldn't continue last night, but hopefully the nice weather today will lend itself to a victory.

"Ladies and gentleman, I feel it's my duty at this time to let you know pretty much where we're at and some things that are likely to occur because they directly affect the amount of time that you will be in the courtroom. It is anticipated that this morning the defense will be rapidly identifying some exhibits and then concluding its case in chief and then we're going into the rebuttal phase which is the people's opportunity to present evidence rebutting what the defense has presented. Rebuttal phases of trials are very unique because they come on very suddenly."

Judd Mudd explained the counsels were working with the schedules of expert witnesses and warned some of the testimonies may be disjointed. He additionally revealed the defense would have one final opportunity to present its own rebuttal witnesses before the trial concluded. Judge Mudd advised jurors to, "clear your calendars," because they would not have Friday off as they had during the trial.

"Okay, Mr. Feldman."

Mr. Feldman called their last witness, Forensic Artist James Gripp. Mr. Gripp presented a series of still images taken from news videos showing the exterior of Mr. Westerfield's house as investigators were conducting the search warrant of his home. Without referencing the content of the images, Mr. Feldman passed the witness to Mr. Dusek.

Mr. Dusek noted Mr. Gripp did not know when the video was shot and was not on the scene at the time. When asked if he knew what was inside the boxes being taken from the house, Mr. Gripp said he did not know. He was also unable to identify any of the individuals in the images. After referencing a woman officer in one of the images, Mr. Dusek asked, "were you ever asked to get that shirt so we could test it to see if it matches any of the fibers we have in this case?"

"No, I was not."

"You were just asked to get a picture with people with orange shirts on, right?"

Mr. Gripp clarified he had been provided the specific clips and asked only to extract still images from the clips.

"Most of the people have orange shirts on, don't they? And they appear to be people who might be affiliated with law enforcement?"

"Yes, it appears that way."

"Do you know if this shirt was requested by the defense to be tested?"

"Objection."

"Sustained."

"Thank you, sir."

In his redirect, Mr. Boyce asked, "can you tell whether or not the people are wearing gloves or not?"

"They do not appear to be wearing gloves."

"I have nothing further, your honor."

Judge Mudd excused the witness.

Mr. Feldman said, "Your honor, subject to our previously articulated reservations, we rest."

"People prepared to go forward with their rebuttal?"

Mr. Dusek confirmed he was ready and called Michael,

the assistant superintendent at the Singing Hills Golf Club, which was across the street from where Danielle's body was discovered. As the assistant superintendent, he was responsible for managing the water on the course.

"As part of your duties regarding the irrigation, is the weather an important factor?"

"It's extremely important." Michael explained how maintaining a healthy golf course required close attention to weather conditions, particularly in the winter months when the temperatures reached freezing. Anytime frost was present in the morning, no activity on the course was allowed until the grass had warmed up, usually sometime in the late morning. He additionally revealed the course featured its own weather station that sent data directly to the computers in his office.

Mr. Dusek presented a large chart showing the dates and temperatures and referenced an additional document that listed all the mornings frost was present on the grass.

"For the month of February, this year, which days were the greens frosted."

"First, second, third, fourth, fifth, sixth, seventh, eighth, nineth, and the eleventh."

"Thank you, sir."

Mr. Feldman started his cross by asking, "sir, if I understood correctly, it frosts when the weather gets below 32 degrees. Is that right, sir?"

"Not necessarily, no. The temperature can range anywhere between 37 and 22 and you could have frost."

Mr. Feldman asked a series of questions about when the course was watered, which animals lived in the area, and how the computer system worked before pointing out Michael was not a botanist or a meteorologist.

"With regard to your calculations, what do you say Singing Hills was on February 11th, sir, the high and low?"

"The low was 34, the high was 73."

Mr. Feldman noted that Michael had only presented the high and the low temperatures for the day, not when those temperatures were reached or the hourly temperatures, which the station also collected. He then inquired about who was in charge of maintaining the weather station. Michael revealed the weather station had not been calibrated since 1999 and said the wind gauge had not been functioning in February.

Mr. Feldman proceeded to discuss wind patterns, the unusually hot days near the end of February, the lack of rain during that month, and how Michael determined how much water the course needed and when.

"Thank you, sir."

Judge Mudd excused the witness and, after the morning break, before the jury returned, Mr. Dusek informed Judge Mudd of his plan to call River Stillwood, a producer for the Rick Roberts Show, a morning show on the radio in San Diego. "Just a heads up, your honor. The next witness is River Stillwood, the on scene observer from channel 760 radio. She doesn't know she's going to testify, but actually at the urging of Mr. Feldlman-"

"I don't want to say urging. I just suggested it might be a good idea to let your honor know."

"That this is going to be coming out of the blue?" Judge Mudd asked.

"Yes. You might want to tune in to 760 to see the reaction."

Judge Mudd allowed the jury and spectators back into the courtroom and Mr. Dusek called Ms. Stillwood who apprehensively took the stand.

After asking her name and profession, Mr. Dusek asked if she had observed the testimony of Patricia who he described as the middle aged lady who walked with a cane and suffered from back problems.

"Were you in present in court when she said she had not taken any alcohol or Vicodin before coming to court?"

"I was indeed."

"Did you hear her say something contrary to that that day?"

Ms. Stillwood confirmed Patricia had and additionally noted she had shared the interaction on the radio.

"Did you see Patricia in the restroom that day?"

Ms. Stillwood recalled seeing Patricia in the restroom shortly before her testimony. While Ms. Stillwood was at the sink, Patricia entered the room. "She was having difficulty coming in. She was shaking. The door was a little stiff and she was having trouble navigating it. I asked her if she needed help."

"What did she say?"

"She said no. She moved over to the sink and then started to tell me about her back trouble, apparently a couple of crushed discs in her back."

"Did she talk about any medication she takes for her back?"

"She said she needed to take some more medication."

"Did you see her take any more?"

"I did not. I asked her if she needed any more help and I quickly left." As Ms. Stillwood walked out, Patricia was digging in her purse.

"Then you heard her testify that she had not taken any Vicodin that day?"

"I did."

"Thank you, ma'am."

In his cross examination, Mr. Feldman confirmed Ms. Stillwood never saw Patricia take any pills and that she said she was in severe discomfort.

"You heard her in court that she did not take any Vicodin, is that right?"

"I did hear her say that."

"That was consistent with your observations because you didn't see her take any drugs, did you?"

"No, sir. That's not consistent with my observations. I saw her in a great deal of pain and I heard her say she needed to take more medication."

After remembering Patricia had drank some water with her hand, Mr. Feldman asked, "because there's no cups in the bathroom, right?"

"That's correct."

"Been a problem in that facility, supplies?"

"I haven't found that to be a problem."

Judge Mudd chimed in, "the county appreciates that last comment."

"That's why I asked, Judge. How much total time would you estimate you spent with her?"

"Two or three minutes."

"The whole period of time that you saw her, she never took any pills?"

"That's true."

"No further questions."

After Ms. Stillwood stepped down, the prosecution called Mr. Westerfield's son, Neal. Because the defense had claimed Neal was responsible for downloading the child pornography onto the computers, the prosecution was forced to refute the claim the only way they could; by calling Neal. The state used the opportunity to refute a wide range of additional claims made by the defense about Mr. Westerfield's activities the weekend Danielle disappeared. Judge Mudd instructed the camera crew not to film or photograph Neal in any way at any time.

"Good morning Mr. Westerfield."

"Good morning."

"I assume you don't want to be here."

"Correct."

Neal informed the court he was one day shy of his nineteenth birthday and since his parents divorced ten years ago had split his time between his parents, spending two weeks every month with his father and two with his mother who also lived in Poway. Neal was a freshman at San Diego State University and drove a 1987 Dodge Aries. Before Danielle disappeared, he did not know and had never seen any of the Van Dams.

Neal discussed the motorhome and recalled the process of dropping his father off at the RV before they would drive back to the house in separate vehicles. When asked about the desert vehicles, Neal disclosed they had a 1998 Yamaha Banshee and a 92 Honda 250x four wheeler as well as a dune buggy.

"Where would you go?"

"We would either go to the beach, out to the desert, or further out to the desert to Glamis. We went to the state park in Borrego Springs most often."

"What would you do at Borrego, the activities when you'd get there?"

"We would hike, go for bike rides, sit in the sun."

When asked if they ever drove to Glamis without the sand vehicles, Neal replied, "I remember six years ago going without the toys." The shortest time they had every spent in Glamis was two nights.

"What would you do at the beach?"

"Walk on the beach, go swimming."

"What would your father do down at the beach?"

"Sit in the sun, go on bike rides."

Before road trips in the motorhome, Neal and his father would clean the inside, replace the water, and pack it with supplies.

"How much in advance of the trip would you do this?"

"Anywhere from a couple of days and a couple of hours.

"Have you ever been to the desert on Super Bowl weekend?"

"No," Neal answered and said they usually stayed home and watched the game.

When asked if he had ever seen Danielle Van Dam near

the motorhome, Neal replied, "no."

Neal explained the wash system and said they usually turned in at the fourth or fifth wash, which was a good distance from the crowds that were loud. They had never traveled farther than the twelfth wash. Although a couple of years ago they had gone to Borrego and Glamis on the same weekend, they had only gone to Borrego to dump the waste from the motorhome. They never camped at both locations on the same trip. When they returned home from trips, Neal and his father parked the RV in front of the house before unloading and cleaning the inside.

"Now, sir, I'd like to direct your attention to Super Bowl weekend, February 1st of this year. Have you paid any attention to the media coverage since the trial started?"

"I've been trying not to."

"Have you seen any of the media coverage regarding the computer use in your father's house?"

"I've been trying to avoid it."

On Friday, February 1, Neal attended school until 3:00, drove to his mother's house, then went to his friend's house for the night. They ate dinner and played video games on their big screen TV until 3:00 the next morning.

"Do you remember what games you were playing?

"*House of The Dead*."

The following morning, Neal woke around eleven and went back to his mother's house where his older sister, Lisa, was getting ready for work. When his mother returned that afternoon, she asked him to go with her to his father's house to make sure the front door was locked.

"Was it your understanding, sir, that the information had basically come through your sister to your mom?"

"Yes."

"What did you do when you got there?"

"I went into the house to pick up some things and make sure the door was locked and my mother noticed there was a blockade in the street and had inquired what it was about."

"Was the front door locked or unlocked?"

"It was locked."

After grabbing some school books, Neal left the house. As he was closing the door, his mother handed him a flier for Danielle, which he put on a short dividing wall just inside the front door. On Sunday, Neal watched the Super Bowl with his uncle.

"Were you supposed to switch that Sunday, Super Bowl Sunday?"

"My father informed me he was going to be out of town that Sunday and to simply come over on Monday."

"Did he tell you where he was going?"

"He said the desert, I believe."

"When did he tell you he was going?"

"The week before."

On the night of Sunday, February 3, Neal spent the night at his mother's house and on Monday went to school. He left school at 3:00 and drove to his father's house where he found him in his office on the computer. After playing video games for a couple of hours in the extra upstairs bedroom, Neal left the house and ran a few errands. When Neal returned around 6:00, his father was gone.

"When was the next time you saw your father?"

"That evening. About midnight."

"When you returned to the house, what did you do?"

Neal recalled checking his email, eating some food, and playing video games. Regarding the computer set up in Mr. Westerfield's house, Neal revealed there was an eight year old Gateway computer in his bedroom he had purchased from his father two years before. The computer contained numerous files and programs his father had used including a digital rolodex that contained numerous business contacts.

"Did it have internet access?"

"No," Neal replied.

In addition to the computer in his bedroom, Neal owned a laptop previously used by his father who had given it to him about a year before. He primarily used the laptop for a C++ programming application for school.

In his father's office there were two Hewlett Packards. One he used for work, the other he used for the internet and contained his digital rolodex.

"Was there a bookshelf in that bedroom?"

"Yes."

"What types of things were kept in that bookshelf?"

"Books, software books, engineering manuals, the actual software as in CDs, and tools."

"Whose stuff?"

"His."

"Is that where he kept all of his work materials?"

"Yes."

Neal often used the office computers to access the internet so he could check his email and work on school projects that required online access.

"Have there been occasions when you've accessed pornography at his house?"

"Yes."

"How did you do that?"

"Either through a link through my email or using a search engine."

Neal discussed receiving spam emails from pornography sites and discussed his inability to stop most spam emails from reaching his inbox.

"Are you able to tell us what types of stuff you were looking at through that computer?"

"Japanese drawn pictures, some, I don't know, big breasted women. I don't remember."

"Is there a name for this Japanese art or animation?"

"There are two names. One is Anime, the other is Hentai." Neal explained that Anime was a style of animation from Japan that was not pornographic. Hentai was a style of Japanese animation that was pornographic.

"Have you ever downloaded any of that material?"

"No."

"Do you know if your father had any pornography in the house?"

"Yes. I found some on his computer and I found some on disks in his office. I was looking for one of my games which was stored on the bookshelf and I found it behind some books."

Neal recalled finding the CDs and zip drives, and revealed he had looked at a small portion or the images.

"Did some of them appear to be males attacking a female?"

"I never came across any."

Judge Mudd jumped in. "We're going to go ahead and take the lunch break. Have a pleasant lunch."

Following the lunch break, before the jury returned, Judge Mudd chastised the media. "Ladies and gentleman of the media. Not since this case was assigned to me on the very first day when I described a tsunami of people rushing to this courtroom have I seen a feeding frenzy by the media as I have this noon hour in their efforts to photograph Neal Westerfield. It is absolutely appalling to this court. I have prided myself in my entire career of having my courtroom accessible to the media. This case is changing all of that and this conduct is not going to help.

"The young man and his family have requested that the court honor his right to privacy. I don't know what's so hard about that to understand. The court has exercised that very same right with juveniles and adults who have made the same request, law enforcement that have made that same request. Neal Westerfield is entitled, if he so elects, not to be filmed, not to be shown on television.

"Now, Neal Westerfield has been filmed, and it was shown on television it has been reported to this court in violation of the court's order. I have been assured by the person that took it that it will not see the light of day. Leave this man alone and don't film him. This conduct is so detrimental to access that it is unbelievable the impact it may have not only on this case, but in future cases as well. If the media is so concerned about their right to access, they need only look at their conduct in this case to know why many judges will not tolerate any of this at all. Having said that, let's get the witness. Turn everything off."

The jury returned to their seats and Neal Westerfield returned to the stand.

"When we quit for lunch I think you had told us about the media you had found in your father's office. Did you copy that to any other computers?"

"Yes. To the one in my room. The gateway."

"Did you ever look at it after you copied it there?"

"Yes."

Mr. Dusek moved back to the night of Monday, February 4.

"On that date, did you access any pornography?"

"I don't remember doing so," Neal answered before discussing screen shots Mr. Feldman had shown him that Mr. Feldman thought indicated he had.

"And he told you what they proved?"

"Yes."

"Do you recall accessing any pornography on the 4th of February?"

"No."

"In the materials that you have accessed over time, were there any small children, elementary school age children?"

"No. They looked all to be adult women."

Jumping back to the night of Monday, Februrary 4, Mr. Dusek asked, "about what time did you see your father again?"

Neal recalled being asleep when he heard loud banging on the front door around midnight. He dressed, walked downstairs and opened the door where an officer instructed him to leave the premises. When he asked if he could take his school work, the officer said no. After grabbing his keys, shoes, and wallet, Neal exited the house and found his father in the driveway talking to detectives.

"The information that you provided us here today about finding the loose media with the pornography in your father's office, did you tell law enforcement about that?"

"Yes."

"All right. Thank you, sir."

"Cross examination?" Judge Mudd asked.

"No questions. Thank you, your honor."

Judge Mudd dismissed the witness and the state recalled Forensic Examiner James Watkins who worked at the Regional Computer Forensics Laboratory and had previously testified about his investigation of Mr. Westerfield's computers.

Mr. Clarke showed him the three page document listing the Internet Explorer history of the office computer on February 4 between 3:50 and 8:29pm.

After verifying the clock was accurate, Mr. Clarke asked, "were any pornographic websites visited during that period?"

"No, there were not."

Mr. Clarke then asked if Mr. Watkins had found on the office computer any videos labeled with the word "Attack." Mr. Watkins confirmed he had.

"Objection, your honor. This is improper rebuttal."

"It's foundational. I will allow it."

Mr. Watkins revealed he had found a folder called "Attack" that contained numerous video files; including the videos shown to the jury that were located on the CDs and zip drives.

"Can you describe for us where they were located?"

"The main folder was My Documents, then there was a subfolder Spectrum Files, and then a subfolder below that called Stuff For Files."

In the Spectrum Files folder, Mr. Watkins found a variety of work related documents that included letters and spreadsheets related to Mr. Westerfield's business Spectrum Design. Within the folder labeled Stuff For Files he found the Attack videos.

Mr. Watkins then explained for the jury that Windows Media Player was the program used to watch videos on Windows based operating systems. When a user opens the program, a history of all the clips previously viewed appears.

From the Stuff For Files folder, there were ten "Attack" videos as well a video labeled "Baby 010" and "Ass Rape 1." Each video had been watched been watched between one and five times. These numbers included only the video files found on the hard drive, not the files on the CDs and zip drives.

Mr. Clarke then moved on to the digital rolodex system on the office computer where Mr. Watkins recalled finding a number of cards with work related contact information that included phone numbers and email addresses as well as twenty-nine cards that each contained a website link, the majority of which were pornographic. Each card contained the web address and a specific label. The labels included, "Young 1s," and "Too Young." The websites included "Lolita.com, YoungVirgins.nu, and those sorts of names."

"Thank you. I have no further questions."

Mr. Feldman started his cross examination focusing on the afternoon of Monday February 4. He noted that Neal had checked his email in which he had received a message from "PinkForFree.com." that contained a link to the site.

After confirming Mr. Watkins had reviewed the testimony of the defense's computer forensic expert, Mr. Lawson, Mr. Feldman asked, "did you forensically determine whether or not Mr. Lawson was making use of EnCase?"

"He wasn't making a proper use of EnCase, but he used it."

Referring to a meeting Mr. Watkins and other investigators had with Neal and his mother sometime before the trial started, Mr. Feldman asked, "and it's true Neal told you, did he not, that he went to the office at about 5:00 o'clock to look at porn?"

"What he said was he wasn't sure whether he did or didn't."

"Screen captures specifically indicate, do they not, that at 4:40pm Lesbian Bordello was accessed, is that right?

"No. The image, Lesbian Bordello, is actually embedded in one of the emails. All it indicates is that he looked at the email."

Moving on to the Windows Media Player, Mr. Feldman pointed out that Mr. Watkins could not determine who watched the "Attack" videos or when, only that the last time one was accessed was on November 18, 2001.

"Did you ask Neal Westerfield in the presence of the four other men and his mother whether or not he was viewing pornography?"

"I believe Mr. Dusek did."

Throughout his lengthy cross examination, Mr. Feldman bounced from one topic to another and back, at times misstating the evidence, possibly confused by the computer data, but at times seemingly over complicating the issue on purpose. He spent significant time pouring through the nonpornographic sites Neal did visit that afternoon, asking for detailed explanations at every step. Despite his attempts to prove Neal had been looking at porn during that time, Mr. Feldman only confirmed again he had not.

"Now, the internet history that you generated, you just went out into the computer and did what, printed out the history?"

"I found a file that maintains a history and then printed it out."

"If somebody wanted to alter the history, could they go into that file and delete out some of the entries?"

"It would be very difficult to do."

"Is it the case that one who had the knowledge, who might be described as a computer nerd, hypothetically, could go into the history file and delete out an address?"

"Objection." Mr. Clarke said. "Argumentative."

"Overruled. You can answer."

"I suppose it would be possible."

Mr. Feldman continued to stumble through a prolonged cross examination with irrelevant questions about the route emails travel, how email time stamps are determined, which links in the internet history were associated to Neal's email, and how he learned Neal had access to the office computers.

Judge Mudd intervened a few minutes before 4:00. "It's time for the break so obviously we're not going to conclude this witness today. Ladies and gentleman, have a pleasant evening, we'll see you at 9:00am."

DAY 22

After a prolonged proceeding not made part of the public record, the jury returned.

"Welcome back, ladies and gentleman. At least you know the reason for the delay. All right, Mr. Feldman, you may continue."

With Mr. Watkins back on the stand, Mr. Feldman continued his poor attempt to show Neal had been looking at pornography on the afternoon of Monday February 4, as if further humiliating Mr. Westerfield's son could somehow separate Mr. Westerfield from the child pornography found on his computer.

"In your review of Mr. Lawson's report, you noticed various GIF and JPG files captured by Mr. Lawson showing access to pornography websites on February 4, isn't that right?"

"No, sir."

Mr. Feldman proceed to slither his way through another convoluted inquiry that focusing on a variety of extraneous topics including email headers, whether an email could be received before it was sent, how long it takes an email to reach its destination, the difference between Greenwich mean time and Pacific standard time, deleted files, and the file names of certain internet related system files.

"Is it correct, sir, that it's your testimony that PinkForFree.com was not accessed on February the 4th?"

"Objection. Asked and answered, also beyond the scope."

"Overruled. You can answer."

"It was not accessed."

Before concluding his exhausting cross examination Mr. Feldman repeated the fact that on numerous occasions Neal had checked his email before viewing pornography.

"Your honor, at this time I have no further questions."

After Mr. Watson was excused, Mr. Dusek called

Forensic Anthropologist Dr. William Rodriguez. Since 1990, Dr. Rodriguez had worked as a Forensic Anthropologist and Chief of Special Investigations for the Armed Forces Medical Examiner at the Walter Read Medical Center where there were twenty-two different pathology departments. His responsibilities included examining very decomposed, skeletalized, burned, or fragmented remains to determine identification and cause of death.

Dr. Rodriguez had examined bodies from all over the world and in every possible climate, and had worked on many high profile cases including war crimes in Kosovo and soldiers who died during the Gulf War. He was a certified member of the American Board of Forensic Anthropology, where he had also served as a vice president, and was a member of the National Association of Medical Examiners. He had taught extensively for law enforcement, students, medical examiners, and coroners, and had written numerous articles about forensic anthropology, particularly human decomposition patterns, postmortem taphonomy, and the process of fossilization. Because forensic anthropologists frequently studied decomposed remains, they are experts at the decomposition process.

After walking the jury through a basic lesson on the process of decomposition and mummification, Dr. Rodriguez confirmed he had reviewed the transcripts of Mr. Faulkner, Dr. Haskell, and Dr. Blackbourne's testimonies as well as the autopsy report, multiple investigative reports, photos of the recovery site and autopsy, and weather data from several nearby weather stations. He had also visited the site where Danielle's body was discovered.

When asked his impression of the photos he had viewed of Danielle's body Dr. Rodriguez said what struck him most was the extreme level of mummification. "The hands are very shriveled. You have blackening of the tissues, and taken into account this is a little girl, we're not talking about a full adult body, which should take much longer to mummify."

Dr. Rodriguez continued. "In looking at the weather conditions for the area, that was a key indicator this was a very rapid mummification that we know occurs with small individuals." Regarding how long the mummification process might have taken, Dr. Rodriguez said, "it can occur very fast, it can occur within twenty-four hours."

Mr. Dusek then asked if the body being fed upon and opened up by scavengers would make it more ideal for flies and insects. Dr. Rodriguez confirmed that would release decompositional odors and provide insects with a source of nutrition. Although insects in some cases do feed on the eyes and inside the nose and mouth, those areas are not preferred if open wounds are available. He also discussed the possibility that insect eggs laid in the hours after Danielle was left in the desert might have been eaten by other animals.

"If the ants and beetles and other animals eat or remove the fly larva and eggs, does that have an impact on estimating through insects how long the body has been there open to insects?"

Dr. Rodriguez said it did.

"Is it scientifically predictable how quickly a scavenging animal will show up on a body and start feeding?"

"No, it's not. I've seen cases where human remains have laid out for a very extensive period of time in a heavily wooded environment that is very infested with all types of animals and never be touched."

"The fact that the golf course is irrigated, does that have any impact on the mummification process on this child where she was located?"

Dr. Rodriguez answered that it did not, confirming that watering the golf course could not have postponed mummification.

"If that body were transported in a dry environment either inside a motorhome or in a storage area, would that begin the mummification process?"

"Yes, it could."

Mr. Dusek moved on to how determining time of death is an imperfect and complicated process with numerous variables and no perfect answer.

As advanced as science is today, Dr. Rodriguez explained, "there is no precise, accurate method for determining time of death or that postmortem interval. If someone tells you that, they were either there at the scene or committed the murder."

Mr. Feldman stood up. "Your honor, motion to strike as speculative. No foundation, it's a pathology issue."

Judge Mudd overruled his objection.

"Why can't we precisely set it?"

Dr. Rodriguez discussed the numerous variables involved, particularly for a body left in the desert and said, "it is not an exact science and so we use our best estimate, based on the scientific methodologies, to simply make an estimate, what is our best scientific estimate."

"Ladies and gentleman, we're going to take a lunch break." After the jury exited the room, Judge Mudd dismissed the gallery. "At this time, the court and counsel need to discuss a security matter. The courtroom will be closed and all the television and media coverage will be terminated."

Following the lunch break, Dr. Rodriguez explained that entomologists estimate a time period from when the "insects inhabited the body to the time at the point they were collected and analyzed. When we look at the insect estimate, that is only telling us when those insects inhabited the body. It gives us just a minimum time period."

Mr. Dusek then mentioned the number of nights the temperature had dropped to frost levels and asked how that affected insect activity. Dr. Rodriguez explained that even in warm temperatures and with open wounds, flies did not like cold bodies.

"After you reviewed all the materials and based upon your experience and background, were you able to come to an estimation of the post-mortem interval?"

"I did." Dr. Rodriguez estimated, based on the gross physical changes and environmental factors, that Danielle had been laying in the desert "approximately four to six weeks." Dr. Rodriguez explained how the longer a body was exposed to the elements, the harder determining time of death became do to the increased number of variables.

"Again, it's an estimate. There is no accurate method. I'm relying solely on experience to provide a window of possibility."

"Thank you, doctor."

Mr. Feldman started his cross examination by noting Dr. Rodriguez was not a medical doctor, forensic pathologist, or forensic entomologist, then highlighted the differences in San Diego weather with the weather in Indiana where he received most of his training. He then reminded the court that Dr. Blackbourne, who had performed the autopsy and had decades of experience with bodies in San Diego had determined the post-mortem interval was ten days.

Discussing an additional pathology report written by Dr. Cyril Wecht, Mr. Feldman noted that, "he too, agreed with Dr. Blackbourne that the post-mortem interval on this case, based upon his review of virtually the same information you had, was ten days, agreed?"

"He reported ten days to four weeks," Dr. Rodriguez clarified.

"Ten days was his start point, is that correct?"

"That was his minimum."

Regarding Dr. Rodriguez's estimated time of death of four to six weeks, Mr. Feldman asked, "would your opinion change any if you knew there were live witnesses that said this is completely impossible?"

"I'm just giving my estimate based on the mummification how long a body could have taken to get to that particular stage."

"You told Mr. Dusek that one of the variables that you consider in evaluating the post-mortem interval is entomology, right?"

"That is correct."

"What you're proposing today, though, is that somehow the natural evolution of things got interrupted by virtue of a mummification that occurred at the earliest twenty-four hours post mortem."

"That's correct," Dr. Rodriguez answered before discussing the various factors that helped form his conclusion, including environment and weather.

"You've told us that mummification could set in within seven days or less, is that a fair statement?"

"Yes."

"So, it's fair to say, is it not, that you would not disagree that the body could have been laid out say from the 18th?"

Dr. Rodriguez answered, "no."

"Based on the mummification process, based on the weather, based on the rainfall, isn't that true?"

"That's incorrect."

"Now, does the absence of the Santa Anas between at least the 1st and 6th in any manner affect your opinion regarding when mummification occurred or the postmortem interval?"

"Not really."

"Isn't it true that the blow flies are less attracted to postmortem incisions than to natural body openings?"

"Not necessarily."

Mr. Feldman continued his strategy of lengthy, convoluted cross examinations by prodding Dr. Rodriguez on a large number of peripheral topics including how freezing bodies decompose, the feeding preferences of blow flies, and if mummification preserves stab wounds. When the time arrived, Judge Mudd intervened.

"We are going to go ahead and take the afternoon break. Before we do, however, I need to talk to you ladies and gentleman about the matter we discussed this morning. As a result, I'm going to conclude the public portion of this, including the media. We will be back in court at 2:45 when I anticipate making a statement to the proper folks." Judge Mudd's subsequent conversation with the jury was not made part of the public record.

Following the afternoon break, before the jury was invited to return, Judge Mudd spoke directly to the media. "Ladies and gentleman of the media. Yesterday afternoon the court experienced a serious breach in the integrity of this trial. A person who has been described, but not yet identified, followed two of the jurors in this case to where they park their cars and wrote down their license numbers. At this point in time, I don't know who's responsible for this, but one can well imagine that with the media coverage we have had where the source of that individual may lie.

"My one and only concern in this case is that Mr. Westerfield gets a fair trial before twelve jurors who are going to make a decision based solely on the evidence they see and hear in this courtroom, unintimidated by any outside source. I like to think that the people in here on a daily basis are not the source of the problem, but at this point in time I don't know who this individual is. I don't know what his motivation is, but I am telling you right now one thing; if it happens again, the television camera goes off."

Judge Mudd advised those in the media present to police their own. "It is in your best interest to do something about it because I can assure you if there is another incident of this kind, it's all shut off. All right, let's get the jury in."

Mr. Feldman resumed his lengthy cross examination by

continuing his approach of suffocating the jury with distracting details. He discussed wind conditions, how the nearby tree effected decomposition, the vegetation under the body, the eating habits of scavenging animals, whether blow flies are more attracted to natural orifices or open wounds, the weights of the organs in the body at autopsy, and whether ants feeding on larvae actually remove all the larvae thus disrupting postmortem interval estimates. Each step of the way Mr. Feldman asked numerous general questions that did little, if anything, to dispute the possibility that Danielle's body had been in the desert longer than the two weeks the defense had claimed, and had likely been in the desert since shortly after her abduction.

"Is it your testimony, sir, that you've rendered a guesstimate as to the postmortem interval based upon your review of the records, but which fundamentally really puts the time of death at a time when it was impossible for Danielle Van Dam to have been dead?"

"Objection. Argumentative, compound."

"Sustained."

"No further questions."

In his redirect of Dr. Rodriguez, Mr. Dusek reviewed the specifics of his timeline.

"Because we have testimony in this case that Danielle Van Dam was put to bed on February 1st, how do you correlate that with your opinion that the time of death could have been from four to six weeks from the time of recovery, which would at least some of those times predate the last time she was seen alive?"

Dr. Rodriguez explained that his estimation was based solely on how long a body in her condition would have likely been exposed to the elements given the environmental and weather conditions. "Looking at the postmortem changes, this is what we would expect a body to look like in that four to six week period."

"Based upon that, does that mean she could not have been

killed on February 1st, 2nd, 3rd, 4th, 5th, or 6th?"

"That would open the possibility to any of those days, yes."

"And your opinion does not preclude that possibility, does it?"

"That's correct."

When asked how the repeated nights with frost would have affected insect activity, Dr. Rodriguez said, "certainly these cooler temperatures can have some delayed effect in their development. Adults are not going to deposit their eggs on a body that has frost on it. It's too cold. It's not a hospitable environment."

"Thank you, Doctor."

"All right, Doctor, thank you very much for coming in and disrupting your plans."

After dismissing the witness, Judge Mudd informed the jury they would not have trial on Monday due to scheduling issues with the prosecution's final professional witness. "Okay, ladies and gentleman, I'm going to close the courtroom so we can discuss some more about what we've talked about earlier. At this time, we're going to close the public section of the trial including the media involvement as a result of the concerns I've previously discussed.

After a long proceeding not made part of the public record, Judge Mudd excused the jury and planned to meet with the counselors on early Monday to discuss jury instructions. "All right. We'll be in recess until Monday at 8:30."

DAY 23

On Tuesday July 30, Judge Mudd welcomed the jury back before providing an update on where the trial stood. "First of all, of course, we all know the Padres haven't won a game since you were last here, which is rather tragic. As I explained to you last week, the closer we get to the end of this case it seems like the harder it is to get to the end because of scheduling conflicts involving the witnesses." Judge Mudd informed the jury there would be no court on Wednesday, but a full day on Thursday. He believed the trial would end on Monday.

At that time, Judge Mudd had not decided whether or not the jury would be sequestered during deliberation and noted that multiple jurors had requested they be allowed to go home. "As of right now my plan is to have you in deliberation without sequestration, but I'm letting you know that is an option I may or may not impose. Obviously, you will be the first to know.

"In addition to that, we've had this case up in Orange County that has gotten a great deal of publicity. It has taken on a life of its own as so many cases do in our society today including national television and it is permeating the media. Many of the kinds of things that are involved in that case may or may not appear to be similar here, but the fact is that the case is not similar in any way, shape, or form, nor are the issues, the personalities, or anything else. So, unless you really need to read about that case up there, I suggest you move on to other things. That brings us to what I thought were very safe television stations for you to watch; the *Discovery Channel* and the *Nature Channel*. All right, Mr. Clarke."

Mr. Clarke recalled Detective Maura Parga who had previously testified about her initial interview with Mr. Westerfield outside his home on the morning of Monday, February 4. Mr. Clarke showed Det. Parga the still images taken outside of Mr. Westerfield's while the search warrant was being served. In the images, she was wearing a white jacket along with a shirt that appeared orange. Det. Parga described the image as, "distorted."

"What was the color of the shirt you were wearing that day?"

"It's red. It's a red instructor's shirt." Det. Parga explained the shirt was used in her role with the mounted units and was red so instructors were easily visible to trainees riding horses.

"In the last several days, were you asked to provide some of your shirts to the San Diego Police Department laboratory?"

"Yes."

Mr. Clarke presented for the jury four red polo shirts belonging to Det. Parga.

"In February of this year, Detective Parga, did you even own an orange shirt?"

"No."

"Thank you."

In his cross examination, Mr. Feldman first explained what a screen capture was then asked if the image of her had been taken before or after the house was searched by the dogs. She did not know.

After pointing out Mr. Frazee and his dog in one of the images, Mr. Feldman asked, "do you recall whether or not he was wearing an orange shirt?"

"Yes. It's a search and rescue shirt."

"It looks like you're wearing, it's kind of a light blue shirt. Is that close?"

"No. It's a cotton jacket, actually."

"What color is it?"

"White."

"So, our color's a little off in the photo, is that right?"

"I would say so, yes."

Before concluding his cross examination, Mr. Feldman noted that none of the officers in any of the still images taken from the video were wearing gloves.

"Detective, thank you for coming in," Judge Mudd said and allowed her take two of her shirts on the way out.

The prosecution next recalled Homicide Detective Brian Le Ribeus who recalled collecting orange shirts from several of the individuals visible in the news videos including the Sherriff's K-9 unit and Mr. Frazee, the scent dog handler. He also collected a dog vest. Det. LeRibeus delivered the items to Criminalist Tanya Dulaney at the crime lab who was Mr. Clarke's next witness.

Ms. Dulaney reported she had analyzed the fibers taken from each of the items collected by Det. LeRibeus and conducted the same examination she had performed on the previous fibers. She photographed the fibers, analyzed them under a microscope and infrared spectrometer, and determined their composition.

When asked if any of the items were acrylic, Ms. Dulaney answered, "no," and confirmed that none of the red or orange fibers collected matched any of the fibers found on Danielle or in Mr. Westerfield's house or motorhome.

After confirming only one dog vest had been tested, Mr. Feldman concluded his cross examination.

For the prosecution, Mr. Clarke next recalled Sgt. William Holmes who remembered on the night Danielle's body was recovered, the Fire Department had raised with a truck ladder a large light that illuminated the scene. While searching the body and surrounding area he had also used a flashlight.

"When you looked at the head, did you observe any maggots in or about the head area?"

"I saw one in one of the eye sockets." Other than that one, Sgt. Holmes had not observed any maggots in the ears, nose, or mouth. He had seen numerous maggots, "where the chest and abdominal area had been."

"Did you note any ants at the scene?"

"Yes. There were ants around her body."

"How close were the ants to the body?" Mr. Clarke asked.

"Inches."

"Thank you. No further questions."

Mr. Feldman started his cross by unsuccessfully attempting to imply that other investigators had observed more than one maggot in the area of her head before emphasizing that Sgt. Holmes was not an expert in maggots or forensic entomology.

"It was your idea to bring Faulkner in, is that right?"

"Yes, sir, it was."

"And that's because you recognized early on in the case that it would be necessary to evaluate the entomologic evidence to assist you in determining time of death, isn't that right?"

"Not time of death. How long she had been there."

"You brought in David Faulkner to help you determine how long Danielle Van Dam had been at the Dehesa site, is that right?"

"Objection. I think we're beyond the scope at this point."

Judge Mudd agreed and added, "and it's been asked and answered repeatedly. Sustained. Move on."

"Who was present with you when you first saw the bugs around Danielle Van Dam?"

As Sgt. Holmes answered, Mr. Feldman was trying to bring up a photo of the recovery site on the large monitor and instead raised a photo of Danielle's body. Mr. Clarke and Mr. Feldman exchanged words not recorded by the court reporter as the Van Dams left the room, crying.

"Your honor, I'm trying to find-"

"I understand."

"Sorry, Judge."

Mr. Feldman located the exhibit he was searching for and reviewed with Sgt. Holmes how the scene had been secured and processed.

"And just with regard to the issue of the presence of maggots, you heard Det. Collins testify that there were maggots in the area, didn't you?

"Objection. Hearsay, your honor."

"Sustained."

"So, you're not sure whether or not there were ants in the area of the body on the night of the recovery, that's a fair statement, correct?"

"I wouldn't say that's a fair statement."

Mr. Feldman again proceeded on a long, disjointed inquiry that focused on a wide variety of peripheral issues that bore little relevance to the substance of Sgt. Holmes' testimony. Finally, he returned to the ants.

"Did you see any ants carrying maggots?"

"No, sir."

"Thank you very much. Nothing further.

Following the morning break, the state called its last witness of the trial, Dr. Madison Lee Goff, Chair of the Forensic Science Department at Chaminade University of Honolulu. Dr. Goff had earned a bachelor's degree in Zoology in 1966 before obtaining a master's degree in biology at California State University. In 1977, he earned a doctorate in entomology from the University of Hawaii where he had worked in the Entomology Department for the past twenty years. He was a member of the Entomological Society of America, the American Academy of Forensic Sciences, the National Association of Medical Examiners, and the American Board of Forensic Entomology.

In addition to his teaching at the university, Dr. Goff had instructed classes at the FBI as well as numerous other law enforcement groups, and had consulted for Honolulu's medical examiner. In his approximately twenty-five court appearances, Dr. Goff had testified on behalf of both the prosecution and defense. Prior to testifying about Danielle Van Dam, Dr. Goff had reviewed the crime scene and autopsy reports as well as the reports written by David Faulkner and Dr. Neal Haskel, had viewed the photographs, and had analyzed the weather data from seven different locations

After providing the jury another lesson on the science of cadaver flies, Dr. Goff discussed the multiple predators who feed on maggots including beetles and ants. He recalled a study in which a pig cadaver was placed near an ant colony. "These ants were so voracious coming onto the pig, looking for the eggs, looking for the maggots, they pick up the maggots, they pick up the eggs and carry them back to the colony. They were so effective that they actually managed to completely eliminate the blow flies for a period of six or seven days. By that time, the carcass had dried out."

Dr. Goff said that once the body became dry, flies had no place to colonize because they required a habitat with soft tissue. In addition to ants, small scavengers like raccoons, feral cats, and rats can consume maggots as they remove flesh, which also depletes the source and increases the rate a dead body dries.

Moving on to the weather, Dr. Goff explained his process of determining accumulated degree hours to estimate how long it would take the collected larvae to reach their stage of development.

Mr. Dusek asked, "based upon your calculations with the data from Singing Hills, did you make calculations as to how long the insects had been on the body?"

Dr. Goff explained how he calculated the temperatures and the accumulated hours each day starting on the day the body was recovered and working backwards. "Based on the data from Singing Hills, this would mean that the body was available anywhere from the 2nd of February. Minimum time would be on the 12th of February."

When reviewing the weather data from Brown Field, Dr. Goff reached a similar conclusion plus or minus a day. Dr. Goff then discussed the stages of growth in maggots as well as the limitations of using insects to determine how long a body had been exposed to the elements.

"You've told us that the starting point is when eggs are laid on a receptive body, is that correct?"

"That's correct."

Are you able to tell us how long that body had been present before the eggs were laid?"

Dr. Goff responded, "no."

For much of the morning, Dr. Goff explained in precise detail his methodology and discussed how his differed from the other entomologists who had testified. At noon, Judge Mudd initiated the lunch break.

After another round of questions regarding Dr. Goff's scientific process, Mr. Dusek asked about mummification.

"To me, this means a body where you've had a significant amount of water loss, drying out, start seeing the skin become hardened, somewhat shriveled. Typically, you see this where it's either very hot or very cold and it's very dry."

"How receptive is a body in that condition to the flies and the laying of the eggs?"

"Objection. Foundation. Beyond this witness's expertise."

"Overruled."

"Request to take him on voir dire," Mr. Feldman asked, referring to the process in which an attorney may question a witness about their background before determining if they are a qualified expert.

After Judge Mudd allowed the request, Mr. Feldman emphasized Dr. Goff was not a forensic anthropologist or forensic pathologist, had never specifically studied those fields, and had never participated in a decomposition study involving actual humans. Mr. Feldman repeated his objection. Judge Mudd overruled.

Mr. Dusek continued. "What effect does a mummified body have on the receptive nature for flies to deposit their eggs?"

"The natural body openings, particularly the head, are not attractive to the flies for oviposition. They want to be some place that's going to be moist where maggots are able to adequately feed and complete their development."

"If an animal came by and started eating the stomach or chest region and opened her up, would that change the receptiveness of this body to insect activity?"

"Objection. Assumes facts not in evidence."

"Overruled."

"If a carnivore or scavenger came through and did open up the body, then I would certainly anticipate that the flies would begin to exploit this as an alternate portal of entry to get into the abdomen and deposit their eggs."

"Then if an animal came by and started eating the stomach or chest region and opened her up, would that change the receptiveness of this body to insect activity?"

Feeling his last line of defense slipping away, Mr. Feldman objected. "Assumes facts not in evidence."

"Overruled."

"If the internal tissues were still moist and a carnivore or scavenger came through and did open up the body, then I would certainly anticipate that the flies would begin to exploit this as an alternate portal of entry to get into the abdomen and deposit their eggs."

"Based upon your experience and what you've determined here in this case, are you able to tell us when this little girl was killed?"

"No, I cannot. I am an entomologist. Basically, I'm analyzing a period of insect activity on the body. My science does not deal with estimation of actual time of death. We are dealing with the estimation of the period of insect activity on the body, not the postmortem interval."

"Based on your assessment of the insects and your knowledge of the field, are you able to say that our victim, Danielle Van Dam, was not dead from February 1st through February 12th?"

"I would defer that to a pathologist or forensic anthropologist."

"Thank you, sir."

Mr. Feldman started his cross examination by referencing a speech Dr. Goff had given at Chico State University and asking if he had stated, "when the insects go into the body, we look at those with the most advanced development. Then we work backwards to measure the time of death?"

"Partially," Dr. Goff answered.

"And you've written time and again that it's the understanding within the forensic entomologic community that once a body is deceased, the flies are there within minutes to hours, that's one of the basic premises of forensic entomology, isn't that true?"

"That's true. Assuming there are no barriers to their accessing remains."

"And in this case, you're aware of no barriers to the remains, isn't that true?"

"I don't know of any physical barriers to the remains," Dr. Goff conceded.

Mr. Feldman then launched a series of questions attacking Dr. Goff's credibility. He revealed Dr. Goff was a friend of David Faulkner's and had full confidence in his abilities, revealed Dr. Goff had written in books and spoke in lectures that insects could, in fact, estimate time of death, and sited a book in which Dr. Goff claimed using mean temperature readings was as reliable as using accumulated degree hours. Dr. Goff also had previously testified that the weather data from Brown Field was appropriate.

"You never inspected the evidence in this case, correct?"

"That's true."

"How often do you testify without inspecting the evidence in a case, sir?"

"Very rarely. Maybe twice before."

"Between the two, it's your opinion, is it not, that a forensic pathologist has a much greater degree of qualification to render an opinion concerning time of death than does an anthropologist, isn't that right?"

"Objection."

"Sustained."

"You've written time and again that it's the understanding within the forensic entomologic community that once a body is deceased the flies are there within minutes to hours. That's one of the basic premises of forensic entomology, isn't that true?"

"That's true."

"Your conversations with Mr. Dusek concerning whether or not carnivores would have come in, that was all speculative, wasn't it? Because you have no evidence that's what occurred, true?"

"Looking at those photographs, the impression which I received was it was very similar to carnivore activity that I had observed on pigs that we used in studies at the FBI academy in Quantico."

"Now, if it's the case that in your view the initial onset would be on the 9th and it's true based on your writings that the bugs get to the fresh body from minutes to hours, she could have been dead as early as the ninth, isn't that true?"

"Yes."

Mr. Feldman conducted a long, detail focused examination of Dr. Goff that started with a thorough review of the growth process of maggots and continued with questions about the length of instar stages and the temperature of maggot masses. Dr. Goff revealed that many of the maggots collected were at their maximum third instar size and were almost ready to become flies.

"Now, if it's the case that in your view the initial onset would be on the 9th and it's true based on your writing that the bugs get to the fresh body from minutes to hours, she could have been dead as early as the 9th, isn't that true? In other words, she could have been killed on the 9th?"

"Objection. Beyond the-"

"Sustained."

Mr. Felman moved on to how Dr. Goff used weather data in his analysis and Dr. Goff explained the mathematical equation for daily accumulated degree hours, which was the thermal unit used to convert temperature to time.

"If I understand you correctly, you're telling us that in order for the mass or the bugs to develop to the prepuparial stage they have to aggregate accumulate degree hours in the number of 2492.1, correct?"

"That's correct."

"However, in your own work and in your own evaluation, you only accumulated 2117.4 hours, isn't that true?"

"Yes."

"Did you have enough accumulated degree hours to account for a stage that was collected?"

"Yes."

"You did use Haskell's data on February 9th, is that right?"

"That's correct."

"Can you please tell me on February 9th what was your conclusion as to his number? It was 55. Could you please run the numbers that are Haskell's and tell us what the accurate number?"

Dr. Goff complied. Surely knowing the answer, Mr.

Feldman asked, "what number did you get?"

"Well, unfortunately it appears I made an error in addition."

"Whoops," Mr. Feldman responded.

"A big one."

"What does that mean?"

"It means that using what I have here instead of 55 is 143."

"Isn't it true that the hotter it is the quicker bugs develop?"

Dr. Goff responded, "that's correct."

"This is not a minor typographical error, is it, sir?"

"No, it is not," Dr. Goff answered.

Mr. Feldman then moved on to some of his other calculations.

For the data on February 8, Dr. Goff had originally determined the ADH was 40.1, it was actually 55. For the data on February 7, Dr. Goff wrote 59.1 when it was actually 40.7. For the data on February 14, he wrote 62 when it was 49.5. The data for February 15 was also wrong.

When asked how the mistakes occurred, Dr. Goff admitted he had made a mistake with his computer. Mr. Feldman clarified that he had made at least five mistakes.

"And these mistakes affect the accuracy of your estimates with regard to the post mortem interval. Isn't that true?"

"Yes."

"No further questions."

In his redirect, Mr. Dusek immediately addressed the mathematical errors. He pointed it out that errors in the math for the dates after February 9 would not make a difference because they were not factored into the overall calculation anyway. Mr. Dusek then revealed that the data for February 14 and 15 were not wrong, they had just been switched.

"So, would that not change your estimate?"

"My estimate would remain the same. Unfortunately,

while entering things in the computer I made a mistake and transposed those figures."

Shortly after the afternoon break, Dr. Goff was excused and the prosecution's case reached its end.

"You're honor, we will be resting again."

"Okay, ladies and gentleman, we've gone through the people's case in chief, we've gone through the defense, we've now gone through completely the people's rebuttal to the defense. What remains of the trial, basically, is any subrebuttal evidence that the defense elects to present and I am informed they anticipate a full day on Thursday for their presentation. Whether it goes beyond Thursday or not I do not know at this time. I should be able to advise you on Thursday. We will be off on this matter tomorrow. You'll be able to go to work or do whatever else you'd like to do on a day off. Hopefully, the Padres can beat the Chicago Cubs. I mean, I don't know if it's possible they're going to win another game, but, at any rate, we'll see you on Thursday morning."

DAY 24

"Welcome back, ladies and gentleman. How about the Pads, two games in a row. All right, Mr. Feldman."

The defense called Dr. Robert Hall, the Vice Provost for Research at the University of Missouri and an expert in the area of forensic entomology. Mr. Hall had graduated from the University of Maryland with a master of science degree and later earned a Ph.D. in entomology from the Virginia Polytechnic Institute and a J.D. degree from the University of Missouri. He had taught forensic entomology and forensic science and was a member of the Entomological Society of America and the American Board of Forensic Entomology. He was also a commander in the 7228 medical support unit with the Army Reserves. He had testified in dozens of trials and had been consulted by a variety of law enforcement agencies.

Prior to his testimony, Dr. Hall had read the autopsy report written by Dr. Blackbourne as well as the reports written by David Faulker, Dr. Neal Haskell, Dr. William Rodriguez, and Dr. Lee Goff. He additionally reviewed the photographs from the autopsy and recovery site, and analyzed the available weather data.

"Is insect arrival the same as the amount of time that the person was dead?"

"In some cases it can be."

"And your position with regard to the accuracy of the entomologic evidence, how accurate is it?"

"In many cases remarkably accurate."

"With regard to the insect evidence in this case, after your review of the evidence and after your consideration of the testimony and after your review of the weather data and all of the other information that you were provided, did you form an opinion as to how long the decedent was exposed to blow fly oviposition?" Mr. Feldman asked, referring to the moment flies laid eggs on the body.

"Yes. My opinion is that blow fly oviposition occurred no later than February 23rd and not earlier than February 12th."

"So, in your view, any time between February 23 and February 12 is the window of time within which the decedent may have been available to insects, is that right, sir?"

"That's correct," Dr. Hall answered and explained how insects required a certain amount of accumulated thermal energy that could be calculated by analyzing the hourly temperatures. "Because the development of flies is a function of accumulated temperature, one can infer from the experimental data how long it would have taken for development to occur at temperatures measured under other circumstances."

"Do you know William Rodriguez?"

"Yes."

"Is he board certified in the area of forensic entomology?"

"No."

"Do you know him as an anthropologist?"

"Yes."

When asked if he agreed with Dr. Rodriguez's postmortem interval estimate, Dr. Hall said, "I do not. It's inconsistent with the insect evidence I've examined."

Dr. Hall additionally noted, "blow flies will arrive within minutes to hours after a decedent has died," as long as the body was outside and not covered. "If the body was put out under the cover of darkness, when the sun rose the next day and the temperatures became sufficiently warm for fly activity, I would expect fly activity to occur almost as soon as the opportunity presented itself."

"If the body was out, hypothetically, on February 4th, would you expect blow flies to wait five days before they got to the body?"

"No, sir, I would not expect that."

"How do you understand the term mummification, sir?"

After clarifying he was not an expert on mummification, Dr. Hall said, "mummification has little, if any, effect on blow fly colonization."

Asked how his estimation would be affected if Danielle's face had mummified within forty-eight hours of being left at the recovery site, Dr. Hall answered, "that wouldn't change my earlier conclusion."

"Do ants scavenge blow fly larva?"

Dr. Hall confirmed ants are scavenging predators, but did not believe enough ants were present at the scene to have removed a significant quantity of larva and noted the prolific nature of flies to successfully lay eggs. "If ants were that effective, we would no longer have blow flies because the ants would have eaten them all."

"So, what you were trying to do was incorporate all of the data and give the fairest possible opinion you could as to what the postmortem interval would have been in this case?"

"That was my goal."

"Thank you very much, sir."

Mr. Dusek began his cross examination by revealing Dr. Hall was good friends with Dr. Haskell with whom he had written several articles previously and was in the process of publishing two more.

"You were working in collaboration with Dr. Haskell on this case?"

Dr. Hall recalled receiving several specimens from the case he was asked to identify because one of his specialties was identifying the species of unknown flies. After identifying the sample, Dr. Hall spoke with Dr. Haskell via phone.

"The use of your insect data, Doctor, provides us with the minimum postmortem interval, doesn't it?"

"Yes, sir."

"And that's what entomologists do is give us the

minimum time the body has been out there, correct?"

"Yes, sir."

"That's when forensic entomology is most helpful, isn't it?"

"I'd say it's a time when it can be very helpful, yes."

Mr. Dusek emphasized that in the case of Danielle Van Dam they needed the maximum time the body could have been out in the desert and not the minimum. He then noted that larvae could be eaten and removed from the scene by not just ants, but small animals including rats and racoons as well. "And if any of those situations occur, you would be losing evidence to accurately assess the beginning of your minimal postmortem interval, correct?"

"You might lose some of the evidence, yes."

"There's no way of knowing how much we've lost, is there?"

Dr. Hall conceded, "there's a certain amount of variability that occurs in the biological world."

"If we were to give three or four qualified entomologists the same data to work with, would you expect them to get the same answer?"

Although every entomologist used their own preferred scientific method, he believed the estimations would be similar. He and Dr. Haskell had arrived at slightly different estimations because he had calculated according to accumulated degree days not accumulated degree hours.

"Based upon your review of the findings and conclusions of the other people who have testified in this case, has anyone else had the beginning date of February 12th?"

"I'm the only one."

"How can everybody come to different numbers in your field?"

Dr. Hall again said he had used a slightly different mathematical equation and noted, "my conclusion would be that the estimates are more consistent than remarkably inconsistent."

Regarding the time between when Danielle's body was dumped and when flies first laid eggs, Dr. Hall said, "It occurs very quickly. Although I cannot quote to you the exact number of minutes, I can tell you that it does not take days. It takes minutes to hours."

"That's assuming the body is fresh, correct?"

"From my experimental work, I noted that bodies that have been dead up to four days and protected from insect attack continue to be highly attracted to insects within minutes to hours."

Mr. Dusek pointed out Dr. Hall's experimental work had occurred in Missouri where the climate was hot and humid. During his experiments, there were no hot and dry Santa Ana winds.

"You told us earlier that you're familiar with Dr. Rodriguez, is that right?"

"Yes. I know him professionally."

"As what?"

"A forensic anthropologist."

"He's not qualified in entomology, right? He should not be rendering opinions regarding the life cycle and how long flies take to develop, correct?"

"I would think that would be the province of the entomologist, that's correct."

"Are you an anthropologist?" Mr. Dusek asked.

"No, I'm not."

"What is an anthropologist?"

Dr. Hall explained an anthropologist was an expert on the study of the human body and skeleton, particularly skeletal remains.

"And how they go through the decomposition process, correct?"

"I would put that in the province of the forensic

pathologist."

"Have you ever studied yourself any bodies that are placed out in a dry, desert like environment?"

"No."

Referring to the autopsy photos, Mr. Dusek asked, "is that body mummified based on your understanding of the term?"

"I would rate that body as partially dried out."

After establishing that flies are initially attracted to natural openings including the mouth, ears, and nose, Mr. Dusek noted that the body of Danielle Van Dam was not a typical situation.

Dr. Hall reluctantly agreed. "From what I've seen of the photographs there was not the extent of insect infestation in the facial area I would consider typical."

"They need moisture in a fresh body in those openings to survive, right?"

Dr. Hall concurred flies required moisture and would not lay eggs on top of a body's skin where they would be exposed. "If the body is completely dried out, there's nothing there to attract the flies."

"The maggots that were found in this case were where?"

"The majority of the maggots were found in the abdominal area."

"And you're also informed that region had been attacked by animals, right?"

"In the reports that I read it was suggested there had been animal activity in that area."

"Doesn't that then indicate to you that the flies arrived on this mummified body after an animal had started to eat on her and cause trauma?"

"Not necessarily."

"Is that one realistic possibility?"

"Objection. Calls for speculation."

"Overruled."

Dr. Hall answered, "I've never seen a situation where that occurred."

"In your experience, you've never seen a body who's been attacked by an animal?"

"I've never seen a situation where it was documented that an individual had dried out so quickly that the insect activity was a product of a subsequent opening by a scavenging animal. I'm unaware of any case that would be similar to that."

"How many murder scenes have you been to when the body's still at the scene?"

"A couple."

"How many murder scenes have you been to when the murder victim is in the condition of this child?"

"I don't think I've seen a decedent in exactly that condition."

"How many murder scenes have you been to where coyotes or outdoor animals attack the body before you got there and had a chance to examine the body?"

"I can't think of any."

"The location of the maggots in this case were in this case were in the chewed out area of this body, correct?"

"Objection. Argumentative." Mr. Boyce attempted to disrupt Mr. Dusek's momentum, but Judge Mudd overruled.

"That's what the reports say," Dr. Hall conceded the point while continuing to insist the maggots had been present before the animal activity. He could not admit the animal activity occurred first without also admitting his postmortem interval estimation was severely flawed if not completely wrong. Despite the damning forensic evidence placing Danielle in Mr. Westerfield's bedroom and motorhome, if the jury concluded Dr. Hall's postmortem interval estimation was correct, they would have to in turn decide Mr. Westerfield could not have killed Danielle. Dr. Hall's dedication to pride over reason possessed the profound power of negating the prosecution's entire case.

Mr. Dusek asked again if Dr. Hall agreed the maggots found were located in an area previously fed upon by animals.

"I'm not sure whether it was a chewed out location or not."

"If the body is dry and not appealing to the flies we would not expect the flies to lay their eggs on the body, would we?"

"Under that fact pattern, that's correct."

"If we then bring in an animal to eat at the chest region and the thoracic region, opening up that fluid, that muscle, those organs, would that area then be receptive to your flies?"

Stumbling through a response without answering the question, Dr. Hall said, "under the situation where you have a – an attractive medium for flies, and maybe I could characterize that best as a situation where you'd have a decedent inside a plastic bag, the flies might very much want to get to that decedent but until the integrity of the plastic bag is concerned they can't get in. And if that's the sense of the question then the answer is yes."

"I'll try to make my question as simple as possible. If we have a dried out body that's not receptive to flies, are you with me that far?"

"Okay."

"Outdoor animals come along and find that body and take chunks, bites out of the thoracic region and abdomen region. Are you with me?"

"Yes."

"That would then expose the entire organs, fluids, and muscles of that body, wouldn't it?"

"Under those facts, yes, it would."

"And wouldn't that then become attractive to your flies to come in and lay their eggs?"

"Under those facts it would."

"Why?" Mr. Dusek asked.

"If the theory is that there's a barrier in place, such as a plastic bag, and the integrity of that barrier is broken, then flies can go through it."

"The situation I gave you, the barrier was the dried skin, wasn't it?"

"Analogous to the plastic bag."

"I don't need analogies, I'm talking about real things."

"Objection, your honor. Argumentative."

"Overruled."

"Dry skin would be the barrier in the situation I gave you, wouldn't it?"

Dr. Hall continued his obstinate defiance. "In the fact pattern you were representing, the dry skin is what I believe is what you consider to be the barrier."

"Dry skin would not be a barrier to this dried out body?"

"I don't believe you can have a situation where you can have moist inside and so dried outside the flies, with which I am familiar, cannot find a way to deposit their eggs that will hatch and give rise to larvae that will get inside that body."

"And you have no way of knowing how long the body was out there before animals got to it, do you?"

"I don't know."

Unable to bend Dr. Hall, Mr. Dusek moved on to the temperatures in the month of February and Dr. Hall's criticism of Dr. Goff for using daily high and low temperatures to calculate accumulated degree hours.

"He used the only temperatures available, didn't he?"

"As far as I know, yes."

"Did you do the same thing?"

Dr. Hall answered, "yes," confirming he had used the high and low daily temperatures recorded at the Singing Hills golf course. He then clarified he had calculated accumulated degree days instead of hours.

"Didn't you just criticize Dr. Goff for using the highs and lows and the averages?"

"Objection. That misstates the evidence, your honor."

"Overruled."

"What I criticized Dr. Goff for doing was to make an unwarranted calculation of accumulated degree hours from daily maximum and minimum temperatures."

Noting Dr. Hall had been provided hourly temperatures from Brown Field, Mr. Dusek asked, "let's assume we would like to know the most accurate minimum postmortem interval period, wouldn't you use the hourly temperatures you were provided?"

"Objection. Asked and answered."

"Overruled."

"Not necessarily."

"The hour lists are going to be the best, aren't they?"

"Not necessarily."

"Weren't you simply asked to find ways to criticize Dr. Goff?"

"No, sir."

"Objection. Argumentative."

"Overruled. The answer was no, it will stand."

A few minutes before noon, Judge Mudd halted the action. "Ladies and gentleman, we'll go ahead and take the lunch break. Please remember the admonition of the court not to discuss any of the evidence or testimony among yourselves or with others, nor for or express any opinions on the case until it is submitted to you. Have a pleasant lunch."

Following the break, Judge Mudd welcomed the jury back and informed the court the Padres were losing by two, but had a runner on third with no outs.

Mr. Dusek remained focused on Dr. Hall's temperature calculations and estimating how long each instar stage would have lasted. There were three different methods of computing the data, each named after a particular scientist; Anderson,

Greenburg, and Kamal. When estimating the date flies had first laid eggs on Danielle's body, Dr. Hall used only calculations related to the controlled studies of Greenburg and Kamal, which were performed at 71 and 84 degrees, temperatures higher than the averages where Danielle's body was found. As discussed by previous expert witnesses, insects are more active and grow faster in warmer temperatures.

"What was the average temperature in the month of February at Singing Hills?"

"I didn't calculate a monthly average, it looks like it ranges from about a daily average of about 43.6 degrees on the 1st, but winds up with an average of about 60.8 on the 28th."

"18 millimeters is the approximate size at the end of the third instar, is that correct?"

"That's correct. The larvae were measured at 17.2."

"And what size are they when they begin that stage?"

"Around 11 millimeters."

"How long did it take him to get there?"

"Well, according to the Kamal's data, it took about nine days."

"No, Anderson's data."

"I didn't calculate the end point."

"If you had, wouldn't we be able to know how long he had been there in that stage?"

"According to that data set, yes."

Mr. Dusek noted that Dr. Hall had said he made calculations using Kamal, Greenburg, and Anderson, but had only actually recorded the data from Greenburg and Kamal. Mr. Dusek asked Dr. Hall to review his notes and find the numbers related to the Anderson data which rated the development at temperatures under 60 degrees, far more accurate to the conditions at Dehesa Road in February.

"Okay. Dr. Anderson studied the development at two temperatures; 16.1 and 23 Celsius and it would have required 66.3

accumulated degree days to reach the third instar at 16.1 degrees." 16.1 degrees Celsius is 61 degrees Fahrenheit, nearly identical to the conditions in the area of Dehesa Road during the month of February.

When asked what day that computed to, Dr. Hall said, "13 February."

"When did it exit the third instar under Anderson's data?"

"Her data would say that at 16.1 degrees, it would exit the third instar at 93.4 accumulated degree days. During the period of time in February at Singing Hills, the maximum number of accumulated degree days at a base ten that were accumulated was 86.9. Therefore, according to Anderson's study, there would have been insufficient thermal energy for it to exit the third instar."

"So, you can't give us a date on the Anderson data?"

"No."

"And the Anderson data is the one that most closely approximates the temperatures at Singing Hills for the month of February, isn't it?"

"It's important to understand that in accumulating this sort of data it really doesn't matter what the temperature was during the experiment. It is the calculation of the number of accumulated thermal units or the amount of temperature accumulated over a period of time to make the insect go from one stage to the other. At 23 degrees Celsius, it takes on the average about 68.6 accumulated degree days at a base 10 for the fly to reach the third instar. If you do the same experiment at 16.1 degrees, it will take 66.3 accumulated degree days to reach the third instar."

"It takes approximately nine days to get from the beginning of third instar to the end of third instar, correct?"

"That's correct."

Mr. Dusek noted that Dr. Hall had estimated the third instar began on February 23 and asked, "so that would get us back to the 14th or 16th, correct?"

"Yes, sir."

"Now, using Anderson's data, which relies on lower temperatures, we have February 13th as entering the second instar, correct?"

"Yes, sir."

"And if we go back nine more days from February 13th, what do we get to?"

"You get to about the beginning of February."

"Which means if we have maggots toward the end of the third instar, they could have been laid there the beginning of February, correct?"

"If you are going to rely solely on Anderson's data."

"You chose not to compute that for Anderson, didn't you?"

"That's correct," Dr. Hall responded.

"Why didn't you apply Anderson's data which uses temperatures in the 60 degree range?"

Dr. Hall explained he had already calculated using alternative data that the maggots would require 93.4 accumulated degree days. The Anderson data would indicate 103.8 accumulated degree days, but the "total amount of thermal energy available at Singing Hills was 86.9. With Anderson's data set there was insufficient energy for the flies to get out of the third instar."

"Some of them were at the extreme end of the third instar, weren't they?"

"Some of them were measured at 17.2 millimeters."

"Some of them were at the extreme end of the third instar, weren't they?" Mr. Dusek repeated.

"They were well into the third instar."

"Some of them were at the extreme end of the third instar, weren't they?"

"Objection. Asked and answered three times."

"Overruled. He hasn't answered the question. Answer the question, please, Doctor."

"I – I – I – when you say the extreme end, I'll say they were toward the end. That's the length of that fly would indicate that it was toward the end of the third instar."

"How much farther did it have to grow?"

"I don't know."

Mr. Dusek presented the chart created by Dr. Goff showing the daily temperature averages at the golf course throughout the month of February.

"Starting at February 2nd, how far do we have to go before we find a temperature that is at or above 61 degrees?"

"The first time that you get a daily average that is above 61 degrees is on the 10th when the average is 63.1."

"And up until that point the daily averages are in the forties and fifties, correct?"

"That's correct."

"Which means the flies are developing at a slower rate than even at 61 degrees, correct?"

"So, to try to be responsive to your question, during the first part of February there was not a lot of thermal energy available to support fly development."

"Does that mean they would develop slower than at higher temperatures?"

"Flies develop slower at lower temperatures, yes, sir."

"Continuing our way through that month, when's the next time we come to a temperature at or above 61 degrees?"

"February 22nd."

After noting several other warm days at the end of February, Mr. Dusek asked, "so, for the entire month of February, based upon the median temperatures that you were provided, only four days exceeded the 61 degree temperature that Anderson was using, is that correct?"

"Well, I count five days that exceeded 61 degrees."

"If we were looking for temperatures that most closely matched the average at Singing Hills, we would be using the 61 degrees Fahrenheit, 16 degrees Celsius for our comparisons, wouldn't we?"

Defiant to the end, Dr. Hall answered, "no, sir, not necessarily."

"Nothing further."

Following the afternoon break, Judge Mudd informed the court the Padres had blown a four run lead in the eighth before Mr. Feldman began his redirect.

"Now, there is in your professional community an agreement as to the manner in which accumulated degree hours ought to be calculated, isn't that right?"

"Entomologists have gone over this and I believe most entomologists are in agreement as to how that should be done."

"But Dr. Goff apparently utilized a method that's inconsistent with those of most entomologists?"

"Yes, sir. In my opinion."

Referring to Dr. Goff's claim the postmortem interval could have been as early as February 9 based on the weather data from the golf course, Mr. Feldman noted that Dr. Blackbourne, Dr. Haskell, and Mr. Faulkner had all determined that oviposition, the moment flies initially laid eggs on the body, could have occurred ten days before the autopsy, approximately February 16. He additionally noted that although each expert provided slightly different estimations, they all overlapped and included the dates of February 14 through 16 as the likely time oviposition occurred.

"All the entomologists plus all the pathologists in the case agree that oviposition, or time of death, both could have occurred between the 9th and 23rd of February, is that right?"

"That would be the conclusion, yes."

"In your professional experience, have you testified in a case where two forensic pathologists and four forensic entomologists put the parameters within the unique time sets that we see in this case?"

"No, sir. It is unusual in my professional experience.""

When asked if he had relied solely on the work of either Anderson, Greenburg, or Kamal, Dr. Hall said, "I did not rely solely on any of those works."

After pointing out that Dr. Hall had been hired by the defense not to affirm or contradict a specific position, but, "to tell us what you believed to be the case based on your professional training and experience," Mr. Feldman asked, "based on your professional training and experience, and based on what's been going on today, do you have an opinion as to the dates within which the decedent was exposed to blow fly oviposition?"

"Yes. 12 through 23 February."

"Thank you very much, sir."

In his recross, Mr. Dusek asked, "and your date 12 would be the date that the eggs were laid on the body?"

"Yes, sir."

"That's when the eggs got to the body?"

"That's the earliest time the eggs could have been there."

"All the maggots were at the end of the third instar stage up to the prepuparial stage, correct?"

"That's what Faulkner's report states."

Mr. Dusek discussed the finding of a maggot in the soil underneath the body, which indicated the maggots had started migrating away from the body prior to becoming flies. He then reviewed the various time of death and oviposition estimates, which, between all the experts, ranged between ten days and six weeks. "And you're saying that this, in your experience, in your field, is remarkable concordance?"

"I'm saying what we see here from the standpoint of the entomological evidence is good concordance."

"Usually it's worse than this?"

"I've seen it worse," Dr. Hall confirmed.

"Thank you, sir."

"Thank you, Doctor, for coming in. You're free to leave

these proceedings. Remember, you're under an admonition not to discuss your testimony until the matter is concluded."

After a brief and private discussion about the defense's plans, Judge Mudd informed the jury the possibility of one more witness, but confirmed they would still have Friday and Monday off. When court resumed on Tuesday, there would either be one last witness, or both sides would conduct their closing arguments. "The bottom line is, we're on the home stretch, folks. The end is in sight and I am anticipating you will be in deliberation next week. Have a pleasant four days off. We'll see you Tuesday at 9:00am."

DAY 25

"Good morning, ladies and gentleman. Welcome back. About the best we can say about the Padres' performance since you left is that football season is about ready to start. Okay, since you were last here a number of things have occurred so let me bring you up to speed. The defense has rested. Now, what remains of the trial are the two concluding phases."

Judge Mudd explained the first phase was his instructions for the jury. "What I tell jurors to do, especially those of you that have never had this experience before, is sit back, relax, and absorb as much of this material as you can, and realize a copy of these instructions will be in the jury room with you during your deliberations."

Following instructions, the prosecution would make their closing argument followed by the defense. Judge Mudd expected a full day and planned just a one hour lunch.

"Ladies and gentleman of the jury, it is my duty at this time to instruct you on the law that applies to this case. The law requires that I read these instructions to you. You must base your decision in this case on the facts and the law. You have two duties to perform. First, you must determine what facts have been proved from the evidence received in the trial and not from any other source.

"Second, you must apply the law that I state to you to the facts, as you determine the facts to be, and in this way you will arrive at your verdict. You must not be influenced by pity for or prejudice against the defendant. You must not be influenced by sentiment, conjecture, sympathy, passion, prejudice, public opinion, or public feeling. Both the people and the defendant have a right to expect that you will conscientiously consider and weigh the evidence, apply the law, and arrive at a just verdict regardless of the consequences."

Judge Mudd reviewed the process of defining what is and is not fact, directed the jury not to independently research any matters related to the case, and discussed the weight of circumstantial evidence.

"If the circumstantial evidence permits two reasonable interpretations, one of which points to the defendant's guilt and the other to his innocence, you must adopt that interpretation which points to the defendant's innocence. If one interpretation of the evidence appears to you to be reasonable and the other interpretation to be unreasonable, you must accept the reasonable interpretation and reject the unreasonable."

"Evidence of dog tracking has been received for the purpose of showing, if it does, that the defendant is the perpetrator of the crimes of kidnapping and murder. This evidence is not by itself sufficient to permit an inference that the defendant is guilty of the crimes of kidnapping and murder. Before guilt may be inferred, there must be other evidence that supports the accuracy of the identification of the defendant as the perpetrator of the crimes of kidnapping and murder. In determining the weight to give to dog tracking evidence, you should consider the training, proficiency, experience, and proven ability, if any, of the dog, the trainer, and its handler, together with all of the circumstances surrounding the tracking in question."

Judge Mudd explained the jury's role in determining the reliability and accuracy of witnesses along with establishing potential biases, but instructed them against dismissing the testimony of any one witness due to favoritism for one side or another. For expert witnesses, the jury was directed to analyze the quality of the facts presented when weighing the importance of their testimony. "Give each opinion the weight you find it deserves."

Although showing motive was not required to establish guilt, the presence of motive could be used to establish guilt and the absence of motive could be used as a reason to decide the defendant was not guilty.

Judge Mudd reminded the jury the defendant was presumed innocent and emphasized the people held the burden of proving him guilty beyond a reasonable doubt, which he defined as a condition that left a person without a strong conviction the defendant was guilty. The judge reviewed the conditions necessary for guilt on all three counts and discussed specific intent. Intoxication did, "not relieve the defendant of the responsibility for those crimes."

"The defendant in this case has introduced evidence for the purpose of showing that he was not present at the time and place of the commission of the alleged crimes for which he is here on trial. If after consideration of all the evidence you have a reasonable doubt that the defendant was present at the time the crime was committed, you must find him not guilty.

"The killing of a human being, whether intentional, unintentional, or accidental, which occurs during the commission of a kidnapping is murder of the first degree. If you find the defendant in this case guilt of murder of the first degree, you must then determine if the following special circumstance is true or not true. The special circumstance reads as follows: The murder of Danielle Van Dam was committed by the defendant David Alan Westerfield while the defendant was engaged in the crime of kidnapping."

Judge Mudd further explained the process of determining special circumstances and reminded the jury again such a finding required evidence of guilt beyond a reasonable doubt.

"In your deliberations, the subject of penalty or punishment is not to be discussed or considered by you. That is a matter which must not in any way affect your verdict or affect your finding as to the special circumstance alleged in this case."

After discussing the charge of kidnapping a person under fourteen years of age, Judge Mudd reviewed the third charge, possession of pornography involving people younger than eighteen. For each charge, the jury was read detailed definitions of the crimes and what constituted guilt. Animated images of children in sexual positions were not considered child pornography.

Having completed his instructions, Judge Mudd gave the jury a fifteen minute break before giving Mr. Dusek the floor.

"Ladies and gentleman, when I stood in front of you a little over two months ago now, I told you this case was about two people and only two people. David Westerfield and Danielle Van Dam. We have sat here for two months. David Westerfield's been in court, as he's entitled and as he should be, but I think at times we've lost track of the other person. We've lost track of Danielle, the other person this case is about, and what happened to her, what he did to her.

"We're talking about a young girl, four feet three inches tall, seven years old, who will never see her eighth birthday. We're talking about what the defendant, a fifty year old man who lived two doors away, did to this child. This case, if you step back and look at it all, is a simple case. It is not a complicated case, although there may be times when it seemed that way. The facts and the reality of what this case is about is very simple.

"On February 1st going into February 2nd, somebody kidnapped Danielle Van Dam out of her own house, out of her own bedroom. Approximately fifty-five hours later, the defendant showed up at the dry cleaners in Poway, in his motorhome at the crack of dawn, in his underwear, white t-shirt, thin shorts, no shoes, no socks, no personality, when it's cold out in February. He hauls in his laundry, two comforters, two pillow shams, and his jacket. On one of the comforters Layla's hair was found, the family dog. On the jacket was Danielle Van Dam's blood. That in and of itself tells you he's guilty beyond a reasonable doubt. That alone. But it doesn't stop there."

Mr. Dusek proceeded to recount Mr. Westerfield's initial

conversations with police, which included a series of inexplicable claims about his weekend. He recounted the steps detectives took in their investigation which continued to reveal signs of Mr. Westerfield's involvement. Due to the hard work of search volunteers and some good luck, Danielle's body was found more than three weeks after the investigation began, providing the family some closure, and confirming everyone's worst fears. "She had been taken, and killed, and dumped like trash.

"But when they found her body, they also found evidence." Mr. Dusek proceeded to meticulously review the complicated and abundant trace evidence linking Danielle to Mr. Westerfield.

In Mr. Westerfield home, six of Danielle's hairs were found in his bedroom, one of her hairs was found on a pair of his boxer shorts collected from the dryer, and three of her hairs were found in dryer lint recovered from the trash in his garage. Blue fibers found with Danielle's body matched fibers found in both Mr. Westerfield's laundry room and in his motorhome. An orange fiber discovered in a clump of hair tangled in her necklace matched orange fibers found with laundry in Mr. Westerfield's washing machine, clothes on top of his dryer, a pillowcase in his bedroom, and a towel in his SUV.

In his motorhome, Danielle's middle and ring finger prints were discovered on a headboard cabinet in the bedroom, her blood was found on the floor by the bathroom, and her hair was collected from the bedroom floor and bathroom sink. Hairs consistent with the Van Dam's dog, Layla, were collected from both Mr. Westerfield's house and RV.

"But there is more to this horrible crime, this evil, evil crime because of his conduct and what he did afterwards to get away with this evil crime." Mr. Dusek noted that Mr. Westerfield had taken some bedding to the cleaners and had thrown away Danielle's pajamas and blanket, which were the likely sources of the blue and orange fibers. He then cleaned his own clothes as well as the bedding at his house.

"But it gets worse. As we saw in the presentation of this case, he tried to blame his son for that porn. And we know that's not true." In addition to the numerous images of naked underage girls, some involving sexual acts, some in videos, Mr. Westerfield also possessed suggestive images of the teenage daughter of his ex-girlfriend.

"She was laying on a chair by a pool, clothed in a swim suit with a towel over her head. Look at that pose and ask yourself why was that picture taken?" Mr. Dusek noted the images were found on a CD along with a variety of other images depicting underage girls.

Focusing on the count of kidnapping, Mr. Dusek returned to the night Danielle disappeared and revealed his theory of what happened. Before Brenda and her friends returned home, he believed Mr. Westerfield snuck into the house through the open side door and walked quietly upstairs into Danielle's room. After entering the room, Brenda arrived home, trapping him upstairs where he waited for everyone to go to sleep. Once the house was quiet, Mr. Westerfield abducted Danielle and exited through the sliding glass door by the kitchen, passing through the back gate on his way home.

"She was certainly kidnapped and she was killed during that kidnapping. She was kidnapped for who knows how long. Kidnapped over to his house, kidnapped again when he took her up to the RV, kidnapped wherever he took her to kill her. She was kidnapped until she was dead. He was smart enough to know, as soon as she saw his face and recognized him, he'd have to kill her."

Mr. Dusek addressed the defense's claim that Mr. Westerfield could not have killed Danielle because it was impossible for him to have placed her in the desert at the time scientific experts claimed she had been dumped. Mr. Dusek admitted not knowing anything about insect evidence before the trial began and confessed his lack of knowledge limited his ability to ask the right questions of entomologist David Faulkner.

"But I think when you look at all the entomologists that testified, we came to a basic understanding of what they do, how they do it, and where the problems are." Mr. Dusek recalled learning from Dr. Goff and Dr. Hall the importance of measuring the maggots to determine how far into their growth process they were as well as applying the correct temperature data when determining how long it took them to reach that size. Insects grow slower at colder temperatures. If the calculations involved temperatures that were warmer than the environment in which the body was found, the estimation will be too short.

Postmortem interval, the time between when a person dies and their body is discovered can be measured in part by examining the age of maggots found with the body, but that only provides an absolute minimum time the body had been outside and exposed. "We can use the bugs to try to help fill in some of that time, but it doesn't tell us all of it. Because we don't know when the flies got there, for one thing."

In a normal setting, a situation with moderate temperatures and humidity, flies will access natural openings like the eyes, ears, nose, and mouth. Danielle's body was left in the desert at a time it was very cold at night and very dry, even for San Diego, which had caused her to mummify very quickly, making her not accessible to insect activity until eventually wild animals fed on her and opened up her abdomen. The fly population was also notably decreased that winter. There was no way of knowing for sure how long after she died flies laid their eggs.

In addition to the abnormal weather conditions distorting an accurate time of death estimate, Mr. Dusek accused the defense of, "cooking the books, making sure you get the results you want," regarding their guess of when oviposition occurred because they purposefully used higher temperatures then were present at the recovery site during the month of February. When calculating accumulated degree hours, the defense experts were using numbers consistent with a daily average of 80 degrees during a month when the highest daily average was only 60 and in many days was far colder. When using an average daily temperature of 60 degrees, the data indicated that the flies had laid eggs in the early days of February, much closer to when Danielle disappeared.

"Robert Hall tried to hide it. Here we have two guys that apparently know what they're doing." Referring to Dr. Hall's analysis using the Anderson data, which computed the weather data at 60 degrees, much closer to the conditions at the recovery site, Mr. Dusek said, "he gave you a mouthful of all the numbers, all the thermal units, all of the computations, but he didn't put a date over there. He'd ask you to believe he didn't have enough time. Yeah, sure. If he'd put a date there he knows his client would be guilty. He knows the promise would have been broken. That's why he didn't put the date there."

"This is not an exact science, this is not DNA, this is not radiology," Mr. Dusek stated before pointing out that even the most accurate and honest calculations could only determine the absolute minimum date oviposition had occurred. There was no way of definitively know the maximum time, which was the only question of importance with regard to Danielle Van Dam.

Confirming a timeline more consistent with Danielle being left in the desert in the first days of February was Forensic Anthropologist Dr. Rodriguez who determined, based on the severe level of decay and mummification, that the body had been deceased for approximately four weeks.

Having addressed the first two charges, kidnapping and murder, Mr. Dusek moved to the child pornography and noted the defense's own expert witness, Mr. Lawson, refused to travel or take possession of some of the images because he didn't want to be arrested. That fact alone, proved the defendant guilty of possessing child porn.

"The only question is, who possessed them?" Mr. Dusek noted the CDs and zip drives containing the illegal images had been found in Mr. Westerfield's office hidden on the top shelf of his bookshelf behind some of his work books.

After noting the defense had initially claimed the pornography was all adult women engaged in consensual sex, Mr. Dusek said, "we now know it's way beyond that. You saw the videos. You had to sit through and watch those, we all did. And we saw what they depicted. His fantasies of that young, little girl being assaulted by those men in all ways imaginable. Not only silent movies, but the screams that came with it. The screams were in his private collection. Fantasies breed need. He got to the point it was growing and growing and growing. What else is there to collect? What else can I get excited about visually, audibly?

"That's the man we're dealing with. If you can answer me why an individual, a normal fifty year old man would collect that stuff, I can tell you why a fifty year old man would kidnap and rape, kidnap and kill a seven year old child."

Mr. Dusek then recalled that during his testimony, Mr. Lawson had focused only on the porn they could blame on Mr. Westerfield's son, Neal, not the images and videos on the CDs and zip drives where the damning content was found. "He was a hired gun and he was unnecessary. If we want to know who the porn belongs to ask Neal. You saw him testify. He shouldn't have had to get up there and testify. He shouldn't have had to do that. Marcus Lawson and others forced it."

Mr. Dusek recounted Neal's admission to sometimes viewing porn and reminded the jury that Neal had not downloaded it, organized it, or put it on CDs or external drives. "Who does? We had to ask him. And he had to say my dad. That stings. It wasn't necessary."

"I would imagine most guys, and maybe even most

ladies, have taken a peak at *Playboy* through the years, maybe even bought one or two. But how many young boys are going to hide their *Playboy* in their dad's office? Who's going to do that? That's what the defense is telling you happened in this case. Neal Westerfield created the porn, labeled it, hid it in his dad's office. No. His dad did it. And all the blame from the defense comes down on his own flesh and blood."

Referring to Mr. Westerfield's state of mind, Mr. Dusek noted he had been having a difficult time coping with the reality his girlfriend had left him and was seeing another man. "We know that alcohol plays a role in the defendant's personality, how he behaves, how he acts, that there is a change in character when he's out drinking. Sometimes he becomes quiet, might become depressed. According to Susan, he had become forceful. Forceful when he's had too much to drink."

Mr. Dusek attacked the defense's claim that Mr. Westerfield's odd and impulsive behavior the weekend Danielle disappeared was normal. He walked the jury step by step through Mr. Westerfield's weekend from the spontaneous departure with no advanced planning to returning home for his forgotten wallet, departing the Strand after just a few hours, driving all around the desert before reaching Glamis, and getting stuck in the sand farther into the desert then he had ever before journeyed on one of the least busy weekends of the year.

"He's still trying to find a place to put that body and there are too many witnesses there. He says he goes to Superstition Mountain, he goes to Borrego where he gets stuck again going down some offbeat path." Mr. Dusek wondered why he would be driving down an isolated road he had never driven down before.

On the night of Sunday February 3, Mr. Dusek recalled that Mr. Westerfield had purchased gas at a station near his home. "And here's where he starts fudging big time." Mr. Dusek doubted Mr. Westerfield's claim he went to the Strand that night only to find the gate closed. "We know he went down there a little bit because we have another cell phone hit near Miramar at 7:33 in the evening. But he didn't go to the Strand. Why didn't you just go home? You're a couple of miles from home, you had a miserable weekend, you had been driving forever. But he still had the body. He still had to get rid of Danielle. He finally got rid of her alongside of the road in Dehesa. Naked."

Mr. Dusek continued recounting the timeline of unusual activity by discussing his peculiar behavior with detectives that Monday morning; the missing sheets on the bed, the multiple loads of laundry being washed, the smell of bleach in the garage. In an interview with police later that day, Mr. Westerfield had revealed he thought Damon was out of town and only a sitter was at the house.

After completing the timeline of events, Mr. Dusek again reviewed the hard evidence.

Danielle's fingerprints were found on a cabinet over the bed in the motorhome. "She was alive when she was in that motorhome. She was alive when she placed that print there. She was alive laying on that bed. It was her blood in that motorhome and on that jacket. She was alive in that motorhome when it dropped to the ground and got on his jacket."

Mr. Dusek believed more blood had been on Danielle's pajamas and blanket as well as Mr. Westerfield's clothes and black boots, all of which had been thrown away and never recovered. Mr. Dusek was grateful Mr. Westerfield had taken the clothes and bedding to the dry cleaners and left the receipt in his car.

"He tried to destroy the evidence that showed he committed the murder of a seven year old child."

In Mr. Westerfield's motorhome, Danielle's blood was found on the floor between the bedroom and bathroom, and her hair was found in the bathroom sink and bathmat. In his house, six hairs belonging to Danielle were discovered in the bedroom on the pillowcase, flat sheet, and fitted sheet. One of Danielle's hairs was found on a pair of boxer shorts recovered from the dryer in the laundry room and three of her hairs were collected from dryer lint found in the garbage in the garage. All of these hairs were proven to be Danielle by mitochondrial DNA testing. Since mitochondrial testing could only match the mother's genetic line, Danielle's mother and two brothers would have also been a match, however, the boys had short hair and Brenda's hair was treated. The hairs found in Mr. Westerfield's house and motorhome were long, blonde and natural. They could only have belonged to Danielle.

In addition to Danielle's hair, hair matching the Van Dam's dog, Layla, was found in the motorhome as well as on clothes found in the dryer. Danielle's mother recalled how Danielle had loved playing with the dog at night before bed while wearing her pajamas.

Mr. Dusek then reviewed the fiber evidence. Blue fibers collected from the sheet used to wrap Danielle's body at the recovery site matched blue fibers found in both Mr. Westerfield's laundry room and on the headboard in his motorhome. An orange fiber discovered in a clump of hair tangled in her necklace matched orange fibers found in Mr. Westerfield's SUV as well as with orange fibers found on clothes in his washing machine, clothes on top of his dryer, and a pillowcase in his bedroom.

Mr. Dusek showed the jury a picture of Danielle at the autopsy. "Not fun to look at. But from that body Danielle Van Dam gave us clues. She helps us solve this case. There have been times where there's been some levity in this courtroom. There have been times for laughter, breaking the mood, I suppose. That time is over. It's now time to focus on Danielle Van Dam and what the defendant did to her that weekend. Let's get into the real heart of this case because the case is not where were these crimes committed. The heart of the case is who did them, who's responsible. Who was responsible for these horrible, evil crimes. There's only one answer. David Westerfield. He is guilty of these crimes, of this ultimate evil he committed. He's guilty to the core."

Following a thirteen minute break, Mr. Feldman began his closing argument.

"Thomas Jefferson said that jury duty is one of the great honors and privileges of our society. You are what separate us from the Taliban. This responsibility that you have as citizens is unique to our courtroom system. We've just been through hours of intensely emotional experience, all of us in this courtroom. The judge told you in jury instructions under no circumstances can you allow passion, that's feeling, human emotions, tears, affect your judgement because your job as jurors is to be completely one hundred percent objective. Not to show tears, not to allow yourselves to feel in the wake of the death of a seven year old child. This has been a life changing experience for all of us for two months. For this side, for that side, for you.

Mr. Feldman reminded the jury they had been instructed every single day not to form an opinion or reach any conclusions until both sides had completed their case. He emphasized the importance of continuing that admonition. "You can't form an opinion until the case is finally submitted and the case is not finally submitted. You don't have it for deliberation. You've all sworn you will follow that law."

"I look throughout the trial at you. I see during the presentation of evidence, tears. There's an intensity. There's a passion in all of us as human beings. But it makes me nervous, frankly, because if I see prospective jurors whose job is to be impartial crying during an argument, during the presentation of evidence, I get rattled. That's the truth because it infers, rightly or wrongly, that people are starting to form opinions. People are getting prejudiced. The prosecution showing the pictures of Danielle Van Dam is succeeding in his effort to prejudice you, to create passion, to raise the emotional tenor in a courtroom. I got the emotions, folks. You're not allowed. You're the objectives judges, not the lawyers."

Regarding the defendant's right to not testify, Mr. Feldman reminded the jury that not testifying was not evidence of guilt. "He has the right to remain silent. He has the right to rely on the constitution." Holding that decision against the defendant was considered a bias they needed to set aside.

Mr. Feldman then discussed burden of proof, reasonable doubt and presumption of innocence. He explained how they should weigh the credibility of witnesses and encouraged the jury to completely dismiss the statements of witnesses who made conflicting statements and who were clearly biased against the defendant. "If there's a discrepancy in the testimony that's material, you can disregard, throw out the entirety of the witness's testimony. You have that right."

Mr. Feldman moved on to the nature of the evidence. "There is no direct evidence in this case, ladies and gentleman. There's none. There's only circumstantial evidence. That's evidence from which you must infer or draw inferences of facts. If there's any other reasonable interpretation of the evidence, you must return a verdict of not guilty."

Regarding the heavy media presence in the courtroom, Mr. Feldman expressed his concern that the increased scrutiny was negatively affecting the jury, particularly in the shadow of the OJ Simpson trial. "So, I think it's daunting, which to me it means intimidating, to have to look out at these folks. They're not threatening you, but you know every time you walk outside they are all over you. You have not seen, hopefully, the intensity of what all the other people, everybody else in the city is completely obliterated by the media."

"Objection. This is improper, your honor."

"Overruled."

Mr. Feldman continued. "By the intensity of the press, by the newspapers. This is not something you can consider, but it is something I am concerned you will consider in doing your job. We ask you only to evaluate the evidence. Don't allow yourselves to feel the passion that we've seen many times whether walking out of the motor home, during the presentation of the movies, during the closing argument. You can't do that."

After completing his long, at times, condescending and scolding introduction, Mr. Feldman turned his attention to the night of Friday, February 1 and clarified that it was not the defense who introduced evidence about, "sex, drugs, and rock and roll." By calling Brenda's friends as witnesses, Mr. Feldman noted, the prosecution had introduced the of line of questioning.

"We don't blame the Van Dams. We don't think they recognized the dangers of the lifestyle they led. We don't think they understood they put their children at risk by engaging in these behaviors. We do not blame them. If you engage in risqué sexual and drug behaviors, what happens to your children when you don't check on them. Who are you inviting into your house?

"This isn't the first time Brenda Van Dam has gone to a bar and made open invitations to anyone whose attention she could get."

"Objection. He's arguing facts not in evidence."

"Overruled. It's argument. Argument, ladies and gentleman, is argument. It is up to you as to what the facts prove."

Mr. Feldman referred back to reasonable doubt before questioning why the prosecution had not called Cherokee or Patricia. "This is an adversary symptom. They are trying to convince you, okay. That's what's up. What's up is this is an adversarial system. That is what protects us from the Taliban. No kidding. So, they made tactical decisions. We know that parties at the Van Dam residence have been going on for about two years. We don't know who's come in. We do know what's going on. I confess to you there's no pleasure in that at all. The judge ruled it was relevant."

Mr. Feldman then discussed multiple areas in the Van Dam's home where fingerprints of unknown individuals were found, including the wall by Danielle's bedroom door and on the back patio table. None of the unknown prints had been compared to each other. He then jumped to the fibers.

"Jennifer Shen agreed that dancing could transfer up to at least a hundred fibers. I think it was Dulaney that said somebody could shed in an hour. There's reasonable interpretations of that, folks. If a single piece of evidence is susceptible of two reasonable interpretations, you can't use it. That's what the instruction says."

Mr. Feldman recalled Danielle and her mother had been inside Mr. Westerfield's home for twenty minutes. "Those kids were running around. The kids were up and down, upstairs, downstairs, in the garage, in a backyard. That's undisputed.

"For fifteen or twenty minutes, I don't know what those kids were doing. I know the uncontradicted evidence is they were in the house, they were upstairs. Two reasonable interpretations of the same fact. The instruction says you have to interpret that in the light most favorable to the defense.

"There were loose articles of clothing and material on the couches and in the family room and the kids were all over there. That's one explanation as to how they got there, isn't it? Huggy, huggy dirty dancing is another. Mrs. Van Dam's wearing an orange acrylic sweater is another."

"Objection. Misstates the evidence."

"Sustained. The jury is to disregard the last portion as to color. It's red. Move on."

"We don't know based upon prior inconsistent statements whether it was red or orange because we have a circumstance where Mrs. Van Dam didn't tell you the truth."

Mr. Feldman criticized Brenda and Damon Van Dam for not revealing their marijuana use or their previous sexual relationships during their initial conversations with detectives and accused them of colluding in advance to purposefully mislead investigators. Mr. Feldman argued that because they lied and were deceitful in the hours following Danielle's disappearance, nothing they said could be trusted, particularly concerning the color of her shirt, which Mr. Feldman again insisted was orange.

Regarding the fiber evidence as a whole, Mr. Feldman dismissed the matches. "Because all the experts on the fiber issues certainly said they could have come from a common source, could not have come from a common source. Two reasonable explanations. No issue."

As the end of the day grew near, Mr. Feldman began jumping from one point to another with little bridge between. "I confess it's late in the day. Maybe my blood pressure goes up a little bit so maybe I'm a little bit out of sequence to you. I apologize. I'm sure tomorrow morning I will be much more chronologically focused.

"Understand, never once did the defense suggest to you, nor would we, that Neal Westerfield had anything whatsoever to do with the disappearance of Danielle Van Dam. That was absurd. What they did to Neal, it was disgraceful. There was no reason to do that, period. We asked not a single question. The absurdity of the notion that the dad would accuse his son of the crime. Never happened."

Judge Mudd intervened. "Ladies and gentleman, we are going to break for the evening." He warned the jury of the increased number of stories in the news about the case and stressed the importance of avoiding all media, "in order for the court to abide by its commitment not to sequester you. Right now, I have the utmost confidence in every single one of you. I am impressed with how you have handled things, but I want to make sure you know and understand there are going to be things out there that clearly you should not hear, see, or deal with because they don't relate to your job and your commitment to make your decision based solely on what you have seen and heard in this courtroom.

"So, having said that, the Padres have a new foe this week, it will be on TV, so, if nothing else, there's a Padre game on. Have a pleasant evening. We will see you at 9:00am tomorrow morning."

DAY 26

Before either the jury or public was allowed back inside the courtroom, Mr. Feldman informed the court about disturbing information he had received the night before. Co-counsel Rebecca Jones, of the defense, had received a telephone call from a local Walmart employee who notified her about an incident in which, "Brenda Van Dam manifested a request or a desire to purchase a firearm that would get past courtroom security. I took that seriously because the information was serious.

"For some reason, the Van Dams have chosen to park in the lot that Mr. Boyce and I have used for years. Every day we keep our distance. I'm just asking you to please keep your eyes on this. This is completely distracting. It's not reasonable. I've communicated to law enforcement my concern. The court knows there's been three threatening letters that have come to me that were different than just the nastygrams. All that I've given to Sgt. Holmes."

"I'm very concerned to hear about weapons of any kind in the hands of Mr. or Mrs. Van Dam," Judge Mudd began, "because obviously that's of extreme concern, although I don't know of any firearm that is capable – well, I shouldn't say that, I suppose anything is possible to get through medical detectors."

Mr. Dusek chimed in, skeptical of the claim, which, was possibly an attempt to remove the Van Dam's from the courtroom as a way of characterizing them as problematic and not trustworthy while keeping their emotions away from the jury who Mr. Fefldman feared had become too emotionally invested. The defense had only one more opportunity to persuade the jury of Mr. Westerfield's innocence and needed every shred of help they could muster.

"I think some initial investigation has begun already. I think it's third or fourth hearsay. Perhaps Sgt. Holmes could let us know what he has found so far."

"Good idea," Judge Mudd said. "Sergeant?"

"It's at least second hand at this point, your honor. We contacted the person who called Mr. Feldman's office. He said the source of his information was from another employee who was off until Friday, not due back to work until Friday. We are trying to find out where he lives now and interview him."

"Is there any record, though, that a weapon was actually purchased at that store?"

"No, there was no weapon purchased by the Van Dams at that store," Sgt. Holmes responded and said he had informed the Sheriff's Department who was in charge of courthouse security.

"I can tell you I have been watching very carefully Mr. and Mrs. Van Dam. They haven't done anything disruptive," Judge Mudd said before directing one of the Sheriff's deputies to keep an eye on her. If they observed her staring intensely at the defense in a threatening manner, she would be asked to take a break.

"Your honor, I'm not feeling, you know, I'm getting looks from her," Mr. Feldman protested. "It's not those looks that I'm addressing."

"I can image that," Judge Mudd responded. "We will do everything we can to ensure that there, number one, is no disruption, and number two, they abide by the conditions the court has set for them being here."

"Also, your honor, I just want it clear, I'm very sensitive to what's going on in this case. I'm an experienced trial lawyer, I've tried cases for almost three decades now. I've never been in a position where I needed to communicate to law enforcement the specifics of what my telephones are doing. Your honor knows we are getting more than nastygrams sent in the mail to your honor's courtroom that are addressed to me. There are three letters now that are in red ink, two of which I have given to law enforcement."

"Well, the red ink seems to be consistent with an individual," Judge Mudd commented.

Mr. Feldman then mentioned that Sgt. Holmes had requested he not open any suspicious envelopes in hopes of recovering fingerprints.

Judge Mudd agreed to do the same before starting the twenty-sixth day of trial.

"Okay, let's start the parade."

Once back in their seats, Judge Mudd greeted the jury. "Good morning, ladies and gentleman. Welcome back. The ballgame was entertaining and long, but at least it kept you viewing something other than this trial. All right, Mr. Feldman"

"Maybe last night it started to hit you," Mr. Feldman began. "Maybe some of the intensity started to set in, but the judge said to you yesterday when you left the courtroom, you're not allowed to form or express any opinions because that's your obligation as jurors.

"I have to start by saying I've been thinking about this. I know my personality, I've done this for years. I know there are many people that will turn off to my clients because they'll look at his lawyer and say this guy, uh-uh. I know that we're dealing with extraordinarily experienced, competent lawyers. Mr. Dusek is a veteran prosecutor. Mr. Clarke is an extraordinary lawyer. You can't use that against Mr. Westerfield. This is not a personality contest. This is a pursuit for the truth.

"If there's anything I've done, if there's anything I've said that has caused any of you, I'll say, heartburn, please don't hold it against Mr. Westerfield. We are doing the best we can under these extraordinary circumstances."

Picking up from where he left off the day before, Mr. Feldman emphasized the improbability Mr. Westerfield had been able to enter and exit the Van Dam's home without detection. "Like our stealth jets, under the radar, in the dark of night when it was pitch black, snuck in somehow into the Van Dam residence. Mr. Dusek's argument is that Mr. Westerfield snuck in through the side door, left no fingerprints, left no physiology, left no trace. There's no evidence and the truth of the matter is Mr. Westerfield was never in the house. There's no proof. It's nothing but speculation."

Mr. Feldman also emphasized that Mr. Westerfield had never been inside the home previously and would not have known where Danielle's room was located. "How do we know who's where? He's never been there."

Mr. Feldman reminded the jury of the unknown hand print on the banister at the top of the stairs and called the prosecution's theory that Mr. Westerfield had become trapped in Danielle's room implausible. Mr. Feldman believed Danielle must have known the individual who took her because she never screamed for help.

"Their theory is, he killed her. Their theory is he killed her in the bed. That's the only way to shut her up. You heard it yesterday. We didn't advance it, we didn't raise it. They did."

Despite his claim, the prosecution had never suggested Danielle died at home in her bed and in fact pointed out that she was alive in the motorhome when she left the fingerprints by the bed and bled on the floor. If, however, the jury decided she was killed in her bed and not murdered during a kidnapping, he would be not guilty of the special circumstance and spared the possible penalty of death.

"So, let's examine if there is any merit to Mr. Dusek's theory that he killed Danielle Van Dam in her bed."

Mr. Dusek interrupted. "That misstates our argument, your honor. We never said that."

"Clearly misstates the argument, Mr. Feldman. Move on."

"I'm sorry, folks. Again, this is an argument, okay? I'm doing the best I can. I heard the argument dead in the bed."

"Objection. Misstates the argument, your honor."

"It misstates the argument, Mr. Feldman. Move on."

"If you look into their instruction, this was Mr. Dusek's instruction, that required forcible movement while alive."

"Objection. It's not our instruction, it's the court's instruction."

"It's the court's instruction, Mr. Feldman."

"Thank you, your honor. The court's instruction that was written by Mr. Dusek in the effort to save $46,000 because that's what he spent on the DNA. I'm sorry, I told you this is an extraordinarily intense experience."

Judge Mudd intervened. "The words are from the instruction, Mr. Feldman. Let's limit it to an argument as to what the instructions say, not who prepped them, not who wrote them, but how they were given."

Mr. Feldman continued. "One of those elements he has to prove is the movement with regard to the kidnapping had to occur when she was alive, the inference being that if she is dead in the bed, there's an acquittal. It's a problem."

Mr. Feldman persisted in his attempt to convince the jury Danielle died before she was kidnapped and used the few drops of blood found on the bean bag as indisputable proof. Referring to the count of kidnapping, Mr. Feldman proclaimed, "if she was killed before she left that room, he's not guilty."

Moving forward, Mr. Feldman referred to the multiple unknown prints found at the Van Dam's house and repeated his dismay that Damon did not discuss with officers his marijuana use or sexual history until fifteen hours after the investigation began.

"We got no evidence Mr. Westerfield was in the house. They don't got the smoking gun." Mr. Feldman described the likelihood of Mr. Westerfield walking down the street to his home with Danielle as unbelievable.

Mr. Feldman paused and switched tone.

"Who is David Westerfield? Who's this person they say would in the dark of night stealthily sneak into somebody's house and kidnap a seven year old? He has no history of ever engaging in such behavior. He's a fifty year old design engineer. He's got patent, he's had numerous relationships with adult women. He's the father of two college age children. He'd been married fifteen years before he was divorced. He's got mortgage payments. Payments for his kids to go to college. And all of a sudden he's going to decide for no reason, because he's depressed over the break up with Susan, an adult woman, a large breasted adult woman, he's going to suddenly go across the street because he's depressed? That's going to cause him to instantly change into a child killer? That's not logical, that's not reasonable. That's not a reasonable interpretation of the evidence."

Regarding the pictures of Susan's teenage daughter in a bikini, Mr. Feldman noted it was not known who took the photos and dismissed the idea they were sexual in nature. "They are not racy pictures. Because it's in Mr. Westerfield's computer suddenly he's a child pornographer? The argument is one of prejudice, it's not logic. We need you to be objective, not emotional. And this is kiddy porn? A picture of Susan's daughter sunbathing in her bathing suit? They have to stretch. There's too many holes, there's no smoking gun, there's too many explanations, they can't put it together. That's the problem, it doesn't come together."

Mr. Feldman discussed how, in a clear display of his good nature, Mr. Westerfield had helped Susan's other daughter escape an abusive relationship, and then jumped back to when Brenda and Danielle were in his home.

"We know they were in the living room. We know they went upstairs. We know they wanted to go in the garage."

"Objection. Misstates the evidence."

"It will be up to you, ladies and gentleman, to determine what was actually said," Judge Mudd responded. This is just an argument of counsel. You can proceed, Mr. Feldman."

Mr. Feldman repeated his misleading claim that the kids were, "all over," the house, which explained how fibers, dog hair, and Danielle's hair ended up in Mr. Westerfield's home. "All over they were. Fifteen, twenty minutes. Think about it."

A few minutes before 10:00, Judge Mudd initiated a fifteen minute break.

When Mr. Feldman resumed, he confessed his team had chastised him for claiming the kids had gone in Mr. Westerfield's garage. He apologized and said, "you're the final judges of the evidence, not me. I give you my best recollections." The strategy of apologizing for a minor untruth while ignoring the numerous blatant lies that came first was peculiar and disingenuous.

Moving on and again jumping topics, Mr. Feldman reviewed a number of actions taken by Mr. Westerfield, that, he said, were in no way unusual. Washing the bedding early Monday morning, doing laundry after a trip, leaving on a whim without previous plans, going to multiple destinations, getting stuck in the desert, keeping all the curtains closed, going to the desert on Super Bowl weekend, driving long, out of the way routes, and not taking the sand vehicles were all within the normal range of behavior for Mr. Westerfield. He additionally claimed Mr. Westerfield always had plans to go away that weekend. "It was spontaneous, but it wasn't as though I've just kidnapped somebody and now I've got to drive away immediately. That's not what happened. Go back to the evidence."

After dismissing Mr. Westerfield's activities at Silver Strand State Park on Saturday February 2 as completely ordinary if not mundane, Mr. Feldman wondered why, if Danielle was in the trailer, she was not yelling and screaming. "Mr. Westerfield was behaving normally," he emphasized.

Once out in the Glamis desert, stuck in the sand at wash fourteen, more normal behavior according to Mr. Feldman. On

Sunday, when Mr. Westerfield drove back to the beach instead of going home, perfectly understandable given the lack of parking due to all the police and media vehicles in his neighborhood. Also not at all interesting in Mr. Feldman's estimation was Mr. Westerfield's disheveled appearance at the dry cleaners first thing Monday morning. After a long weekend of driving all around southern California and getting stuck in the sand twice, what normal person would not appear a little rough? What mattered was not the blood on the jacket or the fact that Mr. Westerfield was walking around in his underwear, what mattered was the fact that the woman who took his clothes at the counter saw no blood on the jacket.

Returning to the substantial media presence in his neighborhood on Monday morning, Mr. Feldman asked, "if he had done something, why not go to Mexico? That's seventeen miles down the road. This is a circumstance which demonstrates Mr. Westerfield's innocence, not a consciousness of guilt."

Noting Mr. Westerfield's cooperation with detectives in their initial conversation on Monday morning, Mr. Feldman asked why, "when the Van Dams were cooperative it was okay, but when Mr. Westerfield was cooperative it was sinister?" Leaving the hose out on his otherwise immaculate lawn? Also normal. The fresh scent of bleach in the garage? Normal.

"Anyone knows if you use bleach it will destroy DNA? Really? Did you know that? News to me. We have an explanation for the presence of the trace evidence in Mr. Westerfield's residence. Brenda Van Dam, her son, and her daughter came to the residence. No question about it. No dispute. The fibers get picked up off the ground, get plopped into the washing machine, they spin around, they transfer, transfer, transfer. It doesn't prove guilt. Also, that assumes it's the same fibers and remember the testimony, they could not say there was a common source."

Because forensic examiners could not definitively and exclusively determine the matching fibers originated from an identical source, Mr. Feldman instructed the jury to dismiss all the fiber evidence. He also highlighted the large number of different bright colored fibers found with Danielle's body that were not found in Mr. Westerfield's motorhome or house.

Referring to the one dyed blonde hair found in the motorhome, Mr. Feldman theorized its owner was Danielle's mother. "If it were the case that Brenda Van Dam was in the motorhome, would she tell you? And wouldn't it be a fatal blow to the prosecution's case if the defense could show you one time ever innocently that Danielle Van Dam was in the motorhome? That would slay their case. Kids bleed all the time. They don't want to go there. You claim you only just learned his name with your girl friend's dirty dancing? You leave your phone number and not your girl friend's? What is this invitation about? Maybe Mr. Westerfield is too much of a gentleman to have confessed what happened with Brenda Van Dam and maybe Brenda Van Dam didn't want someone to know about it. Bottom line, they cannot prove where the fibers and hairs originated from. They can't prove the source.

"Because this case is only circumstantial evidence, there's nothing more. There's no video tapes. I'm afraid there's so much public passion, so much bias, so much pity, so much empathy, all of which are completely human emotions, completely worthy of respect, and I'm not in any manner trying to be nasty about it, I'm just being honest, you got to be objective, folks, in the face of the intensity of the emotion. Please."

Jumping to the dog hairs found in Mr. Westerfield's motorhome and house that were consistent with the Van Dam's dog, Layla, Mr. Feldman said, "it doesn't matter. You know David Westerfield had dogs, a dog, at least one dog. We know law enforcement found other animal hairs in the motor home." Mr. Feldman concluded any hairs belonging to Layla that might have been discovered had been transferred when the Van Dams were in Mr. Westerfield's home. "It is evidence of tertiary transfer preceding the disappearance of Danielle Van Dam."

Judge Mudd stepped in and initiated the lunch break. "We will see you outside the door at 1:00 o'clock."

When Mr. Feldman resumed his closing argument after the break, he reminded the jury Denise had told a detective Damon did not come downstairs when they returned to the Van Dam's home after Dad's and then told the court he had. He then referred again to the adversarial nature of the justice system and said, "we don't fight our wars in the streets. Literally, our wars come to the courtroom. We don't have lynchings anymore, we don't have gun fights at the OK Corral, we bring them into the courtroom. It's how our democracy works and it's why it's so important each of you understand your individual duties."

After Mr. Feldman proceeded to discuss the problems with the reliability of Mr. Frazee and his scent dog Cielo, he jumped back to the pornography. "Another way the government was grasping was in the pornography. They recognize they got a serious problem. That's no joke. The photos have to show children having sex or depicting sexual conduct. They don't."

"Objection. Misstates the law, your honor."

Judge Mudd addressed the jury. "The law is laid out for you in this instruction, ladies and gentleman. It's in black and white. You can read it yourselves."

Mr. Feldman continued by referring to a photo that had been shown to the jury the day before. "And I looked at that photo and I thought, what is this? They're trying to shock you. They're trying to say she's under eighteen? The rape videos that you all, all of us had the experience with. If those females are over eighteen, there's no crime. End of discussion. Gross, okay. Disgusting, okay. Inappropriate, okay. Enough to shock you, enough to bias you, definitely. Enough to prejudice you against Mr. Westerfield, absolutely. The plan. Those pictures don't depict females under the age of eighteen, period. What they did was take two or three videos out of thousands and claim this is a true and accurate representation of Mr. Westerfield."

Regarding the still images, Mr. Feldman noted there were only approximately eighty-five questionable images. "You decide whether any of those fit the definition of pornography, fit the definition of the crime as the judge has defined it. I submit to you that's not going to happen. Those charges aren't about those pictures, they're about their desperation, their search for a motive. How do you explain why a fifty year old would do this? There's no explanation. There's no history. By that logic, any of us who may possess anything like that are going to go out and kill children. Isn't that the logic? We're going to act on our fantasies. Because we possess these we're going to go out and commit crimes? No."

Judge Mudd interrupted and addressed the gallery. "I realize it's after lunch. If you can't keep awake out there, you're out of here. It's that simple. Sorry, Mr. Feldman."

After noting the unfair position Neal Westerfield had been put in as a result of the prosecution, he again accused Neal of looking at porn on the afternoon of Monday, February 4 and dismissed the internet history showing he had not. "The only person it could have been was Neal. No question." He then referred to the site "Anime.com," a favorite of Neal's that in no way was pornographic, and claimed it was proof that Neal had been the one looking at porn on the computer.

"So, the mere presence of photographs of adults engaged in sexual behaviors does not infer acting out except in the speculative arguments of counsel. There's a major difference between the priests and the Bobby-soxer coaches who are out doing what they're doing than David Westerfield. They have nothing else on David Westerfield as a pedophile. It's this or nothing." The term "Bobby-soxer" originated in the 1940s and referred to adolescent girls who worshiped Frank Sinatra.

"Is possession of twenty-nine or eight-five pictures out of ten thousand, twenty-five thousand, is that proof? Is that less than .00001 percent? Maybe good enough for government work. Not good enough for a jury trial."

Mr. Feldman again switched topics suddenly with no bridge. "At the body scene, intensity of the focus shifts. By now David Westerfield is in jail. They think they got him because they found the fingerprint and some DNA in the motorhome. Okay, it's there, I'm not going to come in here and tell you it's not. It's there. Where's the smoking gun? Can you tell me when it got there? How it got there? How long it's been there? Nope."

Mr. Feldman stressed the importance of the unknown 7cm long hair found underneath Danielle's body and wondered if it belonged to the unknown person who left the fingerprint on the banister at the Van Dam's house. He then referenced the orange fiber found attached to Danielle's necklace and noted the source had not been found in Mr. Westerfield's home.

Recalling his cross examination of Criminalist Jennifer Shen, Mr. Feldman falsely stated that the orange fiber from the necklace had been excluded as a potential match to the orange fibers found in Mr. Westerfield's home.

"Objection. Misstates the evidence."

Judge Mudd addressed the jury. "That misstates the evidence, ladies and gentleman, you're to disregard the last statement."

Mr. Feldman requested a side bar which was granted. Beyond the hearing of the jury, Mr. Feldman complained about the court, "interjecting itself into my closing argument in ways that over twenty-eight years I've never seen."

Mr. Feldman emphatically insisted the orange fiber had not matched the orange fibers found at Mr. Westerfield's home and RV. Because he was giving a closing argument, he believed he was, "entitled to give wings to his imagination. I have been at all times within legitimate argument bounds. Frankly, Judge, I've never had so many interruptions by a court in an argument."

"I think the record will speak for itself how many times that has occurred. Your wings of imagination, however, Mr. Feldman, are grossly misstating a lot of the evidence in this case and it has not been objected to. The last piece of evidence is quite clearly, the witness did not exclude it. You said she excluded it and she did not."

Mr. Feldman discussed the difference in opinion between analysts about the exact color of the fiber.

"You said the witness excluded it and she did not. The make up of the fibers is identical. You misstated what the witness said and that was the objection. It was sustained. When a blatant misstatement is made before this jury I will not tolerate it. End of discussion."

Mr. Feldman resumed his analysis of the orange fiber and focused on a minor discrepancy in Criminalist Shen's descriptions of the color, which he believed excluded the fiber. "You decide based on how her face looked when she realized her notes contradicted her testimony. If that's not an implied exclusion, there is none. Remember the expression on her face. It will never go away. There's a difference between an orange acrylic fiber that's dull and a bright orange acrylic fiber and the testimony will show that she was caught."

Regarding the many different fibers found with Danielle's body that did not match any fibers in Mr. Westerfield's home or RV, Mr. Feldman agreed with Mr. Dusek. "Danielle was speaking to you from the grave. She was telling you there's a universe of fibers that didn't apply to David Westerfield. It's somebody else. That's a message." Additionally, a number of bright colored fibers found in Danielle's bedroom were not discovered in Mr. Westerfield's environments.

"On the issue of DNA, on the issue of what was in the motorhome, we know the motorhome was in the neighborhood parked in the area of Mr. Westerfield's home for days on end."

After another fifteen minute break, Mr. Feldman informed the jury, "this is the home stretch. The defense is going to rest probably within thirty minutes, forty minutes. Please remember, this is the last opportunity the defense has to address you."

Mr. Feldman transitioned to the site where Danielle's body was found and asked, "why would the guy drive several hundred miles," to leave the body in an area where the motorhome could barely park. "Where's the evidence that anybody saw any motorhomes? Where's any evidence of David Westerfield at Dehesa?

"At autopsy we discover there's no fracture of the hyoid bone or the thyroid cartilage. That means she wasn't strangled. Although they tried to argue that asphyxiation, suffocation was the manner in which she was killed, there's no evidence of that. They want you to speculate as to cause of death. But we don't ask you to speculate. We presented evidence as to time of death."

Mr. Feldman recounted the testimony of entomologist David Faulkner who estimated Danielle's time of death at somewhere around February 16. He disputed the prosecution's argument that mummification had occurred so fast the insects didn't have a chance to lay eggs.

Conceding the absence of insect activity around the head, Mr. Feldman stressed they were not the only areas attractive to insects. "They also go to the anus and genitalia. The vaginal area. If Mr. Dusek is right when he inferred she was raped, that was what his pounding was about yesterday, folks. When Mr. Dusek was trying to explain, he pounded up, that's what he was arguing. The downside to his theory is that creates an opening for the bugs.

"Faulkner estimates the 16th to the 18th. We already know David's under constant surveillance. If Faulkner's right, not guilty."

Although the most important aspect of the defense's case,

Mr. Feldman struggled to present the insect evidence in a clear, precise and scientific manner that would plant reasonable doubt in the minds of the jury.

Rather than emphasizing the scientific results, which, if true, proved his client innocent, Mr. Feldman frequently meandered down meaningless alleys that distracted from the most crucial substance in the defense's case, the facts upon which their entire case relied. On several disjointed occasions he was able to focus and clearly articulate the weight of the issue.

"There is a remarkable, unique, undisputable, indisputable, beyond a reasonable doubt concordance of a combination of professions that make impossible David Westerfield's ability to have deposited Danielle Van Dam in Dehesa. This is absolute certainty."

Mr. Feldman combined his choppy recounting of the insect evidence with attacks against the state's witnesses, and dismissed the possibility insects did not access the body until after animals fed upon the body.

Well into the afternoon, Mr. Feldman reached the conclusion of his closing argument. He repeated his doubt that Mr. Westerfield could have snuck in and out of the Van Dam's house undetected and emphasized the significance of unknown fingerprints at the house, an unknown hair under the body, and the unknown blood on the bean bag in her room.

"David's behavior. They want to say it's sinister, guilty, terrible, awful. He's guilty. No. Two reasonable interpretations. We want to know when did that physical evidence get there. Beyond a reasonable doubt. When? Convince us when did it get there. And finally, where is the earring back?"

"Ladies and gentleman, this has been an extraordinary experience. It's been hard. It's been emotional. It's been tense. It's been at times overwhelming. The burden that the lawyers have is coming your way. The tension, the angst, the pain is coming your way. You are the conscience of our community. You save us from lynchings. You protect us. Thank you."

Judge Mudd initiated the afternoon break in advance of the state's rebuttal.

Fifteen minutes later, Judge Mudd welcomed the jury back. "All right, Mr. Dusek. Your closing comments please."

"Thank you, your honor. After hearing what we just heard I hardly know where to start when you're given falsehoods, misrepresentations, total distortions throughout the closing argument. We all sat through this trial and heard the evidence and know what the truth is. I agree we do have a moral problem with what he did to that child. We also have a legal problem with what he did to that child. They are the same. They both violate the law, morality, all that is right in this world. Make no mistake about that. Morality and law are on the same footing here."

Mr. Dusek started with the insect evidence, which he accused Mr. Feldman of misrepresenting. He repeated Dr. Goff's estimation, based on temperatures at the Singing Hills golf course, which was between February 2 and 12 and noted that Dr. Hall had purposefully not included the weather data that most accurately represented the weather at the recovery site because it contradicted the defense's claim that time of death occurred in mid-February. He then emphasized that David Faulkner and the other entomologists could only definitively estimate the shortest possible time the body had been at the site, they could not determine the maximum amount of time, which was the only date of value in the case of Danielle Van Dam. Mr. Dusek emphasized that none of the witnesses could determine how long the body had been in the desert before insects laid their eggs and reviewed how mummification had likely delayed the time flies could have accessed the body.

Moving on, Mr. Dusek addressed the focus on reasonable doubt and circumstantial evidence. Referring to Mr. Feldman's claim that if there were two reasonable explanations for the existence of fibers and hairs the jury must side with the defendant, Mr. Dusek noted they needed to actually side with the scenario that was most reasonable. "What are the possibilities of that really happening in my common sense?

"Perhaps the court's Padres might be an example. How reasonable is it that the Padres are going to the World Series this year? It's possible. It's not reasonable. Sorry, guys, the chance of that is virtually nil. Yet the possibility of that is greater than all of these other factors coming together in one case and leading us down the path of not guilty. The Padres have a greater chance than all of these facts coming together at one time in one place.

"Surely, we have to prove this case beyond a reasonable doubt. Reasonable doubt subject to reason, based upon facts. Based upon evidence, not based upon questions, misrepresentations and fantasies. I do not have to rise to the level of eliminating all possible doubts. I don't have to do that. There are imaginations that can run wild with conspiracy theories. I do not have to prove this beyond an imaginary doubt."

Mr. Dusek clarified Danielle never ran all around Mr. Westerfield's home, never went upstairs, never jumped on the furniture, and was never near any laundry laying around that might have collected her hair or fibers from her clothes. "You're being misled."

Regarding the ability of Mr. Westerfield to find Danielle's room, Mr. Dusek reminded the jury the doors were clearly marked, hers with pink and blue stickers, and advised them to look at the pictures.

Mr. Feldman interrupted. "Your honor, excuse me. I'm sorry, but it does appear that the audience is assisting Mr. Dusek in closing."

"Ladies and gentleman of the audience, please remain silent. Go ahead, Mr. Dusek."

Mr. Dusek reviewed a number of specific areas including Mr. Westerfield's conversations with police in which he provided an alibi while leaving out the dry cleaner visit, his extensive cleaning of the motorhome, his clothes, and his bedding, the lack of access neighborhood children had to the motorhome, Mr. Westerfield's gas receipts, the cell tower data, and whether detectives were wearing gloves during their search of Mr. Westerfield's home. He additionally dismissed the accusation that the Van Dams lived a risqué lifestyle that invited an attacker into their home.

"And now the big ones. The DA should be embarrassed. They should be disgraced for calling Neal Westerfield." Mr. Dusek recalled the prosecution had not called Neal until the defense's witness blamed him for the child porn. "It stings that he had to testify when his dad's on trial. They played the hand. They're still trying to put the heat on Neal."

The next example Mr. Dusek presented of the defense's overt dishonesty was the source of the orange fibers found in Mr. Westerfield's home. The defense had claimed orange shirts worn by detectives and Mrs. Van Dam were the source. "But it is not orange. It is red. The defense witnesses testified it was red. That is how desperate the defense is. Let's try this case on the facts, on the realities, on the truth.

"The defense says they're not picking on the Van Dams, then they proceed to jump right on them with both feet. It's their lifestyle, their choices, they contributed to the death of Danielle. It has nothing to do with who committed this crime. What they did has no bearing unless you're saying they did the crime themselves.

"Did I hear right that Danielle Van Dam was killed in her own bed? Did we hear right that's how it happened? First of all, it didn't happen that way because there is no sign, no physical evidence of that. Nobody believes after hearing all the evidence that she was killed in that bed. That was not our theory, you were misled again. She was taken out of that house alive. She was in the motorhome alive. She was in his house alive."

Mr. Dusek moved on to Mr. Westerfield's long drive

through the desert which he described as anything, but normal. "Line these facts up when you're determining what is reasonable and what isn't. The defense wouldn't even concede that the defendant lied at any time."

Judge Mudd paused the closing argument for the night and warned the jury about the substantial media coverage and probable increased appearance of the trial in conversations throughout the city. He directed them to remain vigilant. "Folks, I have a lot of faith in you. You've told me you don't want your lives disrupted. The only other choice I have is to put you in isolation. I don't want to isolate you from your families while you're deliberating. I believe in you, but you have to abide by the orders I have set to make this work.

"Hope springs eternal, maybe we can beat Cincinnati tonight. We'll see you at 9:00 o'clock tomorrow morning."

DAY 27

On Thursday, August 8, before the jury was brought in for the final day of trial, Judge Mudd opened with concerns about the, "conduct of Mr. and Mrs. Van Dam. Who can tell me about that?"

Mr. Clarke for the prosecution responded. "I have spoken to both of the Van Dams as well as their attorney, Mr. Busby. I don't think what occurred, at least from what they tell me, is as it's been characterized." Mr. Clarke recounted an incident that occurred in the courthouse, but not in the courtroom, in which Mr. Van Dam said he must be very proud of his son. Coincidentally, Mr. Feldman's parents were nearby and assumed the comment had been aimed their direction.

"Mr. Busby says the comment by Mr. Van Dam was said loud enough that he felt uncomfortable because of the relative close presence of Mr. Feldman's parents. It was not directed at Mr. Feldman's parents."

"All right. Mr. Feldman, how far do you want to take this?"

Mr. Feldman informed the court that one of the camera operators had witnessed the event and described it to him as, "completely inappropriate." He then stated, "it may not be inappropriate, it seems to me the court has the ability, and I thought through this last night, to issue a restraining order. Just tell them you keep away from the defense lawyers, you keep away from their families, you keep away from the Sabre Springs residence. That seems to me could possibly accomplish something."

"That I have no problem with. Mr. Clarke, you can convey to them in no uncertain terms that I expect them to stay away from the primary lawyers in this case and I expect them to stay away from the Westerfield house. I can't do much more than that. What they're doing is not helping the situation one bit."

"Judge," Mr. Feldman continued. "There's also been Mr. Westerfield's family around, at least during the last two days. If you're issuing that order, I would also ask you to extend it to have them stay away from Mr. Westerfield's family. And it doesn't reference the fact that at some point yesterday Brenda Van Dam walked up to my family as they were seated on the bench and stood there and glared. It's not just him, it's her." In addition to their actions toward the defense, Mr. Feldman said in the hallway, "their behavior borders on flirtatious almost with people. They're tittering. Our jury is right out there. I was hoping you would also consider the possibility of at least at recesses finding some place the jury can go so they're not exposed to this."

"Mr. Clarke, you've got to make it clear that their conduct is just bordering being contemptible on the prior court order. If they really, truly want to participate in this, get their act together."

"I will tell them that. The only question I have is bear in mind they live two doors away from the house."

"I understand that, but the representations that have been made are basically verbal confrontations with individuals interested in buying the house. And that kind of conduct, it's something I don't need, nor do you, nor does anyone else."

Mr. Boyce of the defense then recounted an additional event that occurred two days prior when Brenda Van Dam purposefully walked past one of the defense attorneys, Ms. Schaefer, and said, "some people will go to hell," as she passed.

Judge Mudd hoped his order would prevent any further incidents and said if it happened again, "I'll contempt them, Mr. Clarke. I'm just not willing to tolerate it."

With the first issue complete, Mr. Feldman then discussed concerns he had about the prosecution's closing argument. "There was prosecutorial misconduct yesterday and I'm concerned it will continue today. There were personal attacks on counsel, personal attacks on me. It's misconduct and there were arguments the defense was trying to confuse the jury and obscure the facts. Our concern is the attack will be personal, not professional. I don't think that was appropriate

"My second motion is to have the court consider a mistrial based on the court's statements yesterday in front of the jury which undermined the defense's credibility. The defense has a right to argue the facts. The court, by telling the jury the sweater was red, specifically undermined the argument that the witnesses may not have been accurate. I don't think that's appropriate for the court to have given in closing argument."

"Number one, Mr. Feldman, your attack on the people was personal, including finger pointing at Mr. Dusek. Maybe in the heat of battle you don't hear what your mouth is saying, but it was a personal attack. He's attacking what you said, not you personally. That is the nature of the beast.

"Number two, I told you at sidebar and I will tell you again, in my courtroom gross misstatements of evidence will not be tolerated. On at least two occasions yesterday I remember sustaining objections for the misstatement of evidence. One was the red sweater that Mrs. Van Dam was wearing. Three witnesses said that and no one in this trial said it was orange. The only evidence in this case is red. You made a specific, unequivocal statement relative to the color of her sweater and it was wrong. It wasn't supported by the evidence.

"You did the same thing with the evidence technician. Your interpretation may be that it's an exclusion and you're free to argue that, but that's not what you said. You said she excluded it. I will not allow gross misstatements of evidence. You went far beyond that in many areas of your argument that were not objected to, far beyond. Including references that you drew that were unbelievable. When it comes to gross misstatements that I know are wrong and I get an objection, I'm not going to let them go by. Let's get the people in."

After the jury reached their seats, Judge Mudd again warned about the increased trial coverage on the radio and television and stressed the importance of self-policing. "How about those Pads? They finally won a ball game. All right, Mr. Dusek, your closing comments, please."

Mr. Dusek informed the jury he was almost finished before again summarizing the physical evidence. He noted first that Mr. Westerfield had dropped off a load of laundry and bedding at the drycleaners before cleaning the motorhome so thoroughly none of his fingerprints were found inside. When he returned home, he immediately started three loads of laundry. After his initial conversation with detectives he returned to the dry cleaners a second time with more clothing and then vacuumed the motorhome.

"This is not just a let's wash the clothes at the end of a trip. He was washing and cleaning every piece of incriminating evidence. He was cleaning like a dervish, like Hazel on steroids. You young folks that don't know Hazel, ask some of the older folks."

Mr. Dusek discussed the high level of efficient professionalism exhibited throughout the investigation by detectives and evidence technicians, and reminded the jury that one team of investigators processed the Van Dam home and another handled Mr. Westerfield's residence. At the lab, a variety of steps were implemented to separate evidence related to the suspect from evidence associated to the victim. "They knew how important this little child was. They were professionals, they were experienced, they were objective, and they were thorough. There was no possibility of cross contamination."

As far as the possibility that Danielle, Brenda, and Dylan had left trace evidence in Mr. Westerfield's home during their fifteen minute visit, Mr. Dusek disputed the defense's accusation they had run all around the house and jumped on furniture. "Look at what was in that bedroom. If you assume there was a comforter over the top of that bed and we know there was because he washed it, how did the other evidence get underneath that comforter, on the pillow, on the top sheet, on the fitted sheet, if she wasn't placed on that bed?"

Mr. Dusek reviewed the list of fibers and hairs found in the house and RV and discussed the impossibility they had all been left there by Danielle. He asked the jury to recall how high the motorhome's door was, how difficult it was to open, and how absurd it was to suggest Danielle had snuck in, run all around and left her hair, blood, dog hair, and fibers inside.

"The hair, the prints, the fibers, the variety of locations. The numbers we have, the variety we have, there was too many types, too many numbers for anything other than guilt. The hair in the sink of the bathroom. How did that get there with the root? There was force involved, it doesn't just fall out. Something forced that out. And why is it in the sink? Was she being cleaned up before she was dumped? Trying to take away the evidence, the DNA, the blood, anything that would link him to her. Don't be misled. Rely on the evidence. This evidence is alone good enough to convict.

And now the big one. This is the smoking gun right here. Danielle's blood is on the jacket. Danielle bled on him. There is no explanation except that he did it."

Mr. Dusek addressed the idea of reasonable interpretations Mr. Feldman so often repeated the day before. "You don't ask it after each piece of evidence, you ask it at the end, after you've decided what has been established beyond a reasonable doubt. When you destroy evidence, that is a circumstance of guilt. There is only one reasonable interpretation that takes into account all of those known, established facts. Only one. That's guilty."

"Murder cases are different because unlike most other cases, we are missing our best witness." Mr. Dusek explained although Danielle could no longer speak in person, she had nonetheless communicated some of the details of what she endured in the final hours of her life, where she had been, and with whom. "I told you with my hair. I told you with the orange fiber found on my choker. I told you with the blue fibers that were on my naked body. I told you with my fingerprints and I told you with my blood. Please listen."

Immediately following the conclusion of the prosecution's closing argument, Judge Mudd began his final instructions for the jury. He directed the jurors to reach a decision only after reviewing all the evidence and discussing the case with other jurors. He warned against overruling their own judgement in favor of the majority opinion and prohibited the deciding of any issue by flipping a coin. He requested they begin deliberation with an open mind and not consider the subject of punishment. During deliberation, they were forbidden from discussing with anyone how the numbers were divided unless specifically asked by the judge. Lunch would start at noon during which time the case could not be discussed. Deliberation could only occur when all twelve jurors were present.

Judge Mudd again stressed the importance of avoiding the media while reaching a verdict based solely on the information discussed in the courtroom. If any problems developed, they would be sequestered.

"You will now start deliberations. You shall now retire and select one of your numbers to act as a foreperson. He or she will preside over your deliberations. In order to reach verdicts, all twelve jurors must agree to the decision."

Judge Mudd briefly explained the process once a decision was reached and discussed the large number of exhibits they would have access to in the jury room. Items including fibers, hair, clothing, and bedding would be available only if requested. Deliberations would end each day at 4:00, but if they wanted to stay longer, they could.

"All right. Those of you in the twelve numbered seats,

pick up all your personal items, your bottled water, coffee, notebooks. You will be going to a jury deliberation room."

At 10:10 in the morning on Thursday, August 8, 2002, the jury started their deliberation.

THE VERDICT

At 9:00 in the morning on Wednesday, August 21, after nine full days of deliberation, Judge Mudd reconvened the court for the verdict. Before the jury entered, Judge Mudd discussed penalty phase scheduling if Mr. Westerfield were found guilty of the special circumstance, which would make him eligible for the death penalty. Although the prosecution would be ready next Monday, Mr. Feldman requested an additional week.

"On Monday, we're obtaining a declaration from San Francisco that will perfect the record regarding a motion we intend to file attacking the death penalty for failure of the special circumstances to adequately narrow the class of death eligible defendant, but we can't get it in our possession until Monday."

Judge Mudd planned, if necessary, to instruct the jury to return for the penalty phase on Wednesday. If the jury found Mr. Westerfield not guilty, Judge Mudd would meet privately with the jury before allowing them access to the media if they desired. If the verdict was guilty, the gag order would remain in effect.

Following a two hour recess, Judge Mudd welcomed the jury back.

"Juror number ten, I understand the panel's made a decision. Is that correct?"

"That's correct."

"If you would kindly hand the verdict forms to my bailiff. All right. Each of the forms has been properly executed. Please recite the verdicts for the record."

"The people of the State of California, plaintiff, versus David Alan Westerfield, defendant. Case number SCD165805," the clerk began. "Verdict. We, the jury in the above entitled cause, find the defendant, David Alan Westerfield, guilty of the crime of murder, in violation of Penal Code Section 187, as charged in count one of the information, and fix the degree thereof as murder in the first degree.

"We, the jury in the above entitled cause, find the special circumstance that the murder of Danielle Van Dam was committed by David Alan Westerfield while the said defendant was engaged in the commission of the crime of kidnapping, in violation of Penal Code Section 207, to be true.

"We, the jury in the above entitled cause, find the defendant, David Alan Westerfield, guilty of the crime of kidnapping, in violation of Penal Code Section 207 as charged in count two of the information. We further find that the victim of the kidnapping was under the age of fourteen years at the time of the commission of the kidnapping, within the meaning of Penal Code Section 208.

"We, the jury in the above entitled cause, find the defendant, David Alan Westerfield, guilty of the crime of possessing matter depicting a person under eighteen in sexual conduct, in violation of Penal Code Section 311."

"Ladies and gentleman of the jury, were these and are these your verdicts as read?" asked Judge Mudd.

The jury, in unison, answered, "yes."

Mr. Feldman requested each juror be asked individually and the clerk obliged. All twelve jurors answered, "yes," for all three counts and the special circumstance.

"Ladies and gentleman, as you are acutely aware, this is a rather unique case in the state. The jury will now, as a result of the allegations and findings, come back together and hear more evidence on what an appropriate penalty will be."

Judge Mudd informed the jury the penalty phase would begin in exactly one week, the following Wednesday, at 9:00am. He directed them to continue abstaining from all media covering the trial and additionally requested he be informed if anyone in the media contacted them directly.

"We'll see you next Wednesday at 9:00am. Have a pleasant week off, folks."

PENALTY PHASE
DAY 1

On Wednesday, August 28, before the jury and public returned to the courtroom, Mr. Boyce of the defense objected to the state admitting multiple photos of Jennifer, one of the state's witnesses, when she was between approximately six and nine years old.

"We object to these photographs as not relevant. We ask they be excluded."

Mr. Dusek explained they possessed a range of photos, but would only show the photo that depicted her age after, "Jennifer comes in and is able to tell us which age she was at the time of the assault."

"Therein lies the relevance," Judge Mudd proclaimed and informed the defense, "once the foundation is laid as to the photo they seek to introduce, I'll deem it over the objection of the defense."

Mr. Boyce persisted. "Your honor, just for the record, though, they are not relevant to prove any element of the offense."

"They are relevant and probative as to what the child looked like on or about and at the time of the alleged conduct," Judge Mudd responded. "Therein lies the relevance. Whichever one they elect will come in over the objection of the defense and it's duly noted. Was there something else you wanted to discuss?"

Mr. Feldman said there was before noting his displeasure about photos of memorials to Danielle that had been built at the park near the Van Dam's home and at the recovery site off Dehesa Road. Each memorial was filled with flowers, toys, stuffed animals, cards and other items of tribute. "In our view this is not relevant to any issue concerning whether or not Mr.

Westerfield should live or die."

Mr. Dusek explained the memorials exhibited the impact of Danielle's death on the community. Judge Mudd agreed and allowed the images in over the objection of the defense.

At 9:10, the jury was seated.

"Good morning, ladies and gentleman, and welcome back. I am hopeful that during the week you were able to kick back and relax and enjoy your family and friends for a little while before entering into this very important second phase of the trial. Like the first phase of the trial, the second phase will start with an opening statement. The lawyers have an opportunity to give you a roadmap of what they are going to be showing. Keep in mind, again, that what the lawyers have to say is not direct evidence of anything. All right, Mr. Dusek."

"Welcome back," Mr. Dusek began. "I think you will find that the second part of this trial will still be about David Westerfield and Danielle Van Dam. Whereas the first part of trial focused upon what David Westerfield did to seven year old Danielle Van Dam, this part of the trial will focus upon what should happen to him for what he did to Danielle Van Dam. What is the appropriate punishment for David Westerfield for what he did to Danielle."

Mr. Dusek informed the jury his case included three segments. The first reviewed the evidence already presented during trial. "You will be able to consider the evidence that he took her to his house, to his bedroom, to his bed, and what he did to her there. You will be able to consider evidence that he took her to the motorhome, to the bed of the motorhome, and what he did to her there. You will be able to consider that he dumped her down in Dehesa, naked." Additionally, Mr. Dusek said they would be able to consider all the steps Mr. Westerfield took while covering up his crime.

The second category of evidence, "will come from the people that knew Danielle Van Dam, what we call the victim impact, which will indicate the magnitude of what the defendant did to Danielle Van Dam, what his actions caused to that little child, to her parents, to her siblings, and to the community at large.

"The third category of evidence will give you some insight into David Westerfield, some insight that most people don't know about and few people suspect. In the end we will be back in front of you asking for a verdict based upon what he deserves, not based upon what he wants. Thank you."

Mr. Feldman began his opening statement by saying, "We respect your verdict. We know that as citizens we ask you to do the task that you've done. We know you did everything your hearts, your minds would permit. We don't question your verdict, but we do continue to have doubts that linger. The community pressure is great. You've been out in the community. I speak truthfully. I'm concerned that you will be influenced not by what happens in the courtroom, but by what's happening in the streets of our community. It's hard to imagine walking the streets of our city and not seeing the headlines that appeared on every street corner throughout the county, throughout the state. It's hard to imagine missing the pressure. It's hard to image your ultimate responsibility is to decide whether or not David Alan Westerfield lives or dies. It is only your decision, no one else's. We accept your verdict."

Mr. Feldman discussed his plans to show the positive impact Mr. Westerfield had left in his wake. "We will show you that Mr. Westerfield is, to a certain extent, an inventor. He's developed numerous patents which have been manufactured by companies the he's worked for." Mr. Feldman revealed that Mr. Westerfield had "developed or participated in the development," of a knuckle joint replacement prosthesis for patients suffering from rheumatoid arthritis as well as a pully that helped patients recover following shoulder surgery. The defense would also show how he had helped other people in his day to day life.

"We don't try and justify the crime, there's no justification. We don't try and excuse the crime, there's no excuse. We can't minimize the horror. It's terrible. But Mr. Westerfield is not the worst of the worst."

Mr. Feldman emphasized that Mr. Westerfield was a family man who had two children for whom he cared. "You will hear his children. You heard Neal Westerfield testify as a prosecution witness, you'll hear him again, he's coming back. You'll hear from his daughter. You will hear from the dozens of people who've known this man and are shocked. Just shocked."

Mr. Feldman asked the jury to approach the process with an open mind while removing intense emotions. "This is a case where none of us will ever be at peace. There'll always be questions. Doubts will always linger. But now, although you disagreed, and we respect your verdict, it didn't erase the doubts. Now, you will need a deeper sense of resolution than before because this is now a life or death situation. Each of you, and only you, will decide whether or not David Alan Westerfield will live or die. Thank you."

"All right, Mr. Clarke, call your first witness."

The prosecution's first witness in the penalty phase was Amy, Danielle's school teacher during kindergarten and first grade at Creekside Elementary School who remembered Danielle as, "a very sweet, polite, hardworking little girl. She really enjoyed school. She enjoyed doing her best and learning new things. She liked to write and would often stay into recess and continue working on her writing because she enjoyed it so much."

"How about the way she dealt with other children in the class?"

"She was just a very caring little girl. She wanted to make sure that nobody had their feelings hurt. She wanted to make sure everyone was included. She got along with everyone. Everyone was Danielle's friend."

"Do you recall how she would share with others?"

"She loved to talk about her family. They seemed to do wonderful activities on the weekends, going to Sea World, going camping, those kinds of things."

Amy said Brenda Van Dam was very active in school activities and often volunteered to help in class when needed, which Danielle especially enjoyed.

"What about her as a person stands out about her?"

"Her caring personality. The fact that she never wanted anyone to feel alone or sad."

"Thank you, no further questions."

Mr. Feldman had no questions for Amy. Mr. Clarke next called Ruby, Danielle's second grade teacher. Ruby described Danielle as an intelligent student who always worked hard and finished her work, and who was well liked by others and who treated people well.

"I would like to take you to the time when Danielle first was determined to be missing. Do you recall that?"

Ruby recalled assigning the class a writing project that week Danielle was very excited about. On Friday, February 1, as Danielle was leaving for the day, Ruby reviewed her progress. "And then she left. And I told her I will see you on Monday. I never saw the paper back because that Monday never came."

Ruby discussed occasions when Danielle completed extra work not assigned and remembered how attentive and likeable she was.

When school resumed without Danielle on Monday, February 4, Ruby remembered the children being very afraid. They knew she was missing and had witnessed the search teams, the police activity, the dogs, and the helicopters. While Danielle was missing, Ruby kept Danielle's desk in its usual position and told the other students, "we were going to leave her desk until we knew what happened to Danielle." After Danielle's body was found, the students became very concerned about what they would do with the desk. Ruby collected all of Danielle's belongings for her parents and the class rearranged the desks in a completely different order.

At that time, Mr. Clarke admitted into evidence a number of Danielle's writing projects, one of which was about a frog and a toad.

"Ruby, what do you recall most about Danielle?"

"Ever since Danielle disappeared, there has not been a day that passed that I have not thought about Danielle." Although young, Danielle was a, "delightful student," who cooperated, listened to instructions, and got along with everyone. "She was a very obedient child and a very pleasant child." If Danielle were alive, she would have just started third grade that week.

"Do the other kids at school miss her?"

"Yes."

"Do you miss her?"

"Yes."

"Thank you."

The defense did not ask any questions.

After the morning break, Mr. Dusek called Danielle's father, Damon Van Dam, who recounted his daughter's life.

When Damon was twenty-nine years old and living in Dallas, Texas, Danielle was born. She was a big baby, eleven pounds, and was delivered via c-section. From the beginning, Danielle was very easy and calm. "She was just a great gift."

After briefly living in Phoenix when Danielle was two, they moved to San Diego where Danielle started school at Creekside Elementary in kindergarten and did very well right away. Instead of becoming frustrated and upset when she encountered tough assignments like most kids, Danielle was able to figure out where she was wrong and fix the problem.

She enjoyed helping around the house, taking care of the dog, and assisting her dad with projects in the garage. She particularly enjoyed the annual father daughter dance when she was able to dress up and go out with Damon alone. She was a

Girl Scout Brownie, took dance classes, and had just started piano lessons. At night, she loved reading before bed and had recently started reading to her younger brother. Because Derek was a little older, Danielle and Dylan were best friends and did everything together.

When asked how Dylan reacted to Danielle's death, Damon said, "he reverted back to more baby like, stopped reading, started wetting the bed again, needed to sleep with us for quite awhile and now still needs to sleep with his brother. They have separate rooms, but they sleep together in Derek's room now because they're still afraid."

"Does he ask any questions?"

"He mostly just misses her, he gets really sad. We had a function a while ago with the Brownie troop and a lot of people talked about Danielle and he got very sad there, as did I. We had to leave. So I think he understands it better than we think."

Derek, Damon said, had become very introverted. At first he refused to talk about it, then he started having emotional outbursts and would start crying over unrelated, insignificant issues. Everyone had seen a therapist after Danielle was killed, but had stopped when the trial began.

"Have you done anything to Danielle's bedroom?"

Damon said they had repainted her room a brighter color, but left everything else the same. They had also put a video game system in her room so Derek and Dylan could spend time with her.

"Do you go in there?"

"Yeah, sometimes to play with the boys and sometimes at night just to cry."

When asked about Danielle's hopes for the future, Damon recalled that she wanted to be a mother, a teacher, or a veterinarian."

Mr. Dusek admitted several pictures of Danielle happy and smiling. "She was always happy in her pictures," Damon said.

"Let me go back to February, Mr. Van Dam. The morning you discovered her missing, do you recall what your reaction was?"

"Shock and disbelief at first. Kind of still doesn't seem real. I just didn't know what to do."

"Did there come a time when you thought she might be dead?"

"At the beginning I held out a lot of hope, but after awhile we started searching the desert and I went out to map areas for doing searches with a friend of mine. And I think as we drove around out there I kind of realized, I still hoped, but kind of realized she was probably gone and I knew what we were looking for. I had a couple of breakdowns with him."

Damon remembered participating in the searches and not talking with Brenda about the likelihood she was gone forever because Brenda, "held out a lot more hope than I did."

At the time Mr. Westerfield was arrested, on February 22, Damon and Brenda had not given up hope Danielle was alive.

"When we told you the charges would be murder did you still have hope?"

"Not much. I think Brenda had a lot more than I did."

Where were you when you received word she had been found?"

"At home. I remember we were out back and it was the first call we had gotten from the search center saying they had found someone. We had heard stuff on the news before and I never really put much in that. But this was the first time we were called from the search center and I kind of braced for it right away because it was them telling us. It wasn't till later that night it was confirmed that it was her."

Damon remembered that a detective had visited their home that night with Danielle's necklace and earrings. "That was pretty much when Brenda finally realized, I had kind of slowly eased into it."

For the funeral, Damon and Brenda chose the church and the location of the memorial service with significant help from friends who managed the details and logistics. Danielle was cremated and her ashes placed in the house upstairs.

While Danielle was missing, Demon recalled how people had created a memorial in front of the house where visitors, "would leave notes and lots of flowers, lots and lots of teddy bears and stuffed animals, lots and lots of angels." Eventually it was moved to the park down the street.

Mr. Dusek introduced photos of the memorial at the park followed by pictures of the site Danielle's body was found where angels hung from the tree along with a variety of other items and trinkets.

Mr. Dusek then admitted a card Danielle had written to her father after she had been disciplined for fighting with Dylan. She had placed heart stickers around her writing which read, "to Dad, I am sorry. I will try to be nice. Will you forgive me? I love you. You are the best dad ever."

"What was it like being her father?"

"It was fun. She was very adventurous. She liked to try anything, she loved to help other people, she loved to be involved with Brenda and I and things we did."

"Thank you, sir."

Mr. Feldman did not ask Damon any questions.

Due to some scheduling issues, Judge Mudd broke for lunch early, giving the jury extended time to enjoy, "the gorgeous day. Hopefully you'll be able to find something to do. Have a pleasant lunch."

After the jury left the room, Mr. Boyce of the defense objected to some of the preceding testimony, specifically discussions about the effect on the community, how other students reacted, and Danielle's future hopes and dreams. "We feel they exceeded the permissible victim impact and move for a mistrial on that basis."

"The motion for mistrial is denied. The court has previously ruled on all of the exhibits that have been shown to the jury and has found they fit within the appropriate parameters. All right, we'll be in recess till 1:00 o'clock."

Following lunch, Judge Mudd restricted the media to using only the first name of the next witness and prohibited any photography or video. Mr. Dusek next called Jenny, Mr. Westerfield's former niece. Her father's sister was Mr. Westerfield's ex-wife, Jackie.

"I would like to direct your attention back about twelve years. Was there a time when your family got together with his family?"

Jenny remembered an occasion when she, her parents and her younger sister stayed at Mr. Westerfield's home along with her cousins and aunt, Mr. Westerfield's wife and kids. After revealing she was seven years old when the incident occurred, Mr. Dusek showed the jury a picture of Jenny at that time.

That night, Jenny and her sister went to sleep in their cousin Lisa's room while the adults stayed up late downstairs.

"What's the next thing you remember?"

"Waking up and my uncle Dave had his fingers in my mouth and he was kind of playing with my teeth. Then I was still pretending I was asleep. Then he went around to where my sister was sleeping, she was to the right of me, and I kind of rolled over to see what he was doing over there, but I don't remember seeing him doing anything.

"Then he came back over to where I was and did it again. So, I bit him really hard for as long as I could. He kind of adjusted the sides of his shorts and then left the room."

"Did you act like you were awake the first time?"

"No. I was too freaked out. I didn't understand what was

going on."

"Describe for us as best you can what he was doing."

"He just had a couple of fingers in my mouth, like rubbing my teeth or massaging them. And that's it."

"How long would you say it lasted?" Mr. Dusek asked.

"Maybe a minute or two."

"If one hand he was using to put fingers in your mouth, do you know what he was doing with the other hand?"

"No."

"What was he wearing?"

"He was wearing dark colored little running shorts."

When asked if Mr. Westerfield was sitting, standing or kneeling while touching her, Jenny said she thought he had been kneeling. After Mr. Westerfield left the room, Jenny waited a little while before going downstairs and telling her mom, "that uncle Dave was in the room and he was being weird and it bothered me."

Jenny did not share the specific details with her mother who then tucked her back into bed. "She told me later on that she had talked to him."

"When was the next time the subject was raised, as far as you know?"

"When a police detective called in February."

Jenny revealed she had not disclosed all the details in her initial conversation with police because she did not want to upset her family, but, after discussing the issue with her boyfriend and mother, she later called Marion Pasas, the defense investigator, with whom she shared some of, but not all of the details.

After a conversation with her father who encouraged her to reveal the full truth, Jenny called Mr. Dusek's office.

"When you first spoke with Marion Pasas, did you mention the part about the defendant adjusting his shorts?"

"No. It scared me too much. I don't know if it meant anything or not, it just freaked me out a lot so I didn't say anything."

"Thank you, ma'am."

After criticizing Jenny for adding details to story, Mr. Feldman noted Jenny did not, "remember in great detail what happened. When talking about Mr. Westerfield's shorts, that's something that's come back to you since you first started talking about the event, is that right?"

"Well, I remembered it back when I remembered everything else, but I didn't say anything about it to anybody except my boyfriend. I actually did remember that the whole time. I just was too afraid to say anything to anybody."

"Mr. Dusek started his questions by saying about twelve years ago. You don't have a specific memory exactly how long ago this was, do you?"

Jenny agreed that she did not know for sure how long ago this occurred.

"It could have been thirteen years ago?"

"Yes."

"It could have been fourteen years ago?"

"I guess."

"So, fourteen years ago you would have been five?"

"Yes."

"He didn't do anything other than that, did he?"

"No."

"In fact, he never bothered you again, did he?"

"No."

"You never felt uncomfortable around him ever again, did you?"

Jenny said, "no," and admitted that her family continued to attend parties at his house and socialize with his kids after that nigh. Jenny and her mother had never spoken about the event again until recently.

Mr. Feldman then noted Jenny had told his investigator the event occurred when she was five or six, younger than when the photo shown had been taken.

"Your honor, before I ask the next question, I think I better ask for a sidebar."

"All right, Bob."

Out of the hearing of the jury, Mr. Feldman requested permission to ask, "and I didn't want to just throw this out, whether she has an opinion as to whether or not the jury ought to vote to kill her uncle because I think it relates to her bias. My expectation is that she will say no."

Mr. Dusek responded, "that's improper, she doesn't get to be asked that kind of question in this type of case."

Judge Mudd agreed. "And her feelings on the subject are irrelevant." He did however, allow the defense to explore her feelings about testifying.

Mr. Feldman did not think her feelings were irrelevant, "if she believes he should be put to death."

"Whether she wants it or thinks the jury should or shouldn't is not relevant so don't get into it."

Back in front of the jury, Mr. Feldman asked, "you're very close to your cousins now, aren't you?"

"Yes."

"And you're not real comfortable being here, are you?"

"No."

"Thank you. Nothing further."

In his redirect, Mr. Dusek conceded that Jenny might have been younger than seven then introduced pictures of Jenny when she was five and six.

"Thank you ma'am."

"Jenny, thank you very much for coming in. You are free to leave these proceedings."

Mr. Dusek next called Jeanne, Jenny's mother and Mr. Westerfield's ex-sister in-law. Judge Mudd again restricted the media from using her last name and prohibited any photos or video of her face.

Jeanne recalled socializing with Mr. Westerfield and his family on multiple occasions when he was still married to his ex-wife, Jackie. On the night in question, she took Jenny and her sister up to Lisa's room and put them to bed on the floor in their sleeping bags.

"Did there come a time when your daughter, Jenny, contacted you that evening?"

"Yes. She came downstairs at ten or elevenish. She said Dave had been up in the room and was bothering her. I don't remember the specific language used or anything like that. I just got the impression she was uncomfortable with whatever it was that he did."

Jeanne reported that Jenny had been taught in elementary school to report any adult behavior that made them uncomfortable. Jeanne calmed Jenny down, put her back to bed, and spoke to Dave.

"I told him Jenny was upset, that he had been up there bothering her, what was going on? He said she had been fussing in her sleep and he was comforting her."

"Where was the bedroom?"

"Upstairs."

"Where were you guys partying?"

"Downstairs."

"Did he explain to you how he knew she was fussing in her sleep?"

"I can't recall any specific words, just the general idea of what the discussion was. It seemed like a reasonable explanation. I didn't question it further."

"So, you let it go?"

Jeanne answered, "yes," and said the subject was never again discussed until a detective called her in early February, a few days after Danielle disappeared.

"She said Dave had mentioned an incident-"

"Objection. This is hearsay, your honor."

"Overruled. This is the basis for the action she's taken."

"Could the court please give an admonition?"

"Ladies and gentleman, the purpose of this answer is solely to allow the witness to describe what she did based on that answer. It's not for proof of what the officer said to her. You may answer, ma'am."

"They called Jackie to find out who I was and get my phone number and called me." Jeanne recalled recounting the incident for the detective and said a month later Jenny told her she was upset, stressed, and nervous, and wanted to contact investigators to reveal additional information.

"Thank you, ma'am."

In his cross examination, Mr. Feldman noted that Jeanne could not say for certain when the event occurred, just that Jenny had been approximately six years old.

"With regard to the specifics, you don't really have a clear memory of the specifics because you were partying, is that right?"

"Correct."

"You didn't observe any injuries on her, did you?"

"No."

"She never told you, I guess until just within the past couple weeks, anything about claiming that her uncle had put his fingers in her mouth, right?"

"Correct."

"For years, she never said a word?"

"Correct."

Referencing the instructions Jeanne had received from Jenny's school about identifying inappropriate physical contact from an adult, Mr. Feldman asked, "there were no red flags, correct?"

"No."

"When you talked to David about what your daughter had said, he was composed, he was appropriate, correct?"

"Correct." Jeanne confirmed she continued to socialize

with Mr. Westerfield and Jackie and had spent the night in their home about five other occasions. They additionally went camping on once and took several family vacations together, including trips to the desert and Silver Strand.

"Your interactions with David continued to be the same with him as they had always been, correct?"

"Yes."

"Thank you very much, ma'am."

"All right. Ma'am, thank you very much for coming in. You are free to leave at this time."

Following the afternoon break, the prosecution called its last witness, Brenda Van Dam. Brenda recalled her difficult pregnancy and living in Dallas at the time Danielle was born.

"Do you remember the first time you got to see her?"

"They had to do a c-section because Danielle was so big and when they took her out they brought her to me and I got to see her and I was very happy."

Once they moved to San Diego, Danielle started school at Creekside Elementary. Brenda drove her to and from school every day and was very involved in classroom activities. She volunteered as a chaperone on field trips and helped out in class when needed.

"How did Danielle react to you being in the classroom?"

"She loved me being in the classroom. She would run up and hug me and she wanted to show me all of her work."

"How did she like first grade?"

"She loved school, she's always loved school."

Brenda described Danielle as a girly girl who loved pretty dresses and said she was caring and kind. She was a Girl Scout Brownie, took dance classes, and had just started piano lessons. Brenda discussed many of the details Damon had previously revealed about Danielle's habits, routine, and personality, including her desire to become a mother and veterinarian.

"Since she's been gone, how have the boys reacted?"

Brenda recalled a time Derek revealed he had woken up the night Danielle disappeared and felt guilty for not getting up, thinking maybe if he had he could have, "stopped that bad man from taking her."

Derek was having difficulty coping with the trauma, was holding in his feelings and then having outbursts of anger triggered by small, insignificant moments. "What I do is I take him upstairs, I lay down with him and I tell him it's okay to cry. We talk about it and he tells me what he misses about her and that he really misses her."

"How did Dylan react?"

"Dylan knows and he's very upset. He kind of regressed a little bit and started wetting the bed and kind of went back to his baby talk."

"Did you try to keep some of her writings?"

"I have them all."

Mr. Dusek introduced the small purple journal in which Danielle had been writing in the months leading up to her disappearance. Purple and pink were her favorite colors. He also introduced an orange folder with dolphins on the cover that contained the school work sent home with Danielle on her last day.

"How was Danielle disciplined?"

"Well, Danielle was a very strong headed little girl and I learned early on there were some battles worth fighting and some that weren't. She was very independent and I wanted her to grow up being strong and independent. If she did something that deserved punishment, I would ask her to think about what she had done wrong, how she could have done it a different way and then, when her time was done, I would go up and we would discuss it."

Mr. Dusek then showed the jury a video showing various photos of Danielle throughout her life, including images from their trip to Disneyworld, Halloween, her first bath, Christmas with their extended family, and sleeping with Brenda. After the video ended, Mr. Dusek transitioned to Danielle's disappearance.

"Do you recall how long it was until you first had the thought she might be dead?"

"Damon had talked to me about it at one point and told me that he kind of thought she was. I told him I couldn't, I couldn't give up hope until I knew for sure so I really didn't believe it until they came and told me they had found her.

"How about after the defendant was arrested and you met with our office?"

"Before they arrested him, Bejarano called us into his office to let us know that it was happening, and the reason why they were arresting him. When he mentioned blood I had a major breakdown because I still wanted to believe she was alive."

"That was even after we filed the murder charges?"

"Yes."

"Do you recall where you were when you found out her body had been found?"

"My friend, Diana, talked me into getting a massage so I went and she sat outside the room. I had been on the table maybe five minutes and I heard her phone ring and I knew right away what it was. She opened the door and said, 'Brenda, I have to take you home because the search center found something.' So, I got dressed and we went home and waited."

Later that night, two detectives arrived at her home, "and told me it was her. She had the necklace and earrings."

"As you live in your house, do you go by Danielle's bedroom?"

"Yes."

"Do you ever go in there?"

"Yes, a lot of times I can't sleep at night and I go in there to cry. I go in there to try and feel her, try to smell her. Just recently we decided we wanted the boys to feel comfortable in her room so we hooked up a Nintendo 64 in there. I wanted it to be a happy room so now they play in there."

"Can you describe your loss?"

"I don't know where to begin. She was one of the most precious gifts anyone would ever receive and I was so happy the day I found out I was pregnant because I had a miscarriage between Dylan and Derek and I so wanted another child. I was so happy when I found out I was pregnant and, I don't know, I just, it's too hard to explain."

"That will be fine, thank you, ma'am."

The defense had no questions for Brenda Van Dam.

"All right, ma'am, you can resume your seat in the audience. I just want to remind you of the admonition not to discuss your testimony until the matter's concluded."

"Okay."

After confirming the prosecution was finished and the defense was ready to go, Judge Mudd updated the jury. "Ladies and gentleman, we're going to commence with the defense presentation first thing tomorrow morning. Tonight is a couch potato's dream. You got the Pads at 5:00 and the Chargers at 6:00. The remote's going to be going back and forth. So, anyway, have a pleasant evening."

PENALTY PHASE
DAY 2

"Good morning, ladies and gentleman, welcome back. Just because it was a good night for couch potatoes didn't mean it was a good night for San Diego sports franchises, unfortunately. Those of you that watched the football game were exposed to some television coverage relative to the trial. I'm assuming you just looked the other way or tried to see how the Padres were doing. All right, Mr. Boyce."

The first witness the defense called for the purpose of explaining to the jury why David Westerfield should not be sentenced to death was Mr. Westerfield's long time friend and work colleague, Ron. Ron was a self employed mechanical engineer who had been married for twenty-eight years and had three children. In 1977, Ron initially met Mr. Westerfield at Hydro Products, a company that manufactured underwater equipment where they both worked, along with Mr. Westerfield's ex-wife, Jackie, as design drafters.

Together, they had helped design an underwater camera mounted vehicle used by oil rigs to investigate oil platforms so human divers did not have to risk their lives in dangerous waters. "In the year we were working there, they lost twenty-two divers in the North Sea alone."

"So, this was a device that saved the lives of divers?"

"Yes, it was."

In 1980, after leaving Hydro Products, Ron, Mr. Westerfield, and a third individual named Wes started Spectrum Design. About a year and a half later, Ron started his own company, but remained friends with Mr. Westerfield who he last visited two days before his arrest to, "show a little support."

"Thank you."

In his cross examination, Mr. Dusek noted the team Ron and Mr. Westerfield worked with included approximately twenty-five different individuals.

"Did he invent any of these things?"

"No, he did not. We were designers. We were asked to make this fit here and we would design it so it would fit there." Ron revealed that, as designers, they were assigned projects by the engineers. The engineers instructed the designers to solve a specific problem or make a particular aspect of the construction work, the designers figured out how.

"He was there when the project got started?"

"No, he was there to help finish it up."

"Along with a whole lot of other people."

"Yes."

"And he was getting paid during this time, wasn't he? Basically, this was his job."

"Yes."

"And if he couldn't do the job, there were other people who could do the job?"

"Yes. There's two or three people in that department."

After discussing how Mr. Westerfield was using computers way back in the early 80s, Ron was asked if their work required a high level of organization. Ron confirmed it did and additionally revealed Mr. Westerfield adhered to a strict schedule and planned everything in advance.

"It would be very good for someone to have a plan and then carry out the plan, wouldn't it, for what he did?"

"That's a requirement."

"That was one of his strong suits, wasn't it?"

"Yes, very much." In confirming Mr. Dusek's descriptions of Mr. Westerfield, which on the surface appeared very positive, Ron likely didn't realize he was helping the prosecution solidify just how uncharacteristic Mr. Westerfield's erratic behavior had been on the weekend Danielle disappeared.

Regarding Spectrum Design, Ron discussed how they were working regular jobs during the day and then working on their business at night, which mostly involved designing for other companies.

"And part of the accepting or rejecting business would be on whether or not the compensation would be worthwhile, wouldn't it?"

"Yes."

"There were things that you turned down that you wouldn't get paid enough?"

"Yes." Ron recalled they were young and learning and sometimes mistakenly took on projects that were too complex and time consuming to make them worthwhile and stated they learned by trial and error. Eventually, Ron left to, "pursue my own ventures with concept design."

When asked if any of Mr. Westerfield's parties, "were adult parties," Ron answered, "no, no. A lot of families were there."

"Drinking going on?"

"Yes, not too extreme."

"How about the defendant, would he drink?"

"His favorite was rum and Coke."

"To excess?"

"Objection. Scope, relevance."

"Sustained."

"Did you get a chance to observe the defendant around female coworkers?"

"Objection. Relevance, scope."

"Sustained."

"Nothing further."

"Thank you very much for coming in, you're free to leave."

After the witness was excused, Mr. Boyce called Carmen, the Vice President of Engineering and Operations at a company in San Diego she did not name. Carmen had initially met Mr. Westerfield in 1983 at Sutter Biomedical, a company that manufactured CPM devices and implants.

"When you say CPM device, what does that stand for?"

"Continuous passive motion."

Carmen was Mr. Westerfield's boss, but they became friends and socialized occasionally outside of work with their families.

For the CPM device, Mr. Westerfield was the chief architect and primary designer.

"What did this device do?"

"This is a device that's used to rehabilitate individuals that undergo reconstructive surgery; either knee hip, or any of the major joints. He designed a device that was intended to be used at home when patients leave the hospital." Carmen then explained the device was designed to loosen stiff joints, which would allow for accelerated healing. Thousands of devices were distributed all over the country for patients recovering from a variety of orthopedic surgeries. Mr. Westerfield had also worked on an anatomic hand implant for which he had received a patent. The hand implant was used primarily in Europe.

After leaving Sutter Biomedical in 1989, Carmen started working at Technovision where Mr. Westerfield joined him a short time later. At Technovision, Mr. Westerfield, "designed a product that enabled optometrists and ophthalmologists to cast prescription ready lenses in a doctor's office and helped design some of the devices required for that product."

Carmen explained Mr. Westerfield had helped improved the company's overall design efficiency, which in turn made their products more profitable.

"So, Mr. Westerfield's design was responsible for overcoming these technical hurdles in the casting of these molds?"

"Absolutely. It was a very difficult job." Carmen recalled

the specifics of the process, which included, "a combination of chemical, electrical, electrolysis process. Quite a bit of science, a little bit of art, to make it work."

Following Technovision, Carmen started working in 1991 at Primary Access where he hired Mr. Westerfield as the Design Engineer Manager in charge of designing devices related to the telecom industry. "They produced a software definable internet access concentrator. For example, the people that go into the internet, they would dial up a phone number and our device would answer the phone and connect them to the internet. He designed the next generation product which went into the market. That was one of the products that made AOL famous."

"Was that something anybody could do or did this take some creativity and imagination?"

"Obviously there's more than one person that could do it, but he's very creative and designed a product to the point where it was very easily manufacturable. A very talented guy. If he weren't talented, I wouldn't keep hiring him."

"When was the last time you saw David Westerfield?"

"I would say about a year and a half to two years ago, other than a few months ago just before he was arrested."

Carmen recalled visiting Mr. Westerfield at his home with Ron in mid-February.

Referencing the patent Mr. Westerfield had received for the CPM device, Carmen said, "I must tell you, this particular device was very revolutionary for its time. David absolutely deserved congratulations on that."

"And his name appears in that patent as one of the inventors?"

"Even though there was a secondary inventor, he was absolutely the person that designed the device. The other inventor was a contributory manner, he had very little to do with the design. I believe David came up with the idea."

After reviewing the details of the patent for the surgically implanted hand prosthesis, Mr. Boyce thanked the witness and sat down.

Mr. Dusek started his cross examination by asking about Carmen's education, which included electrical engineering at Drexel University and graduate school at UCLA and Stanford. He noted that Mr. Westerfield had attended only junior college.

"You're good friends with him, aren't you?"

"Yes, I am."

"In fact, when you got on the stand you winked at him, didn't you?"

Carmen agreed and then admitted he had given numerous radio, television, and newspaper interviews in which he spoke positively about their friendship.

"In all, how many times have you spoken up on his behalf to show your friendship?"

"Six or seven times."

"Have you been contacted by *Entertainment Tonight*, those types of shows?"

"No, I have not."

Mr. Dusek noted in the twenty years Carmen had known Mr. Westerfield, they had worked together at three different companies and once as a consultant.

"He would quit the job he was doing at the old company to come with you?"

"Objection. Foundation."

"Overruled. You may answer."

"Sometimes, yes."

"And these projects you talked about him designing, somebody would give your company the idea of what they wanted, correct?"

"Sometimes. Sometimes the ideas were initiated inside the company."

Regarding the orthopedic medical device, Mr. Dusek clarified the idea came from a doctor and Carmen's team just designed and manufactured it before asking, "how many people were on the team?"

"I believe six."

"And if any one of those people had not been there, would the project come to a complete halt?"

"Temporarily, yes, until you replace the person."

"Each of those people could have been replaced, couldn't they?"

"Sure, but I don't understand where you're going with that."

"You don't need to."

"Okay."

Mr. Feldman interjected. "Your honor, that was a gratuitous remark. Motion to strike, admonish counsel."

"The jury is to disregard the comment of counsel, just ask a question, Mr. Dusek."

Mr. Dusek next revealed that Carmen was also on the patent as one of the inventors even though he was only a supervisor.

"There were lots of people involved in this project?"

"Right. He was the primary designer, though."

After reviewing the roles of the other three names listed on the patent, Mr. Dusek noted two of the three were engineers with college degrees.

"And they would do the engineering work on this item?"

"Yes."

"And then the defendant would somehow make it look like it's supposed to look?"

Carmen pushed back. "You're making it sound like he gave it a facelift. No, he actually came up with the main design of the product. The most important part of the product is the mechanics and that's what he designed. The main crux of the system, all of the mechanics, and its anatomic design was Dave's idea."

Pointing out this device was created nearly twenty years ago, Mr. Dusek asked if there was a, "newer and better one out there now?"

Carmen assumed there was.

Regarding the hand implant, Mr. Dusek asked why it was used in Europe and not in America. Carmen was not sure, but thought maybe because there were already similar devices being used in America.

"There were other devices doing the same thing?"

"Absolutely."

Regarding his meeting with Mr. Westerfield in February, Mr. Dusek asked, "did you ask him what he did?"

"Objection. Scope."

"Sustained."

"Nothing further."

After the morning break, the defense called Dr. Richard Coutts, the orthopedic surgeon who had initially contacted Sutter Biomedical for help designing his idea for a device that would help patients move their joints after surgery.

"When you contacted Sutter, did you meet with somebody by the name of David Westerfield?"

Dr. Coutts recalled meeting with Mr. Westerfield and discussed the phases of development that followed.

"Do you have any idea how many people have benefited from the use of this device?"

"I would guess it's been used in the millions by now," Dr. Coutts answered before adding that a number of similar devices copying the initial concept were later invented as well.

"Would you say this device is very beneficial?"

"I think so."

"Thank you, nothing further."

Mr. Dusek pointed out the idea originally came from a doctor in Toronto and then discussed some of the other doctors involved in the process as well as the similar devices from which it evolved.

"Did you have a financial involvement in the production of this?"

"I had a royalty agreement with the company. Based on sales, I would get seven percent."

Mr. Dusek noted subsequent generations were later created that did not involve Mr. Westerfield's help.

"Is this the only device being used for this type of work or are there other models being used also?"

"At the hospital where I work there's only one device currently being used. The Sutter device actually doesn't exist anymore."

"Thank you, Doctor."

The defense next called Judy, the owner of PrePak Products, a company that manufactured medical devices for the physical therapy market.

In 1997, she had hired Mr. Westerfield to work on a knee slide, a device patients could use at home to exercise their knee and improve their range of motion. After working on the knee slide for approximately one year, Mr. Westerfield started working on improving their shoulder pulley device.

"He came up with the idea that made that stiff rope work for us, sort of like a fender on a bicycle that sits a little bit above the pulley. That was Dave's idea."

"How is the pulley beneficial?"

Judy explained the pulley helped people recover from shoulder injuries and was particularly useful for those with frozen shoulder, a condition when a person cannot raise their arm. "This is a device a patient would use at home to restore range of motion."

Judy called the product a Flex Ranger and marketed it to the physical therapy, chiropractic, and surgical markets. The Flex Ranger was, "our company's best selling product. We sold at least six hundred thousand of them."

Mr. Boyce noted Mr. Westerfield had a patent in his name for the shoulder pulley and asked, "what is the date for the development of that patent?"

"October 10, 2000."

"Thank you. I have nothing further."

In his cross examination, Mr. Dusek revealed the knee slide Mr. Westerfield had initially worked on had never reached the marketplace because they could not decrease the cost to the required level.

"So, what happened to that device?"

Judy answered, "we abandoned it," and confirmed there were similar devices on the market that cost more than their original target price.

"The pulley device was in existence when it came to your company?"

"The pulleys have been around for years, but we were the first people on the market to design a home device that was easy to use."

"Who designed that?"

"My former partner. He's a physical therapist."

Mr. Dusek emphasized Mr. Westerfield had only slightly modified an existing product and showed the jury both pulleys. The newer pulley, which Mr. Westerfield had worked on, included a small fender that helped control the rope.

"So, he really didn't invent the device we have here in court?"

"No."

"Thank you, ma'am."

"All right. Counsel have asked for an early lunch break, ladies and gentleman. Sun's out, might as well get your head start on the deli or wherever you're going. Please be outside the door at 1:00 o'clock."

Following the lunch break, Mr. Feldman called Mr. Westerfield's sister, Tania. Judge Mudd directed the media to use only her first name and prohibited them from taking photos or video. Judge Mudd additionally instructed the bailiff to escort her from the courtroom to her car at the end of the day.

Tania was four years younger than Mr. Westerfield, who she called Alan, and two years younger than her other brother, Earl. They were born and raised in a small town in Maine in the 1960s where their mother took care of the kids while their father, David, worked and served as a state representative. They lived on a small farm that had been in their family for several generations and enjoyed camping, swimming, water skiing, ice skating, and spending time at St. George Lake where Mr. Westerfield worked as a lifeguard one summer. Another summer, he and his brother worked for their uncle picking blueberries. Tania described her early years as, "a very nice childhood."

In 1967 the family moved to San Diego. Tania was in seventh grade at the time and her brothers were in high school. For vacations, they often drove around the desert. Their father enjoyed the dry heat, sand dunes, and landscape, and often stopped and took pictures.

In San Diego, their parents started a compographics business, which arranged the typesetting for magazines. Mr. Westerfield worked as a dishwasher at Saska's in Mission Beach his junior and senior year and also had a job at the Ramada Inn.

After graduating high school, Mr. Westerfield moved out. Two years later Earl did the same and they became roommates. In 1974, their parents separated, which shocked Tania and her brothers because their parents rarely argued and always seemed to get along. Around that time, Mr. Westerfield was attending junior college at Mesa Community College and working as a junior draftsman. Although busy with his own life, Mr. Westerfield continued to support his sister with her activities and give her rides when needed.

In 1979, Mr. Westerfield married Jackie and in 1981 Lisa was born. He enjoyed hosting parties at his house and traveling to the desert with camper trailers. A few years later, they moved to a nice house where he designed all the landscaping, installed a pool, and built an aviary in which he had several birds. He was always involved in the lives of his children and included them in family decisions and activities.

In 1990, their brother Earl was diagnosed with a terminal illness   and died. Their father passed a few years later. Although depressed about the loss of his father, Mr. Westerfield handled all the funeral arrangements and paid all of the hospital bills. In 1996, Jackie divorced Mr. Westerfield, but agreed to remain in Poway so the kids could stay in the same school, continue seeing both of their parents, and retain a normal life.

When asked who in her family was in court that day, Tania answered, "my mother's here and my aunt is here, but not in the room."

"Do you love your brother?"

"Yes, I do."

"Nothing further."

With his cross examination, Mr. Dusek reviewed Tania's early years and remarked, "It sounds like you had a good life there, is that right?"

"Very much so."

Mr. Dusek pointed out that both her parents had been present and involved, the family had not been poor or impoverished, and all the kids had graduated high school. There was no alcohol or drug abuse and no physical abuse.

Mr. Dusek then highlighted all of the activities Mr. Westerfield enjoyed with his son the Van Dams would never have with Danielle. Watching his son play saxophone, seeing his kids graduate, participating in their activities and seeing them grow into adults. "And he seems to know how important that is to a parent, doesn't he?"

"Yes."

At that point, Brenda Van Dam left the courtroom and Mr. Feldman interjected.

"Your honor, can the record-"

"Yes," Judge Mudd answered. "The record will reflect that Mrs. Van Dam has audibly left the courtroom. Ladies and gentleman of the jury please disregard the outburst."

Tania then recalled that Jackie was Mr. Westerfield's second wife. He had married in 1973 and divorced five years later.

"The divorce with Jackie, whose idea was that?"

"Jackie's."

"Objection. Speculation, foundation."

"Sustained."

"Thank you ma'am."

"Ma'am, your time with us is done, you're free to remain in the courtroom."

Following the afternoon break, Judge Mudd directed the cameras to go dark before Mr. Feldman recalled Mr. Westerfield's ex-girlfriend, Susan.

Susan recounted the time Mr. Westerfield had helped her before and after her father died of liver disease. "He helped in the hospital and then helped with many of the funeral arrangements. He was a big support to the family."

Susan also recalled how Mr. Westerfield had supported her financially after she injured herself and could not work for a little over a year. He paid her bills, hired a cleaning service, and eventually bought her a car. He also helped her daughter, Christina, escape an abusive relationship.

"We went late one night to where she was living and packed up as much stuff as we could and we brought her back to David's house and he took care of her and her son for approximately three to four months."

"Do you still care about David?"

"Yes, I do."

"Thank you very much. Nothing further."

"Christina moved out the same time you moved out, didn't she?" Mr. Dusek asked.

Susan answered, "yes," and confirmed Mr. Westerfield had stopped supporting them financially at that time. Mr. Dusek emphasized that a majority of Mr. Westerfield's support was just financial.

"He made a lot of money at that time, didn't he?"

"Yes."

"He liked to spend it on you?"

"Yes, he did."

"What about your other daughter? She didn't live at the house, did she?"

"Objection. Scope."

"Sustained."

"In spite of these things that you say he's done for you, how many times did you leave him?"

"Objection. Scope." Mr. Feldman repeated.

"Overruled, you can answer."

"I would say approximately three times."

"He would keep talking you back into the house?"

"There was an agreement. There were things that were going on and we would talk about it and resolve them and try to work things out."

"And he would continue to provide for you financially?"

"Yes."

"You'd still leave him, though, wouldn't you.

Susan answered, "yes."

"You're not with him now, are you?"

"No, I am not."

"Nothing further."

Mr. Boyce next recalled Susan's daughter, Christina, who recounted the period when she stayed at Mr. Westerfield's home after leaving the abusive relationship. During that time, he provided food, helped out with supplies for her one year old son, and did not charge her rent.

"Did he throw a birthday party for your son?"

"Yes. Since it was his first birthday party, I did want it to be special, but because of everything that had happened, financially, I was struggling a little bit. So, David threw a party for my son and supplied all the food and bought the birthday cake."

"Do you still care about David Westerfield?"

"Yes, I do."

"Still care what happens to him?"

"Of course, I do."

"Thank you. I have nothing further."

"Birthdays are pretty important, aren't they?" Mr. Dusek started and Christina agreed.

"And there came a time when you moved out?"

"Yes," Christina answered and confirmed she left with her mother when her mother broke up with Mr. Westerfield.

"You felt that your mother was the reason you were able to stay in the house?"

"I don't believe I would have stayed there had she not been there."

"Nothing further."

"Ma'am, thank you very much for coming in, you're free to leave. Ladies and gentleman, just want to remind you, tomorrow we'll be dark, Monday is a state court national holiday so we will not be in session. The next time we'll be gathering is on Tuesday morning.

"Tuesday, based on everything I've seen, is going to be another herky-jerky day as we try and wrap things up. I'm anticipating, at this point in time, that in all likelihood I will instruct you and you'll either be in deliberations or at least have heard all the arguments by Wednesday. Please remember not to discuss any of the evidence or testimony among yourselves or with each other nor form nor express any opinions on the matter until it is submitted to you. This may be the last time you get to see the Padres for the rest of the year so they're on a little bit earlier. Have a nice four days off. We'll see you Tuesday morning at 9:00am."

PENALTY PHASE
DAY 3

Following the Labor Day break, court resumed at 8:58am on Tuesday, September 3.

"Good morning, ladies and gentleman, and welcome back. I understand one of the flock is not feeling too well so if I see a raised hand I am to stop immediately. Accommodations have been made for you to get out the back door so all you have to do is raise your hand."

"Thank you," Juror 7 said.

The defense next called Mr. Westerfield's aunt, Ina, the younger sister of his mother.

Ina lived in Florida and was only eight years older than Mr. Westerfield. When they were young, their families spent the summers together in Maine.

"What memories do you have of that time period in Maine when you would visit him?"

Ina recalled spending time with the kids on the farm where they picked blueberries. In the late 1960s, her family and his both lived briefly in San Diego until she moved back to Illinois. Mr. Westerfield kept in touch and during one summer worked for her husband's landscaping business. During that summer he started learning about how machines worked.

The last time she had seen Mr. Westerfield was about two years earlier when she was vacationing in San Diego.

"Thank you, Ida."

Regarding the last time she saw her nephew, Mr. Dusek asked, "how much time did you spend with the defendant at that time?"

"I was here for five days, I believe."

"How much of that time did you actually spend with

him?"

"Probably about a day."

"Did you know either of his wives?"

Ida answered, "I think I met them," and then revealed she had only met Mr. Westerfield son once and had not met his daughter until the night before her testimony. Since his arrest, she had not seen or communicated with Mr. Westerfield at all.

"Thank you, ma'am."

After calling to the stand another aunt who repeated much of the information about Mr. Westerfield's summers in Maine and who also had not communicated with her nephew in a long time, the defense moved on to Margaret, Mr. Westerfield's first girlfriend in high school.

Margaret recalled meeting Mr. Westerfield in her senior year physics class and discussed going to prom together and dating for awhile after graduation. He often spent time with her family who thought fondly of him. They enjoyed playing pool and chess, going to museums and theaters, and talking about their future. Mr. Westerfield wanted to be an architect and showed artistic talent.

Some weeks after his arrest, Margaret sent him a letter that read,

"Dear David,

You once told me if I ever needed anything I should call you. I carried that gift of love and care with me to various points on the globe. It's a wonderful thing to feel loved. Now, if there's anything I can do for you, please let me know.

Peg Hennon

My mother also sends her love."

"Are you here for David today?" Mr. Feldman asked.

"Yes. And his children."

"Nothing further."

Mr. Dusek started his cross examination by pointing out

she had dated Mr. Westerfield for about one year nearly thirty years ago.

When was the last time you saw him?"

"I think it was in '73 or '74."

"When was the last time you spoke with him?"

"I think it was at my parents' house in 1974."

"Thank you, ma'am."

After the morning break, the defense called Mr. Westerfield's former colleague, Wes, who met Mr. Westerfield at Hydro Products in 1977. At Hydro Products, Wes worked with Mr. Westerfield on the underwater camera mounted vehicle. They became friends, spent Thanksgiving together, and often went camping together with their families. After leaving San Diego in 1980, Wes and Mr. Westerfield remained friend and saw each other every year or so.

"You still care about what happens to him?"

"Yes, I do."

"Thank you."

Mr. Dusek noted that Wes supervised about twelve designers who he assigned various projects. "It wasn't like any of these twelve designers would pick a specific project they wanted to work on?"

"No, they would work on what I felt they would do best on."

After emphasizing that Mr. Westerfield was just one of many individuals involved in the underwater vehicle project, any one of which could have been easily replaced, Mr. Dusek revealed that Wes had arrived in San Diego two days ago and had a long conversation with Mr. Westerfield the day before.

"Did you talk with him about the case?"

"No, we talked about everything else. I didn't feel that it was proper."

"Did he express any remorse for what happened?"

"Objection. Scope."

"Sustained. You need not answer."

Prior to his visit with Mr. Westerfield the day prior, Wes had last seen Mr. Westerfield in February while he was coincidentally on vacation in San Diego.

"We heard, you know, about it, and I was concerned about it so I stopped and talked to him."

Regarding Jackie, Mr. Dusek asked, "do you know why she divorced him?"

"Objection. Relevance."

"Sustained."

"Thank you, sir."

Following another work colleague who repeated much of the testimony already provided, the defense called Alden, a wildlife biologist who had known Mr. Westerfield since 1986 when he was thirteen years old.

Alden recalled meeting Mr. Westerfield when they became neighbors and learned he had a bird aviary in his back yard. Alden described the aviary as large, intricate, and full of birds which later became his career's primary focus. When he encountered problems with his parents, Alden often spoke with Mr. Westerfield who was a good listener and provided sound advice.

Mr. Feldman introduced a photo of Alden in the desert riding one of the sand vehicles along with a photo taken during Christmas with his family and the Westerfields when he brought home his future wife the first time. On many occasions, Alden watched Mr. Westerfield's kids who were very intelligent, respectful, and well behaved. When Alden married in 1998, Mr. Westerfield helped with the wedding logistics and offered his home for people who needed a place to stay. Mr. Westerfield also helped plan a surprise birthday for Alden's mother.

"Do you care what happens in this case, sir?"

"Absolutely."

"Nothing further."

"You talked about baby sitting his kids and how good his kids were," Mr. Dusek started. "Did Jackie have any responsibility for raising those kids?"

Alden agreed she did share some of the credit for how smart and well behaved they were and admitted he had watched as much of the trial as his job allowed. After pointing out that the surprise birthday party exhibited Mr. Westerfield's understanding of the importance of a child's relationship with their mother, Mr. Dusek asked, "how many times have you been able to come home and spend Christmas with your parents?

"Objection. Scope. Relevance."

"Overruled. You can answer."

"Since college it's been very limited."

"But you could come home if you wanted to, couldn't you?"

"No, there's obligations I have. I have a job. I have a wife. In fact, December is very tough for my wife and I."

Alden then revealed he had last seen Mr. Westerfield two years ago when he was in San Diego for a friend's wedding. "I make a point whenever I come to the area to see David."

"Thank you, sir."

The defense next called Alden's brother, Michael, a lawyer who echoed much of his brother's testimony about the close relationship between the two families. He referred to Mr. Westerfield as a mentor and recalled how Mr. Westerfield had helped him start a law publication in college.

"David's really one of those people, I think, that has helped get me where I am today."

"Do you care what happens to David in this case?"

"Absolutely. I love David. David is a family member in my mind."

"Nothing further, thank you."

When asked by Mr. Dusek which parts of the trial he had watched, Michael said he was very busy as a practicing attorney, but had checked in as much as possible and was watching the highlights on the news.

Before the previous weekend, Michael had not seen Mr. Westerfield in nearly two years because he lived in Santa Barbara and his parents had moved to Florida. Since his arrest, all communications went through either his defense team or Jackie.

"Some point during the investigation, in talking with Jackie Westerfield, I indicated that I wholeheartedly wanted to support David and let not only David, but everyone else know what he means to us."

"Based on your contact with him, it was your impression that he was very skilled with knowing how a computer worked, is that right?"

"It was my understanding that was part of his work experience."

Mr. Dusek talked about some of the milestones in Michael's life Mr. Westerfield had attended, including his graduation, and then pointed out Michael had not sent him a card for his fiftieth birthday, which happened to have occurred in February after Danielle disappeared.

"Nothing further. Thank you."

Right at noon, the defense finished its witnesses for the day.

"I hope you're not sorely disappointed at the prospect of having the afternoon off. We'll see you at 9:00am tomorrow morning."

PENALTY PHASE
DAY 4

At 9:20am on Wednesday, September 4, Judge Mudd invited the jury back into the courtroom for the last day of trial. "It sure is hard being a Padre fan at this time of year, isn't it? At least the season is on the downhill slide in more ways than one. All right, Mr. Feldman."

"Your honor, Neal Westerfield."

As Neal entered the courtroom, Judge Mudd reminded the media that no photos or video were allowed.

At Mr. Feldman's request, Neal recalled his father teaching him how to ride a bike, drive a car, and use a computer and discussed how they went on road trips that included hiking and camping. Neal particularly enjoyed their times playing chess and hanging out around their pool. His father had attended his high school graduation and took him on many fun vacations. During his parents' divorce, Neal revealed that his father had been distraught and cried often.

"This is hard, I know. Did you continue to live with him?"

Neal discussed splitting time between his parents; two weeks every month with his mother, two weeks with his father.

"Do you still love your father?"

"Yes," Neal answered and revealed he had visited him in jail often since his arrest.

At that time, Neal was attending San Diego State University and planned to graduate in 2005.

"Do you miss not having your dad there?"

"Yes."

"Plan to get married some day?"

"Yes."

"Plan to have kids some day?"

"Yes."

"Miss having your dad there as a grandfather?"

"Yes."

"No further questions."

Mr. Dusek jumped right into his cross examination.

"Did you speak with your mom about the divorce?"

"Yes."

"Did she tell you why it happened?"

"No."

Mr. Dusek reviewed Neal's visitation arrangement and noted that Lisa had stopped staying at her father's home after she graduated high school and started college even though she never lived on campus.

"Was she living at home when she was in college?"

"Yes."

"So, she chose to live with her mother?"

"Yes."

"Did your father teach you that you should take responsibility for your actions?"

"Yes."

"Did he ever teach you that you should try to blame someone else for your misdeeds?"

"No."

"Did you speak with him after you were blamed for the porn?"

"Your honor, objection. Misstates the evidence, argumentative, request for an admonition."

"As to the latter portion, sustain the objection. Next question."

"Did you ever speak with him about that aspect of the case?"

"Objection. Irrelevant."

"Sustained."

"Nothing further."

"Sir, your time with us is done. You are free to remain in the courtroom if you so elect. You're free to leave if you desire."

The defense's next and last witness was Mr. Westerfield's daughter, Lisa.

After admitting she was nervous, Lisa recalled for the jury her father's active role in her life. He took her camping and to sporting events and movies. He attended her softball games and graduation, and had family parties at his home often. She took care of the many birds in the aviary and enjoyed the time she spent with him.

"Do you miss him?"

"Yes."

"Have you visited him in jail?"

"Yes." Lisa broke down for a moment and Mr. Feldman gave her a chance to recover before continuing.

"Does it matter to you what happens to your dad in these proceedings?"

"Yes."

"Will you miss having him at your college graduation?"

"Yeah."

"Miss having him at your wedding?"

"Yes."

"Miss having him be the grandfather of your kids?"

"Yes."

"No further questions."

Mr. Dusek used his cross examination to again show all the events Mr. Westerfield had enjoyed with his daughter the Van Dams would never experience with Danielle; her graduation, wedding and kids.

"Because of what's happened here, have you had to go to counseling?"

"Yes."

"Your brother, also?"

"Yes."

"When this happened, when your father was arrested, how long had it been since you lived with him?"

Lisa recalled that she had stopped living with her father when she was sixteen. Although her mother lived just a long walk away, Lisa rarely saw her father.

"You don't have that much time, huh?"

"Yeah."

"Thank you, ma'am."

In a quick redirect, Mr. Feldman asked, "You would visit your dad after you moved out?"

"Yes."

"You would visit him regularly?"

"Yes."

"Did he help you buy a car?"

"Yes."

"Is he helping to pay for your schooling?"

"Yes."

"Thank you."

"Ma'am, I'm not sure there's a courtroom seat available, but you are free to leave or you can remain in the courtroom if you desire. Thank you for coming in. Mr. Feldman?"

"The defense rests."

"All right, ladies and gentleman, you've now heard all of the penalty phase evidence. What remains of this phase of the trial are the two concluding parts. Number one, the law that is applicable to a penalty phase, and number two, the arguments of counsel." Judge Mudd explained he would deliver brief instructions before each side gave their closing argument. "Then you'll be deliberating sometime today."

After a short break, Judge Mudd began his instructions.

"Ladies and gentleman of the jury, the defendant in this case has been found guilty of murder in the first degree. The allegation that the murder was committed under a special circumstance has been specifically found to be true. It is the law of this state that the penalty for a defendant found guilty of murder in the first degree shall be death or imprisonment in the state prison for life without the possibility of parole in any case in which the special circumstance alleged in this case has been found to be true. Under the law of this state, you must now determine which of these penalties shall be imposed on the defendant."

Judge Mudd directed the jury to remain unbiased despite public opinion and stressed the importance of considering all the evidence and following the law. He reminded jurors to discuss the case only with each other and only when all twelve jurors were present. He reviewed the definition of circumstantial evidence and reasonable doubt, and discussed the credibility of witnesses.

"In determining which penalty is to be imposed on the defendant, you shall consider all of the evidence which has been received during any part of the trial of this case. You shall consider and be guided by the following factors if you find them to be applicable; the circumstances of the crime of which the defendant was convicted, the presence or absence of criminal activity by the defendant other than the crimes for which the defendant has been tried in the present proceedings, the presence or absence of any prior felony convictions, whether or not the offense was committed while the defendant was under the influence of extreme mental or emotional disturbance, whether or not the victim was a participant in the defendant's homicidal conduct, whether or not at the time of the offense the capacity of the defendant to appreciate the criminality of his conduct was impaired as a result of mental disease or defect, or any other circumstance which extenuates the gravity of the crime and any sympathetic or other aspect of the defendant's character or record that the defendant offers as a basis for a sentence less than death."

Judge Mudd further instructed each juror to reach their

own conclusion independently and warned against going along with the group as a path of least resistance. He reminded the jury to remain open minded at the beginning of deliberation and not immediately declare a position pride might prevent them from subsequently reversing in light of conflicting evidence.

"It is now your duty to determine which of the two penalties, death or imprisonment in the state prison for life without the possibility of parole, shall be imposed on the defendant. After having heard all of the evidence and after having heard and considered the arguments of counsel, you shall consider, take into account, and be guided by the applicable factors of aggravating and mitigating circumstances upon which you have been instructed."

Judge Mudd defined an aggravated factor as a factor that increased the seriousness and enormity of the crime and a mitigating circumstance as an extenuating circumstance for which the sentence of death might not be an appropriate punishment. "You are free to assign whatever moral or sympathetic value you deem appropriate to each and all of the various factors you are permitted to consider. To return a judgement of death, each of you must be persuaded that the aggravating circumstances are so substantial in comparison with the mitigating circumstances that it warrants death instead of life without parole.

"In deciding whether life imprisonment without parole or death is the appropriate sentence, you may not consider for any reason whatsoever the deterrent or non-deterrent effect of the death penalty or the monetary cost to the state of execution or maintaining a prisoner for life. At this time, you'll hear the people's presentation."

"Thank you, your honor," Mr. Dusek began. "Let me let you in on a little secret. Probably not that big of a secret. As much as you folks watch us, we watch you. We watch your reactions and we saw you come in here today, this morning, and just now.

There was a change, a difference. You knew it, we knew it. Because of what today represents, what's going to happen today for us and what's going to begin to happen for you.

"We have reached that point that has been discussed, questioned, hinted about for several months, and now it's time, at this point, to determine from the relevant evidence which penalty is justified and appropriate. You will have to determine does he get what he deserves or what he wants. And you probably know what your answer should be. You'll probably do that. You know what it should be, what it must be. This man has gone so far beyond the line of a decent society that he has to pay the ultimate price.

"This is not easy, not easy at all. It's easy for people out in the public to talk about do you approve the death penalty. It is tougher when you have to come into court. This is tougher in reality, tougher when you have to make that decision on guilt, which you did, knowing the next step will come. Now we are at that next step and it is tough. We know that and we will not minimize it. Do not shirk that responsibility. Do not question your beliefs.

"Another truth. This is not fun. This is not fun for anybody. Nobody wants to be here. You know the Van Dams do not want to be here on a murder trial because of the murder of their daughter. You know the Westerfield family did not want to have to come here and beg for the life of their father, brother, nephew. This is not fun.

"Do not let anybody make you feel guilty for doing your job, what you took an oath to do. Do not let anybody put you in the same category as David Westerfield. He is the one that brought all of us together. His conduct brought us all to this point. Make no mistake about that."

Mr. Dusek proceeded to review some of Judge Mudd's instructions, particularly about not debating the morality of the death penalty, and advised the jury that death was the most severe punishment even if they thought life long imprisonment might be far more torturous.

"If he is deserving of the greatest punishment, that's what he gets."

Mr. Dusek discussed each of the potential mitigating factors previously listed by Judge Mudd and noted that none of the evidence of prior behavior, good or bad, needed to be proven beyond a reasonable doubt in order to be considered.

"To return a judgement of death, each of you must be persuaded that the aggravating circumstances are so substantial in comparison with the mitigating circumstances that it warrants death instead of life in prison without parole."

In weighing the mitigating factors against the aggravating factors, Mr. Dusek started with the mitigating factors, which he believed were his absence of previous felony convictions and his life experiences. Mr. Westerfield had grown up in a good household with no major obstacles to overcome. He had lived a good life and understood with full clarity the severity of his crime. He had no excuse.

"Each and every family member, each and every friend, you have to feel for them for what he made them do. Come into court and try to save my life."

Observing the irony of Mr. Westerfield relying on his sister's help while Derek and Dylan no longer had a sister, Mr. Dusek stressed, "they lost their sister. They will not know the love of a sister and how neat that is. They will not get a birthday card from their sister. He took that away from them."

Regarding Mr. Westerfield's first girlfriend, he noted she had worn a pair of earrings he had given her in high school. Mr. Dusek reminded the jury about another important pair of earrings; the Mickey Mouse earrings taken off Danielle's body, placed in a clear evidence bag and shown to her mother as proof her daughter was dead.

Mr. Dusek questioned whether the testimony from the

friends of Mr. Westerfield carried much weight at all. He additionally wondered why Mr. Westerfield had so many parties with kids, why he had close relationships with teen boys, and whether something had ever happened at any of those parties that had never been reported.

Although Mr. Westerfield's ex-girlfriend, Susan, still possessed feelings for him, she admitted he had a drinking problem and said his personality changed with alcohol. He had become violent in the past and stalked her after she moved out. Her daughter Christina also spoke well of Mr. Westerfield, but when her mother moved out, so did she. Susan's other daughter, also named Danielle, had never lived in Mr. Westerfield's home. Why not?

Regarding Mr. Westerfield's work, Mr. Dusek conceded he was a talented man who worked hard and became friends with the people he worked beside. "But that is really what everyone's supposed to be doing, isn't it? Before we put him in the category of Jonas Salk, understand he had a job. He was given an assignment to work on this project and he did it."

Moving on to the testimony of Mr. Westerfield's children, Lisa and Neal, Mr. Dusek said they were victims, too. "Your heart goes out to them. What he has done to them and their lives and how they had that unconditional love for their father, good for them. But he has trampled over that footprint with what he did in this case. You tell this jury from your evidence Neal Westerfield is responsible for the porn. That's what happened in this case. Blame your son. And he had to come in here and straighten it out. He's a good kid and it looks like his sister is just as good.

"When you sit down and try to determine all of the evidence that has been presented, you should be struck by some of the things you did not hear. Who knows him best? His wife. First wife, second wife. Who knows the David Westerfield of today? Neighbors from the '80s or the neighbors from Mountain

Pass?"

Mr. Dusek discussed how all the testimony about Mr. Westerfield from his friends and family focused on things he did years ago and never who he was or is as a person, nothing about his character. They talked about the public David Westerfield who seemed kind, generous and polite. No one talked about the private David Westerfield the jury learned about during the trial; the man who meticulously organized a massive bounty of pornography that included videos of an underage girl being raped.

"We certainly know about the private David Westerfield with Danielle Van Dam. There are two parts to this guy and that's what makes it scary. The family and friends know a sweet, kind hearted individual who opens up his home and lets you bring your children into the house to sell cookies. Someone you trust. Somebody you like. That's the scary part.

"The private part, the evil part, the black hearted part is the other side. Look at what he had in life. Look at what he utterly obliterated. Danielle Van Dam. The Van Dam family is obliterated.

"There is no doubt that when I sit down you will be asked to show mercy for him. Sympathy. Compassion. What mercy, compassion, sympathy did he show anybody? He had a chance as that weekend progressed. He showed her absolutely no compassion, no mercy, no pity. None to her family, none to no one.

"He had a chance when he stood in front of the TV cameras and gave the interview to show compassion, to show remorse. He showed arrogance, crookedness, lies. He had a chance when he spoke with Paul Redden. You could hear the tone of his voice. I am smarter than you, I can beat you, you can't touch me. He had a chance to show remorse but he showed none."

Regarding the aggravating circumstances, Mr. Dusek recounted Mr. Westerfield's brazen act of sticking his fingers in a seven year old girl's mouth while her parents were downstairs.

"Battery, lewd act on a child. And then we get the defendant doing what he did in this case. Talking his way out of it. Kids were having trouble sleeping, I just calmed them down. Yeah, right. He knew what it was about when he was questioned about this incident. He's the first one that brought up molestation, not Paul Redden. His mind took him exactly where it was supposed to go. This was a molestation, a lewd act on a child. He knew it."

Mr. Dusek believed the incident with his neice was the beginning stage of his fantasies becoming reality. The child porn was another step. "It tells us what he likes, what he wants. Also tells us something else. He did this crime."

Moving on to the kidnapping and murder of Danielle Van Dam, Mr. Dusek, first emphasized that Mr. Westerfield had received a fair and just trial in which the defense had presented all of the expert witnesses they desired and were provided all the evidence in the case for their own analysis. And from all of the evidence and expert witness testimony, "we know he is guilty of this crime. There will always be questions we don't know the answers to, but we know he did this crime.

"We have heard and probably will hear again that the defendant is not the worst of the worst. Don't get caught up in that. Look at the crime he committed, how far over the line he is. It's unimaginable what he did to that child. He was carrying out his fantasies on that child. If we had the technology, would you want to see a video of her last day, her last thirty-six hours, her last hour? Would you want to see what he did to her? I don't think many people could look at. There are problems enough with what you were shown. Is he the worst of the worst? What will Danielle tell you? What will her parents tell you?

"She was a seven year old child who had barely started her way through this world. There are three photographs that best describe, best show what this crime is about and his evil heart, evil mind, and evil conduct.

"First photograph is his bedroom at his house where he

473

first took this young child and did what he did to her. We know the defendant could see the terror in her eyes as she laid there on his bed. We know he could feel her fear as he touched her skin. That gives him pleasure. She was alone, absolutely alone in this terror. Alone with this man in his bedroom."

The second photograph was the bed in the motorhome. "He wasn't done with her in the house and we know she was alive in the motorhome because of the fingerprints and blood. He took her there to further satisfy his fantasies. Did she know it was over, she was never getting out of there? What did she know? Probably very little. This was not an easy death. Not easy at all. This took a while. Where were his family values while this was going on? What had he done with them if he ever truly had them? How can you do this to a young child? He could have let her go, but he chose not to."

The third photo was Danielle's bedroom. "Where the crime started. He took her out of her own bed, in her own house, away from her blanket, her stuffed toys, her security, her innocence, her family. All for his pleasure, to fulfill his fantasies. This was truly an innocent victim."

Mr. Dusek asked the jurors to approach the process with an open mind before reviewing the evidence and reaching a conclusion. "Walk back into this courtroom with your heads held up high knowing you did a good job, you were fair, and honest, and decent. You look at him. Yes, David Westerfield, that's my verdict. Thank you."

A few minutes after noon, Judge Mudd broke for lunch and informed the jury they were taking an abbreviated break to ensure their deliberation began before the day ended.

"Have a pleasant lunch. We will see you at the normal meeting place at 1:00 o'clock, please."

After lunch, Judge Mudd informed the jury the defense

planned to divide their closing argument into two parts. The first section would be conducted by Mr. Feldman, Mr. Boyce would handle the second. "Mr. Feldman."

"This is really one of the saddest moments I've ever attended," Mr. Feldman began. "We listened to the power of the emotion of Mr. Dusek's argument and it was extraordinarily emotional. It was pitched to your hearts. He used words like evil. Emotional words designed to get emotional responses, designed to push you off your obligation. The judge has told you, you shall not form nor express any opinion until the case is finally submitted. It's not finally submitted. So, although you may have been taken by the power of the argument, by the quality of the advocacy, that's not what this is about. You are called upon to make a life or death decision not on the basis of the quality arguments, but on the basis of the quality of the evidence.

"This is about what's the right thing to do to David Westerfield. Don't kid yourself. This man every day for the rest of his life will be in a five by eight cage. He will never walk the streets again no matter what. You guaranteed that already. Don't give him what he wants? That is a subtle way of saying kill him.

"There was cheering in the streets at the verdict. Our community has a lust for the killing of David Westerfield. If you've been out in the community, you know this. None of us has experienced this kind of intensity. As Mr. Dusek said, it ain't fun. No kidding. I fear you'll return a verdict of death to placate the blood lust on the streets of San Diego. That's not the right thing to do."

After stressing the importance of following the law whether or not they supported the death penalty, Mr. Feldman noted the president of Mexico, "Vicente Fox refused to come meet President Bush because the United States has a death penalty. A man named Moussaoui, who is one of the 9/11 terrorists, is on trial on the east coast and Germany won't give the United States evidence against this man because the United

States imposes death. Please take this very, very seriously. This is truly, if not the single most important decision you'll ever make, among the most important decisions you'll ever make.

"Terribly sad. Sad for the Van Dams. We grieve. There's no excuse. There's no justification. We grieve also for David Alan Westerfield. For his family, for his children, for future generations, because no matter what he's done in the past, he has no future.

"The prosecution asks you to take that which is the most sacred, life, in the name of justice, in the name of vengeance. Kill him. We want justice. Kill him. Is this justice? Do two killings justify one?"

Mr. Feldman then sidetracked by informing the jury, probably to their surprise, "you were never asked to find Mr. Westerfield guilty of killing. Remember. That was never presented to you. The only issue was did he commit the crime of kidnapping? Once you found kidnapping, under the felony murder rule, you don't have to find killing. If she died during the commission of a kidnapping, it's automatic first degree murder. The question was never put to you who killed Danielle Van Dam.

"The requirements of the law put in your hands, empower you to make the decision as to whether he lives or dies." Referencing reasonable doubt, Mr. Feldman said, "there's beyond the possible doubt and beyond a shadow of a doubt. You need that because if you have questions, your doubts linger, that's a reason not to kill him.

"The law says you must consider the background and character of Mr. Westerfield. Mr. Dusek says, 'I don't understand,' it is a split personality, a Jekyll and Hyde. Kill him for the Hyde, let him live for the Jekyll. Folks, think about it. We've got a nice theory, but does that mean you should vote to kill David Westerfield? Does that mean you should disregard the emotional testimony? Does it mean you shouldn't consider his contributions?

"The cross examination of the character witness was mean spirited." Mr. Feldman dismissed the state's simplification of Mr. Westerfield's contributions as just assignments he was given at work and reminded the jury that his work had benefited more than a million people. "Isn't that something to consider in deciding whether or not to kill him?

"The process requires you to search your souls, look beyond the emotion, beyond the crime. Every capital murder is terrible. There is no such thing as a good child murder, a good rape murder. There's no such thing. But there's different individuals that commit those crimes and we know from history that it's only the worst of the worst that get death. You heard those words from Mr. Dusek, worst of the worst. Not even close. This is not a man with an institutional background who's committed crimes in prison. This is not a man who spent a single day in prison. This is not a repeat offender.

"He said Jenny was a child molest. Did you hear that? Did that invite your speculation? Did that play very well to your emotions? Not proved nor charged."

Continuing with factors to be placed on the scale in favor of Mr. Westerfield, Mr. Feldman discussed his age, the many good deeds he had performed in his life, the inventions which had helped more than a million people, the lack of a previous criminal record, and the positive role he had played in the lives of his son and daughter.

"I say take the high road. The high road in this case is life, not another killing. It's hardly what David Westerfield wants, to be caged for the rest of his life, to never see the light of day. This man never again will see the sunrise. Don't think he isn't getting punished. He is. Every time he's come in the courtroom look at our security. He'll never take a step again out of chains and shackles ever again. Mr. Dusek says that's not enough. We need to kill him like a dog.

"In order to impose the death penalty, you must find

David Westerfield to be the worst of the worst. Think about Ted Bundy, a serial rapist and murderer, Charles Manson, John Wayne Gacey, Jeffrey Dahmer. These are the names in the news. These are the people who have killed many, many people. Dahmer was a cannibal. This man is not the worst of the worst. The death penalty is reserved for the worst of the worst. You have to be objective. You have to be exercising your rational judgement. If you allow your emotions to overcome you, the right decision won't be made."

While discussing Mr. Westerfield's lack of a criminal history, Mr. Feldman again stressed his outrage over the prosecution accusing him of blaming Neal for the porn, which he clearly had on several occasions.

"The prosecution has abused the Westerfield family. You heard again the scandalous remark that David Westerfield claimed his son did something. Remember the evidence. Marcus Lawson looked at the books. In order to inflame you, prejudice you, to get you to think David is trying to shift the blame to his son, which is a ridiculous, almost obscene, notion. He wants to inflame you because he knows if you're angry enough killing is easier."

Mr. Feldman repeated his insistence that jurors evaluate the evidence without bias or emotion and dismissed the claims of Jenny who, he said, barely remembered what happened and changed her story each time the event was discussed.

He claimed a person who lived, "a relatively blameless life and contributed to his family and society, who commits a single grave transgression does not deserve death, but to remain in prison for the rest of his life. Think about the treatment child killers get in prison."

"Objection. Improper argument."

"Sustained. Move on."

"Think about the prejudice that's been spun from the prosecution about child killers. He's trying to claim that that act somehow is different than killing an old person or someone else, as he puts it, who's innocent. Any capital murder involves that. This is no different.

Again, Mr. Feldman pointed out that Mr. Westerfield did not have a long criminal history filled with violence like most men convicted of capital murder and repeated the good contributions he made to society.

"It makes no sense when you compare it against what happened in this case. It doesn't make sense. No matter how you evaluate the evidence, this doesn't make sense. When you look at this man's personality, we've been thinking about this for months, it doesn't make sense. That's not a reason to kill. Justice and a death sentence aren't the same. You should consider the severity of life without parole. The circumstances in mitigation significantly and substantially outweigh any circumstance in aggravation.

"Thomas Jefferson said until the infallibility of man is proven to me, I will not favor the penalty of death because mistakes can be made. A hundred and one people have been released from death row-"

"Objection. Improper argument."

"Sustained. I will not allow it. Proceed Mr. Feldman."

"We know that there are reversals in the criminal justice system."

"Objection. Improper argument, your honor."

"Sustained."

"One of our concerns is some of you have already stopped listening. Some of you have already decided. Death is not justice in this case. Please, don't be swayed by public opinion. One of the more disgusting images was the cheers on the street on your last verdict. The community is inflamed. My concern is that you're all in a position where it's easier to vote death than it is to vote life. Not on the facts of the case, but because of what we see every time you look out at the streets. You've had to literally be moved to an area to be protected because you couldn't get privacy.

"The easy thing and the popular thing is to kill my client. Men and women who do not think will applaud. The cruel and thoughtless will approve. It will be easy today, but think of tomorrow. You, the jury, stand between David Alan Westerfield and the executioner. I am pleading for life, understanding, charity, kindness, and mercy. I know that a vote for life is a vote for human understanding. It's a vote to temper justice with mercy.

"When you discuss this case with your grandchildren or children, talk about the power you were given in this case. And when they look at you and ask you what happened, tell them, I chose life. It was the right thing to do. I chose life. Thank you."

"All right. Mr. Boyce."

"Thank you, your honor. This is hard, ladies and gentleman. It's hard for all of us and it's no fun. I see how easy it would be for you to automatically impose the death penalty for the crime."

Mr. Boyce reviewed their obligation of approaching the process with an open mind before emphasizing that the defense was not minimizing the severity of the crime. He discussed lingering doubt, which he encouraged the jury to weigh on Mr. Westerfield's behalf. Walking the jury through the night of Friday, February 1, Mr. Boyce recounted all the steps the kidnapper must have gone through in the process of kidnapping Danielle. "It doesn't make any sense. We have David Westerfield over here. You have a horrible crime over there. The two are not reconcilable. You can consider any doubts the circumstances of this case raises for you in deciding penalty."

Echoing Mr. Feldman's prior claims about the worst of the worst, Mr. Boyce highlighted Mr. Westerfield's lack of criminal history as well as his many strong friendships and the positive role he had played in the lives of his son and daughter. He discussed Mr. Westerfield's work history, which, he said, included helping the lives of over one million people.

"Nothing is going to bring Danielle Van Dam back, but that's not what this is about. This is not an excuse for the crime, this is not to justify this crime. This is about Mr. Westerfield. Whether he is the worst of the worst."

Mr. Boyce encouraged the jury to listen to Mr. Westerfield's friends and family and said, "the death penalty is not designed for this defendant. It's designed for the worst of the worst," who Mr. Boyce believed were career criminals who had become institutionalized during a life in and out of prison between repeated violent acts. "That's not David Westerfield."

Mr. Boyce noted that Mr. Westerfield's life was completely ruined and reminded the jury he would live the rest of his days in a cell. "Every life has value. Every single life. That's why we have the death penalty only for the worst of the worst. David Westerfield has value. You heard it from all the people he touched. He will continue to have value, he will continue to be productive, he will continue even in prison because he's worked since he was a teenager.

"The people who knew David Westerfield are good people. They didn't have to come here. Most of them contacted us. They needed to come here and tell you about David Westerfield and what they said went beyond the words they spoke because they shared his life, his dreams, his accomplishments. They care about him. They love him. And they have given you the reasons why they don't want you to kill him. And I hope all of you were listening."

Upon the completion of the defense's closing argument, Judge Mudd gave his final instructions. "Ladies and gentleman of the jury, you shall now retire to deliberate the penalty that is appropriate in this case. In order to make a determination as to the penalty, all twelve jurors must agree. Gather up all your personal belongings, your notebooks and so forth. You're headed back to the jury deliberation room."

At 2:14 on the afternoon of Wednesday, September 4, 2002, the jury began the process of determining whether or not David Westerfield would be executed for his crimes.

PENALTY PHASE
THE VERDICT

At 1:38 on the afternoon of Monday, September 16, after seven days of deliberation, Judge Mudd summoned the counselors and Mr. Westerfield to the courtroom. The gallery was full.

"Counsel, I'm sure you're aware of all of this, but in order to bring everybody up to speed, at approximately a quarter to 12:00 this afternoon or this morning, we received a note signed by Juror 10 which reads: 'We are unable to reach a unanimous verdict at this time and would like further guidance.'

At that time, I instructed my bailiff to put the jurors out to lunch to return after 1:00. I advised counsel to be here so we could discuss the potential ramifications of a hung jury. At approximately 1:25 this afternoon, Mike, my bailiff, was putting the jurors away and immediately the jury foreman rang and the following note was received by the court: 'Subsequent to writing and sending our note this morning, we have decided we want more time to deliberate.' And that was certainly acceptable.

"Approximately ten minutes later, at 1:35, we received the following note signed by Juror 10. It reads: 'We have reached a unanimous verdict.' So, going in chronological order, we have gone from a potential hung jury to now a verdict. At this time, we're going to take a verdict."

Mr. Feldman intervened. "Your honor, it appears as though between 11:45 and 1:25 the jury continued to deliberate in some manner because, as your honor put it, as the jury was being put back in, meaning before they were gathered together and deliberating together amongst their selves, in apparent violation of the court's order not to discuss any aspect of the case unless they're together, another note comes out indicating they want some more time. It's our view that's a direct breach of the court's orders. We move for a mistrial as a result of that breach and disregard of the court's explicit orders to the contrary. We request a hearing conducted by the court of the jury to ensure that any deliberations were done as directed. Thank you."

"People desire to be heard?"

"We're opposed to the motion," Mr. Dusek answered. "The assumptions defense counsel is making are unsubstantiated and there's absolutely no support for them. It sounds like from the description the court gave us they acted properly and well within the confines of the law."

"Yes," Judge Mudd agreed. "Mr. Feldman, the only thing I can say is that your argument is rank speculation. Another point that is equally plausible is that they all decided to think about the positions they were in and come back after the lunch hour. They asked for more time to talk about it and then they made a decision. So, the request is duly noted for the record and denied. Let's get the jury."

After the jurors reached their seats, Juror 10 confirmed they had reached a verdict and handed the forms to the bailiff. Judge Mudd quickly checked the forms and passed them to the clerk. "Please recite the verdict for the record."

"The people of the State of California, plaintiff, versus David Alan Westerfield, defendant. Case number SCD165805. The verdict. We, the jury in the above entitled cause, determine that the penalty shall be death. Dated September 16, 2002. Signed Juror number 10, foreperson."

The clerk polled the jury one by one and one by one each juror confirmed the verdict of death.

"All right. The polling being unanimous, the verdict as decided will be entered for the record. Ladies and gentleman, I think it goes without saying that as a group you are one of the most hardworking citizen panels I have had the experience of dealing with. You folks have had a very difficult case. You've had a trial that has taken many months. You have had gaps to deal with and, in addition to that, you have had to work very hard at self policing yourselves. You are to be commended for your dedication to the task. We didn't lose a single one of you from illness, or conflict, or anything else. Your dedication to the task is monumental to say the very least.

"Now, in some probably ten days to two weeks from now, you're going to receive a letter from me which is the court's official way of thanking you for your jury service. If there are any of you that would like to communicate with me regarding that service, I would be very pleased to respond as soon as I am legally able. The time at which I am legally able to comment on the case is at the time of sentencing, which is a date after you folks leave. You're welcome to attend that hearing. You're having a problem Juror 1?"

"If I could step outside for a minute?"

"All right. You will be welcome to and as soon as you are composed, I need all of you present."

After Juror 1 left the room in tears, Judge Mudd suspended the proceeding. "Ladies and gentleman, Juror 1 has made a very simple request. I'm going to honor that request and take five or ten minutes so she can compose herself."

After the jury left the room, Judge Mudd discussed his plans for both the defense and prosecution to meet in private with jurors willing to answer any questions they had about the case. He also informed the media he was leaving the courtroom open for journalists to interview any willing jurors. Whether they used their real names or allowed photography or video could be decided by the participating jurors.

"Mr. Westerfield, you have a right to be sentenced twenty court days from today's date. The date that has been suggested goes beyond twenty days. Is that acceptable to you?"

"Yes, sir," Mr. Westerfield answered.

"Your honor, I'm sorry, one point," Mr. Feldman started.

"The juror who asked to be excused. It's the defense's request that the court repoll the jury to ensure the confidence is there for purposes of recording the verdict."

"Mr. Dusek?"

"We're opposed. There's no reason for it, your honor. She answered firmly. There's no reason to change the rules in a case like this."

"It's not changing the rules, Judge," Mr. Feldman countered. "She answered the question before you finished the question and she broke down. I don't think that's an unreasonable request."

"All right. First of all, it should be noted that she did answer the question before Peggy fully asked it, but then after she fully asked it Juror 1 answered the question, as did all of the other jurors. It is not uncommon in a case of this importance for jurors to have an emotional reaction and that's what we're seeing. The poll was unanimous and the verdict will be answered as read. The request will be denied."

Once the jury returned to their seats, Judge Mudd continued. "Members of the jury, you have now completed your service as jurors in this cease. On behalf of the superior court I want to thank you for giving your time and efforts to the administration of justice in this community."

Judge Mudd advised the jurors they could speak about their experience with lawyers from each side as well as the media if they chose, and confirmed all of their personal information would remain confidential.

"The sentencing date has been set as November 22nd at 8:30am. You are welcome to attend that hearing if you are so inclined. At this time, with great thanks from your fellow citizens and the superior court, I formally discharge you from further service on this case."

SENTENCING

At 8:38 in the morning, on January 3, 2003, Judge Mudd started the sentencing hearing by acknowledging two motions that had been submitted by the defense. The first motion requested a sentence reduction from death to life in prison without parole. The second motion requested a dismissal of the special circumstance charge. Judge Mudd allowed Mr. Feldman a chance to explain.

"Your honor, it appears today America has changed. America is now a place where the media turns capital murder trials into summer entertainment where local attorneys make disparaging remarks about counsel and the court on a nightly basis and where the entertainment for the evening becomes the nightly scorecard. Our motions address constitutional issues specifically and initially the issue of outrageous governmental misconduct.

"The court specifically indicated they had troubles with some of the testimony that was offered by prosecution witnesses, in specific, three particular law enforcement officers who were involved in the greater than sixteen hour interrogation process of Mr. Westerfield. Our supreme court says death is different. Death is reserved for the worst of the worst people. Not necessarily the crimes, but the people.

"Detective Ott on May 10th was asked whether or not he was aware that he was intentionally violating the constitution rights of Mr. Westerfield and his answer was yes."

Quoting from a private hearing conducted prior to trial, Mr. Feldman read, "so, you made a decision to violate Mr. Westerfield's constitutional rights after talking to your superiors, after running it up the chain of command in the police department? Yes. Why? My emotions had gotten away from me."

Mr. Feldman noted that Det. Ott had admitted committing two separate constitutional rights violations before reminding Judge Mudd, "the court indicated this was, 'the highest dilemma on the chart of stress and blood pressure this court had to deal with.' You said, 'I'm troubled, deeply troubled by the fact there's no tape recordings involving the sixteen hour interrogation of an aggressive confrontation by Ott and Keyser with Mr. Westerfield.' You said, 'I'm troubled because so much of what occurs on that road trip is based on the credibility of Ott and Keyser.' The court knows a lot about them, having dealt with their past, but more important, it appears to the court that they have been less than candid if not outright committed perjury. I'm deeply troubled by that, but your honor, at the time, indicated there was nothing to do."

Mr. Feldman believed there was something the court could do to preserve civil liberties and emphasized, "the ends simply do not justify the means, your honor. Although this court found concern with the veracity of these two key witnesses in this, the most serious of cases, the death penalty cases, those officers continued to act as law enforcement officers, to continue in their egregious pattern of conduct. As to the first part, the request for dismissal on governmental misconduct, the court has the authority to strike death as a sanction for this admittedly perjurious conduct."

Moving on to the second motion, Mr. Feldman discussed the overwhelming abundance of news stories about the case, which he believed frequently targeted the defense. "We're all under attack by doing our jobs. The independence of the court is threated by these behaviors, your honor. We fear that politics in this case had a role in the determination as to whether or not to seek death for Mr. Westerfield. Had the killing occurred in another state, there would be no death penalty. If we went to whichever of the Carolinas Susan Smith was in, and this is in response to Mr. Dusek's argument that there's no more egregious offense than this, we look to Susan Smith, we look to any other state in the union which doesn't impose the death penalty.

"Your honor has demonstrated, by history, you are independent. I don't believe your honor will be influenced by attacks from self promoting, narrow minded journalists posing as commentators who send their minions skulking around neighborhoods in the dark hours of the morning to subvert the system by engaging in personal, vituperative attacks on counsel, the court, and the system, whose only purpose is to generate audience, but who cynically undermine our system of constitutional justice and the faith of our public in our system. Don't allow them to sabotage our system. I ask the court to take the high road. The high road is life.

"If your honor was to compare Mr. Westerfield's background against that of virtually any defendant that's appeared before you, I think you would find his is a mitigated background. You can spare Mr. Westerfield's life. I ask you to take the high road. I ask you don't acquiesce to the heartless killing of another. I ask you don't be swayed by the lynch mob mentality we've seen in our community."

In requesting life without parole, Mr. Feldman additionally noted the death penalty required multiple review stages that would reopen the Van Dam's wounds. Life in prison meant the case would be closed once and for all. "Your honor, I respectfully submit in this case life is the only appropriate resolution."

For the prosecution, Mr. Clarke responded to the motion to dismiss the special circumstance charge. Mr. Clarke acknowledged, "the court had difficulties with some aspects of that investigation," and emphasized the interviewwhich included, "even more damning evidence indicating Mr. Westerfield's guilt," had not been allowed during the trial. He agreed the sanction had been appropriate and emphasized the rest of the investigation had been performed with the highest level of competence. Although the violations were serious, they did not, by themselves, "rise to the level where the court should dismiss the special circumstance or reduce the penalty as a result of that conduct."

Mr. Dusek addressed the second motion. "I am confident, I am absolutely certain this case was tried regardless of the media." Stressing the strength of the evidence presented, Mr. Dusek said he was, "absolutely certain the court will make its decision based upon what happened in this courtroom during the trial. We are not concerned with what happened elsewhere. This was not a politically motivated case. This was a criminally motivated case.

"He showed absolutely no humanity, no remorse, no compassion for what he did or for the Van Dams. He told Paul Redden when he was interviewed someone who does this type of crime ought to be taken out and shot immediately. He knows what it's worth. The guilt evidence was overwhelming."

After stating that what happens in other states is irrelevant, Mr. Dusek reminded the court that the crime was horrific. "There is nothing worse than taking a child out of her bedroom, kidnapping her, and doing whatever he did to her before he killed her. He is deserving of the death penalty. It should not be reduced."

"Okay," Judge Mudd began his response. "The court is first going to address the request and motion to dismiss the special circumstance as a result of police misconduct."

Judge Mudd reminded Mr. Feldman he had conducted a private hearing at the defense's request for the specific purpose of not releasing the contents of Mr. Westerfield's interview to the media as a way of preventing any potential jurors from hearing information that would not be included during trial.

"The court heard all of the evidence, viewed the tapes, heard the testimony of officers and denied the people the right to present that evidence to this jury, evidence that in many respects, many respects, was very damning to the defense. People were deprived of that evidence. The jury never heard it. As a result, it is clear that the defendant suffered absolutely no, zero, zip, nada prejudice in this trial as a result of the conduct of these officers. As a result, the motion is denied.

"Now, Mr. Feldman brings up an interesting point, and I'm glad that he raised it, that we have many pundits across this country that know what we're doing here. They know better than we do. They're all experts. They're on the national media. They determine what the rules should be, they determine what the law in the State of California should be. That's absolutely preposterous. But it is one of the things that everyone in this trial has had to live with and, as a result, I'm going to take just a couple minutes, not to bore the lawyers in the audience, but to educate, to a certain extent, the pundits that think they know everything.

"First of all, the nature of the motion that is being brought in this case is mandatory under the laws of the State of California." Judge Mudd explained he was required to complete five separate obligations when reviewing an application to reduce a death sentence to a sentence of life; reviewing all the evidence, considering aggravating and mitigating circumstances, determining if the jury's decision was contrary to the law or the evidence presented, explaining on the record the reasons for his conclusions, and directing the clerk to enter those findings in the minutes.

Judge Mudd additionally revealed he could only consider evidence presented to the jury. "So even though I've heard a lot of material over the months preceding trial, I am obligated to work with the evidence that was presented in the courtroom. In addition to that, the court may not contrast this case with other cases in which this court has imposed the sentence of death. With this overview, the court will now recite its reasons as required by law as to the motion brought.

After revealing he had independently considered all the

evidence presented during trial, Judge Mudd said, "the circumstances of this case and this crime weigh heavily in favor of the upholding of the jury's verdict of death. The victim, Danielle Van Dam, age seven, was taken out of her home in the middle of the night while sleeping in her own bed. The physical evidence overwhelmingly confirms the defendant returned to his house with the victim, taking her from his bed, to his car, to his motorhome.

"The defendant then drove in an almost aimless fashion for two days. The victim's handprint was found above the bed in the motorhome. Her hair was found in the sink of the motorhome. Her blood was found both on the floor of the motorhome and on the defendant's jacket. The uncontested evidence establishes well beyond any reasonable doubt that the blood, handprint, and hair were from Danielle. The hair length was completely consistent with a recent haircut. The victim's body, when found, was unclothed and had teeth missing, the likely result of trauma to her face. The weight of this factor is of enormous magnitude."

Regarding his consideration of aggravating circumstances, Judge Mudd reviewed the accusations made by Mr. Westerfield's niece. "This incident is disturbing to say the least. Additionally, the defendant was convicted of the possession of child pornography. Both of these instances of criminal activity weigh against the defendant.

"Based on a careful and an independent reweighing of the evidence, the court finds the weight of the evidence as outlined above supports the jury's verdict of death. The motion is hereby denied.

Prior to the reading of the sentence, Judge Mudd allowed Brenda and Damon Van Dam an opportunity to address the court. Damon spoke first.

"Your honor, I've been asked to make a statement to the court to let you know how this has impacted my life. Let's just say my life as I knew it before Danielle's murder has been destroyed. Every day there is something else I am missing because she is not here. Danielle was my only daughter, there will never be anyone else like her.

"I'll never see her grow up. I'll never get to see her be a friend to her brothers. I'll never see her be a teacher or doctor. I'll miss her first date. I know she would be such a smart, independent person. I'll miss seeing her go to the prom. I'll miss her graduation, most likely would have been with honors. She was a hard worker. I'll miss seeing her go off to college and I'll wonder what she would have become. I'll miss seeing her on her wedding day.

"As the years pass and all these things don't happen, all I'll have are the memories of her, some old pictures and videos, and dreams of her which I hope are always as vivid as they are now, and having to know how brutal the last hours of her life were. My heart and my wife's heart have been broken and my other two children have been deeply hurt. It's too soon to measure the full impact of Danielle's abduction and murder on our lives and their lives, but we know we have a hole in our hearts that will never heal and we will miss you for all of our lives. Thank you."

"All right. Thank you," Judge Mudd said as Brenda approached the podium.

"In early November, I started wondering about how I was going to get through the holidays and I wanted to think of some things I had to be thankful for. Even though I went through this horrible year, I am so thankful to have been blessed with Danielle and I thank God every day I had seven years with her. She was such a wonderful, loving child and I am so thankful for my other two beautiful children, whom I love and adore, and my wonderful husband who has been by my side through this entire ordeal.

"I am thankful for a dedicated jury who is not only intelligent, but they're not blind. They saw through all the smoke fields Feldman threw in front of them and they saw the truth. They need to be commended. Most of all, I'm thankful for the justice system because the justice system is what will put him where he belongs. I am thankful to all the men and women who were so dedicated to getting all the evidence done in time to make sure he was put in his proper place.

"Now I have my statement. How can I, as a mother, find meaningful words that would express how this unthinkable crime has affected my family? I can't. Her father can't. Yet this is where our family finds itself. In a courtroom, standing across from the man who murdered our precious daughter and who greedily stole the heart out of our family. Our lives are forever changed. The pain runs so deep you can't reach it to stop it and the missing never ends. The tears are always one memory away.

"Our precious Danielle was taken by a monster seeking self gratification and not thinking about the sweet little child he was harming or how his horrific crime would impact her family and the community. You sat by smugly as thousands of people frantically searched for Danielle and her family anguished over finding her. It disgusts me that your sick fantasies and your pitiful needs made you feel that you needed Danielle more than her family."

Brenda recalled Danielle's birth, her early years, and her evolution into a little girl who loved dressing up, looking pretty, and treating other people well. She loved school, attending dance classes, and writing in her journals. She was smart, thoughtful, kind, and considerate. She was great with her brothers and studied hard in school. Since Danielle's abduction, her brothers have slept in the same room because they are afraid of being alone at night.

"I ask you, why did you not let her go? Why didn't you drop her off in a safe place? If you had done so, she would be with her family now and you would not be facing death. What were you thinking as you killed her? Did she not touch your heart one bit? If not, you are heartless, you are an empty shell, you are nothing. If she did, reclaim some decency and apologize to her brothers, her parents, your own children, and this community. You have victimized your own children just because you wanted mine. Although your children may try to move and change their names, they will always live with the fact their father is a cold blooded killer.

"Danielle was not an object to be taken. She was a human being to be lovingly cared for. You do not deserve any leniency, any mercy, because you refused to give it to Danielle. You have to live with the memory of her death. I will cherish the memory of her life."

After Brenda finished, Judge Mudd invited Mr. Westerfield to speak.

"Mr. Westerfield, is there anything you would like to say, sir?"

"No, sir. Thank you."

"All right. Having ruled on the mandatory motion to set aside the jury's verdict, it is time for the judgement and sentence of the court. Mr. Westerfield, for the crime of murder in the first degree, committed under the special circumstance in which the murder was committed during the course of a kidnapping, you shall be put to death within the walls of the California State Prison at San Quentin in the manner prescribed by law upon a date to be fixed by this court in a warrant of execution.

"As to count two, the sentence for kidnapping, the court concurs in the probation officer's analysis this is an aggravated term based on the extremely cruel and vicious nature of the crime and shows, without doubt, this defendant has a violent propensity to commit crimes in our community. As a result, the court sets the term of eleven years.

"As to misdemeanor count three, possession of child pornography, the sentence of the court is that probation be denied and he be sentenced to credit for time served, which is in the amount of 316 days. I'll set the fine as the maximum fine in the amount of $10,000. As far as restitution is concerned, based on the probation officer's analysis, to the family of Danielle, Mr. and Mrs. Van Dam, the court will set restitution in the amount of $81,571.36. For repayment to the state restitution crime victims board, the court sets the amount of $8,556.54.

"Mr. Westerfield, you're hereby ordered remanded to the custody of the Sheriff without bail to be delivered by the Sheriff within ten days to the warden of the California State Prison at San Quentin.

"Okay, it appears that all the matters have been resolved."

EPILOGUE

As of February 2023, David Westerfield remains incarcerated on Death Row at San Quentin Prison. The last execution in California was in 2006. In 2019, Governor Gavin Newsom placed a moratorium on executions in California and in 2022 announced plans to dismantle death row and transfer its nearly seven hundred inmates to a variety of prisons throughout the state where they would live the rest of their lives in general population.

All of David Westerfield's appeals have been denied.

Also From

MONSTER PUBLISHING

DEATH ROW FILES:
JERRY BUCK INMAN

On May 26, 2006, Clemson University student, Tiffany Souers, was attacked and murdered by Jerry Buck Inman, a mentally deranged sexual predator who had been released from a from a Florida prison the year before where he had served seventeen years for a kidnapping and rape he committed when he was only sixteen.